WORLD RALLY WINNING MANUFACTURERS

Note: these records do not include outright winners of W2L-only events but do include WCD-only res

WINS	MARQUE	TYPE	YEAR & EVENTS WON
24	Audi	Quattro	1981 S, I, GB
			1982 S, P, GR, BR, FIN, I, GB
			1983 S, P, RA, FIN, GB
			1984 MC, S, P, GR, NZ, RA
		Sport Quattro	1984 CI
			1985 I
		200 Quattro	1987 FAK
2	BMW	2002tii	1973 A
		M3	1987 F
8	Citroen	Xsara Kit Car	1999 E, F
		Xsara WRC	2001 F
			2002 D
			2003 MC, TR, D, I
9	Datsun/Nissan	240Z	1973 EAK
		Violet 710	1976 GR
		160J	1979 EAK
			1980 EAK, NZ
		Violet GT	1981 EAK, CI
			1982 EAK
		200SX	1988 CI
21	Fiat	Abarth 124	1973 PL
			1974 P
			1975 P
		Abarth 131	1976 FIN
			1977 P, NZ, CDN, I, F
			1978 P, GR, FIN, CDN, F
			1979 FIN
			1980 MC, P, RA, FIN, I
			1981 P
45	Ford	Escort RS1600	1973 FIN, GB
			1974 FIN, GB
		Escort RS1800/RS	1975 GB
			1976 GB
			1977 EAK, GR, FIN, GB
			1978 S, GB
			1979 P, GR, NZ, CDN, GB
			1980 GR
			1981 GR, BR, FIN
		Sierra RS Cosworth	1988 F
		Escort RS Cosworth	1993 P, F, GR, I, E
			1994 MC, FIN
			1996 RI
		Escort WRC	1997 GR, RI
		Focus WRC	1999 EAK, P
			2000 E, GR, CY
			2001 RA, CY, GR
			2002 RA, GR, EAK
			2003 GR, FIN
74	Lancia	Stratos	1974 I, CDN, F
			1975 MC, S, I, F
			1976 MC, P, I, F
			1977 MC
			1978 I
			1979 MC, I, F
			1981 F
		Rally	1983 MC, F, GR, NZ, I
			1984 F
		Delta S4	1985 GB
			1986 MC, RA, I, USA
		Delta HF 4WD	1987 MC, P, GR, USA, NZ, RA, FIN, I, GB
			1988 MC, S
		Delta Integrale	1988 P, EAK, GR, USA, RA, FIN, I, GB
			1989 MC, P, EAK, F, GR, RA
		Delta Integrale 16v	1989 I
			1990 MC, P, F, RA, AUS, I
			1991 EAK, GR, FIN, AUS, I, GB
		Delta HF Integrale	1992 MC, P, F, GR, RA, FIN, AUS, I
3	Mazda	323 4WD	1987 S
			1989 S, NZ
2	Mercedes-Benz	450SLC5.0	1979 CI
		500SLC	1980 CI

WINS	MARQUE	TYPE	
34	Mitsubishi	Colt Lancer	
		Galant VR-4	
			1991 S, GR
			1992 CI
		Lancer Evolution	1995 S, AUS
			1996 S, FAK, RA, FIN, AUS
			1997 P, E, RA, FIN
			1998 S, EAK, RA, FIN, I, AUS, GB
			1999 MC, S, NZ, I
			2000 MC
			2001 MC, P, EAK
6	Opel	Ascona	1975 GR
		Ascona 400	1980 S
			1982 MC, CI
			1983 EAK
		Kadett GSi	1988 NZ
45	Peugeot	504	1975 EAK, MA
			1976 MA
		504 V6 Coupe	1978 EAK, CI
		205 Turbo 16	1984 FIN, I, GB
			1985 MC, S, P, GR, NZ, RA
		205 Turbo 16 E2	1985 FIN
			1986 S, F, GR, NZ, FIN, GB
		206 WRC	2000 S, NZ, FIN, F, I, AUS
			2001 S, FIN, E, I, AUS, GB
			2002 S, F, E, CY, FIN, I, NZ, AUS
			2003 S, NZ, RA, E
2	Porsche	911 Carrera	1978 MC
		911 SC	1980 F
6	Renault	17 Gordini	1974 USA
		5 Turbo	1981 MC
			1982 F
			1986 P
		Maxi 5 Turbo	1985 F
		5 GT Turbo	1989 CI
6	Renault-Alpine	A110	1973 MC, P, MA, GR, I, F
4	Saab	96V4	1973 S
			1976 S
		99EMS	1977 S
		99 Turbo	1979 S
39	Subaru	Legacy 4WD Turbo	1993 NZ
		Impreza 555	1994 GR, NZ, GB
			1995 MC, P, NZ, E, GB
			1996 GR, I, E
		Impreza WRC	1997 MC, S, EAK, F, NZ, I, AUS, GB
			1998 P, F, GR
			1999 RA, GR, FIN, AUS, GB
			2000 EAK, P, RA, GB
			2001 NZ
			2002 MC, GB
			2003 CY, AUS, F, GB
2	Talbot	Sunbeam Lotus	1980 GB
			1981 RA
43	Toyota	Corolla	1973 USA
			1975 FIN
		Celica	1982 NZ
		Celica Twincam Turbo	1983 CI
			1984 EAK
			1985 EAK, CI
			1986 EAK, CI
		Celica GT-Four	1989 AUS
			1990 EAK, GR, NZ, FIN, GB
			1991 MC, P, F, NZ, RA, E
			1992 S
		Celica Turbo 4WD	1992 EAK, NZ, E, GB
			1993 MC, S, EAK, RA, FIN, AUS, GB
			1994 P, EAK, F, RA, I
			1995 F
		Corolla WRC	1998 MC, E, NZ
			1999 CN
1	Volkswagen	Golf GTI 16v	1987 CI

AFRICAN CHAMPIONS (ARC)		ASIA-PACIFIC CHAMPIONS (APRC)		MIDDLE EAST CHAMPIONS (MERC)	
1982	Walter Rohrl (D) Opel Ascona 400	1988	Kenjiro Shinozuka (J)	1984	Saeed Al Hajri (Q) Porsche 911SC RS
1983	Alain Ambrosino (CI) Peugeot 505		Mitsubishi Galant VR-4	1985	Saeed Al Hajri (Q) Porsche 911SC RS
1984	David Horsey (EAK) Peugeot 504 Pick Up	1989	Rod Millen (NZ) Mazda 323 4WD	1986	Mohammed Ben Sulayem (UAE)
1985	Luc Requile (RWA) Opel Manta 200	1990	Carlos Sainz (E) Toyota Celica GT-Four		Toyota Celica Twincam Turbo
1986	Alain Ambrosino (CI) Nissan 240RS	1991	Ross Dunkerton (AUS)	1987	Mohammed Ben Sulayem (UAE)
1987	Alain Ambrosino (CI) Nissan 240RS		Mitsubishi Galant VR-4		Toyota Celica Twincam Turbo
1988	Satwant Singh (Z) Opel Manta 400	1992	Ross Dunkerton (AUS)	1988	Mohammed Ben Sulayem (UAE)
1989	Satwant Singh (Z) VW Golf GTI		Mitsubishi Galant VR-4		Toyota Celica Twincam Turbo
1990	Walter Costa (RWA) Peugeot 205GTI	1993	'Possum' Bourne (NZ)	1989	Mohammed Ben Sulayem (UAE) Toyota Celica GT-Four
1991	Satwant Singh (Z) VW Golf GTI		Subaru Legacy 4WD Turbo	1990	Mohammed Ben Sulayem (UAE) Toyota Celica GT-Four
1992	Aldo Riva (I) Audi 90 Quattro	1994	'Possum' Bourne (NZ)	1991	Mohammed Ben Sulayem (UAE) Toyota Celica GT-Four
1993	Satwant Singh (Z)		Subaru Impreza 555	1992	Mamdouh Khayat (KSA) Lancia HF Integrale
	Toyota Celica Turbo 4WD	1995	Kenneth Eriksson (S)	1993	Sheikh Hamad Al Thani (QA) Mitsubishi Galant VR-4
1994	Abe Smit (Z) Audi Coupe S2		Mitsubishi Lancer Evolution	1994	Mohammed Ben Sulayem (UAE)
1995	Fritz Flachberger (NAM)	1996	Kenneth Eriksson (S)		Ford Escort RS Cosworth
	Ford Escort RS Cosworth		Subaru Impreza 555	1995	Abdullah Bakhashab (KSA) Ford Escort RS Cosworth
1996	Satwant Singh (Z)	1997	Kenneth Eriksson (S)	1996	Mohammed Ben Sulayem (UAE) Ford Escort RS Cosworth
	Hyundai Elantra/Subaru Impreza WRX-RA		Subaru Impreza WRCar	1997	Mohammed Ben Sulayem (UAE) Ford Escort RS Cos./WRC
1997	Satwant Singh (Z) Subaru Impreza WRX-RA	1998	Yoshio Fujimoto (J)	1998	Mohammed Ben Sulayem (UAE) Ford Escort WRC
1998	Satwant Singh (Z) Subaru Impreza WRX-RA		Toyota Celica GT-4/Corolla WRCar	1999	Mohammed Ben Sulayem (UAE) Ford Focus WRC
1999	Charles Muhangi (EAU) Subaru Impreza 555	1999	Katsuhiko Taguchi (J)	2000	Mohammed Ben Sulayem (UAE) Ford Focus WRC
2000	Satwant Singh (Z) Subaru Impreza 555		Mitsubishi Lancer Evolution	2001	Mohammed Ben Sulayem (UAE) Ford Focus WRC
2001	Schalk Burger (ZA) Subaru Impreza	2000	'Possum' Bourne (NZ) Subaru Impreza	2002	Mohammed Ben Sulayem (UAE)
2002	Johnny Gemmell (ZA) Subaru Impreza	2001	Karamjit Singh (MAL) Proton Pert		Ford Focus WRC/Subaru Impreza WRX
2003	Fernando Rueda (E) Mitsubishi Lancer Evolution	2002	Karamjit Singh (MAL) Proton Pert	2003	Nasser Al-Attiyah (QA) Subaru Impreza WRC

KNOCK OUT

PIRELLI. WORLD RALLY CHAMPIONS 2003.

Petter Solberg in his Pirelli shod Subaru is the new World Rally Champion Driver.
A celebration of Pirelli's 19th World Rally Championship title.

POWER IS NOTHING WITHOUT CONTROL.

If the Focus is a god when it comes to handling…get ready to praise the ST170. From the first drive, the 170PS at 7000rpm from the 2.0 litre 16-valve Duratec engine gets you going. And that's just for starters. You then put the close ratio six-speed Getrag gearbox, unique ST tuned suspension and low profile tyres through their paces. And in return, you get amazing grip, ultra-sharp steering and glue-like road holding. It can handle you - but can you handle it? £16,100* puts you in charge. So call 0845 7111 888 or visit www.ford.co.uk. **Life's better when you take control.**

FordFocus ST170   Designed for living. Engineered to last

World Rallying

MARTIN HOLMES RALLYING

PO Box 117, Woking, Surrey, GU22 8YP

SUSPENSION STROKE
up to 280 mm

HIGH PRESSURE GAS SHOCK
with piggy back design

LOW FRICTION FORCES
hard coating plus
low friction seals

HIGH-STRENGTH STEEL

IMPROVED TEMPERATURE MANAGEMENT

ADJUSTMENT HYDRAULIC
BUMP STOP

BUMP AND REBOUND FUNCTIONS
independently adjustable
in low-and high-speed

DESIGNED TO WIN.

SACHS RACE ENGINEERING

Meeting the demands of the best teams in the most uncompromising rally events
worldwide poses a continuous challenge for us. Ford, Mitsubishi and the Peugeot
world rally teams rely on Sachs carbon clutches and our newly developed release
systems. The Subaru WRC team, too, has chosen a high-tech innovation from Sach
the new multiply variable shock absorber for WRC. Whether Formula 1 or World
Rallying, whether touring cars or club sport – winning teams rely on shock
absorbers and clutches made by Sachs in Germany. Join the winners – contact us a
service.sre@sachs.de, + 49 97 21 98 32 58 or www.sachs-race-engineering.de

SACHS
RACE ENGINEERING

ENGINEERED TO RACE.

Contents

©2003 Martin Holmes

DISTRIBUTORS:

Great Britain	Vine House Distribution, Chailey, East Sussex, BN8 4DR
Argentina	Juan Cruz Mathus, Cordoba
Australia	Simpson Safety Equipment, Jannali, NSW 2226
Belgium	Van + Van Publiciteit, Maarssen, Holland.
Bulgaria	Strasho Dimov, Sofia
Czech Republic	Martin Hlinsky, Mlada Boleslav
Denmark	Tolerance A/s, Viborg
Estonia	Rein Luik, Tallinn
Finland	Vauhdin Maailma, Helsinki
France	Stephane Pichard, Paris
Germany	Jurgen Bertl, Dohla
Hungary	Andras Fekete, Budapest
Indonesia	Trendypromo Mandira, Jakarta 12330
Italy	Tutto Rally, Chieri (TO)
Japan	Tequenitune Corporation, Kamakura City
Kenya	Surinder Thatthi, Nairobi
Latvia	Liga Kalnaca, Riga
Lithuania	Vidmantas Jankavicius, Vilnius
Malaysia	SR Motorsport Sdn Bhd, Kuala Lumpur
Mexico	Guy Lassauzet, Mexico City
New Zealand	Rally New Zealand, Auckland
Norway	Gundersen Motorsport, Oslo
Peru	Ramon Ferreyros, Lima
Poland	Jacek Lewandowski, Warszawa
Portugal	Gatekeepers, Leiria
Russia	Russian Autosport Magazine, Moscow
Spain	JAS Info Service, Vic (Barcelona)
Sweden	Hakan Toner, Vasteras
Uganda	Geoffrey Kihuguru, Kampala
Serbia & Montegra	Nenad Nikolic, Pozarevac
Zambia	Lee-Ann Singh, Lusaka

ADVERTISING AGENCIES:

GB and Europe	Martin Holmes Rallying, Woking, Surrey
Argentina	Juan Cruz Mathus, Cordoba
Indonesia	Helmy Sungkar, Trendypromo Mandira, Jakarta
Japan	Tequenitune Corporation, Kamakura City

ISBN 0-9545433-0-0

British Library Cataloguing-in-Publication Data.
A catalogue for this book is available from
the British Library.

Front Cover photos *Petter Solberg gained his first World Drivers' title in 2003. These pictures were taken in Cyprus, his first of four wins in 2003.*

Foreword

Tommi Makinen
FIA World Rally Champion
1996/1997/1998/1999

All good things have to come to an end! This is the time when I have decided to retire from world championship rallying, and this is may be the final chance that I can have to be asked to write this introduction. My 19 years in active rallying have taken me to the four corners of the world, given me the chance to compete in many different types of car, and to work with so many people who have given all their efforts to help me do well. So I would like to thank everyone who we have worked with, everyone who has shared our emotions, and hopefully this introduction will be in some small way a chance to say thank you.

If I tried to tell someone outside the sport of everything that has happened in my career, I do not think they would ever believe me. Rallying is too extraordinary to be true! But these events did take place and luckily Pirelli World Rallying books have extensively recorded them as they happened. These things happened to me, and just as much has happened to everyone else in the sport. I shall always keep my set of books, to prove that the great days of world championship rallying were real for all of us.

From 2004 a lot of things will change in the sport we love. I am curious to know how they will turn out. I really hope the changes will work well. I won't be taking part any more, but my heart will never be far away from the special stages. Thank you for sharing my life. Please take care, enjoy the future to the full, and hopefully find the sport as fulfilling as I have done.

Tommi Makinen
Jyska
October 2003

Marcus Gronholm

My First Five Years at Peugeot

Evolution in colour! Models of Peugeot 206 WRC on display at the reception to the team's headquarters in Volizy, France.

Ready for the Off! Family group on the morning of the start of the 1999 Acropolis Rally! Xavier Carlotti (Assistant Team Director), Alix Champoiseau (Jean-Pierre Nicolas' secretary), Michel Nandan (Technical Director), Marcus and Vincent Laverne (Team Coordinator).

My life at Peugeot began in July 1998. I had seen pictures of the prototype 206WRC and knew that Peugeot were planning a major rally comeback. I asked someone for the phone number of Peugeot Sport, and rang Jean-Pierre Nicolas asking if we could speak, maybe could I come to meet him. I got the feeling he was not quite sure who I was, maybe he was confusing me with some of the Swedish drivers! He knew I was Scandinavian, anyway! He was polite and asked me to send him my CV, and he said maybe we could meet when he and his assistant Vincent Laverne came to watch the 1000 Lakes Rally. On the event he came up to me when we were waiting outside a service park time control and was immediately a lot more welcoming. He was positively quite excited about having a talk! He came to my hotel in the middle of the rally. We talked for 15-20 minutes, and he then invited me to go and meet them at the Peugeot Sport headquarters at Velizy in France. At that time things were finally beginning to hot up in my career. Previously I had been in touch with both Malcolm Wilson at Ford and John Spiller at Subaru, also I had been talking to Toyota. I did not seem to be getting anywhere though, so I can honestly say this was the first time in my life I did not know what was going on. Suddenly in Finland it had all changed round. Jean-Pierre seemed so excited about us working together. Peugeot immediately offered me five rallies in 1999, starting with their second event, Greece, and before that we were to go testing straightaway. I kept remembering how successful the 205 had been. It was worth accepting the chance of working in a new team if I had a year of testing with just the five rallies, to begin with. I had never done more than five or six world rallies in a season before and then it was effectively only in private teams. When they then offered me ten rallies in 2000 I knew the decision had been correct! The idea was that we would do Monte Carlo but I would miss out the other asphalt rallies. Monte Carlo 2000, what a start, or rather, what a restart it wasn't! When the cars would not restart at Gap on the second day it was a big shock for Mr Provera and the rest of the team. But things soon changed, we won the next rally, the Swedish. At that moment they started to think about me doing the whole season.

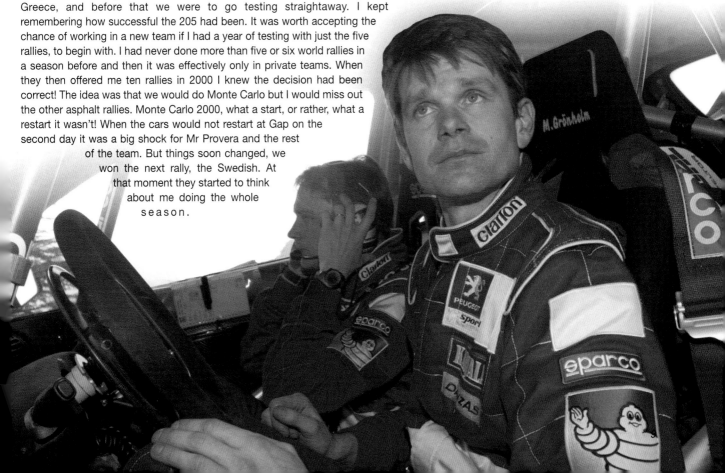

Things went better and by the end of 2000 both Peugeot and I were World Champions.

These were interesting times. How could I, at 1m93, manage to fit into a car whose interior had been laid out for a small person like Gilles Panizzi? Actually it turned out alright. The mechanics were able to move the pedals and the steering wheel and I felt I could live with it. The biggest problem was getting my legs in a comfortable position. There had never been a problem sitting in the Corolla WRC, in that car there was much more room for my legs. After we had done quite a lot of testing I had become comfortable. The first thing I noticed about driving the 206 was the way the car went and how good the handling was. The car was small but turned-in well and it was easy to drive. Many things impressed me, like the high quality of the detailed work on the car. People kept on thinking the smallness of the 206 would mean it was inherently unstable, but it wasn't like that. At the beginning the rear used to kick up a bit, but the engineers were always confident they could overcome that problem. Things progressed quickly. The main problem in the early days was the gearbox.

With Michel Nandan.

We had to change the gearbox on a rally every evening as a routine, but they found the weakness and overcame that. There were many little problems, but none of them were a catastrophe. The thing that spurred everyone on was that the speed was there all the time. While other teams were struggling to get their cars fast enough, our only problem was getting reliability.

I could never have believed that my first full season would end up with me winning the title, particularly having to do four events which were completely new to me. Over this time I also learned to be quite a good mechanic. I got to know how to repair various things! Sometimes the problems were because I hit things, but the car was usually capable of being brought back to service for a proper repair. I knew that we were going forwards all the time in my career, and looking back it is difficult to remember much about the other cars I had rallied. The car had quite a similar feeling to the Corolla, but the 206 had much better suspension with more travel. Both were so much smaller than the old Celicas, where you always had to worry about how wide you could slide out of the bends for fear of hitting things. Even during my days with Peugeot the style of driving required from rally drivers has changed. Now everyone has to drive smoothly and not slide around. In this respect the Celica ST205 did me quite a favour! That car taught me to drive neatly.

So much has changed since we started the 206 programme. As we progressed and entered the active transmission era, other technical problems emerged, notably with the hydraulics which gave a lot of troubles. We were usually lucky to be able to reach service when we had these problems, and happily still the car was fast enough to let us catch up after delays. The biggest mechanical change

Marcus outside the family farm in Inkoo, Finland.

Celebrating victory in New Zealand.

in the last few years has been with the differentials. We started life with the 206 using mechanical differentials. With hydraulic systems we had so many more opportunities to adjust the set-up. Every year the car got better. On faster rallies the improvements are not so big, we could go just as fast with mechanical differentials. It is on the more twisty roads you especially notice the improvements. But it works both ways. You can find the correct set-up much quicker with hydraulic systems, but you can also get lost in finding the correct set-up as well. That has happened to a lot of drivers. The latest technical development is the controlled anti roll bar,

The Family Gronholm

I do not think life as world champion has really changed me. I belong in Finland, not in some lonely tax resort abroad. Finland is the home of our family. There is now a fourth generation of Gronholms living in our house in Inkoo, 50 kilometres west of Helsinki, in the essentially Swedish speaking part of the country. We live on an arable farm, and this is where my grandfather settled. My father, Ulf, was more of a farmer than a rally driver. He had two children, me and my sister. My wife Tessa and I have three children, Jessina 12, Johanna 10 and Niclas 7. Sebastian Lindholm, who is seven years older than me is my cousin (his mother is my father's sister) and my sister Mia married my codriver Timo Rautiainen. While Sebastian and I are busy away on rallies, Sebastian's brother Thomas is taking care of the family farm. While my grandparents were living here in Inkoo my parents lived nearer Helsinki at Espoo, which is where I was born. My mother is still alive. She did not say anything about me and motorsport, even after my father died in his rally car accident. At that time I was 13 and more interested in motocross and used to compete around Finland. In 1985 I stopped motocross when I had an accident which invalided me out of the sport. I had an insurance policy for such an eventuality, and the money they paid was then spent buying my first rally car. It was about £500. I guess when my mother saw the car she knew the future! In between Sebastian's activities on rallies, his main business is running a rally driving school, and he helped me learn the rally business. My training had been farming and I had been in farming college for three years after I left school and my normal work has always been in farming. We are settled here. My wife has a little shop in Inkoo which gives her some motivation even when I am away. All this probably explains why I want to live my life here and do not want to move abroad. If we leave, we will have to go somewhere where my family will have no friends. Have you seen a happy person who lives in Monte Carlo? There is always something special going on here. The happy days of mid summer, the day of the first snows, things like that. It is always special. Each of the four different seasons give something to look forward to. It is just a good place to be.

which started in 2003. This system is not used on gravel because it is vulnerable to damage, and anyway I could not find it made the car quicker, but on asphalt it works. The purpose is to improve tyre wear.

One of the biggest talking points was at the end of 2001 when Richard Burns joined the team. He had just won the World title with Subaru and then came to Peugeot. The consequence of having Richard as my teammate has been talked about a lot. My engineer says Richard has motivated me but I disagree. People forget that I had won rallies and even been World Champion before he came to Peugeot, so I don't necessarily agree with people who say he made me more motivated. I agree it is true I gained my second championship in Richard's first year with us! Sure, when the 206 programme first started we were so keen to get going every day, but even now the moment the helmet goes on, no problem!

Our team chief is Corrado Provera. He is very good for giving a good image of the team, he pulls the team together, stops people dividing their efforts behind one particular member of the team, demonstrating the personality of what we are doing. He has been very good for me but obviously there have from time to time been some difficulties. I think the worst time was when Richard came to the team. It wasn't as most people assumed just a matter of money, rather than of opinion and policy. It wasn't that one driver was given priority over the other, more the feeling that when Richard arrived they thought that he, as reigning champion, in our car would be unbeatable. There was a feeling that if they had brought me up from obscurity into being champion, think what it would be like if you started with someone who was already champion. Richard is close to being the best driver in the business but I do not know what stops him from being unbeatable. I cannot remember him fighting hard for a long time during a rally, maybe it is that. People say that it is because he is a clever driver and only thinks for the championship chances, but I do not agree. I think it is because he tends to give up a little bit if he thinks he cannot win.

Neither of the two regular drivers at Peugeot in 2003, Richard and me, started the season having won an asphalt world

Marcus and Corrado Provera.

championship rally. It is very strange that people in the press all talk about me being a gravel specialist, but it is just the same for Richard as well! Having Gilles Panizzi in our team for asphalt events has taken this pressure away from us. For me it is basically a lack of asphalt rally background in my career that takes away that final 1% of my speed. I still find I do not know what is expected on asphalt from me. On gravel roads, the moment I reach the end of a stage, I know exactly how well I have done. On asphalt, I never can tell. I just do not know if my time was good or bad until I see the times of the other drivers. It may be something to do with not knowing if we had the right tyres or not.

We are coming to the end of the 206 era and looking to the 307. I have driven the new car and know it will be competitive. I do not know what the new car will be like on asphalt. Even by August I had only driven it on gravel. I just want to be sure the car will be ready for the start of 2004. A lot of the car is working without any troubles now, but there are many new things on the car and it will obviously be a rush to get everything ready. Because new rules are coming, things now are not the same as before. We needed to test in every single type of rally we had the chance to do so, now, before the rules changed and it would be too late. There had to be a hell of a lot of work before the end of the 2003 season. There needed to be two separate test teams in operation, working all the time in as many different types of location as possible. Reliability is much more important these days than ever.

Any regrets? I still want to win more rallies, even asphalt ones! I have not finished my work yet. I can still do it. My contract with Peugeot continues until the end of 2004 and I do not have any specific deadlines in my life. I am now 35 years, I reckon I have a few more years left. I do not think rallying is changing so much. Ford is trying to make this a young man's sport but it has not come to that yet. I predict it will be another five or six years before someone like Jari-Matti Latvala can think of being a champion. Rallying is so much a matter of accumulated experience. The proposed rules limiting recceing do not help the younger drivers. I am looking forward to the next step in my career with the 307. Hope to see you there!

Meeting interesting people.

(left) Jumping on the Cyprus Rally.

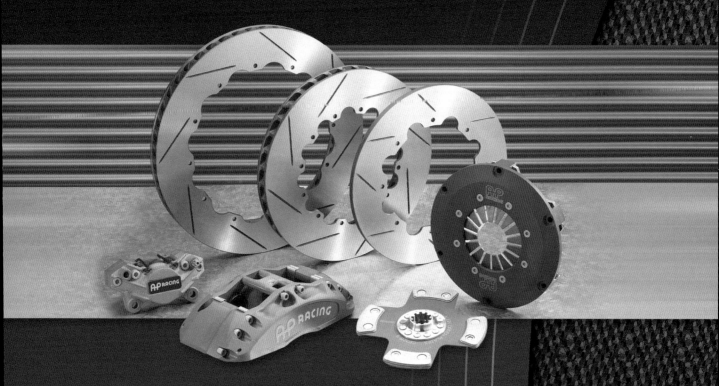

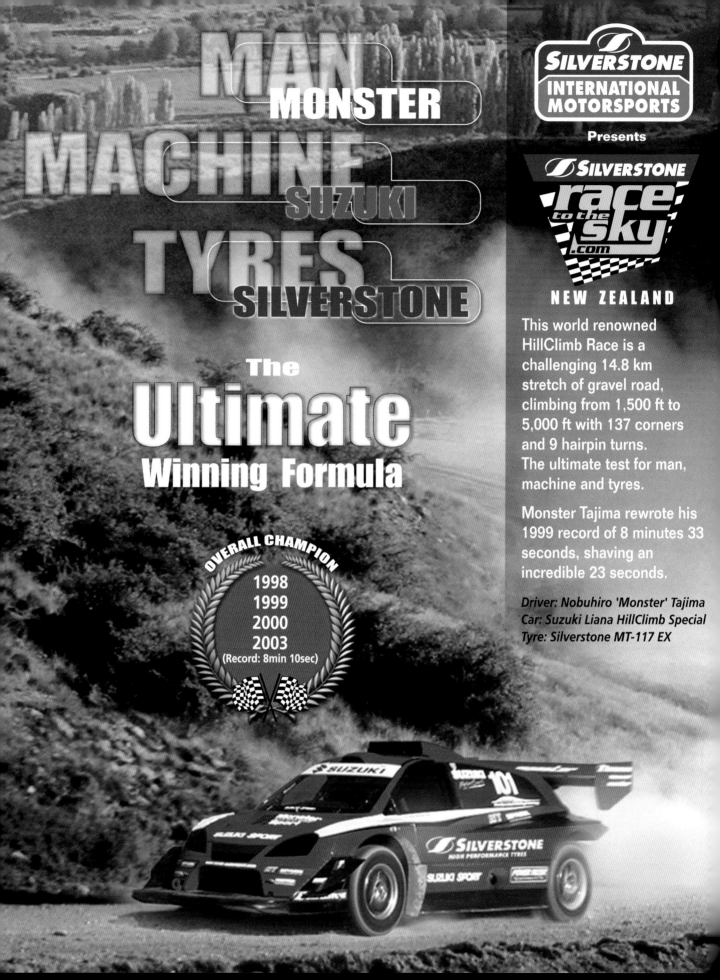

MONSTER

MAN

MACHINE

SUZUKI

TYRES

SILVERSTONE

The Ultimate Winning Formula

This world renowned HillClimb Race is a challenging 14.8 km stretch of gravel road, climbing from 1,500 ft to 5,000 ft with 137 corners and 9 hairpin turns.
The ultimate test for man, machine and tyres.

Monster Tajima rewrote his 1999 record of 8 minutes 33 seconds, shaving an incredible 23 seconds.

Driver: Nobuhiro 'Monster' Tajima
Car: Suzuki Liana HillClimb Special
Tyre: Silverstone MT-117 EX

OVERALL CHAMPION

1998
1999
2000
2003
(Record: 8min 10sec)

SILVERSTONE
HIGH PERFORMANCE TYRES

SUZUKI SPORT CO.LTD 665 Hiehara Ryuyo-cho, Iwata-gun, Shizuoka, 438-0213 Japan. Tel: 81-538-66-6040 Fax:81-538-66-6

From Panamericana to Mexico

News that the Corona Rally Mexico would become a member of the FIA World Rally Championship in 2004 came as a delightful reward for long and hard work by a group of dedicated enthusiasts. This is no sudden inspiration, indeed it is the reward for the imagination, dedication and hard work but the source of the original inspiration is clear. The Carrera Panamericana races of the 1950s! This Mexico-length race was held only five times in its original version, but has done much to generate the chance for Mexicans to discover road sport first hand. And strange to say, without the Panamericana it seems unlikely that Mexico, 50 years later, would be in the position to be part of the FIA's world rally championship.

Rally President Juan Suberville

Rally Director Patrick Suberville

FROM PANAMERICANA TO MEXICO

David Higgins passes a village spectator.

Regularity…?

Regularity sections on rallies demand drivers keep very closely to a required 'regularity' average speed. In old time Mexican rallies there was a twist. The winner was the driver who adhered most accurately to their own previously declared speed, even though the nomination of the speed had to be made without first knowing which roads the route would take. The only navigational instrument in those days was the car's standard distance recorder! Regularity rallying was the basis of Mexican rallying until the early '90s when performance rallying took over.

Franco Soldati at speed in his Ford Mustang on the 1995 London - Mexico marathon.

Mexico has a long motorsport tradition. There were no fewer than 15 Grand Prix races held in the country from 1963. There were the legends of the racing brothers Rodriguez, the dusty endurance Baja 1000 off-road race, the 1970 London Mexico marathon and its 1995 re-run, and recently the CART races at Monterrey and Mexico City. There is a strong motor industry in the country. Ford and Renault have supported motor sport in the country for many years, but through all this variety the Panamericana events are the most emotive. Not only from the memories, but the way one event led on to another, until Mexico now has a rally strong enough to be a world championship event.

The Carrera Panamericana was an amalgam of glory and tragedy. It was the time when the great competition teams from Europe, such as Ferrari, Lancia, Mercedes, Gordini, Alfa Romeo and Porsche, also the top teams from North America, went racing along the open roads in Mexico. The event was conceived as a way for proving to the people of Mexico that, just like similar events had earlier done in South America, arterial roads had now been built to allow people to travel from one end of the country to another. Roads were a way to unite the people in the country, the race was a way to give the people the sense of unity, excitement and importance. The ambitions are very little changed from 50 years ago. A world championship rally serves to demonstrate, now not only to local people but also people from other lands, that a host country is a viable, safe, economic and law abiding country, and also an event able to entertain people who live in faraway regions.

Guy Lassauzet, a long time motor sport enthusiast, recalls how rallying first started in Mexico. "My father Rene was a course official in the Panamericana in the 1950s. It was quite an international occasion. The Panamericana organisers needed help and approached AAA in the USA for ideas and support. Most of the competing cars were American but the event also created considerable interest in Europe. My father became friends with the Monegasque Grand Prix driver Louis Chiron, who came each year to the race. Chiron knew all about the Rallye Monte Carlo, about how regularity sections (then the competitive basis of major rallies) were run, what rallying was all about. He said it was first necessary to form a club before starting to organise an event. Our family was French, coming from Ales in Provence, and with other French ex-patriots my father formed his club called Automovil Club de Mexico." The first rally was called the Rally Morelos and held in October 1954. It was two days long, without a concentration run. In this way, the French had already started to stamp their authority on Mexican motorsport. "Among the Frenchmen who emigrated to Mexico was the rally driver Jean Trevoux. He was four times Monte Carlo winner (when regularity sections were the competition style of the event). He came to Mexico to see the Panamericana, liked the life here so much that he never went home." Trevoux actually renewed his competition career in his exile, proving to be probably the best French driver in the Panamericana races.

The invasion of the first group of French racing enthusiasts in the 1950s was one thing, but a few years later another French group came to prominence, and founded the CAF (French Automobile Club) in 1956. It was the CAF club that the Suberville brothers (Juan and Patrick) joined in 1985 becoming influential in Mexican rallying and organisers of the Corona Rally Mexico. The French were not alone, however. There were many groups of European families living in Mexico and fascinated by motorsport. Franco Soldati, now the outgoing President of the Mexican federation FMAD, came from an Italian background and

Club history...

● 1950s, Rene Lassauzet formed Automovil Club de Mexico. First rally was called the Rally Morelos, held in October 1954. In 1956, the CAF (French Automobile Club), was founded respectful of their French connection but in distinctive and friendly rivalry to the club originally founded by Lassauzet.

● National championship rallying has been a feature of the sport since 1957, with around eight qualifying events each year, with 30 or so cars regularly taking part on each event.

remembered the Panamericana well. "My father used to cook. I remember him inviting all the Italian drivers to our home in Mexico City to cook them spaghetti. I specially remember the driver Felice Bonetto who was at our house the day before he died."

Despite the hopes of the immigrants who came to the country after the war, life was not easy for Mexican motor sport enthusiasts. Mexico was a poor country and import restrictions on cars severely limited the availability of foreign cars. Soldati, "Some foreign drivers were able to import cars to Mexico just for the race, and then drove them to other countries, even as far away as Argentina, afterwards. In 1962 the commercial borders were closed to imported cars, only cars made in Mexico were available to buy which limited sportsmen to GMs, Fords, Chryslers, Nissans and Renaults." At that time Ford were the greatest commercial supporters of rally sport, but only with large American based cars. "The big front engined, rear-drive American cars were spectacular to watch, but tyre wear was a well known problem in Mexico. In the Panamericana days, many of the foreign competitors found the Mexican roads so abrasive that they ended up by using tyres made for trucks. They lasted a long time but they could not withstand being driven fast!"

Drivers from those times may have long been absent but they are still remembered. Perhaps the greatest Mexican rally driver was Sergio Gonzales, seven times national champion, and the only driver successfully to make the transition from driving regularity into driving performance rallies. Emilio de la Parra was champion twice and delighted spectators (and maybe also the tyre industry) by the lurid style in which he handled the big American based cars he rallied. Jorge Serrano was twice champion and also noted for his driving big Ford and GM cars while another old-timer driver Francisco Martinez Gallardo is still active and was recently a challenger for the Presidency of the Federation. He was 1969 champion and also had a wide experience of Mexican motorsport including competing on the Baja 1000.

Enthusiasts in the 1970's had a chance to see more exciting cars in action when they were brought to Mexico by visiting competitors. Soldati, "Some cars were rallied here by foreigners, cars like the Fiat Abarth 131 and the Triumph TR8 which were

Javier and Gabriel Marin

being run on American rallies, when the NARRA organisation also ran qualifying events in our country." The dearth of suitable cars for Mexicans continues. "Only now do we have one-make rally championships. Peugeot and Renault cars have done much to encourage rally drivers at grass roots level and this in turn should give them the chance to progress upwards." Unfortunately the first local rally driver to want to rally regularly in world class championships, Ricardo Trivino who is entered in the FIA Production Car championship, has problems of another kind. The Mexican authorities denied him a licence after a disagreement with the federation and he has to compete under the Spanish flag!

In the 1970s and the '80s, it became obvious that performance rallying was the only serious way to progress in the sport. Soldati: "I had seen in Europe what performance rallying was like and knew we needed to go the same route. The Subervilles felt the same way and they undertook to run special stage rallies for the national championship. These became the standard style in Mexican rallies from the early '90s, and the brothers (Juan and Patrick) have worked all the time to upgrade the standard to a point where Mexico now had a real world championship opportunity." Things finally seem to be pulling together. The present situation in Mexico is that more automotive companies are appearing in the national car market. Of the current WRC participating companies only Ford and Peugeot are strongly active in the Mexican market, but Citroen and Mitsubishi are coming soon, which bodes well for the future of the Corona Rally at world championship level.

Juan Suberville admits he first had the vision of a world championship rally in Mexico in 1999. By 2000 he had put on the first rally in the quest for a world qualifying event. "Money was of course the first major hurdle. Our family put personal assets into the project, and things finally seem to be going in the right direction but it hasn't been easy. There are various specific factors we have to face. For example, to be a world championship rally it is better to be a gravel event, but here in Mexico drivers prefer asphalt events, because these are less damaging on the cars. It is also a pity that Mexican drivers are not competitive with those from other countries but a lot is due to the availability here of cars currently suitable for rallying. This however seems to be changing for the better."

"The next challenge has been to achieve compatibility with international vehicle regulations," continued Suberville. "This has been a major hurdle in our work. Our first major international rally was the Rally America in 2000 when the total number of cars completely complying with FIA rules was one. We have come a long way in the right direction in three years." In 2001 Ramon Ferreyros came from Peru and won in a Toyota Celica GT Four, the

Mexico's 2003 world championship representative: Ricardo Trivino.

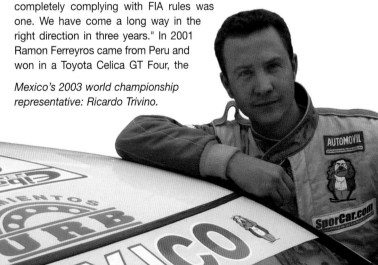

Sergio Gonzalez in his Ford Fairmont.

following year Peugeot (the factory team doubtless encouraged by the future world championship potential of the event) sent Harri Rovanpera with a World Rally Car. "Harri's runaway victory against negligible opposition was not the ideal way to go, whatever the quality of the car and driver. So for 2003 the organisers invited six internationally known Group N drivers, no fewer than five of whom (Daniel Sola, Ramon Ferreyros, Janusz Kulig, Marcos Ligato and Patrick Richard) were active contenders in the FIA Production Car World Rally Championship and the sixth David Higgins, was the reigning US Champion. There was not only a good spread of talent, but even more important, it was a very close run event. In the first six stages there were three different leaders."

The host city for the Corona Rally Mexico is Leon GTO. This city has a heaven-sent head start with its name alone. GTO! How many places with motor sporting aspirations would give their all for a motorsporting connotation like that! GTO is, in fact, an abbreviation for the state of Guanajuato, but does that matter? Leon GTO also once served as a staging-post in the Panamericana events and the nearby town of Silao was the scene of one of the most upsetting moments of those events, when the Lancia works driver Felice Bonetto crashed. Bonetto, even at 50 years old, was an accomplished Grand Prix driver and teammate to the great drivers of his day. He loved the Panamericana, but this was to come to a tragic end. On the 1953 event he was driving a

works Lancia D24 sports car and entered the town flat-out. The car launched itself into the air when it struck a "vado", a washaway which crossed the road at right angles. The racing car cartwheeled through the air for 75 metres before crashing into a roadside building and Bonetto was killed. There is a memorial plaque on the wall.

Corona Rally Mexico will never, hopefully, have anything but good memories for the people of Silao, Guanajuato and Leon who have come to see what was going on and who will come in future years as well. This is a place where little but good can come from hosting an event of world championship standard, for the competitors, the organisers, the people and the country itself. Leon GTO has every reason to hold its head high when it comes to rallying. Memories in Mexico are not just for enthusiasts, they are for everyone touched by the sport.

Regional Connections

One of the major frustrations for local enthusiasts is that Mexico has never yet formed a strong alliance within an international rally framework. Franco Soldati, President of FMAD, "We have pursued many avenues with other countries, trying to make our sport more international, but always the result is the same. Things haven't happened. We worked well in the late 1970s with NARRA, one of the American rallying bodies, but that series was wound up in 1980. Recently we have tried to help NACAM (North American, Caribbean and Mexico) federation to work but about the only support we have had are entries from Costa Rica for the Corona Rally. There has been talk recently about an organisation called Championship of North American Rallies (Canada, USA and Mexico) but it has not really taken off, yet. The trouble is that these associations have become concepts rather than realities. Difficulty of transportation in our part of the world has always been a major problem. It takes ten days by boat to bring a car here from Peru, assuming a boat is available, it even takes three days driving a car up from Costa Rica."

2000

2001

2002

2003

Recent Winners

RALLY AMERICA 17/18.06.2000			23s	8f
1 Douglas Gore/Mark Nelson	Mitsubishi Lancer Evo VI	4h.01m.02s.		
2 Gabriel + Javier Marin	Mitsubishi Lancer Evo V	4h.14m.46s.		
3 Raffaele Cardone/Jorge Bernal	Audi A4	4h.23m.41s.		
CORONA RALLY AMERICA MEXICO 27/29.04.2001			22s	11f
1 Ramon Ferreyros/Raul Velit	Toyota Celica GT-Four	3h.44m.42.8s.		
2 Douglas Gore/Mark Nelson	Mitsubishi Lancer Evo VI	3h.52m.25.6s.		
3 Andres Montalto/Max Rohrmoser	Toyota Celica Turbo 4WD	4h.09m.01.7s.		
CORONA RALLY MEXICO 26/28.04.2002			37s	9f
1 Harri Rovanpera/Risto Pietilainen	Peugeot 206 WRC	4h.23m.21.8s.		
2 Carlos Izquierdo/Angelica Fuentes	Mitsubishi Lancer Evo V	5h.22m.56.1s.		
3 Roberto Sanchez/Mauricio Pimentel	VW Golf GTI	5h.40m.44.7s.		
CORONA RALLY MEXICO 13/16.03.2003			45s	16f
1 Marcos Ligato/Ruben Garcia	Mitsubishi Lancer Evo VII	4h.34m.19.9s.		
2 Janusz Kulig/Jaroslaw Baran	Mitsubishi Lancer Evo	4h.35m.24.0s.		
3 Andres Montalto/Max Rohrmoser	Subaru Impreza	4h.59m.50.2s.		

KNOCK OUT

PIRELLI. WORLD RALLY CHAMPIONS 2003.

Petter Solberg in his Pirelli shod Subaru is the new World Rally Champion Driver.
A celebration of Pirelli's 19th World Rally Championship title.

POWER IS NOTHING WITHOUT CONTRO

Black Magic

In the complicated world of rallying, few topics seem so complex as the black magic of tyres. Questions are only answered with incomprehensible replies. Tyres are always offered as a reason for failure, when no other explanations are available, rather than as reasons for success... Pirelli's Motorsport Director Paul Hembery tries to answer some of the questions which do not appear to have an obvious answer, in a way we can understand.

1   How has rally tyre work changed in recent years?

In the last ten years or so, rally tyre development has changed from being completely innovative into being adaptive to changes in regulations. For example, one regulation which was introduced some years ago was substantially to reduce the permitted dimensions of tarmac tyres. Immediately this meant that rally car tyres now have to be very small compared with the forces and duress to which they are submitted. Cars are therefore now 'under-tyred'. Some of the most recent changes in rallying come from the double usage of stages, the way conditions can change during an event and also the general extent of knowledge about each individual stage. Today there are fewer different types of surface encountered on each event. The calendar, however, is the biggest variable we face in rallying. On some events, a change in a rally date/season can dramatically alter the character of a rally and therefore requirements for a tyre manufacturer.

2   What do you seek to learn from testing?

You look for improvement in acceleration, in braking and cornering performance. On tarmac, you have the opportunity to measure in great detail how the cars and the tyres are working. Gravel remains more subjective than tarmac, it is very hard to measure exactly what the driver is feeling. Drivers have different styles, and the drivers' style has a great effect on how he perceives the tyres are performing. If a driver gains confidence with a specific product, he will push harder than with tyres which scientifically are faster. Understanding the type of surface is the main aim before events, then finding out what the conditions will be. Hot or cold, wet or dry. That information will give the tyre designers the information on which they need to work.

3   What features about the design of tyres actually allow the cars to go round corners faster?

Firstly you need the greatest 'footprint' (surface area of tread) on the ground as possible. Then you need stickiness. A genuine chemical reaction between the tyre and the road surface creates the stickiness. Thirdly, it is the ability of the compound to allow the tread pattern to form itself around the contours of the surface of the road. The contact patch ('footprint') is three dimensional.

4   For the driver, what style of driving gets the car round corners quickest?

These days, you lose time if the car is allowed to slide round corners. Over even just the last few years, driving styles have changed dramatically. With the improved traction control systems on the cars the quickest way round corners is to have a very clean line, to be very tidy. This is coming even to the smoother gravel rallies. I think this change in style is why some of the older drivers in the sport, who are used to driving in other styles, are struggling today. Awesome levels of car control are now not so important. Gravel rally tyres are acquiring more of the structures previously seen in tarmac rallying, with very flexible sidewalls and larger footprints.

5   How important was the rule change some ten years ago which limited the number of tyres to be used on each event?

This was fundamental, and now the FIA are set to move to reduce this number even further. Rule changes are themselves costly, and certainly if the proposed reduction to 40 tyres per car per event goes ahead, we will have to review all the competition tyres in our range and how we use them. Maybe we will have to develop 'double stint' tyres which will not be changed at service areas, if it helps us have a wider range of compound choice. We will have to decide what parameters are more important than others.

6   Tread patterns are controlled, but not compounds or constructions. How many varieties of these are available on each event, and are tyres of exactly the same specification prepared for two different rallies?

There are generally three different compounds for each pattern. We aim to have only one construction for each event. Various rallies have similar characteristics and this allows us to use the same constructions and patterns. Compounds are chosen based on anticipated climatic conditions. All three factors provide performance advantages. Currently the constructions relating to the reinforcements of tyres are providing the most significant advantages.

7   Why control only the number of available tread patterns?

It is a rule which can be easily checked. It was introduced to stop manufacturers being tempted to bring a wide range of tread patterns to events. Cost cutting. Tread patterns can dramatically influence the performance of the tyres. On fast gravel events, tread patterns can be very specific for braking and traction. Different treads can have a very widespread effect. On rough events where the correct construction and durability of the tyres is fundamental, tread patterns are not so important. Compounds are not easily controlled. We believe that a useful limit on costs can be achieved instead simply by limiting the total number of tyres a team can bring to events. This would reduce the number of available compounds, rather than just the number actually used.

8   Why were slick tyres banned?

This happened from the start of 1995 to help reduce speeds. It meant that tread pattern philosophy also became important for dry weather tarmac tyres. The main problem with putting grooves into tarmac tyres is increased wear, so we have to concentrate on minimising the wear on tyres. Also, putting patterns into otherwise slick tyres can create weak points in the tyres which can cause a buckling effect. The skill is to put in the required amount of groove without compromising the rigidity of the belt area (underneath the rubber) and overcoming issues regarding wear.

(top to bottom) This Pirelli truck can carry nearly 1,000 tyres. Discussing suitable tyres at Deutschland Rally. Paul Hembery (right) with Subaru's Technical Director David Lapworth.

9   How are tread patterns designed?

Science and magic together! Experience counts a lot. It has become a habit in the business to evolve tread patterns rather than create revolutions. Various factors have to be considered not the least that the same type of tyre may be used in many different conditions in various parts of the world. Many patterns are compromises. The work of developing patterns has a direct influence on road car technology. Maybe asymmetrical tread patterns are the most important change in recent years. It is a way to get good braking and good lateral grip from the same tyre! The biggest challenge for the future will be defining the surfaces on which the stages will run, and matching patterns to those surfaces in the prevailing conditions. For tarmac rallies this is more straightforward. On gravel we do not have the same standards of analysis because of the subjective factor.

*(top to bottom) Ready to run!
The markings tell us it is a KM type
tyre (a narrower gravel version) with
compound grade 4+ (a medium
grade compound), in set 21, suitable
for fitting to the left side of a car
after first being used as a spare.
Paul with Fiorenzo Brivio,
Pirelli's rally manager.
Running with flat tyres is a
valuable feedback from
Group N, where mousses
are forbidden.*

10 Do drivers prefer specifications of tyres which are not necessarily
the most performant?

Some drivers have preferences. For example, Richard Burns likes cars which are very
precise and rigid and therefore needs very precise tyres while Tommi Makinen
preferred a softer and more forgiving tyre. Drivers still indicate preferences in the way
they want tyres to behave.

11 When you know the characteristics to be encountered on a rally, are there
specific ways ideal tread patterns can be defined?

Yes, and these would be varied according to each type of surface. For example, we
are talking about, the angle of the lateral grooves, do you want to open out the
grooves, is it necessary to have a tread pattern to help expel the gravel from under
the tyre? Or close it up if the conditions are harder? We probably only homologate
one new tread pattern a year. Cutting the tread blocks is a way we can easily change
the patterns, and of course that demands science and experience, and enables us to
modify a design actually on an event. For the future, cutting the tread patterns is likely
to be banned. The effect of this will then have to be incorporated into a new pattern
design instead, so we will have to spend more time evaluating the science of tread
patterns. This is bound to force more research on the effect of tread patterns and their
interrelation with surfaces. This is especially important in relation to the design of off-
road tyres.

12 What has been the impact of the anti-deflation mousse in rallying?

This has not had much effect on the design of tyres, but a big change in how drivers
drive! Strangely enough the most number of punctures our drivers suffer are not on
gravel but on tarmac roads, because the mousses now allow drivers safely to cut
corners and shower the road with stones thrown up from the verges. In terms of tyre
technology, our drivers often prefer to run the same tyres without mousse on some
events, and of course the PCWRC/Group N cars are not allowed to run with them,
anyway. Pirelli has also worked hard over many years developing 'run-flat' tyre
concepts, and indeed these are incorporated into PCWRC/Group N tyres. Personally
I prefer this line of development, it has a lot more relevance to road car tyres.

13 What changes in the escalating technology of the cars have had the greatest
effect on tyre manufacturers?

It must be development of differentials. I believe a consequence of this work is that
the role of the tyres is coming to be less important in world rallying, in the sense that
the current traction systems on the cars are dominating the sport. For example,
whereas tyre wear used to be a major factor, this is not now so because cars can now
use tyres in a more even manner. Suspensions are also developing all the time, and
we are approaching the era of dynamic suspensions which will take this further
forwards. We have already seen major changes in the Peugeot and the Citroen. What
is to say we will not go towards a fully active suspension rally car? That will further
diminish the impact of the tyres on the performance of the car. For us that is not a
problem, it is an evolution of the sport, tyres will still be needed! Ten years ago the
tyres had 60% effect on the performance, now it is 40%.

14 What is the consequence of these changes for a tyre supplier?

Traction control allows tyres to wear in a more even manner. This then allows the use
of softer compounds, especially on tarmac. Traction control has opened up a new
avenue in tyre development. For example cars like Peugeot run at almost zero
camber, so the tyre runs very flat on the ground. This means wear rates are very
low, and so we can soften the tyres more than we used to do in similar circumstances.
I think the immediate future of our work lies in the use of softer compounds.

15 What other characteristics in the design of a rally car makes the work of rally tyres easier?

Anything which allows the car to run with as little camber as possible, both in straight lines and in corners. Even two extra degrees of camber means you lose 18 to 20% of your footprint, almost the equivalent of having a fifth tyre on the road! When Peugeot first came out with their new suspension system, we noticed they were already a half second a kilometre faster. The other advantage of running with low camber angles is the enhanced braking ability. You have more rubber on the road, you can brake later and longer into corners. The French teams are very active on this "camber retrieval" work, which enables you to run with very little camber.

16 What does the future hold?

Shock absorber development is becoming very interesting. One day we may well see a car with fully active suspension which will mean you can get rid of shock absorbers altogether. Shock absorbers help in putting more tyre on the road, on gravel in particular. If you think of the way the suspension rebounds on gravel, the better you cope with the rebound, the longer the tyres stay in contact with the road and that means you are getting better traction. It is all the business of getting more of the tyre on the road more of the time. I think suspension design is the fastest developing area in rally cars at the moment.

17 What are the main challenges in winter tyre work?

Snow! The biggest question is to decide what type of snow you are dealing with. Defining snow is one of the most difficult jobs of all the work in tyre design. So far as winter rallying is concerned, there are other factors such as defining if we are dealing with snow or ice or maybe frozen gravel. Or whether there is a melting situation, when the temperatures rise above zero. Especially in full snow, the pattern of the tyre is paramount so that you prevent the tread blocks from getting clogged up with the snow. In those conditions you need a tread pattern that clings itself to the snow.

18 What about studs?

When it is icy the studs themselves have fundamental importance. The movement and the behaviour of the stud in the tyre make the tyre faster or slower. As soon as the stud starts to move there is a big drop in performance. There are three challenges. Firstly to insert the stud in the tyre in the first place, secondly to keep it there firmly and thirdly to stop it coming out! The fastest way to drive in winter rallies is to ensure you retain your studs. This means you must avoid overly aggressive braking, which can rip the studs out of tyres, also to try to avoid gravel patches that may appear.

19 What are the challenges in Group N work?

On account of the ban on using mousses, puncture resistance becomes a major objective. Although it would be good to be able to use 18 inch tyres on tarmac rallies, to be the same as world rally cars this is not allowed. In other respects, the technology in Group N is the same as in WRCars but maybe one step behind. Also there were new rules in 2003 limiting the quantity of tyres which could be used, so we have already started to gain experience of "double-stint" useage. That will be good experience for when we are going to have to do that on the WRCars as well in future.

20 How does Pirelli feel about rallies today?

We love rallying. In 2003 we were disappointed we could only work with one team in the world championship. Not only did this statistically reduce the chances of victory, but it took away the opportunity of a second team giving us a benchmark in our work. But I must say it was great working with such a highly experienced and competent team as Subaru and we look forward to a very competitive year in 2004.

(top and bottom) Two types of winter tyre: snow type on the left, ice type on the right. EMI mousse inserts waiting to be fitted.

CYPRUS

A HOLIDAY ISLAND IN THE SUN...
...and home to an FIA World Rally Championship event

on't miss the opportunity
combine a first class holiday with
first class event

CYPRUS AA 2004 **CYPRUS RALLY**
14 - 16 MAY

CYPRUS SPORT
ORGANISATION

CYPRUS TOURISM
ORGANISATION

WRC
FIA WORLD RALLY
CHAMPIONSHIP

CYPRUS AUTOMOBILE ASSOCIATION PO Box 22279 Nicosia Cyprus Tel: +357 22 313233 Fax: +357 22 313482
E-mail: caa@cytanet.com.cy Website: www.cyprusrally.org

Go racing with C2

CITROËN SPORT

C2 CHALLENGE

C2 SUPER 1600

100 % compétition | competizione al 100 % | 100 % competition | 100 % competición | 100 % rennsport

Automobiles Citroën DCCO • Design: ® WAKKELI-PIP 10/2003 • Pictures: DPPI, Greg, Pl Lagua

CONTACT

Citroën Sport
Customer Department
Tel.: +33 (0) 1 30 84 04 57
Fax: +33 (0) 1 30 84 04 60

André Péan
C2 Rallycross Challenge
C2 Super 1600 Trophy
Tel.: +33 (0) 1 30 84 04 56

Christine Solibieda
C2 Rally Challenge
Saxo T4 Trophy
Tel.: +33 (0) 1 30 84 04 65

What the Engineers Think...

about their rivals' cars

More and more it is the Engineers in the teams who are becoming the focal point in the evolution of rallying. Each Engineer is extremely proud of their team, happy to let you share their achievements. Each has been responsible for evolving one of the most significant cars in the manufacturer's range, and indeed in the history of the manufacturer they represent. Each Engineer however is only one part of the whole sport, representing one of seven manufacturers at World Rally Car level. Each of them knows they have six rivals to beat before they can succeed. Each rival manufacturer offers a different base from which to produce a World Rally Car design. Each company has a different scale of operation, a different objective. When the Engineers walk around the Service Parks, what they think about their rivals' cars could produce a wide range of emotion. It would be nice to know what each of them thinks about the cars of the teams they are competing against. So we asked them.

Jean-Claude Vaucard, Citroen Total

Ford: is a very good, strong car. Very good on rough roads. The Focus still seems to be getting better and better, even though it is now in its fifth season.

Hyundai: a good job, the car is always improving but it was a serious problem for them having to stop their winter testing.

Mitsubishi: good decision to stop their competition in 2003 to plan a new start for 2004. They had fallen too far behind to carry on as they were.

Peugeot: the best engine, the advantage of having a small car. Their success is that they have made a good job of everything they do.

Skoda: a surprisingly good engine, we have measured this for ourselves. Their problems are that the Octavia was essentially too heavy.

Subaru: often suffers from reliability troubles which come because they are always pushing forwards.

ENGINEERS

Christian Loriaux, M-Sport/Ford Motor Company

Citroen: design is very good, one of the best shapes. The decision to use the transverse transmission was clever. They did their homework right.

Hyundai: performance recently improved a lot largely by changing the under bonnet layout. The Hyundai is quite a tidy little car.

Mitsubishi: Tommi Makinen's driving skills had kept them up at the top artificially. The car is now visibly behind the others.

Peugeot: very nice because it is very small, has a low frontal area and the best engine. Good low-down torque and engine response.

Skoda: the team seem to be getting better, the engine is not bad and their cars have a good top speed. The team people work hard and are enthusiastic.

Subaru: best factor is the boxer engine with its low centre of gravity. The Impreza is a good car and now the reliability is getting better.

Graham Moore, MSD/Hyundai World Rally Team

Citroen: has a very good low down centre of gravity and adapted well from being a tarmac car into being good also on gravel.

Ford: is everything a World Rally Car should be, everything an engineer would want good centre of gravity, weight distribution and a very good engine.

Mitsubishi: seems to be quite a difficult car to drive. It was necessary to use the left foot for braking to get the best out of the car.

Peugeot: the ideal size, everything packaged very well. There is no one item on the car which is fantastic, but put all together it is excellent.

Skoda: has a good engine, very strong chassis, good suspension but, the Octavia cars struggled because they were heavy.

Subaru: my feeling is that it should be quicker than it is. They have good drivers, good weight distribution, the lowest centre of gravity of all.

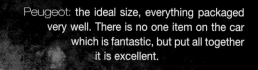

Mario Fornaris, Ralliart/MMSP

Citroen: standard Xsara makes a very good basis for a World Rally Car because of the aerodynamics, the size and the weight.

Ford: speed of development has been helped by computer techniques. I do not think it needs to look so strange, so unlike a production car!

Hyundai: at first sight the Accent looks very nice, with good ideas. Some clever technical solutions. It is surprising they do not achieve more success than they do, but it must all be down to their limit on the amount of testing.

Peugeot: success is because the team is well organised. Design-wise, the parts are never unnecessarily too heavy, their strength is just right, the parts work efficiently.

Skoda: despite competing for so many years the Skodas are always getting better! Becoming an international team has in itself been a great achievement.

Subaru: they still come up with better designs every time! The boxer engine and longitudinal transmission must be an advantage.

Michel Nandan, Team Marlboro Peugeot Total

Citroen: good dimensions, a good compromise for the various conditions encountered and has a good shape so the aerodynamics are good.

Ford: I do not like the look of the 2003 Focus. It looks like a Play Station car! The engine must be one of the best and they have done a really good job on the car.

Hyundai: has good dimensions for a rally car with the length, wheelbase, overhang, and so on. Budget limits are their one big problem.

Mitsubishi: WRC regulations were a big step forward but Mitsubishi stuck with Group A philosophy. Drivers used to World Rally Cars find it hard to drive.

Skoda: the main problem for them is that the Octavia's chassis was not suitable for top line competition. It was too big, the overhang too great but it was strong.

Subaru: the one surprise with the 2003 car, is that they did not gain success immediately. The size, the dimension the weight distributions all make this a most ideal car.

Dietmar Metrich, Skoda Motorsport

Citroen: basically a good car, the chassis is the right size, has a good floorpan and a good wheelbase. After a lot of work they have done a good job.

Ford: perhaps the wheelbase is a little too long, the longitudinal gearbox is not ideal, but I think the new Ford will be competitive.

Hyundai: a good basis, very well engineered in many areas but they always struggle with reliability, maybe because of limits on testing.

Mitsubishi: it did not look right at all. Maybe the car was developed for Tommi? The only car without permanent four-wheel drive or hydraulics.

Peugeot: a complete package, the car, the team, the drivers, everything is done to the maximum. They have a lot of people testing the cars.

Subaru: has a good engine mounted very low. Good suspension, but often with reliability problems. They are advancing in the way they develop things.

David Lapworth, Prodrive/555 Subaru World Rally Team

Citroen: is no more complicated than it needs to be. The car is based on a relatively recent design. It looks very nice and tidy and simple.

Ford: an ideal wheelbase and overall size, and excellent durability. The 2003 car un-does the compromises in the original design.

Hyundai: it is not over-complicated, not over- or under-engineered. It is an effective budget design. What has been done has been done well.

Mitsubishi: Tommi Makinen's brilliance of driving gave the team a false sense of security, which gave them conservative engineering approach.

Peugeot: a well organised team, good resources and good planning. There was no magic about the original design. It is well refined in every area.

Skoda: they got enough out of the Octavia despite limitations of resources for us to take them seriously with their Fabia programme.

IN EVERY KIND OF BUSINESS,

there are times when you only
get one shot at something.
You can't afford to be let down.

WE MAKE SURE YOU WON'T BE.

Trust matters. Whether it's at the FIA World Rally Championship or in the corporate boardroom, you need to know your equipment is going to work. It's something you shouldn't even have to think about. You can believe in Inmarsat technology. Our high-speed, high-quality communications are all about reliability. With our sophisticated satellite network, connectivity is constant. So when something absolutely needs to get through, it does. At the FIA WRC, our high-speed data communications and fast, mobile internet connectivity instantly and reliably relay crucial data to teams and drivers, ensuring everyone can concentrate on the road ahead. When you need one less thing to worry about, trust Inmarsat to deliver.

For more information about Inmarsat solutions, visit www.inmarsat.com/data

inmarsat
Total Communications Network™

EXCLUSIVE GLOBAL PARTNER OF THE FIA WORLD RALLY CHAMPIONSHIP

an **inmarsat ventures** company

Daniel Carlsson

2003 Suzuki JWRC driver

"I have been working with Arne Johansson in the development of this system for the last three years. It is such a consistent system. It really describes the road as I need to know it. There are so many advantages. You can make the notes at any time of day or night, whether you are alert or tired. Always the same pacenotes are produced".

Daniel Barritt

2003 SCCA Rally Champion
US codriver

"David and I have used the system for the last two years. Initially we were very sceptical. When we use the system you can only be impressed. The whole system is an ideal cost-cutting way of using pacenotes, for teams big or small. The notes are clear and well presented, and are very legible at high speed".

David Higgins

2003 SCCA ProRally Champion Driver
2002 SCCA ProRally Champion Driver
2002 Production Car champion, Pirelli British Rally Championship

"I can honestly say that this is a system I completely trust. If personal pre-event reconnaissance of special stages becomes forbidden this is a system which I feel will provide everything that competitors would need. I think this story will tell you something very interesting. It is an extraordinary development in present day rally sport".

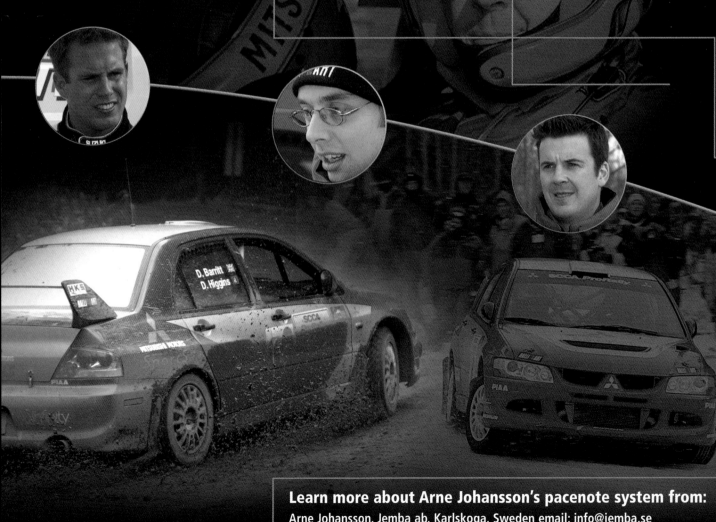

Learn more about Arne Johansson's pacenote system from:
Arne Johansson, Jemba ab, Karlskoga, Sweden email: info@jemba.se

The Virtual Codriver
Listen to the Ideas of Arne Johansson

Champion David Higgins at speed in America, using a machine-made set of pacenotes.

Just occasionally comes an exception in our world of rallying. Something which has never been tried before. My 2003 season started with a journey to Norway to meet someone who could show me the future of codriving. Arne Johansson. Arne is Swedish and is widely known as the designer of the Coralba rally distance recorder. His latest business is making the official pacenotes for rally organisers. On the day we met, he was working with the former Norwegian rally champion Roar Vannebo, making pacenotes for the competitors to use on a small event north of Oslo. Arne wanted me to see what they were doing. When I arrived they had already made their first-time notes and were waiting for me to see them being checked. Actually, they had not made the notes at all. All they had done was to drive along the stage, leaving the work of defining and storing the instructions to a machine. As 2003 progressed and official pressure increased from the FIA to limit rally reconnaissance, so Arne's work began to take on an importance far greater than originally envisaged...

"I started as an amateur codriver in around 1962, when I was training to be an engineer. The more I competed on rallies, the more I wanted to analyse what happened, try to work out why we did not win and make sure I did not make the same mistakes the next time. I was initially competing on orienteering-type rallies (slow speed, precision route finding) but later became involved in high speed rallying as well. There was one famous machine that everyone in rallying used in a rally car, the Halda Tripmaster. This was a distance recorder that was made by a Swedish company that supplied the taxi industry. This machine became an essential tool in the work of any codriver, not only in Sweden but all over the world, and how I used to get angry with it! These machines would often fail to revert back fully to

How it was in the beginning. Under the clocks is a Halda Twinmaster.

zero when instructed to do so. Also you wasted so much time trying to read what the machine was telling you, time when you should have been studying the maps. There was also continual trouble because the cogs used to jump over the teeth, and the accuracy of the machine was always limited by the mechanical ratios of the available gear wheels.

"I gave up getting upset with the Halda machines and planned my revenge. That was when I designed the first of my products, an electronic trip meter, back around 1973. The number displays used glowing wires, it was before the days of LED and LCD. The numbers were so much more easy to read compared with the mechanical ones and could be used at night without the aid of interior lights, which used to reflect on the inside of the protective glass covers. Immediately this led to new ideas. We put a switch on the map light so that I could operate the reset button without having to take my eyes off the maps. Then we found

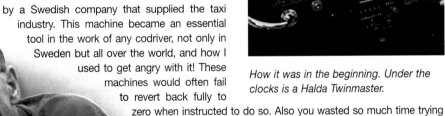

Today's distance recorder, the Coralba.

we could input corrections in the distance readings. This was the start of ongoing work which led to the design and production of the Coralba tripmeter. We realised how much better these were, not the least because electronic machines were much more reliable and very accurate. We are still finding people using Coralba tripmeters which are between ten and 15 years old, and they are perfectly reliable. That was never the case with the old mechanical ones."

Being satisfied that the basic work of codrivers, following the route, had been achieved, Arne started to look at how codrivers could make drivers go faster. "In the early '60s, rallies started to get faster and this made people interested in pacenotes. We started to use pacenotes in international rallies around 1972 and immediately there was a problem which seemed insuperable. This was the difficulty of making them consistent. The weakness was that drivers used their own assessment of the severity and this created the inconsistency. We started to dream of using mechanical sensing devices to create greater consistency, and about ways of recording the sideways forces round a corner, in order to assess what instructions to give the drivers. We tried out a pendulum system, connected to an electric recording meter, but it wasn't very successful. Another idea was to record the angle by which the steering wheel was turned. That did not work very well, either, but at least it gave some information about the shape of the road. We had to wait until the available technology improved before we could make progress at an affordable price level.

"I was thinking about the latest available systems on my way back from the Safari Rally in 1990. An international amateur Swedish rally driver of that time was Fredrik Skoghag, and he urged me to keep working at this system. The starting point was a system where manual judgements were fed into a database

from a digitizer, together with information from a tripmeter. This information could be translated and printed in any type of language or system. This meant we could then make printouts in a recognisable and standardised format. At that time, no sensors were used but this basic system has been used ever since then.

"The next step was to make decisions by machine, not by human judgement. This was combined with a system in which additional human information, which the sensors would not detect but which were important to the driver (for example: cautions and landmarks) could be manually inserted into the machine's instructions. I was eventually able to make the system work and by 1997 it was ready to be tested on an actual event. This was a great breakthrough. It was the Golden Tulip Rally and Mats Andersson was my guinea pig driver. It worked well enough for us to win the class first time out. During 1998 we took part in the British rally championship and gained more valuable experience during actual events."

To make the measurement system accurate enough so that pacenotes can be made by machine was complex work. Always the primary problem was achieving consistency. Presenting the pacenotes in the required style was not difficult. "There was so much available data from recording the dynamics of the car. Deciding what data should be considered depends a lot on what information a driver wants to know. I do not think the information should control him. My idea is to supply the driver with as much relevant information as he wants, then let him be the person who decides what to do with the car!" Curiously, the way the information is given to the driver is not such an issue even if most drivers have a preference for a certain way. There are two different types of pacenotes in common use, a static system which describes the speed at which the corner can be taken and a speed system where the speed you approach the corner is also taken into account. This last system is not suitable for official notes as different competitors face very different conditions and use so many different types of car.

The notes can be presented in two different ways: the number system which gives the grade of a corner as a number, and the descriptive system which tries to tells the driver what the corner is physically like. The descriptive system gives a lot of confusion between drivers as every driver has his own image for every descriptive term. Therefore we prefer drivers to use number system when they start using our notes. Both types of notes however contain the same information and have to be given to a driver at identical moments. "It does not make any difference what system of instruction they want. It ends up by being converted into the required terms and syntax, whether it is the number system, or any other language and type of writing. The main problem is this initial one, selecting the data which is relevant."

There is another factor. The commercial base from which Arne nowadays operate is to provide consistent and friendly pacenotes to organisers so they can issue them to competitors. When competitors are using these notes without having the chance to make their own reconnaissance, they need a lot of additional information. "Just describing the lines is not enough. Drivers will want to be told what the conditions on the road itself are like. Also, remember that organisers' notes will be used by competitors with a wide variety of skills. Beginners cannot

Brave men! Mats Andersson trusts Arne Johansson's machine in Scotland 1998.

With Roar Vannebo in Norway.

cope with too much information so immediately there has to be a compromise. We also had to make the output of information adjustable so that the different preferred ways of receiving the notes can be given, for example the order in which the words like long, caution etc are given."

There is little point in asking Johansson to identify which sensors give the relevant information. If he told us, we would be instantly confused in his technical explanations! What, however, is visible to all is that Johansson uses a small box resting on the floor of the car, under the codriver's legs, and inside this are the sensors. The box is connected to a Coralba tripmeter, so the movement of the car, side to side, front and back, also in the vertical plane, as well as the speed and distances travelled can be correlated together. There is another device, a box which lists the various extra instructions which can be manually inserted into the notes. "The secret is to select which data is needed to give the best notes! I have sensors enough to know how far the car has moved and in which direction. For evaluating the movement of the car in the vertical sense, in other words to know how severe a crest or jump will be, it is also important to know what type of car is being used on the rally. That will tell us whether a crest will become a jump, how far and how high you will jump. The computer will assess all this but usually we set the system up simply to say whether it will be a small, normal or big jump."

When the driver starts to drive down the stage there is nothing for the crew to say to each other, apart from the codriver reading the roadbook, and also to operate a device for manually adding the

additional notes. Whatever the syntax or language used, the format of the pages is kept the same, and opposite the first instruction on every new line is marked the total distance covered so far, and adjacent to the last instruction on each line by the distance still to be covered on the stage. At the moment, the systems do not display the notes on a screen in front of the codriver as they are being written, but that is achievable technically without difficulty. Instead, the display simply produces a usual trace showing the shape of the route being followed, which incidentally has a much higher resolution than a GPS handset can trace. At the moment there is no attempt to trace the altitude pattern of the route but there is no technical problem to do that.

This was the status quo of Johansson's work at the start of the 2003 season. Already he had come a long way. His "First Generation" system had used the DOS (computer operating) system with manual judgement of the instructions. This was developed into the "Generation 1.5" version, in which the instructions were based instead on the Windows operating system. The sensor box arrived for the second generation, which is called Jemba Inertia Notes System, the system provided the desired level of consistency and the ability to create the notes travelling in the opposite direction. Now we start to move into the future with the generation three, nick-named the Virtual Codriver system...

Arne happy at his work. The sensor box is on the floor.

Enter the Virtual Codriver

As soon as I arrived, and without any warning, Arne demonstrated the current state of the art. The Virtual Codriver system. We drove down a road, with the machines switched on, turned round and headed back the way we had come. We listened to an unseen voice reading pacenote instructions in the direction in which we were now travelling! This was a serious glimpse into the future of codriving. Suddenly, before my eyes, the work of the codriver became superfluous. "There is now no difficulty in giving the instructions to the driver without the codriver having to read pacenotes, or even being in the car! We are already capable of doing this, the challenge has been in making the machine read them at a rhythm and in the way drivers want to hear them. To start off there are three available modes, relating to the position during the first time through ('check' mode), then the notes being read at a pace in relation to a simulated drive with the defined car

('simulated driver' mode) and finally at actual rally speeds in relation to actual speed taking into account simulated drive ahead ('race' mode)."

At this time, Johansson does not pay much attention to the revolutionary implications of the work but he knows there is an open door ahead, "My current priority is to make and market pacenotes for organisers in an orthodox manner. Sometimes I wonder what we are doing. Codrivers are there to do a certain job, and that includes pacenote reading. Being a codriver myself I am not quite sure about the ethic of what we do...!" This is a laudable sentiment, but once upon a time there was a sense that pacenoting itself was intrinsically unsporting, later that it was unsociable and dangerous. Rallying is an activity that never stands still. "In fact, now we have finally got to the stage in the development of making notes where we could get the timing of the notes to work well at rally speeds, I have started to become more enthusiastic about developing the item. I think the voice

ARNE JOHANSSON

would be interesting for beginners to use as a back-up for my notes to stop codrivers getting lost." But why just back-up, why not make the talking notes the primary way to instruct a driver? Indeed, why should a codriver speak to the driver at all?

"That will take some more work but, in fact, we are getting there. The rhythm of reading the notes is controlled by sensing how fast the car should be going at any particular point. And this leads us to another science we are developing. We can now calculate how fast the rally car is actually travelling at any particular point on the stages." Now we are entering another huge area of the unknown. "In 2002 we made some advance checks over the stages in Finland and found with our notes system we could immediately calculate, usually to within three percent, the speed of the top cars on the special stages on the Neste Rally and the times the cars would take. Then we started to do more research on Swedish championship rallies and sometimes we were able to estimate the time taken to cover the stage by the crews to a second. This has important benefits to rally organisers from both a safety and an operational aspect. This also opens another huge door, helping to develop rally cars. The system can be used to dictate the standards which should be attained by rally cars, and enable engineers to be able to assess by how much the performance of their cars can still be improved. We have already started to do some tests in this direction, for example we did an experiment by shifting the weight balance in the car, by altering the position of the codriver's seat, and seeing what effect it had on the performance of the car. I am very interested in this and would love to know more."

Where is the work leading? "I can think of situations in which a virtual codriver would be a great asset. We have already proven a lot of the technology which will make the virtual codriver a reality, certainly in the work of using pacenotes." Tomorrow is already here. Stig Blomqvist used the virtual codriver system when he entered Pikes Peak Auto Hill Climb in July 2002, sitting alone in his 600bhp

Ford RS200 (above), knowing well this was the one place in the world when the first error in your pacenotes can easily be the last. "When Stig says something, he has usually thought about it a lot beforehand. He was obviously pleased at Pikes Peak. I kept on thinking about what changes we could make, but he kept on saying he was already happy! We kept on discovering characteristics from our systems about his driving, and we were able to input this into the notes before his next run. The only thing which spoiled his day was when he had a problem with the brakes which slowed him down." Things have come a long way since Arne designed his first electronic tripmeter in 1973, 30 years ago. "My driver started telling other codrivers that I was going to put them all out of business, that my systems were going to make them redundant. Well, the revolution did not come quite as quickly as my colleague imagined, but technology has now caught up with our ideas."

Print-out of the same pacenotes showing how the syntax can be adjusted to drivers' preferences.

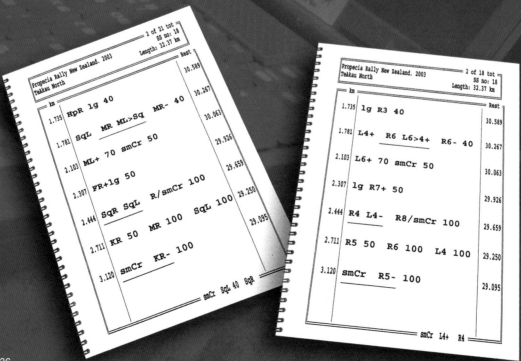

36

MINILITE

the winning wheel

2003 First Overall - PWRC - Rally of Corsica
Niall McShea - Mitsubishi Lancer

2003 First Overall - MSA Historic Rally Championship
Steve Perez - Porsche 911

2002 Second Overall - Rally of Thailand
John Lloyd - Mitsubishi Lancer

2002 First Overall - MSA Historic
Rally Championship
Charles Golding - Escort RS

2002 First Overall - Equator Rally
& Kenyan Rally Champion
Rory Green -
Subaru Impreza

TECH-DEL LTD
Unit 8A, Roughmoor Industrial Estate, Williton, Taunton TA4 4RF United Kingdom
Tel: +44 (0) 1984 631033 Fax: +44 (0) 1984 631044 E-mail: bev.minilite@virgin.net www.minilite.co.uk

YEAR OF

Perhaps the least happy aspect of the 2003 season was the unrest in the sport.

Turmoil came from many sources in 2003, not least the global economic situation, and while it was assumed that Hyundai's departure from the sport was more to do with this than imminent changes in the sport, their withdrawel raised fears that this could be a prelude to other departures. Added to this problem was a belief at the FIA that the ISC might become too powerful for the good of the sport, and the structure of rallying needed to be better defined. The ISC's original plans for promotion of rallying were laudable and exciting but unfortunately became unworkable. Firstly the changes were based on the assumption that all organisers' rights belonged automatically to the FIA and therefore could be assigned to the ISC. After the ISC's contract to acquire the promotional rights had been concluded, the European Union declared that those rights were not assignable. The central theme of ISC's promotion of the sport were the film rights. This immediately forced the ISC to renegotiate their position with organisers, which was largely solved by the ISC agreeing to provide technical facilities regarding timing, safety measures and results.

Based on this new position, the ISC then began to develop plans for a new-style championship, based on a championship calendar with events which provided the best promotional opportunities, even considering ways for events to buy their way into the series. This in turn alarmed the FIA, who felt obliged to state categorically that they, not the ISC, decide which events would form the championship.

In these two steps, much of the promotional powers of the ISC were constricted. The ISC had long declared that their primary work was the marketing of the sport, of which image dissemination was the major part. For a long time the ISC declared strongly that the more events, the more television, the richer the sport would become. During 2003 the ISC was forced to reconsider its stance, declaring it was no longer a marketing operation, and that the television work was their sole major activity. The images of the sport continued to be superb, but gradually the availability of technology to the organisers ebbed away, and this disenchanted the people who most relied on the ISC for cooperation. Journalists became angry that the reduced results services affected their work. Then the ISC admitted that the more events there were in the championship, the more money it was losing!

By this time the FIA was well on its way to restructuring the whole championship based on the premise that 'more was best', and that costs had to be saved to make expansion possible. The FIA never accused the ISC of bad advice but the basic assumption was that, had the ISC not originally been so expansionist, there might not have been any push to expand the championship and in turn change the rules.

Discontent on another front came when the FIA announced details to reduce expenses for the teams. These were outlined at the June 2003 World Council, with instructions to the World Rally Championship Commission (WRCC) to make the system workable in practice. This forced the WRCC into an impossible position. Manufacturers have a minority power in this advisory committee, but they were the only vociferous element. They poured suggestions (often conflicting ideas) into the WRCC but very few of these seemed to have emerged from the WRCC as recommendations. Tensions were escalating all the time. This came to a climax in Australia when Peugeot's Sporting chief Corrado Provera declared the WRCC was 'useless', at an official FIA Press Conference.

'Tensions were escalating all the time'

Beyond the original explanation at the June World Council that rule changing measures were necessary to enlarge the size of the championship, nobody at the FIA would say why there was such urgency to make the changes. The FIA had thrown many revolutionary ideas into the air when they planned the Formula 1 scene for 2003. Now they wanted to do the same for rallying in 2004. In Formula 1

TURMOIL

there were well orchestrated interests ready to catch the balls and throw them back again. In rallying there was no agreed policy between the teams apart from ill defined discontent. The balls bounced on the ground and nobody collected them up.

consequential effects that had never been considered. On a statistical level, every event in the championship could expect a proportionately reduced coverage. No magazine would expand their rally coverage to give greater exposure to the sport just because there are more events.

town. The distaste at the Thursday rather than Wednesday shakedown system which came into force in the 2002 season was profound, the new five-day timetables have only reinforced this.

Through all this it became evident that the FIA and the participants could not understand each other. The participants showed every sign of not understanding how the FIA works, and not knowing the right way to promote their interests. The FIA did not understand why the teams had a passion for building cars which were so expensive, that they spent their money in a way which was acceptable on engineering rather than promotional budgets.

One of the curiosities of the changes is that not all the rules changes are actually bad. The problems are not across the board. For example, the alternative servicing arrangements free the organisers to revert back to a traditional spread of locations. Argentina announced they were going to invoke the 'waiver' option to revisit Santa Maria de Calumachita and Mina Clavero, recent victims of the single Service Park service concept. But the overall signs were bad. Poor consultation, a failure to explain why changes were necessary. It was a bad year for all. And nobody would tell us why.

> ## 'The change from 14 to16 rallies, in times of economic pressure, was most unwelcome.'

Formula 1 by all accounts had been boring and needed an injection of ideas, but this was a sport which had entertainment at its core. Rallying was not only working well, certainly at this time, but it was also an activity which had quite a different foundation, not only financially but also in its sporting protocol and constitution. Decisions were made in quite a different way. The manufacturers were loudly vocal in their unrest, but they over estimated their political power nor could they agree measures between themselves. The FIA could see this clearly, and while paying lip service to certain proposals from the WRCC they went ahead and implemented the majority of the changes.

The change from 14 to16 rallies, in times of economic pressure, was most unwelcome. Not taken fully into account was the fact the two extra rallies were expensive ones to attend. Also that one of them (Japan) was included on a whim without a careful analysis of whether the actual event proposed (Hokkaido) possessed the wider range of qualities which made it suitable for the series. An enlarged championship created so many

Costs may have been reduced for the competing teams, but not for sponsors, organisers, journalists.

Gradually a gamut of consequential effect of the various rule changes became evident. The 'two-driver' rule was flawed. If this was to encourage younger drivers, why should older, world class drivers, have to be thrown out of the sport? Why deliberately reduce the number of top cars? And if teams needed both drivers to score points, experience rather than youth was an essential quality. Then what about the concept of a half-day rally, because of the 'Mille Pistes' recce system? There will be nothing for spectators to see until the afternoon. The whole Service Park rallying epicentre facility, carefully developed over years, was now to become a once-a-day event. Banning gravel note crews takes away the accumulation of countless years of experience in the sport: there had already been an unpopular move to reduce the length of rallies. Journalists had no time to make in-depth interviews at events. Teams had a very limited chance to make their promotions. Organisers found it almost impossible to hold pre-event rally shows in their home

> ## 'One of the curiosities of the changes is that not all the rules changes are actually bad.'

Move & more. OMV

NEIL ALLPORT
Motorsports

Rally Car Leasing

Our Cars are run to the latest full FIA specification and to the current technology from around the world. In 2004 we will have both left and right-hand drive versions of the Mitsubishi Lancer Evo VIII.

We have 20 years of rally experience in National, Asia-Pacific and World championship events with Group A, Group N and World Rally Cars.

Revenge victory for Sebastien Loeb and Citroen after their 2002 debacle.

❖

Yet another bad Monte-Carlo Rally for Peugeot, four years in a row.

❖

Splendid Citroen debut for Colin McRae, his personal Monte Carlo best.

❖

First time victory for a Renault in the Junior WRC after a dramatic performance by Daniel Carlsson's Suzuki.

LEG 1 Marcus Gronholm led all the way, first car on the road. Gilles Panizzi physically disadvantaged and mentally demoralised by a pre-event penalty for a recce offence. Both works Subarus crashed. Remarkable performance by Carlsson in Junior WRC halted by a speeding conviction! Francois Duval lost a wheel but continued.
1 Gronholm 2h07m24.7s, 2 Loeb +20.6s,
3 McRae +1m16.6s, 4 Burns +1m53.9s,
5 Sainz +1m55.7s, 6 Martin +2m30.7s,
7 Robert +4m41.1s, 8 Schwarz +5m03.8s.
JWRC Tirabassi (20th) 2h30m54.4s.

LEG 2 Organisational problems! Stage seven cancelled because of spectator parking trouble. Only the leading cars tackled stages nine and ten because of a motorway blockage. JWRC cars tackled only one stage all day. Gronholm badly delayed allowing Loeb to inherit the lead. Panizzi gave up, Mikko Hirvonen and Freddy Loix went off and retired.
1 Loeb 3h08m54.0s, 2 McRae +1m07.9s,
3 Sainz +1m45.0s, 4 Martin +2m24.4s,
5 Burns +3m38.9s, 6 Robert +5m11.5s,
7 Kresta +6m16.2s, 8 Duval +6m36.0s.
JWRC Tirabassi (14th) 3h41m07.8s.

LEG 3 Loeb held an unchallenged lead to the finish. Carlos Sainz delayed by wheel bearing collapse. Gronholm fought back into the Driver points and was again first car on the road, as a result of reverse running order. No fewer than five Junior WRC cars retired and afterwards second-placed Kosti Katajamaki was excluded for technical reasons. Splendid result for Cedric Robert, on only his second World rally in a WRCar, who just beat Duval.
1 Loeb 4h29m11.4s, 2 McRae +38.1s,
3 Sainz +52.2s, 4 Martin +55.5s,
5 Burns +3m16.5s, 6 Robert +5m16.7s,
7 Duval +5m17.1s, 8 Schwarz +6m42.3s.
JWRC Tirabassi (17th) 5h12m36.1s

Citroen swept to victory in very convincing style, gaining control of the rally on the second day when Peugeot failed on this event once again. Marcus Gronholm had been leading the event for the first day in his Peugeot, but while he was systematically being caught by Sebastien Loeb the World Champion went off the road. From then on it was

untouchable Citroen, and particularly Loeb, all the way. Although outwardly the same as ever, the Citroen cars sported not only a new sponsorship colour scheme, but also a hydro elastic suspension system which interlinked the anti roll bars front and rear. Gronholm finished 13th (albeit gaining one point under the new championship scoring rules based on the top eight, not six, qualifying competitors) while his teammate

Hopes were to be dashed for World Champion Marcus Gronholm, who led for over half the rally.

Richard Burns finished fifth after he lost time with poor handling on the second day. Five of the six manufacturers registered for the 2003 series went home with scores to their credit.

The 2003 season's opening event was run in traditional Monte Carlo conditions, maybe with not as much snow as purists would have liked, but in clear weather and on treacherously icy mountain roads. For French fans it was not so much a matter of whether a red painted car would win, but whether it would be a Peugeot (now sporting the colours of their sponsor Marlboro) or a Citroen. The Monte Carlo Rally was as usual its controversial self however! Bad spectator parking caused stage seven to be cancelled, while a motorway blockage caused more trouble. A pre-rally reconnaissance offence had led to Stewards imposing a one-minute penalty on Gilles Panizzi, an act which could hardly be more calculated to destroy his morale. By the end of the first day he was in a hopeless physical condition. Doctors detected low blood pressure and were relieved when he withdrew on the second day.

Hyundai's financial woes prevented pre-event testing. Freddy Loix (seen here) went off the road for the second year running.

44

Star of the Show

A new Superstar has arrived. Suzuki driver Daniel Carlsson was clearly the fastest driver in the JWRC category. He was leading after two stages, despite having had a puncture, but was then baulked by a slower driver, had another puncture and went off and hit a telegraph pole, which dropped him to sixth. By stage five, however, Carlsson had bounced back to second and on stage six, the last of the first day, he was leading again! Then he met an implacable obstacle that would not make way for him. French police stopped him for exceeding the speed limit through a town. He was held up for so long that he was beyond the time limit when he returned to Monte Carlo. "For me it didn't matter, I had never enjoyed myself so much in my life. On one stage I caught and passed a World Rally Car. I've got a fantastic car!"

What's New in 2003

● As in 2002, the maximum number of competitors was limited to 60, with no Group N cars admitted.
● There was free liaison for the competitors from the Ceremonial start to Tallard. It was only necessary for the cars to arrive at Tallard in time to take the restart on the Friday. This obviated the need for a Service Park between the restart and the first stage.
● The rally revisited the region of Gap where the Friday stages were run, allowing a return to the 47km Plan de Vitrolles stage, run consecutively as stages five and six.
● Tallard (Gap airport) replaced Dignes-les-Bains as the Friday Service Park. Monte Carlo remained the location of the Service Park on Saturday and Sunday.

The speed at which Gronholm disappeared into the distance on the first day was very encouraging for Peugeot, but this was not entirely surprising. The World Champion started car number one, on stages clear of snow but often with snowbanks alongside the road, ready to be hit by passing cars. After the first two or three cars passed, drivers told stories of snow and gravel liberally scattered across the road which slowed them down. When the stages were repeated later in the day, the later running drivers had more equal conditions, and this was when Loeb's challenge took shape. Peugeot's hopes plummeted on the second day when first Gronholm damaged his steering on stage eight (dropping him to 15th), then Burns tackled stages nine and ten with dampers and tyre set-ups which were too hard for the conditions. This

First time with Skoda, Didier Auriol bought two points to the team.

meant the efforts of the Peugeot privateers Cedric Robert, the French young driver scholarship winner, and ex-Skoda works driver Roman Kresta were attracting the attention the works team might have expected.

The misfortunes of Peugeot were good news for Citroen! Colin McRae felt that running second to Loeb on this rally was as much as he could hope for. Carlos Sainz was gradually getting the feel of the car and, apart from a few driving errors in the opening stages, did well. Citroens were now running 1-2-3 but then the Spaniard was delayed on the final day when a rear wheel bearing broke, wrecking the brakes and costing him enough time to allow Ford driver Markko

Petter Solberg's first encounter with a bridge ended harmlessly. On the next stage it was more final.

Twenty-two year old Mikko Hirvonen entered a whole new world at Monte-Carlo. On this occasion his Ford Focus was devoid of overt commercial support.

Martin to pass him into third place. Finally Sainz regained third place, when Martin spun and hit a wall, and established the Citroen walkover. Ford's young team leader, however, had done them proud despite feeling weak as a result of illness on the second day. His teammate Francois Duval was also going well but he damaged the suspension and lost a wheel, although he fought hard to recover lost ground, eventually finishing seventh.

Subaru were the only team to run new World Rally Cars on this event. The 2003 version Imprezas were engineering masterpieces and enabled Petter Solberg to lie second behind Gronholm early on and was therefore in front of the Peugeots for most of the first day. Then it went wrong. Twice Solberg hit bridges and

damaged the car, the second time terminally. Teammate Tommi Makinen was delayed on stage four by a freak brake problem, an unlucky delay from a curiously damaged wheel rim. He was lying 14th when he went off the road on the same stage that saw the end of Solberg's efforts. Skoda were, however, happily in the frame. Bolstered by pre-rally declarations that their future competition programme was assured for the next three years, one of their cars finished in the points even if the other retired on the first morning with fuel injector failure. Hyundai were hampered by the absence of dedicated pre-event testing and suffered from poor set-up choices for most of the event. Freddy Loix crashed close to where Gronholm went off, but Armin Schwarz managed to finish in the points.

Junior Championship

Once again Monte Carlo was the first qualifying round of the Junior WRC, a total of 28 entries were received, and eventually 22 cars took the start. Carlsson attracted all the attention on the first day, but when he had to retire Brice Tirabassi took over, held a steady pace and maintained the lead to the end. For a long time the sight of the four yellow Suzuki team cars (now based in Britain and run by mechanics who until two weeks before had never worked together) was a delight. After Carlsson retired, they then lost Salvador Canellas with a broken driveshaft and finally the young ex-kart driver Ville-Pertti Teuronen went off the road. So Urmo Aava was in fact the only Suzuki finisher. The 2003 version Super 1600 Volkswagens were going well. Both Kosti Katajamaki and Oscar Svedlund had reliable drives until curiously both suffered a blocked gearbox, at the same place on the same stage, and both had to drive to service with the gearbox stuck in fifth gear! After the event, Katajamaki's car was inspected by technical officials and was found to be fitted with under-size rear brake pistons. His ensuing exclusion was ironic. "All rally I had a handbrake problem and our team couldn't find out why. It took the FIA to tell us what the problem was!" Tirabassi's success complemented the performance of Simon Jean-Joseph, too old to be eligible for the JWRC, running an identical Renault. Although Jean-Joseph's times were often overshadowed by drivers who qualified for the JWRC, he led the 1600cc class from start to finish of the event and finished a creditable 14th overall on the rally.

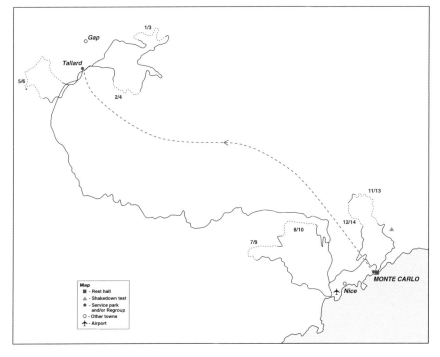

Map
- ■ - Rest halt
- ▲ - Shakedown test
- ● - Service park and/or Regroup
- ○ - Other towns
- ✈ - Airport

Double success came to Renault. This is Brice Tirabassi

71ST RALLYE AUTOMOBILE MONTE-CARLO

POSITION/ LAST STAGE COMPLETED	ENTRANT	DRIVER/CODRIVER	NAT.	COMP NO.	CAR	CAT.	REG NO.	TOTAL PENALTY/ CAUSE
1	Citroen Total	SEBASTIEN LOEB/Daniel Elena	F/MC	18	Citroen Xsara	WRC	32CSP92 (F)	4h.29m.11.4s.
2	Citroen Total	COLIN McRAE/Derek Ringer	GB	17	Citroen Xsara	WRC	15DDM92 (F)	4h.29m.49.5s.
3	Citroen Total	CARLOS SAINZ/Marc Marti	E	19	Citroen Xsara	WRC	31CSP92 (F)	4h.30m.03.6s.
4	Ford Motor Company Ltd.	MARKKO MARTIN/Michael Park	EE/GB	4	Ford Focus RS	WRC	FX02OBD (OD)	4h.30m.06.9s.
5	T. Marlboro Peugeot Total	RICHARD BURNS/Robert Reid	GB	2	Peugeot 206	WRC	206NLM75 (F)	4h.32m.27.9s.
6	Equipe De France FFSA	Cedric Robert/Gerald Bedon	F	20	Peugeot 206	WRC	3076XR69 (F)	4h.34m.28.1s.
7	Ford Motor Company Ltd.	FRANCOIS DUVAL/Jean-Marc Fortin	B	5	Ford Focus RS	WRC	EX02OBE (GB)	4h.34m.28.5s.
8	Hyundai World R.T.	ARMIN SCHWARZ/Manfred Hiemer	D	10	Hyundai Accent	WRC	X18HMC (GB)	4h.35m.53.7s.
9	Skoda Motorsport	DIDIER AURIOL/Denis Giraudet	F	14	Skoda Octavia	WRC	2S5 1180 (CZ)	4h.36m.25.2s.
10	Bozian Racing	Roman Kresta/Milos Hulka	CZ	22	Peugeot 206	WRC	206NAP75 (F)	4h.37m.02.3s.
13	T. Marlboro Peugeot Total	MARCUS GRONHOLM/Timo Rautiainen	FIN	1	Peugeot 206	WRC	206NLL75 (F)	5h.02m.43.2s.
14	-	Simon Jean-Joseph/Jack Boyere	F	106	Renault Clio	S1600	872AMC83 (F)	5h.09m.19.6s.**
17	-	Brice Tirabassi/Jacques-Julien Renucci	F	61	Renault Clio	JWRC	871AMC83 (F)	5h.12m.36.1s.*

LEADING RETIREMENTS

1	Skoda Motorsport	TONI GARDEMEISTER/Paavo Lukander	FIN	15	Skoda Octavia	WRC	2S5 1190 (CZ)	fuel injector
4	555 Subaru World R.T.	PETTER SOLBERG/Philip Mills	N/GB	7	Subaru Impreza	WRC	S40WRT (GB)	accident
4	555 Subaru World R.T.	TOMMI MAKINEN/Kaj Lindstrom	FIN	8	Subaru Impreza	WRC	S30WRT (GB)	accident
8	T. Marlboro Peugeot Total	GILLES PANIZZI/Herve Panizzi	F	3	Peugeot 206	WRC	206NDQ75 (F)	driver ill
8	Ford Motor Company Ltd	MIKKO HIRVONEN/Jarmo Lehtinen	FIN	6	Ford Focus RS	WRC	EX51HXZ (GB)	accident
8	Hyundai World R.T.	FREDDY LOIX/Sven Smeets	B	11	Hyundai Accent	WRC	X19HMC (GB)	accident

MANUFACTURER'S REGISTERED DRIVER. *JWRC winner. **S1600 winner.

THE ROUTE

		SPECIAL STAGES	TOTAL DISTANCE	CREWS RUNNING
Leg 1 (1-6)	Monaco (Thursday 1830) - Tallard - Tallard - Monaco (Friday 2244)	6 asphalt-196.30km	706.88km*	40
Leg 2 (8-10)	Monaco (Saturday 0640) - Monaco - Monaco (Saturday 1745)	3 asphalt-82.41km	413.99km	36
Leg 3 (11-14)	Monaco (Sunday 0800) - Monaco (Sunday 1500)	4 asphalt-104.20km	269.16km	30
		13 stages-382.91km	1390.03km	

*free liaison from Ceremonial Start to Tallard (distance not included above).
Stage 7 cancelled-spectator security. Weather: clear, many icy patches but very few snowy stretches. One stage in darkness.

OVERALL LEADING SPECIAL STAGE POSITIONS

	1	2	3	4	5	6
Loeb	5	1	-	1	3	-
Sainz	3	2	1	1	2	1
Gronholm	3	-	3	3	-	-
McRae	2	3	2	3	-	1
Martin	1	2	2	2	-	3
Solberg	-	3	-	1	-	-
Duval	-	1	2	-	1	1
Burns	-	-	2	-	4	3
Makinen	-	-	1	-	-	-

JWRC Carlsson won 4 stages, Tirabassi 3, Baldacci (Fiat) 2, Ligato (Fiat) & Katajamaki (VW) 1 each.
S1600 Jean-Joseph won 5 stages, Carlsson 4, Katajamaki & Baldacci 1 each.

STARTERS 51 (22 JWRC). **FINISHERS** 30 (13 JWRC).
OVERALL LEADERS Gronholm stages 1-8, Loeb 9-14. (stage 7 cancelled)
JWRC LEADERS Tirabassi stage 1, Carlsson (Suzuki) 2, Carlsson 3-5, Carlsson 6, Tirabassi 8-14. (Stages 9 and 10 not run by S1600 cars).
S1600 LEADER Jean-Joseph stages 1-14.
WINNER'S AVERAGE SPEED OVER STAGES 85.35kph.
WORLD CHAMPIONSHIP FOR MANUFACTURERS
Citroen 18 points, Ford 10, Peugeot 6, Hyundai 3, Skoda 2.
WORLD CHAMPIONSHIP FOR DRIVERS
Loeb 10 points, McRae 8, Sainz 6, Martin 5, Burns 4, Robert 3, Duval 2, Schwarz 1.

RECENT WINNERS

1993	Didier Auriol/Bernard Occelli Toyota Celica Turbo 4WD (95.33kph)	
1994	Francois Delecour/Daniel Grataloup Ford Escort RS Cosworth (94.83kph)	
1995	Carlos Sainz/Luis Moya Subaru Impreza 555 (83.58kph)	
1996	*	Patrick Bernardini/Bernard Occelli Ford Escort RS Cosworth (85.50kph)
1997	Piero Liatti/Fabrizia Pons Subaru Impreza WRC (89.50kph)	
1998	Carlos Sainz/Luis Moya Toyota Corolla WRC (80.42kph)	
1999	Tommi Makinen/Risto Mannisenmaki Mitsubishi Lancer Evolution (80.42kph)	
2000	Tommi Makinen/Risto Mannisenmaki Mitsubishi Lancer Evolution (86.80kph)	
2001	Tommi Makinen/Risto Mannisenmaki Mitsubishi Lancer Evolution (76.77kph)	
2002	Tommi Makinen/Kaj Lindstrom Subaru Impreza WRC (Loeb's speed 88.37kph).	
Note	*	=W2L-only event.

Once again the Scandinavian drivers proved uncatchable on the Swedish Rally.

❖

Tommi Makinen was finally back in form!

❖

Classic wintry conditions made this a rally to remember.

❖

After Toshihiro Arai retired it was a fight to the finish in the Production Car WRC category. Janusz Kulig won but was subsequently excluded, 56 year old Stig Blomqvist gained the honours instead.

LEG 1 After an initial stage victory by Sebastien Loeb, Gronholm led all the way. Organisational crisis as Stewards could not quickly resolve a stage five dilemma when Francois Duval blocked the route. In the end the stage was cancelled. Bad day for Citroens slowed by having to run 1-2-3 on the road, especially when Colin McRae's car ingested snow through the air intake.
1 Gronholm 48m54.1s, 2 Makinen +27.0s, 3 Burns +30.8s, 4 Rovanpera +36.2s, 5 Pykalisto +59.3s, 6 Gardemeister +1m03.9s, 7 Martin +1m05.0s, 8 Solberg +1m09.4s. PCWRC Arai (29th) 53m41.3s.

LEG 2 More dilemmas for the Stewards, when Juuso Pykalisto rolled his car and was hit by Harri Rovanpera's, and another stage blockage ensued. This time the problem was compounded by the reverse running order system but was solved amicably. Gronholm damaged his steering but retained the lead. Recovery began for the Citroens.
1 Gronholm 2h03m29.1s, 2 Makinen +38.8s, 3 Burns +1m00.9s, 4 Martin +1m46.0s, 5 McRae +2m02.5s, 6 Solberg +2m12.1s, 7 Gardemeister +2m25.8s, 8 Sainz +2m30.1s PCWRC Arai (24th) 2h14m45.5s.

LEG 3 Strong finish by Loeb, who rose to seventh place overall. Long time PCWRC leader Arai retired with engine trouble while the battle between Kulig and Blomqvist, initially resolved in Kulig's favour, but several days after the rally was decided by the Scrutineers in Blomqvist's favour.
1 Gronholm 3h03m28.1s, 2 Makinen +50.8s, 3 Burns +1m17.9s, 4 Martin +1m45.8s, 5 McRae +2m15.8s, 6 Solberg +2m19.1s, 7 Loeb +3m14.7s, 8 Gardemeister +3m19.2s PCWRC Kulig (26th) 3h22m24.9s.

Four wins in a row for Peugeot in Sweden! The team that can never, it seems, win a present-day Monte-Carlo, more than avenged its most recent disappointment when reigning world champion Marcus Gronholm scored his third win in Sweden. The Monte-Carlo Rally winners Citroen suffered badly because of the regulation requiring that the first leg be run in order of Driver Championship position. This meant that their three cars were running at the head of the field. It was a major disadvantage and consequently they did well to finish with all three cars in the top nine places. The new Subaru showed a lot of promise, a smile was once again to be seen on the face of Tommi Makinen, while Markko Martin once again achieved an enviable points

What's New in 2003

● New Service Park was located at Hagfors Airport.
● Different Shakedown location close to the Service Park.
● A new 'sprint' (one at a time) publicity stage at Hagfors.
● Of the 12 different stages, eight were the same as last year.

scoring result for Ford.

The theme of the rally again was red, but this time it was the red of Peugeot rather than Citroen and, in the unusually heavy snow covering in Sweden's Varmland region, the speed of the French cars was more dramatic than ever. The rally itself, however, was marred by organisational confusions on the first day when the route was blocked by the crash of Ford driver Francois Duval. It took three hours for the Stewards to decide not to use available mid-stage split time records and cancelled the

No mistakes this time for Marcus Gronholm, who led virtually throughout.

stage. This decision was unfortunate because the stage concerned was of critical importance on account of its length and newness, and reduced the competitive distance on this leg by a quarter. This was bad enough, but then another stage was stopped on the second day when the semi-works Peugeot of Juuso Pykalisto crashed and his car was impacted by the works Peugeot of Harri Rovanpera. This time, however, the artificial

Colin McRae was not so happy in Sweden this year.

Production Car Championship

The opening round of the 2003 PCWRC could hardly have finished with more excitement when Janusz Kulig, who spent a long time recovering from a first-stage spin, took the lead on the final stage! Right from the start, until halfway through the final day, Toshihiro Arai held the lead in front of the veteran Stig Blomqvist, both in Subarus. On the final day, however, Arai had an engine failure and retired, but Blomqvist had Kulig chasing him hard, and finally the Polish driver's Mitsubishi achieved its aim. Success, however, was temporary. Scrutineers discovered an illegal flywheel on the Mitsubishi, so in the end it was Blomqvist who claimed another victory. A most remarkable drive also came from reigning PCWRC champion Karamjit Singh finishing third in the category, despite being visibly daunted by the temperatures. Although the three rally days saw temperatures close to zero, it had been minus 23 during Shakedown on the day of the start. "A Malaysian would only survive a few minutes if left alone in these conditions," he joked. Local team Mitsubishis were dominant in the overall Group N category, with Stig-Olov Walfridsson leading until the middle of the final day when he had an engine failure and Kenneth Backlund went on to win. Faster than Backlund on the stages, however, was a surprise, the Italian driver Gianluigi Galli, who incurred road penalties on the second day when the differential had to be changed.

....until halfway through the final day, Toshihiro Arai (seen above with codriver Tony Sircombe) held the lead in the PCWRC category when the engine failed.

Fourth place for Markko Martin avenged his Shakedown indiscretion 12 months earlier.

results were happily, fairly and quickly, decided. These two incidents were massive frustrations for the organisers who themselves were powerless to intervene.

The rally started strangely. The first car on the road, the Monte-Carlo winning Citroen of Sebastien Loeb, made best time, but the conditions here had been abnormal. Overnight snow-fall did not clear with passing cars on that stage but it did on the subsequent stages. Gronholm, running ninth car on the road, went into the lead which he held until the end of the event. Chasing Gronholm hard were Makinen and Richard Burns, Burns being the only non-Scandinavian close to the front. He drove steadily but seldom fast and finally achieved a solid third place.

The rally was run with a high degree of reliability among the top cars. The only non finishers among the works drivers were Duval and Rovanpera and the guest works car of Jussi Valimaki whose Hyundai had a clutch shaft failure.

Here in Sweden Rovanpera drove the third works Peugeot while Pykalisto was encouraged to show his paces in a car run by Gronholm's private Peugeot team. Once again Pykalisto went well for a while, holding fifth place for most of the first day, only to end with his crash the following day. Citroen had made technical changes since last year to prevent snow from entering the air inlets, but the modifications did not prevent McRae's car suffering a recurrence of the problem and he

Toni Gardemeister finished just in the points.

And Still There's Stig...

Stig Blomqvist's first Swedish Rally was in 1965, the first year the rally was run as a winter event. It began in his home town Orebro, went to Ostersund and returned to Orebro. He drove a very unusual car, a two-stroke Saab Sport fitted with dual foot controls! Stig's father was a driving instructor, and acted as codriver. Driving instructors often want to feel they should have ultimate control, but this time control was not complete, because at one point they overturned. A nice thing about the old Saabs was that they usually, of their own accord, rolled back on to their wheels again. They finished the rally, and a life story began which has seen Stig win this event seven times outright, his first back in 1971. On the 1979 event he became the first driver ever to win a World rally in a turbocharged car.

The legend continues. In 2003 the 56 year old drove one of the David Sutton team PCWRC Subaru Imprezas, and was fighting Janusz Kulig for the lead in the later sections, with as much determination as ever. It had been a great fight, and Stig was the first to acclaim the fine drive by Kulig, even if Kulig was ultimately to be denied the win. There was one strange affair, however. Stig's sponsor. Together with his 38 year old compatriot Joakim Roman, Stig's car was sponsored by Pfizer, the manufacturers of a renowned and popular personal stimulant for men. Could Stig endorse the product from personal experience? "I certainly can't, and wouldn't tell you if I could. I can tell you some of my friends already need the product, but I am still as good as ever!" He is still in love with rallying.

Freddy Loix cuts a corner.

dropped to 22nd place after having to drive stage two with snow starving the air inlet system. McRae drove well for the rest of the event, eventually pulling up to fifth. His teammates Loeb and Carlos Sainz both performed well and finished in the top ten. Ford had their young driver team, Martin finishing fourth for the second rally running, Duval crashed once again (but this time leading to retirement) and Mikko Hirvonen, who had originally been told he could drive as fast as he liked, was later told to

finish at all costs which he did in 11th place! Second place for Makinen was a convincing performance by Subaru, though Solberg was less confident. Only when Solberg reverted to the suspension set-up originally proposed by his teammate did he start to go better, but this time he was off the pace of his Finnish colleague.

Skoda was the surprise star of the first day. Toni Gardemeister had driven his Octavia into fifth place and finished eighth, but teammate Didier Auriol, who lost considerable time in testing, drove uncertainly. Hyundai started the rally surrounded by rumours of impending financial doom, even to the extent of suggestions that they would cross the start line and then go home. As it transpired, they were able to announce a pre-event corporate commitment to carry on in the sport, and Freddy Loix in particular again drove well, running as high as seventh in mid event. Hyundai just missed out on the points this time suffering badly from cancelling their testing before the rally. Loix's teammate Armin Schwarz, however, was unhappy with his car and was slowed by engine trouble on the final day.

The rally was a classic in the weather but a disappointment for the Swedish fans, who had no top driver of their nation to cheer. The potentially fastest Swede, Andreas Ericsson, crashed his Focus on stage two and hospitalised his codriver. The highest placed Swede at the finish was the Group N winner Kenneth Backlund.

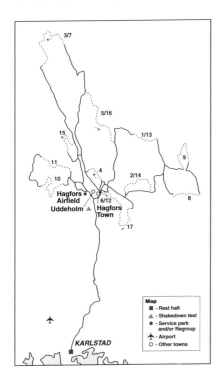

Map

- ■ - Rest halt
- ▲ - Shakedown test
- ● - Service park and/or Regroup
- ✈ - Airport
- ○ - Other towns

POSITION/ LAST STAGE COMPLETED	ENTRANT	DRIVER/CODRIVER	NAT.	COMP NO.	CAR	CAT.	REG NO.	TOTAL PENALTY/ CAUSE
1	T.Marlboro Peugeot Total	MARCUS GRONHOLM/Timo Rautiainen	FIN	1	Peugeot 206	WRC	810NVT75 (F)	3h.03m.28.1s.
2	555 Subaru World R.T.	TOMMI MAKINEN/Kaj Lindstrom	FIN	8	Subaru Impreza	WRC	S50WRT (GB)	3h.04m.18.9s.
3	T.Marlboro Peugeot Total	RICHARD BURNS/Robert Reid	GB	2	Peugeot 206	WRC	624NZT75 (F)	3h.04m.16.0s.
4	Ford Motor Company Ltd	MARKKO MARTIN/Michael Park	EE/GB	4	Ford Focus RS	WRC	EX02OBB (GB)	3h.05m.13.9s.
5	Citroen Total	COLIN McRAE/Derek Ringor	GB	17	Citroen Xsara	WRC	26CSP92 (F)	3h.05m.43.9s.
6	555 Subaru World R.T.	PETTER SOLBERG/Philip Mills	N/GB	7	Subaru Impreza	WRC	S60WRT (GB)	3h.05m.47.2s.
7	Citroen Total	SEBASTIEN LOEB/Daniel Elena	F/MC	18	Citroen Xsara	WRC	27CSP92 (F)	3h.06m.42.8s.
8	Skoda Motorsport	TONI GARDEMEISTER/Paavo Lukander	FIN	15	Skoda Octavia	WRC	MBO90-41 (CZ)	3h.06m.47.3s.
9	Citroen Total	CARLOS SAINZ/Marc Marti	E	19	Citroen Xsara	WRC	20CSP92 (F)	3h.06m.52.3s.
10	Hyundai World R.T.	FREDDY LOIX/Sven Smeets	B	11	Hyundai Accent	WRC	X23HMC (GB)	3h.07m.04.5s.
11	Ford Motor Company Ltd	MIKKO HIRVONEN/Jarmo Lehtinen	FIN	6	Ford Focus RS	WRC	EK51HYA (GB)	3h.09m.33.8s.
12	-	Kristian Sohlberg/Jakke Honkanen	FIN	35	Mitsubishi Lancer Evolution	WRC	KR02DLZ (GB)	3h.09m.45.5s.
13	Hyundai World R.T.	ARMIN SCHWARZ/Manfred Hiemer	D	10	Hyundai Accent	WRC	X24HMC (GB)	3h.10m.49.3s.
18	Skoda Motorsport	DIDIER AURIOL/Denis Giraudet	F	14	Skoda Octavia	WRC	MBN15-48 (CZ)	3h.16m.14.9s.
21	-	Kenneth Backlund/Bosse Holmstrand	S	105	Mitsubishi Lancer Evo VII	N	SSO427 (S)	3h.18m.55.8s.**
-	Kulig Promotion	Janusz Kulig/Jaroslaw Baran	PL	61	Mitsubishi Lancer Evo VI	PCWRC	KBC.V034 (PL)	3h.22m.24.9s.#
26	-	Stig Blomqvist/Ana Goni	S/YV	65	Subaru Impreza GD	PCWRC	OE52WXH (GB)	3h.22m.28.2s.*

LEADING RETIREMENTS

4	Ford Motor Company Ltd	FRANCOIS DUVAL/Jean-Marc Fortin	B	5	Ford Focus RS	WRC	EX02OBC (GB)	accident
6	Hyundai World R.T.	JUSSI VALIMAKI/Tero Gardemeister	FIN	12	Hyundai Accent	WRC	X14HMC (GB)	clutch
7	T.Marlboro Peugeot Total	HARRI ROVANPERA/Risto Pietilainen	FIN	3	Peugeot 206	WRC	814NVT75 (F)	accident
7	-	Juuso Pykalisto/Esko Mertsalmi	FIN	32	Peugeot 206	WRC	206MWJ75 (F)	accident

MANUFACTURER'S REGISTERED DRIVER. *PCWRC winner. **Group N winner. #excluded.

THE ROUTE

		SPECIAL STAGES	TOTAL DISTANCE	CREWS RUNNING
Leg 1 (1-4,6)	Karlstad (Friday 0600) - Hagfors - Karlstad (Friday 1850)	5 gravel-94.13km	660.17km	70
Leg 2 (7-12)	Karlstad (Saturday 0530) - Hagfors - Karlstad (Saturday 1904)	6 gravel-122.23km*	706.76km	59
Leg 3 (13-17)	Karlstad (Sunday 0600) - Hagfors - Karlstad (Sunday 1705)	5 gravel-120.75km	568.20km	54
		16 stages-337.11km*	1935.13km	

Ceremonial Start on the Thursday evening in Karlstad. Stage 5 cancelled and Stage 8 stopped-blocked stages. Weather: always dry except for some falling snow on the first day, snowy or ice covered stages. Two stages in darkness.

OVERALL LEADING SPECIAL STAGE POSITIONS*

	1	2	3	4	5	6
Gronholm	7	2	3	1	-	2
Makinen	2	6	2	2	-	2
Loeb	1	2	4	-	-	-
Burns	1	2	1	6	1	3
Martin	1	2	1	3	3	2
Rovanpera	1	1	2	-	1	-
McRae	1	-	2	1	6	1
Solberg	1	-	-	1	3	2
Sainz	-	-	1	1	1	-

PCWRC Arai won 8 stages, Kulig & Blomqvist 3 each, Singh (Proton) 1.

GROUP N Walfridsson won 6 stages, Galli (Mitsubishi) 4, Backlund & Salo (Mitsubishi) 2 each, Arai 1.

*Note: includes Stage 8.

STARTERS 75 (18 PCWRC). **FINISHERS** 53 (13 PCWRC).

OVERALL LEADERS Loeb stage 1, Gronholm 2-17.

PCWRC LEADERS Arai (Subaru) stages 1-15, Blomqvist 16, Kulig 17. Blomqvist after event.

GROUP N LEADERS Walfridsson (Mitsubishi) stage 1, Arai 2, Walfridsson 3-15, Backlund 16+17.

WINNER'S AVERAGE SPEED OVER STAGES 110.24kph.

WORLD CHAMPIONSHIP FOR MANUFACTURERS
Citroen 24 points, Peugeot 22, Ford 15, Subaru 11, Hyundai & Skoda 3.

WORLD CHAMPIONSHIP FOR DRIVERS Loeb & McRae 12 points, Gronholm, Burns & Martin 10, Makinen 8, Sainz 6, Robert & Solberg 3, Duval 2, Schwarz & Gardemeister 1.

RECENT WINNERS

1993	Mats Jonsson/Lars Backman Toyota Celica Turbo 4WD (107.34kph)	
1994 *	Thomas Radstrom/Lars Backman Toyota Celica Turbo 4WD (102.60kph)	
1995	Kenneth Eriksson/Staffan Parmander Mitsubishi Lancer Evolution (103.16kph)	
1996	Tommi Makinen/Seppo Harjanne Mitsubishi Lancer Evolution (106.21kph)	
1997	Kenneth Eriksson/Staffan Parmander Subaru Impreza WRC (106.52kph)	
1998	Tommi Makinen/Risto Mannisenmaki Mitsubishi Lancer Evolution (107.49kph)	
1999	Tommi Makinen/Risto Mannisenmaki Mitsubishi Lancer Evolution (109.85kph)	
2000	Marcus Gronholm/Timo Rautiainen Peugeot 206 WRC (112.61kph)	
2001	Harri Rovanpera/Risto Pietilainen Peugeot 206 WRC (110.10kph)	
2002	Marcus Gronholm/Timo Rautiainen Peugeot 206 WRC (114.83kph)	

Note * =W2L-only event.

Rally vs Winter

WELCOME TO KARLSTAD

Inaugural world championship rally in Turkey. An event which for nearly every driver was new.

❖

Carlos Sainz's 25th WCR win equalled teammate Colin McRae's record.

❖

Responsible drive by 22-year old Ford driver Francois Duval, brought him a personal career best result.

❖

Extraordinary pre-event organisational efforts ensured the rally took place despite unexpectedly severe winter storms.

LEG 1 Marcus Gronholm took an initial lead but was then slowed by persistent power steering trouble. Petter Solberg took over the lead but crashed so Harri Rovanpera went ahead. Sebastien Loeb ran out of fuel after taking a wrong turning. Markko Martin delayed by gearbox trouble. Colin McRae unhappy with the Xsara's handling. Rocks all over the roads!
1 Rovanpera 1h14m50.5s, 2 Sainz +20.7s,
3 Duval +29.5s, 4 Makinen +31.4s,
5 Panizzi +37.9s, 6 Burns +56.5s,
7 McRae +1m03.3s, 8 Schwarz +1m07.1s.
JWRC Carlsson (15th) 1h23m18.1s.

LEG 2 At half distance leader Rovanpera slid off the road and ensuing damage led to retirement. Sainz went into the lead. Armin Schwarz retired with suspension failure. Gronholm went off the road but still continued to regain lost ground. Toni Gardemeister's Skoda's handling improved. Tommi Makinen had power steering trouble. Freddy Loix had sticking throttle problems.
1 Sainz 3h26m49.9s, 2 Burns +1m19.5s,
3 Duval +1m44.0s, 4 McRae +2m26.0s,
5 Panizzi +2m45.1s, 6 Gardemeister +3m39.7s
7 Martin +3m54.3s, 8 Makinen +7m01.0s.
JWRC Katajamaki (15th) 3h55m12.7s.

LEG 3 Finally the surfaces of the stages were cleaner. Sainz cruised to victory. Gardemeister lost time after a spin. Gronholm finally scored a point for Peugeot.
1 Sainz 4h32m14.1s, 2 Burns +47.9s,
3 Duval +1m46.5s, 4 McRae +2m09.1s,
5 Panizzi +2m41.6s, 6 Martin +3m24.9s,
7 Gardemeister +5m13.0s, 8 Makinen +7m18.6s
JWRC Katajamaki (15th) 5h08m56.6s.

This was the first world championship rally to be run in a country where the borders of Europe meet the Middle East, and was one of constantly changing fortunes. Four different drivers took turns to lead in three makes of car but, for the third rally running, the winner still drove a red coloured car built in France. This time Peugeot, the favourites, were out of luck. The number three Citroen driver Carlos Sainz went into the lead at half distance when the number three Peugeot driver Harri Rovanpera, who was leading, slid into rocks, wrecked his suspension and retired three stages later.

Just how hard a challenge it was for the rally organisers to run the event nobody could predict. Quite unseasonably severe winter weather had devastated the roads. Many had to be rebuilt several times, while the single central Service Park could only be surfaced days before the start. To have held the rally at all would have taxed many organisers beyond their capabilities. To have achieved this in a country new to top level sport was astonishing. The rally was

Carlos Sainz is always at the top when the going is a little unusual! He scored his first win for Citroen, the fifth manufacturer he has won with.

based at the Mediterranean resort of Kemer, south of Antalya, in the low tourist season. Many large hotels were vacant to accommodate the visitors and facilities were available waiting to be used. The

What's New in 2003

The route was very similar to that run when the event (the Anatolian Rally) was a Candidate rally in 2002. The main differences were as follows:

● The headquarters was moved from the Pyramid complex, on the western side of Antalya, to the resort region of Kemer.

● The Superspecial was only run once, on the Thursday evening on the way from the start in Antalya to Kemer.

● It had been less than five months since the trial Anatolian Rally was held and four since the event's inclusion in the 2003 WRC was confirmed.

● Traffic streaming was introduced to encourage spectators to use the main road, Antalya and Kumluca, rather than venture into the small roads in the hills behind Kemer.

One point for Marcus Gronholm was reward for persistence after a terrible event.

Surprises for Peugeot's Technical Director, Michel Nandan.

weather, however, was quite unusually cool. At night it was often freezing, even at sea level.

As at Monte-Carlo, Subaru's hopes were short lived, but on the first two normal gravel stages Petter Solberg was fastest before he crashed. Tommi Makinen took up the challenge, reaching second place in the middle of the first day, before falling back with suspension troubles caused by hitting the stones at the side of the road.

Peugeot had a bad event, saved only by a steady drive by Richard Burns to second place. World Champion Marcus Gronholm showed his driving style to good effect, beating teammate Burns in a head-to-head race round the Antalya superspecial course. Then it all went wrong for the Finn. Power steering problems dropped him down to 11th, and on the way to the following stage after service, the same problem happened again - and by the end of the first evening he was 19th. From then on it was a thankless effort to recover lost ground, but finally he was responsible for gaining one extra point for Peugeot. Punctures

and spins upset Burns' drive but he delivered a result when Peugeot most needed it.

It was Sainz who saved Citroen's day. Sebastien Loeb was out very early on in disgrace, after taking the wrong road on the way to a refuelling halt in the mountains, and running out of fuel. Later the team admitted they had miscalculated the quantity of fuel the car required and it was fortunate the other Citroens escaped this problem. Colin McRae meanwhile had differential troubles with his Xsara, and even though this was changed he never found a set-up which gave him full confidence in his driving. So it was the time for the old master Sainz, and he did not disappoint. When Rovanpera damaged his car, Sainz gained a lead of around a minute which he maintained until the end of the event.

Ford felt confident, the rough conditions traditionally promising them a chance to win, but instead it turned out to be a consecration of determination. Markko Martin lost considerable time on the third stage with transmission failure which was something from which he could not recover, though he finally pulled back to sixth. Francois Duval, meanwhile, showed a new maturity in his driving. Apart from a spin and a power steering problem, and then frighteningly a sticking throttle, Duval had a clear run, finished third and earned the first podium finish of his WCR career and gained the majority of the team's championship points.

Skoda hoped the conditions would also work in their favour, but Didier Auriol had engine trouble right from the start,

then Toni Gardemeister found the car very difficult to handle on surfaces that were covered by gravel. As the surfaces of the stages cleared later on in the event, so Gardemeister went better, and only a couple of spins on the final day dropped him from sixth down to seventh, Hyundai's optimism continued and Armin

The Magic of Mumtaz

Turkey became the 26th different country to host a world championship rally in the 31 year history of the series. The speed of evolution of the event to top status came as a surprise to outsiders, but not to those who have followed its four-year story. Events on the scale of a successful world championship rally do not happen by themselves. First major decision was to plan the event. The organisers decided this would be a purpose-designed rally based on current event concepts, not an adaptation of an existing one. But flair was needed as well. The Rally of Turkey has been the work of the businessman Mumtaz Tahincioglu. Mumtaz's family business has been in confectionery, the biggest sweet making company in Turkey, and above all it was Mumtaz's business acumen which put the rally into the championship. This is no eyes-closed dream, it was the culmination of a solid business project, focussed on the objective of bringing Turkey to the forefront of motorsport. Mumtaz is President of the Turkish Federation and, one suspects, that now the rally is on a firm footing, maybe Formula 1 will be coming to his country in the near future. Racing is not far from the mind of Mumtaz. His son Jason was competing in Formula Renault events in Britain in 2003.

Mumtaz Tahincioglu (left) with adviser Jonathan Ashman.

Shock absorber and suspension damage slowed Tommi Makinen.

TURKEY

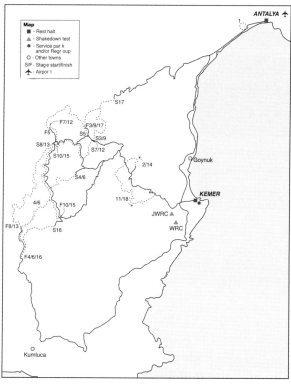

Armin Schwarz, high in the hills.

Schwarz was lying second on the first day but he had to retire on the second day when a suspension bolt sheared. Freddy Loix, however, had many troubles, including a sticking throttle and then turbo trouble. In the end Hyundai fell just out of the points.

Even Sainz had a few disquieting moments when the alternator light kept flashing in the last two stages, but it did not lead to disaster. "This was very much like Cyprus - but with bigger stones beside the roads. It was a challenge to know the correct pace." As usual, the Spaniard had judged it right. Burns: "If you go fast or slow, you are never going to avoid every stone! You just have to hope you will avoid trouble." The rally was a huge success for everyone involved, setting new standards of attitude and determination to succeed. It happened in a country that wants to move on in life. It lit up latent enthusiasm in a lot of people. The organisers asked for volunteer helpers, saying there were a thousand vacant jobs needing to be filled. Five thousand applied. The locals had the chance to see the greatest drivers in the world for the very first time, it was an occasion not to be missed.

Junior Championship

The rough conditions did no favours for the Junior WRC cars, which were plagued by punctures and steering troubles. Once again Daniel Carlsson was the pace setter though it was Brice Tirabassi who was fastest initially. Tirabassi retired after overturning and from then on there seemed to be no stopping the Swedish driver's Suzuki. Behind Carlsson was Kosti Katajamaki's new version VW Polo *(below)*. On the final stage of day two Carlsson stopped to repair his broken steering and restarted in third place. On the final day the suspension failed and the Swede retired. So the VW was ahead, but suffering from clutch bearing trouble which they hoped to repair before the final leg. Unfortunately it was beyond repair in the time allowed, so the faulty unit was reassembled. The crews crossed their fingers all the way to the end and the car survived. Suzukis led the category nearly all the way, on day one lying 1-2-3. The classification oscillated wildly according to who had to stop and change a flat tyre on a stage (mousse inserts being forbidden in S1600) but there was delight when the young British driver Guy Wilks was lying second with five stages to go. The 22 year old, however struck trouble, when his Puma was stuck in gear, but finally he finished third, behind the VW of Katajamaki and the Suzuki of Salvador Canellas.

POSITION/ LAST STAGE COMPLETED	ENTRANT	DRIVER/CODRIVER	NAT.	COMP NO.	CAR	CAT.	REG NO.	TOTAL PENALTY/ CAUSE
1	Citroen Total	CARLOS SAINZ/Marc Marti	E	19	Citroen Xsara	WRC	39CSP92 (F)	4h.32m.14.1s.
2	T. Marlboro Peugeot Total	RICHARD BURNS/Robert Reid	GB	2	Peugeot 206	WRC	334NQZ75 (F)	4h.33m.02.0s.
3	Ford Motor Company Ltd	FRANCOIS DUVAL/Stephane Prevot	B	5	Ford Focus RS	WRC	EX02OBE (GR)	4h.34m.00.0s.
4	Citroen Total	COLIN McRAE/Derek Ringer	GB	17	Citroen Xsara	WRC	14DDM92 (F)	4h.34m.23.2s.
5	Bozian Racing	Gilles + Hervé Panizzi	F	21	Peugeot 206	WRC	341NQZ75 (F)	4h.34m.55.7s.
6	Ford Motor Company Ltd	MARKKO MARTIN/Michael Park	EE/GB	4	Ford Focus RS	WRC	EX02OBD (GB)	4h.35m.39.0s.
7	Skoda Motorsport	TONI GARDEMEISTER/Paavo Lukander	FIN	15	Skoda Octavia	WRC	MBO72-24 (CZ)	4h.37m.27.1s.
8	555 Subaru World R.T.	TOMMI MAKINEN/Kaj Lindstrom	FIN	8	Subaru Impreza	WRC	S30WRT (GB)	4h.39m.32.7s.
9	T. Marlboro Peugeot Total	MARCUS GRONHOLM/Timo Rautiainen	FIN	1	Peugeot 206	WRC	290NNN75 (F)	4h.43m.06.3s.
10	Hyundai World R.T.	FREDDY LOIX/Sven Smeets	B	11	Hyundai Accent	WRC	X19HMC (GB)	4h.43m.54.5s.
14	-	Simon Jean-Joseph/Jack Boyere	F	101	Renault Clio	S1600	872AMC83 (F)	5h.04m.21.2s.*
15	-	Kosti Katajamaki/Miikka Anttila	FIN	54	VW Polo	JWRC	H-RM388 (D)	5h.08m.56.6s.**

LEADING RETIREMENTS

3	Ford Motor Company Ltd	MIKKO HIRVONEN/Jarmo Lehtinen	FIN	6	Ford Focus RS	WRC	EX02OBC (GB)	steering
3	555 Subaru World R.T.	PETTER SOLBERG/Philip Mills	N/GB	7	Subaru Impreza	WRC	S70WRT (GB)	steering
3	Citroen Total	SEBASTIEN LOEB/Daniel Elena	F/MC	18	Citroen Xsara	WRC	16DDM92 (F)	no fuel
6	Hyundai World R.T.	ARMIN SCHWARZ/Manfred Hiemer	D	10	Hyundai Accent	WRC	X18HMC (GB)	suspension
6	Skoda Motorsport	DIDIER AURIOL/Denis Giraudet	F	14	Skoda Octavia	WRC	MBO90-42 (CZ)	engine
12	T. Marlboro Peugeot Total	HARRI ROVANPERA/Risto Pietilainen	FIN	3	Peugeot 206	WRC	344NQZ75 (F)	accident damage

MANUFACTURER'S REGISTERED DRIVER. *S1600 winner. **JWRC winner.

THE ROUTE

		SPECIAL STAGES	TOTAL DISTANCE	CREWS RUNNING
Leg 1 (1-6)	Antalya (Thursday 1800) - Kemer - Kemer (Friday 1733)	6 gravel-95.35km	389.55km	41
Leg 2 (7-13)	Kemer (Saturday 0600) - Kemer - Kemer - Kemer (Saturday 1824)	7 gravel-158.52km	483.35km	29
Leg 3 (14-18)	Kemer (Sunday 0700) - Kemer - Antalya (Sunday 1600)	5 gravel-84.02km	320.95km	26
		18 stages-337.89km	1193.85km	

Weather: Mainly sunny but cool. Dry throughout. One stage in darkness.

OVERALL LEADING SPECIAL STAGE POSITIONS

	1	2	3	4	5	6
Gronholm	4	2	1	-	3	1
Rovanpera	4	1	1	1	-	1
Sainz	3	-	3	6	-	3
Martin	2	3	5	1	1	2
Burns	2	2	3	4	1	1
Solberg	2	1	-	-	-	-
Duval	1	2	2	1	2	2
McRae	1	2	1	1	3	2
Makinen	-	2	1	-	3	2

JWRC Carlsson won 8 stages, Teuronen (Suzuki) & Katajamaki 3 each, Ligato (Fiat) 2, Tirabassi & Wilks (Ford) 1 each.
S1600 Jean-Joseph won 12 stages, Carlsson & Katajamaki 3 each.

STARTERS 60 (22 JWRC). **FINISHERS** 26 (7 JWRC).
OVERALL LEADERS Gronholm stage 1, Solberg 2+3, Rovanpera 4-9, Sainz 10-18.
JWRC LEADERS Tirabassi (Renault) stage 1, Carlsson (Suzuki) 2-12, Katajamaki 13-18.
S1600 LEADERS Jean-Joseph stage 1, Carlsson 2, Jean-Joseph 3-18.
WINNER'S AVERAGE SPEED OVER STAGES 74.47kph.
WORLD CHAMPIONSHIP FOR MANUFACTURERS
Citroen 39 points, Peugeot 31, Ford 25, Subaru 13, Skoda 6, Hyundai 3.
WORLD CHAMPIONSHIP FOR DRIVERS Burns 18 points, McRae 17, Sainz 16, Martin 13, Loeb 12, Gronholm 10, Makinen 9, Duval 8, Panizzi 4, Robert, Solberg & Gardemeister 3, Schwarz 1.

RECENT WINNERS
2000 * Volkan Isik/Yusuf Avimelek Subaru Impreza WRC
2001 * Serkan Yazici/Erkan Bodur Toyota Corolla WRC
2002 * Ercan Kazak/Cem Bakancocuklari Subaru Impreza WRX
Note: * =National-only event.

Peugeot gained their sixth maximum points result in the past ten rallies. Marcus Gronholm led from start to finish.

❖

Peugeot gained their 43rd world rally win, equalling the total of Ford and Toyota and headed only by Lancia.

❖

Impressive demonstration of speed by the new Ford Focus but a bad event for Citroen.

❖

Huge financial penalties imposed, on competitors for a variety of offences, by the Stewards.

LEG 1 Citroen drivers had visibility troubles in the rain, Colin McRae then hit a bank and retired. Francois Duval had hydraulic problems which took a long time to resolve. Tommi Makinen unhappy with his car. Big crash for Armin Schwarz. Smaller crash for Harri Rovanpera.
1 Gronholm 1h18m25.5s, 2 Martin +38.1s, 3 Solberg +43.6s, 4 Burns +55.0s, 5 Rovanpera +1m03.6s, 6 Loeb +1m26.2s, 7 Makinen +1m29.4s, 8 Sainz +1m47.2s.
PCWRC Arai (20th) 1h24m50.1s.

LEG 2 Markko Martin also had hydraulic trouble but lost little time, then had a spin and finally retired with engine failure. Carlos Sainz went off the road and regained it by an unorthodox route. Brake trouble for the Peugeots. Freddy Loix slowed by handling trouble. Gronholm crashed on to the car's side but kept his lead. Many cars suffered serious tyre wear.
1 Gronholm 2h42m43.7s, 2 Burns +1m00.9s, 3 Solberg +1m50.7s, 4 Loeb +2m23.7s, 5 Loix +5m51.6s, 6 A.McRae +6m28.8s, 7 Gardemeister +6m33.5s, 8 Auriol +7m45.7s.
PCWRC Arai (12th) 2h55m52.9s.

LEG 3 Big crash for Loix. Sebastien Loeb slowed by transmission trouble but finished a consistent fourth.
1 Gronholm 3h45m21.2s, 2 Burns +1m08.7s, 3 Solberg +2m09.8s, 4 Loeb +4m15.4s, 5 Gardemeister +8m13.8s, 6 A.McRae +9m14.2s, 7 Makinen +9m50.2s, 8 Auriol +10m08.6s.
PCWRC Arai (11th) 4h03m30.3s.

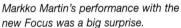

Marcus Gronholm led the Propecia Rally NZ from start to finish at the wheel of his 206 World Rally Car heading teammate Richard Burns, who once again had a consistent points-scoring run. The surprise of the event, however, was Markko Martin in the 2003 Focus WRC. Despite very limited personal experience of this highly specialised event and the competition debut of the car, Martin held second place for more than half the rally. Citroen had an event they would prefer to forget, their misfortunes enabling Peugeot to pass into the lead of the Makes championship.

Technically there was a remarkable number of innovations among the cars for such a faraway event. The spotlight was on the 2003 version Focus, the first time in the five years of Focus world championship rallies that designers prepared the car starting with a "white sheet" of paper. Citroen also featured many engine changes and had joined Peugeot, Subaru and Ford in fitting vertical fences on the transverse rear wing, designed to keep a more constant download (and therefore stability) when the car was being driven sideways. Hyundai had made some engine changes and also joined the other teams

Markko Martin's performance with the new Focus was a big surprise.

by beginning shock absorber design in-house. There were changes to the engine of the new Group N version Impreza (of which the only example to finish the event won the category). Finally there was an unexpected World rally debut of the Mitsubishi Lancer Evo VIII in the hands of a private driver, who crashed the car three kilometres into the first stage.

What's New in 2003

● The rally had never been held at this time of year before. Sixth different month in the past seven years!

● Two days were spent in Northland. The rally did not go to the west coast stages in the region of Raglan. On the first day the stages were mostly run twice, thus reducing the problem of running first car on the road. Damp conditions also made things fairer.

● The cars spent Friday night out of town, at Paparoa, some 140km north of Auckland. The event's first away night halt since 1996, when the rally went to Rotorua.

● This was absolutely the final year for the Superspecial stage at Manukau! A new site is being sought for future rallies.

Running first car on the road, in the damp conditions, was not the expected problem for Richard Burns.

Francois Duval makes his peace with the Maoris.

Production Car Championship

The most impressive driver in the category was Toshihiro Arai in his latest version Subaru, while initially lying behind him was Possum Bourne in a similar car. Bourne *(below)* had just taken the lead on stage four when his engine failed and Arai was ahead again and on his own from that moment on

until the finish. Sadly it was to be the final time we would be with Possum. Second place went to the Argentine driver Marcos Ligato. "This car was the one in which we won Corona Rally Mexico, but still stuck in the US docks are our spare engine and transmission. We were nervous all the time." Behind came battles between Ramon Ferreyros, who was delayed by punctures, Martin Rowe who was consistently speeding up, as he continued to learn the best way to drive Subarus, and Hamed Al-Wahaibi who had not entered a major rally for a year. While the Omani was trying to brush off the rusty style in his driving, champion Karamjit Singh stayed behind and finished sixth in front of the British driver Niall McShea, who had been admitted into the series only in time for this event. The rally ended with a three-way tie for the lead in the PCWRC between Singh, in the official Proton entry (albeit the Proton Pert being in reality a lookalike Evo VI), equal with the two Subaru drivers Stig Blomqvist and Martin Rowe, run by the private David Sutton Cars team.

Carlos Sainz lost a lot of time off the road.

The Citroen team itself had never competed on this event before, but their chief chassis engineer Jean-Claude Vaucard knew a lot about the rally. He had been Peugeot's engineer when they won in 1985. This year the speed of the event shot up, for two reasons. Slower stages were cut out from the route, in an effort to contain the region where the event is run, and faster stages were used twice. Double usage of stages on the first day of competition also served to make the event fairer. The traditional covering of little stones on the road, which are cleared away by the passage of fast moving cars, normally works badly against the front running cars. The cleaning of these stones on the first run therefore lessened the disadvantages of running first car on the road. Wet weather helped as well to bed down the stones into the surface. Richard Burns said "The moment we heard it had

Tommi Makinen was off the pace and out of pocket in New Zealand.

started to rain, as we drove up to stage two, was the best of the rally. It meant that (as befits the current championship leader) running first car on the road would be even less of a disadvantage than we feared." But Gronholm (running in sixth place on the road) was taking strides forward on the opening stages and was uncatchable for the rest of the rally. Burns' second place gained points which helped him keep his championship lead.

It was not Burns however who shadowed Gronholm for the first half of the event, it was Martin, "The new Focus is so much better on fast roads, it is more stable, overcoming the one big disadvantage of the previous version Focuses." The Estonian was there behind Gronholm all the time until he had a spin on stage 14 and the engine stopped shortly afterwards. As the sleek white Ford was parked alongside the road, Burns moved up to second where he stayed for the rest of the event. Behind, there was mayhem. All three Citroens suffered serious demisting trouble in the rain in the early sections. Petter Solberg was chasing the Peugeots in his Subaru but his efforts were frustrated by broken tyre mousse inserts and then by sliding off the road for a while. His teammate Tommi Makinen had a miserable event, firstly feeling his car was lacking performance

but not being able to identify why, then being penalised for upsetting the police.

Hyundai had a bad event. Armin Schwarz crashed right at the start, Freddy Loix on the final day and Jussi Valimaki slid off the road on the first day as well. It was a good event, however, for the ageing Skoda Octavias with both cars (like Peugeot) finishing in the points, although, there was something quite strange. Didier Auriol had a lot of trouble with the handling, which defied detection, until suddenly there was a huge bang from the front of the car - and the car was fine! By this time his teammate Toni Gardemeister had pulled well ahead, finishing fifth. One welcome aspect of the event was the return of Mitsubishi, with two cars (for regular driver Alister McRae and privateer Kristian Sohlberg) although this was a 'wiping off the dust' exercise, rather than a chance to test out new engineering. Alister finished a splendid sixth, his best

result in over a year, but Sohlberg crashed on stage 14 and was too late to carry on.

Severe Penalties

Financial penalties from the Stewards began being imposed during reconnaissance with Carlos Sainz starting the rally USD11,200 poorer after a report for speeding. Huge fines continued to be meted out by the Stewards not only on their own initiative, based on reports from officials, but also acting on police reports. This included Tommi Makinen for a speeding infringement for which the Stewards issued a monetary fine and then also a five minute penalty because he failed to stop when the police wanted to question him about the incident. As a result Makinen dropped from fifth to seventh. Harsh sentences from the Stewards did not stop when the event had come to an end. They also penalised Daniel Sola USD250 (for bad driving on the highway) and Kristian Sohlberg (right) USD5000 and a suspended loss of licence (for a particularly serious offence) for bad

driving. The climax came with a USD2500 penalty imposed in absentia on the Uruguayan driver Gustavo Trelles - for not being present in New Zealand, as he

had promised to be, and USD5000 on Luca Baldini, for a similar but second offence (having already missed Australia in 2002).

POSITION/ LAST STAGE COMPLETED	ENTRANT	DRIVER/CODRIVER	NAT.	COMP NO.	CAR	CAT.	REG NO.	TOTAL PENALTY/ CAUSE
1	T. Marlboro Peugeot Total	MARCUS GRONHOLM/Timo Rautiainen	FIN	1	Peugeot 206	WRC	286NNN75 (F)	3h.45m.21.2s.
2	T. Marlboro Peugeot Total	RICHARD BURNS/Robert Reid	GB	2	Peugeot 206	WRC	952NVB75 (F)	3h.46m.29.9s.
3	555 Subaru World R.T.	PETTER SOLBERG/Philip Mills	N/GB	7	Subaru Impreza	WRC	S50WRT (GB)	3h.47m.31.0s.
4	Citroen Total	SEBASTIEN LOEB/Daniel Elena	F/MC	18	Citroen Xsara	WRC	30CSP92 (F)	3h.49m.36.6s.
5	Skoda Motorsport	TONI GARDEMEISTER/Paavo Lukander	FIN	15	Skoda Octavia	WRC	2S5 1190 (CZ)	3h.53m.35.0s.
6	Ralliart Europe	Alister McRae/David Senior	GB	32	Mitsubishi Lancer Evolution	WRC	KP51RWL (GB)	3h.54m.35.4s.
7	555 Subaru World R.T.	TOMMI MAKINEN/Kaj Lindstrom	FIN	8	Subaru Impreza	WRC	S80WRT (GB)	3h.55m.11.4s.
8	Skoda Motorsport	DIDIER AURIOL/Denis Giraudet	F	14	Skoda Octavia	WRC	2S5 1180 (CZ)	3h.55m.29.8s.
9	Ford Motor Company Ltd	FRANCOIS DUVAL/Stephane Prevot	B	5	Ford Focus RS	WRC	EJ02KMV (GB)	3h.56m.32.9s.
10	Ford Motor Company Ltd	MIKKO HIRVONEN/Jarmo Lehtinen	FIN	6	Ford Focus RS	WRC	EX02OBB (GB)	3h.59m.03.5s.
11	-	Toshihiro Arai/Tony Sircombe	J/NZ	54	Subaru Impreza WRX	PCWRC	GMG300NO9070 (J)	4h.03m.30.3s.*
12	Citroen Total	CARLOS SAINZ/Marc Marti	E	19	Citroen Xsara	WRC	19DDM92 (F)	4h.03m.34.4s.

LEADING RETIREMENTS

0	Hyundai World R.T.	ARMIN SCHWARZ/Manfred Hiemer	D	10	Hyundai Accent	WRC	X24HMC (GB)	accident
5	Citroen Total	COLIN McRAE/Derek Ringer	GB	17	Citroen Xsara	WRC	18DDM92 (F)	accident damage
6	Hyundai World R.T.	JUSSI VALIMAKI/Tero Gardemeister	FIN	12	Hyundai Accent	WRC	X14HMC (GB)	accident
9	Stohl Racing	Manfred Stohl/Ilka Minor	A	35	Peugeot 206	WRC	206MWP75 (F)	accident
13	T. Marlboro Peugeot Total	HARRI ROVANPERA/Risto Pietilainen	FIN	3	Peugeot 206	WRC	938NVB75 (F)	accident
13	Ford Motor Company Ltd	MARKKO MARTIN/Michael Park	EE/GB	4	Ford Focus RS	WRC	EJ02KMU (GB)	engine
13	-	Tomasz Kuchar/Maciej Szczepaniak	PL	34	Ford Focus RS	WRC	Y129XEV (GB)	accident
16	Blue Rose T.	Kristian Sohlberg/Jakke Honkanen	FIN	33	Mitsubishi Lancer Evolution	WRC	KP51RWN(GB)	too late
17	Hyundai World R.T.	FREDDY LOIX/Sven Smeets	B	11	Hyundai Accent	WRC	X23HMC (GB)	accident

MANUFACTURER'S REGISTERED DRIVER. *PCWRC/Group N winner.

THE ROUTE

		SPECIAL STAGES	TOTAL DISTANCE	CREWS RUNNING
Leg 1 (1-9)	Auckland (Thursday 1915) - Auckland - Paparoa - Paparoa (Friday 1700)	9 gravel-139.10km	387.69km	62
Leg 2 (10-16)	Paparoa (Saturday 0800) - Paparoa - Manukau - Auckland (Saturday 2020)	7 gravel-150.43km	455.57km	51
Leg 3 (17-22)	Auckland (Sunday 0600) - Manukau - Manukau (Sunday 1545)	6 gravel-113.81km	454.36km	46
		22 stages-403.34km	1297.62km	

Weather: Leg 1 and 2 - very changeable, Leg 3 - dry. Two stages in darkness.

OVERALL LEADING SPECIAL STAGE POSITIONS

	1	2	3	4	5	6
Gronholm	10	8	1	-	-	-
Burns	7	5	3	2	1	1
Martin	3	3	1	3	2	1
Solberg	1	2	7	4	3	3
Duval	1	-	-	-	-	-
Rovanpera	-	1	6	1	1	-
C. McRae	-	1	1	-	-	-
Loix	-	1	-	1	-	-

Ligato and Arai scored one second fastest time each.

PCWRC Arai won 9 stages, Al-Wahaibi (Mitsubishi), Ferreyros (Mitsubishi) & Sola (Mitsubishi) 3 each, Bourne, McShea (Mitsubishi), Ligato (Mitsubishi) & Singh (Proton) 1 each.
GROUP N Arai won 7 stages, Crocker 5, Sola 3, Al-Wahaibi & Ferreyros 2 each, Bourne, McShea & Ligato 1 each.

STARTERS 80 (22 PCWRC). **FINISHERS** 46 (15 PCWRC).
OVERALL LEADER Gronholm stages 1-22.
PCWRC LEADERS Arai stages 1-3, Bourne (Subaru) 4, Arai 5-22.
(stage 14 not contested by Group N cars.)
GROUP N LEADERS Crocker (Subaru) stages 1-9, Arai 10-22.
WINNER'S AVERAGE SPEED OVER STAGES 107.39kph (record).
WORLD CHAMPIONSHIP FOR MANUFACTURERS
Peugeot 49 points, Citroen 44, Ford 26, Subaru 22, Skoda 12, Hyundai 3.
WORLD CHAMPIONSHIP FOR DRIVERS Burns 26 points, Gronholm 20,
Loeb & C.McRae 17, Sainz 16, Martin 13, Makinen 11, Solberg 9, Duval 8, Gardemeister 7, etc.

RECENT WINNERS
1993   Colin McRae/Derek Ringer Subaru Legacy 4WD Turbo (92.39kph)
1994   Colin McRae/Derek Ringer Subaru Impreza 555 (88.73kph)
1995   Colin McRae/Derek Ringer Subaru Impreza 555 (89.87kph)
1996 * Richard Burns/Robert Reid Mitsubishi Lancer Evolution (91.25kph)
1997   Kenneth Eriksson/Staffan Parmander Subaru Impreza WRC (93.48kph)
1998   Carlos Sainz/Luis Moya Toyota Corolla WRC (92.08kph)
1999   Tommi Makinen/Risto Mannisenmaki Mitsubishi Lancer Evolution (95.95kph)
2000   Marcus Gronholm/Timo Rautiainen Peugeot 206 WRC (99.47kph)
2001   Richard Burns/Robert Reid Subaru Impreza WRC (100.88kph)
2002   Marcus Gronholm/Timo Rautiainen Peugeot 206 WRC (103.39kph)
Note: * =W2L-only event.

Remarkable win by the world champion
Marcus Gronholm, recovering from
suspension trouble on the first day.

❖

Carlos Sainz lost the lead due to a
time control misunderstanding with
his codriver.

❖

Markko Martin led despite gearbox troubles
and retired due to dust ingestion by his
Focus on the final morning when leading.

❖

Extraordinary confusion over timing on
the first day, and security on the second,
both of which were eventually overcome
by the organisers.

LEG 1 A long leg, 13 stages and almost half
the competitive distance! Gronholm damaged
his suspension which let Carlos Sainz go
ahead. Extraordinary fire caused Colin
McRae's retirement. Petter Solberg went
off and dropped to 14th. Freddy Loix retired
because of electronic problems. Tommi
Makinen broke his gearbox exactly where it ha
failed last year, and lost a lot of time. After ear
puncture Martin was steadily catching the
leader Sainz. Considerable timing problems.
1 Sainz 1h54m01.2s, 2 Martin +22.4s,
3 Burns +40.1s, 4 Rovanpera +41.8s,
5 Loeb +50.2s, 6 Gronholm +1m04.0s,
7 Duval +2m38.3s, 8 Solberg +2m43.3s.
PCWRC Arai (12th) 2h02m53.6s.

LEG 2 Gearbox troubles for Martin delayed
his efforts to catch Sainz. Sainz entered
service one minute too early and the ensuing
one minute penalty dropped him to third.
Sebastien Loeb went off the road and retired
Confusion over safety issues, led to two stage
being abandoned and held instead on Leg 3
1 Martin 3h01m02.6s, 2 Gronholm +15.2s,
3 Sainz +23.3s, 4 Burns +26.6s,
5 Rovanpera +1m21.4s, 6 Solberg +2m49.3s
7 Duval +4m22.8s, 8 Schwarz +4m58.0s.
PCWRC Arai (11th) 3h14m48.6s.

LEG 3 Martin retired. Gronholm regained
the lead. Richard Burns caught Sainz who
had misfiring troubles, but lost second place
on the final stage with turbo troubles.
Armin Schwarz retired.
1 Gronholm 4h14m45.0s, 2 Sainz +26.6s,
3 Burns +1m12.8s, 4 Rovanpera +2m19.3s,
5 Solberg +3m11.4s, 6 Auriol +7m58.5s,
7 Gardemeister +8m33.7s, 8 Duval +11m55.3s
PCWRC Arai (9th) 4h34m46.7s.

Q uestion: "How have you reacted to Burns' attack?" Marcus Gronholm: "Oh, sorry, I had not noticed it!" Q: When will the new car be ready?" MG: "This car seems to be good enough..!" The memory of this year's Argentina Rally will linger for a long time. Two days before the start, Ford announced the immediate replacement of Sporting Director Martin Whitaker as part of an internal

What's New in 2003

● All servicing, including Shakedown, took place at the same location, outside La Cumbre.

● The tradition of running each leg of the rally in different regions around Cordoba was dropped. All the stages were run in the area or in and around the Punilla valley to the north of Villa Carlos Paz.

● New Shakedown location north of La Cumbre.

● The superspecial stages at the Pro-Racing complex were held in darkness on the Thursday evening, not as last year in daylight during the Friday.

● The rally finished one hour earlier, to be more media-friendly in European and Asian countries.

reorganisation. In the days before the event, there was an organisational crisis after ISC were unable to give training in their new timing systems, which in any case failed, or in the back-up systems. This was a disaster for the event, particularly for the organisers whom people initially, and mistakenly, assumed were responsible for the succession of wrong timings. On the

Both works Skodas finished in the points.

second day of the event, there followed a catastrophic misunderstanding by the FIA Safety Officer about security, and for no evident reason stages were delayed, and the third day's route had to be rescheduled so that the requisite competition distance would be run. It was a miracle

Petter Solberg, notwithstanding his evident effort, lost time off the road and was off the pace all rally.

of determination that the organisers overcame those problems.

Gronholm came to Argentina hoping to avenge his exclusion in 2002, and did so in style. Richard Burns, as championship leader, started first car on the road, but conditions favoured neither the first or the later cars in any discernable measure. Burns, once again, drove a steady and rewarding event. Burns had hoped at least to finish second and was very upset when turbo trouble on the final stage dropped him to third. On the first day when Gronholm wrecked his suspension, team manager Corrado Provera was supportive. "The timing mistakes on the first day could only have distracted a driver. It is no surprise Marcus made a mistake and hit a rock." Peugeots generally went well. They won more than half the stages and finished with three cars in the top four.

Citroen had another unconvincing event as to their performance, despite being the final team to have tested in the country before regulations prohibited this. Sebastien Loeb crashed. Carlos Sainz was the rally's second fastest driver and would have won but for moving too early into a Service Park and incurring a one minute penalty. Colin McRae had a slow start and then the car caught fire. When he parked it to the side of the track and walked back to warn following cars, the car moved on its own, across the track, without occupants, still burning. Armin

Schwarz claimed (and received) a time compensation for being delayed, but only thanks to in-car video evidence. Would anyone have believed the story otherwise?

What would become of the 2003 Fords? Technical trouble persisted for both Francois Duval and Markko Martin having transmission trouble, while the 2002 car of Mikko Hirvonen was slowed by a flattened exhaust. Martin was leading when his engine expired due to entry of dust.

Subaru came with high hopes. Having a long run of Argentina wins for Pirelli behind them and a new supply of shock absorbers from Sachs, but hopes again were dashed as Petter Solberg lost time off the road, and Tommi Makinen had a major delay when he was stuck in second gear. The gearbox broke, at the very same corner where he had transmission trouble 12 months before, which led to continued transmission troubles. At the end of the second day he was 13th overall, and 10th in the manufacturers' points chart and the chances of ever getting into the points seemed zero. He had reasons to go home quickly (his second child had been born while he was away) and so did not collect his car from parc ferme on the Sunday morning. Unfortunately for him, however, the series of misfortunes for other drivers meant he missed out on a point and gave Ford a point they did not deserve. Both Skodas finished in the points, although

Farewell, Friend

Saying goodbye is not easy, and in the case of motorsport can be exceedingly expensive. Hamed Al-Wahaibi walked away from his life in motor sport after the first two stages of the Rally Argentina. He did not turn up at the Friday morning restart. This was no temperamental reaction, but a genuine personal decision about the things which are important in life. It is easy to typify the people behind the wheels of rally cars, to prejudge their ambitions and motivation. Hamed however was never a person who fitted the norm in motorsport. He once listed the three things which were most important to him as his faith, his family and his country. Motorsport was a luxury, an indulgence. Why go to Argentina and make your decisions so far from home? It seemed that the memorial stickers the PCWRC crews placed on their cars, to honour Possum Bourne, was the turning point. It was an indication of the risks which not everyone needs to take, especially with the depth of personal responsibilities that Hamed possesses. He told this to the FIA, but they did not see it in the same personal light. For them it was a broken contract, the like of which they had not encountered before, and handed down a fine of USD20,000.

Hamed and team chief Manfred Stohl.

Didier Auriol drove with an injured wrist and Toni Gardemeister (who suffered a one minute pre-event penalty for a reconnaissance infringement) had differential pressure problems. As for the Hyundai team, Freddy Loix had a sensor fail which led to a damaged engine, and most disappointingly for Schwarz, when he was lying in sixth place, a core plug blew out with three stages to go.

The crisis of timing and the cancellations highlighted, at the expense

One last time for Gabriel Raies and what a fine result! Highest placed South American driver.

Production Car Championship

Local driver Marcos Ligato looked like being a sure fire winner in the category. He scored fastest time on the first four stages but then flew too high and damaged his car at the end of the fifth stage. He struggled to the start of stage six but then the engine stopped and would not restart. Ramon Ferreyros damaged his car at the same place as well. Toshihiro Arai took over the lead which he kept until the end of the event. Daniel Sola (below) settled into second until he had transmission trouble, with Giovanni Manfrinato third, but then both had punctures and fell back. By the end of the second day Niall McShea, notwithstanding earlier gearbox troubles, was up to second and looked like a splendid finisher but with three stages to go the oil cooler was smashed and he was out. Sola therefore finished second with Karamjit Singh, who had struggled after damaging his Proton against a rock which had been maliciously placed in the road, third. Of the 16 starters only seven reached the finish, with Riccardo Errani coming last, having had to stop on the stages to add water to his engine. Arai's second win placed him in the lead of the series with Singh in second place.

A time control misunderstanding denied Carlos Sainz victory.

of trust in the Argentina organisers, rallying's current problems of interference by outside authorities. In New Zealand, it had been the police, in Sweden it had been poor results availability. With the ISC's new high technology timing system there have been constant troubles, but the back-up system normally works well. On this occasion the marshals could not be given proper advance instructions. Quite why the stages on the Saturday were ordered to be cancelled, but whatever the reason, it was heart rending to realise how many thousands of spectators had camped out all night, for nothing. For Burns the loss of a possible second place was upsetting but still he held his championship lead, and Peugeot pulled ahead in the Makes series. Red French cars took the top four places on the event and the red cars continued to hold the top five places in the Drivers' championship.

Just the motivation he needed! Marcus Gronholm pulled back from this distaster to win.

23RD RALLY ARGENTINA

8/11.05.2003

POSITION/ LAST STAGE COMPLETED	ENTRANT	DRIVER/CODRIVER	NAT.	COMP NO.	CAR	CAT.	REG NO.	TOTAL PENALTY/ CAUSE
1	T. Marlboro Peugeot Total	MARCUS GRONHOLM/Timo Rautiainen	FIN	1	Peugeot 206	WRC	206NDQ75 (F)	4h.14m.45.0s.
2	Citroen Total	CARLOS SAINZ/Marc Marti	E	19	Citroen Xsara	WRC	36CSP92 (F)	4h.15m.11.6s.
3	T. Marlboro Peugeot Total	RICHARD BURNS/Robert Reid	GB	2	Peugeot 206	WRC	206NLM75 (F)	4h.15m.57.8s.
4	T. Marlboro Peugeot Total	HARRI ROVANPERA/Risto Pietilainen	FIN	3	Peugeot 206	WRC	206NLL75 (F)	4h.17m.04.3s.
5	555 Subaru World R.T.	PETTER SOLBERG/Philip Mills	N/GB	7	Subaru Impreza	WRC	S90WRT (GB)	4h.17m.56.4s.
6	Skoda Motorsport	DIDIER AURIOL/Denis Giraudet	F	14	Skoda Octavia	WRC	MBN15-48 (CZ)	4h.22m.43.5s.
7	Skoda Motorsport	TONI GARDEMEISTER/Paavo Lukander	FIN	15	Skoda Octavia	WRC	MBO90-41 (CZ)	4h.23m.18.7s.
8	Ford Motor Company Ltd.	FRANCOIS DUVAL/Stephane Prevot	B	5	Ford Focus RS	WRC	EJ02KMU (GB)	4h.26m.40.3s.
9	Subaru Production R.T.	Toshihiro Arai/Tony Sircombe	J/NZ	54	Subaru Impreza GD	PCWRC	GMG300NO9070 (J)	4h.34m.46.7s.*
10	J.Lopez	Gabriel Raies/Jorge Perez	RA	33	Toyota Corolla	WRC	not registered (RA)	4h.34m.48.4s.
16	Ford Motor Company Ltd	MIKKO HIRVONEN/Jarmo Lehtinen	FIN	6	Ford Focus RS	WRC	EX02OBC (GB)	4h.51m.37.4s.
LEADING RETIREMENTS								
0	-	Gabriel Pozzo/Daniel Stillo	RA	32	Skoda Octavia	WRC	MBN44-30 (CZ)	engine
6	Hyundai World R.T.	FREDDY LOIX/Sven Smeets	B	11	Hyundai Accent	WRC	X21HMC (GB)	withdrawn
8	Citroen Total	COLIN McRAE/Derek Ringer	GB	17	Citroen Xsara	WRC	28CSP92 (F)	fire
19	Citroen Total	SEBASTIEN LOEB/Daniel Elena	F/MC	18	Citroen Xsara	WRC	17DDM92 (F)	accident
20	Ford Motor Company Ltd	MARKKO MARTIN/Michael Park	EE/GB	4	Ford Focus RS	WRC	EO03YWC (GB)	engine
20	555 Subaru World R.T.	TOMMI MAKINEN/Kaj Lindstrom	FIN	8	Subaru Impreza	WRC	S70WRT (GB)	withdrawn
23	Hyundai World R.T.	ARMIN SCHWARZ/Manfred Hiemer	D	10	Hyundai Accent	WRC	X22HMC (GB)	engine

MANUFACTURER'S REGISTERED DRIVER.*PCWRC/Group N winner.

THE ROUTE

		SPECIAL STAGES	TOTAL DISTANCE	CREWS RUNNING
Leg 1 (1-13)	Villa Carlos Paz (Thursday 1830) - Villa Carlos Paz - Villa Carlos Paz (Friday 2043)	13 gravel-175.14km	586.33km	48
Leg 2 (15-20)	Villa Carlos Paz (Saturday 0655) - Villa Carlos Paz (Saturday 2022)	6 gravel-98.70km	544.20km	41
Leg 3 (21-25)	Villa Carlos Paz (Sunday 0635) - Villa Carlos Paz (Sunday 1439)	5 gravel-105.49km	386.01km	33
		24 stages-379.33km	1516.54km	

Stage 14 cancelled-spectator security. Weather: dry throughout. Two stages in darkness.

OVERALL LEADING SPECIAL STAGE POSITIONS*

	1	2	3	4	5	6
Gronholm	11	8	3	-	-	-
Sainz	7	3	2	4	5	1
Martin	2	3	4	3	1	3
Burns	1	3	3	4	4	2
Makinen	1	2	1	3	1	3
Rovanpera	1	-	1	3	4	3
Solberg	-	2	6	4	4	2
Loeb	-	2	2	2	1	2
McRae	-	-	1	-	1	1

*not including stage 15.

PCWRC McShea (Mitsubish) won 8 stages, Arai 6, Ligato 4, Sola (Mitsubishi) 3, Singh (Proton) & Manfrinato (Mitsubishi) 1.
GROUP N McShea & Arai won 6 stages each, Ligato 4, Sola 3, Singh, Sanchez (Subaru), Villagra (Mitsubishi) & Manfrinato 1 each.

STARTERS 78 (16 PCWRC). **FINISHERS** 33 (7 PCWRC).
OVERALL LEADERS Gronholm stages 1-8, Sainz 9-19, Martin 20, Gronholm 21-25.
PCWRC/GROUP N LEADERS
Ligato (Mitsubishi) stages 1-4, Arai 5-25. (Group N drivers did not contest stage 15)
WINNER'S AVERAGE SPEED OVER STAGES 89.34kph.
WORLD CHAMPIONSHIP FOR MANUFACTURERS
Peugeot 65 points, Citroen 52, Ford 29, Subaru 27, Skoda 19, Hyundai 3.
WORLD CHAMPIONSHIP FOR DRIVERS
Burns 32 points, Gronholm 30, Sainz 24, Loeb & C.McRae 17, Solberg & Martin 13, Makinen 11, Duval & Gardemeister 9, etc.

RECENT WINNERS

1993		Juha Kankkunen/Nicky Grist Toyota Celica Turbo 4WD (91.51kph)
1994		Didier Auriol/Bernard Occelli Toyota Celica Turbo 4WD (96.68kph)
1995	*	Jorge Recalde/Martin Christie Lancia HF Integrale (82.41kph)
1996		Tommi Makinen/Seppo Harjanne Mitsubishi Lancer Evolution (88.81kph)
1997		Tommi Makinen/Seppo Harjanne Mitsubishi Lancer Evolution (90.93kph)
1998		Tommi Makinen/Risto Mannisenmaki Mitsubishi Lancer Evolution (91.50kph)
1999		Juha Kankkunen/Juha Repo Subaru Impreza WRC (92.24kph)
2000		Richard Burns/Robert Reid Subaru Impreza WRC (88.60kph)
2001		Colin McRae/Nicky Grist Ford Focus RS WRC (90.45kph)
2002		Carlos Sainz/Luis Moya Ford Focus RS WRC (Gronholm's speed 87.02kph)

Note: * =W2L-only event.

50
GOLDEN
ACROPOLIS
RALLY

ΕΛΠΑ   6   WRC FiA
FIA WORLD RALLY

4-8 JUNE 2003

First world rally win for the 2003
Ford Focus WRC and also Estonian
Markko Martin, despite spectacular
incident when he drove with his vision
impared by his opened bonnet.

❖

Endless problems for Peugeots,
Richard Burns struggling to finish fourth
with a broken gearbox.

❖

Baulked on the final stage, Petter Solberg
was denied second place.

❖

Eighteen year old Jari-Matti Latvala
finished tenth overall!

LEG 1 Francois Duval took an initial lead
but retired after an accident. Mikko Hirvonen
also retired. Disaster for Hyundai. Sebastien
Loeb retired straightaway. Gronholm retired
end of day. Burns had gearbox trouble.
Good start by late running Harri Rovanpera.
Spectator control mayhem at Superspecial.
1 Martin 1h47m35.0s, 2 Rovanpera +4.8s,
3 Solberg +23.9s, 4 Sainz +37.9s,
5 Makinen +38.2s, 6 Panizzi +48.2s,
7 McRae +56.8s, 8 Auriol +1m29.7s.
JWRC Tirabassi (19th) 1h59m21.0s.

LEG 2 Gearbox problem for Rovanpera and
more gearbox trouble for Burns. Solberg
had a broken driveshaft. The reliable Citroens
gradually improved their placings.
1 Martin 3h30m25.8s, 2 Sainz +55.8s,
3 Solberg +1m17.0s, 4 McRae +1m33.6s,
5 Makinen +2m05.0s, 6 Burns +2m10.7s,
7 Rovanpera +3m31.1s, 8 Panizzi +3m34.9s.
JWRC Tirabassi (18th) 3h55m26.1s.

LEG 3 Burns continued with a broken
gearbox. Solberg spun and hit a tree.
Colin McRae slowed by electronic problem
and baulked Solberg.
1 Martin 4h53m40.5s, 2 Sainz +46.0s,
3 Solberg +52.7s, 4 Burns +2m06.6s,
5 Makinen +2m12.3s, 6 Rovanpera +3m44.7s
7 Panizzi +3m54.3s, 8 McRae +4m05.0s.
JWRC Tirabassi (17th) 5h27m34.0s.

Even if the new Ford Focus cars led all the way, this was a four team race. Peugeot, Citroen and Subaru all took turns at chasing Ford. The starting order advantage of running further back enabled Harri Rovanpera's Peugeot, running on cleaner tracks, to give chase on the first day. Then when reverse order came in on day two, firstly Petter Solberg (before he had a driveshaft failure on his Subaru) then Carlos Sainz's Citroen were challenging the Ford. Solberg, who scored

Finally it all came good. Markko Martin completed unfinished business from 2002.

the most fastest stage times, spent more than a day fighting back and with three stages to go was up to second place. Then firstly he spun into a tree, and was later baulked by Colin McRae's misfiring Citroen. In desperation Solberg drove his Subaru into the back of McRae's car and finally got past, but by 6.7 seconds he was just too much delayed to keep his second place. McRae's teammate Sainz

What's New in 2003

● 50th anniversary Acropolis Rally. Many winners of previous Acropolis Rallies attended as VIP guests and a display of contemporary cars.
● Based at Lamia, at the National Trade Centre.
● Figure-of-eight Superspecial held at Lilea, on the site used in recent years for the Service Park at the end of the Friday and the Saturday legs.
● Single Service Park at Lamia for all the event and Shakedown as well. The complex was also used for scrutineering, a rally show, the start and finish of each leg and the finish ceremonies.
● The more northerly location of the Service Park meant the rally was able to revisit stages further north, for example the old "Tarzan" stage, which recently had been unavailable because of reservoir construction work. The last time the mountainous stages in central Greece were included in the route of the Acropolis Rally was for the 2-litre event in 1995.
● New Shakedown location, north of Lamia.
● The ceremonial start reverted to its traditional location, beneath the Parthenon, instead of outside the Zappion.

All the Hyundais were out of the rally very early on. Jussi Valimaki (here) just survived until the second day.

First retirement of the season for Marcus Gronholm.

The Magic of Castrol

This was not the first or even the second time that Castrol had brought good fortune. Their win first time out with the Ford Focus team was truly a matter of deja vue. Ten years previously, the company was aligned with Toyota, and Didier Auriol gave them victory first time out, at Monte Carlo 1993. But the magic started even before this, 25 years earlier when Castrol joined up with Ford on the Escort RS1800 on their first appearance together in Sweden. Bjorn Waldegard gave them victory on that occasion as well.

Jari-Matti Latvala youngest ever works rally driver, at 18 years old.

was there instead. Solberg was unhappy with McRae. "The Citroen did more damage to my car than the tree ever did", the Norwegian joked but in the heat of the moment it had seemed to have been a deliberate ploy to help Carlos.

The rally was moved a little northwards this year, being based on the city of Lamia although the ceremonial start was again 220km away in Athens. This was the first European round of the world series for three months, since

Sweden, and a full entry was received. There were some interesting novelties as well. Ford had a new sponsor, the BP group, and a fourth team member, Finn Jari-Matti Latvala, competing on his first World rally, and remarkably finishing tenth overall. Inmarsat, the technical partners for the ISC, experimented with transmitting timing information by satellite, as part of a new initiative to use this system exclusively on world championship events from every control.

Peugeot experimented once again with air conditioning, encouraged by an FIA request that cockpit temperatures in rally cars should be strictly controlled, particularly as the drivers were required to wear fireproof overalls made of three layers. To make the air-con fully effective it was necessary to fit a special radiator, with a water spray injection, and certainly Richard Burns spoke enthusiastically about its benefit. Subaru fitted roof scoops for the first time on their 2003 models but other teams relied on fans and air ducts to cool the cockpits. Citroen Spain ran a works specification car for the reigning JWRC champion Daniel Sola. Ford had spent a lot of effort since Argentina checking on transmissions and hydraulic problems which manifested themselves in South America, as well as finding ways to deflect dust away from the engine induction system. Hyundai, smitten by many recent crashes, built a brand new car for Freddy Loix (their first of the season!) and also made their first dedicated test of the season as well. Skoda had done no Octavia testing, but plenty of work on the Fabia, and proudly announced they would make the World rally debut for the car in Germany. Subaru were anxious. Pirelli tyres had shod the Acropolis winners for many recent years, and now Subaru were

Unhappy rally for Colin McRae.

the only Pirelli users in the WRC.

This was to be another Acropolis disappointment for Peugeot. Their gearbox problems were unprecedented, due to the effects of using a different type of clutch and the retirement of Marcus Gronholm through another problem with the fuel management system, was a shock. While Peugeot Sport entered three cars, their favoured preparation associates Bozian entered another three, notably for Gilles Panizzi (prepared alongside the works cars at Velizy), Juuso Pykalisto and Roman Kresta. Pykalisto's run was short but not sweet, overturning on only the third stage, but Kresta was lying tenth at the end of the second day, the top non-factory car, when he jumped badly and smashed the radiator. Citroen started off unhappily when Sebastien Loeb retired on the first stage with an engine fault due to a casting error. Then McRae had an electrical problem and arrived late at a stage on the first day. Finally, and most seriously on the final day, he had an overheating ECU and lost more time which dropped him down to eighth. Sainz, once again in a very old Xsara, had the most reliable run and maintained a steady pace despite pressure from Petter Solberg in the leading Subaru near the end of the event.

Of the other two teams, Hyundai had a dreadful event. On the first stage Armin Schwarz hit a rock which bent the chassis and damaged the engine pulley, the camshaft belt failed and his event was over. At the same time Loix had a suspension strut punch its way through the bodywork and cause a fire from the damper fluid, and he was forced to retire.

Petter Solberg's second third place of the season so far.

One more point for Skoda, thanks to Didier Auriol.

Guest team driver Jussi Valimaki retired with an obscure clutch problem while test driver Manfred Stohl drove a development Accent to the finish, delayed by gearbox and oil pressure troubles. Skoda lost Toni Gardemeister when the turbocharger failed and the driver was unable to cut off the oil supply, which then caused the engine to fail, but Didier Auriol survived various suspension troubles to claim the last manufacturer point. So four different manufacturers finished in the top four places and five gained championship points, three of them scoring ten points each!

The event, however, was Markko's. It was very encouraging to win on the first event with a new sponsor, a car which was still very young on the scene, and with a new team chief, Jost Capito. It was a rally on which Fords traditionally do well (this was their 12th win on the event, their fourth in succession) but was also a surprise because the 2003 Focus was a car suspected of being better on faster rather than slower events.

Junior Championship

Brice Tirabassi *(below)* started the event as joint leader in the category with the VW driver Kosti Katajamaki. The Frenchman led all the way, the Finn retired on the second day with gearbox failure when lying third. Suzukis had tested hard for this event and Daniel Carlsson showed a new measured approach which paid off handsomely, lying second virtually all the way. The attrition rate was as high as ever, only six out of the 20 starters reaching the finish. All the Puntos retired, only one Puma finished, and that after seemingly endless suspension and steering problems, but three of the four Suzukis reached the end. All the stages were won by either Tirabassi or Carlsson, behind whom there was a great battle on the first day between Mirco Baldacci, Ville-Pertti Teuronen and Katajamaki. Going well early on was Guy Wilks in a Puma, but he then had considerable trouble and eventually finished sixth, and last. Strangely enough, only six JWRC cars had also finished here last year!

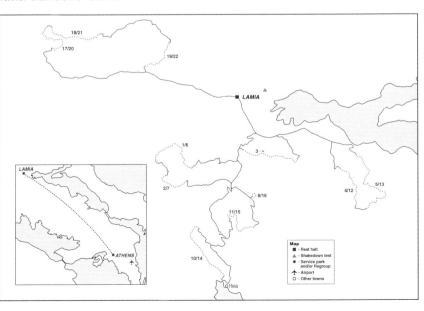

50TH ACROPOLIS RALLY

POSITION/ LAST STAGE COMPLETED	ENTRANT	DRIVER/CODRIVER	NAT.	COMP NO.	CAR	CAT.	REG NO.	TOTAL PENALTY/ CAUSE
1	Ford Motor Company Ltd	MARKKO MARTIN/Michael Park	EE/GB	4	Ford Focus RS	WRC	EO03YRJ (GB)	4h.53m.40.5s.
2	Citroen Total	CARLOS SAINZ/Marc Marti	E	19	Citroen Xsara	WRC	29CSP92 (F)	4h.54m.26.5s.
3	555 Subaru World R.T.	PETTER SOLBERG/Philip Mills	N/GB	7	Subaru Impreza	WRC	S100WRT (GB)	4h.54m.33.2s.
4	T. Marlboro Peugeot Total	RICHARD BURNS/Robert Reid	GB	2	Peugeot 206	WRC	81UNVT75(F)	4h.55m.47.1s.
5	555 Subaru World R.T.	TOMMI MAKINEN/Kaj Lindstrom	FIN	8	Subaru Impreza	WRC	S200WRT (GB)	4h.55m.52.8s.
6	T. Marlboro Peugeot Total	HARRI ROVANPERA/Risto Pietilainen	FIN	3	Peugeot 206	WRC	624NZT75 (F)	4h.57m.25.2s.
7	Bozian Racing	Gilles + Herve Panizzi	F	21	Peugeot 206	WRC	341NQZ75(F)	4h.57m.34.8s.
8	Citroen Total	COLIN McRAE/Derek Ringer	GB	17	Citroen Xsara	WRC	21DDM92 (F)	4h.57m.45.5s.
9	Skoda Motorsport	DIDIER AURIOL/Denis Giraudet	F	14	Skoda Octavia	WRC	2S5 1180 (CZ)	5h.00m.07.7s.
10	Ford Motor Company Ltd	Jari-Matti Latvala/Carl Williamson	FIN/GB	20	Ford Focus RS	WRC	Y6FMC (GB)	5h.05m.13.9s.
12	Citroen Sport	Daniel Sola/Alex Romani	E	25	Citroen Xsara	WRC	20CSP92 (F)	5h.06m.54.0s.
16	-	Simon Jean-Joseph/Jack Boyere	F	105	Renault Clio	S1600	872AMC83 (F)	5h.26m.27.7s.*
17	-	Brice Tirabassi/Jacques-Julien Renucci	F	61	Renault Clio	JWRC	871AMC83 (F)	5h.27m.34.0s.**

LEADING RETIREMENTS

POSITION/ LAST STAGE COMPLETED	ENTRANT	DRIVER/CODRIVER	NAT.	COMP NO.	CAR	CAT.	REG NO.	TOTAL PENALTY/ CAUSE
0	Hyundai World R.T.	ARMIN SCHWARZ/Manfred Hiemer	D	10	Hyundai Accent	WRC	X19HMC (GB)	engine
0	Citroen Total	SEBASTIEN LOEB/Daniel Elena	F/MC	18	Citroen Xsara	WRC	20DDM92 (F)	engine
2	Hyundai World R.T.	FREDDY LOIX/Sven Smeets	B	11	Hyundai Accent	WRC	X26HMC (GB)	suspension
2	Bozian Racing	Juuso Pykalisto/Esko Mertsalmi	FIN	24	Peugeot 206	WRC	3976XR69 (F)	accident
4	Ford Motor Company Ltd	FRANCOIS DUVAL/Stephane Prevot	B	5	Ford Focus RS	WRC	EJ02KMV(GB)	accident
4	-	Armodios Vovos/"El-Em"	GR	34	Ford Focus RS	WRC	EX02OBE (GB)	accident
5	Ford Motor Company Ltd	MIKKO HIRVONEN/Jarmo Lehtinen	FIN	6	Ford Focus RS	WRC	EX02OBB(GB)	suspension
5	Skoda Motorsport	TONI GARDEMEISTER/Paavo Lukander	FIN	15	Skoda Octavia	WRC	2S5 1190 (CZ)	engine
7	T. Marlboro Peugeot Total	MARCUS GRONHOLM/Timo Rautiainen	FIN	1	Peugeot 206	WRC	814NVT75 (F)	fuel feed
7	Hyundai World R.T.	JUSSI VALIMAKI/Tero Gardemeister	FIN	12	Hyundai Accent	WRC	X14HMC (GB)	clutch
16	Bozian Racing	Roman Kresta/Jan Tomanek	CZ	22	Peugeot 206	WRC	4854VW69(F)	engine
19	-	Tomasz Kuchar/Maciek Szczepaniak	PL	33	Ford Focus RS	WRC	Y129XEV (GB)	engine

MANUFACTURER'S REGISTERED DRIVER. *S1600 winner. **JWRC winner.

THE ROUTE

		SPECIAL STAGES	TOTAL DISTANCE	CREWS RUNNING
Leg 1 (1-7)	Athens (Thursday 1930) - Lamia - Lamia (Friday 1938)	7 gravel-145.56km	498.22km*	52
Leg 2 (9-16)	Lamia (Saturday 0600) - Lamia - Lamia (Saturday 1955)	8 gravel-148.53km	608.75km	42
Leg 3 (17-22)	Lamia (Sunday 0800) - Lamia - Lamia (Sunday 1620)	6 gravel-105.04km	336.83km	37
		21 stages-399.13km	1443.80km	

*not including distance from Ceremonial Start. Stage 8 cancelled-security.
Weather: dry and warm throughout. No stages in darkness.

OVERALL LEADING SPECIAL STAGE POSITIONS

	1	2	3	4	5	6
Solberg	7	4	1	1	1	2
Martin	5	4	1	4	3	3
Rovanpera	4	-	4	2	2	2
Sainz	2	4	3	4	2	2
Gronholm	1	1	1	1	1	-
Duval	1	-	3	-	-	-
Makinen	1	-	-	3	3	5
McRae	-	4	5	3	1	2
Burns	-	2	3	3	2	3

JWRC Tirabassi won 13 stages, Carlsson (Suzuki) won 8.
S1600 Jean-Joseph won 12 stages, Tirabassi 5, Carlsson 4.

STARTERS 82 (20 JWRC). **FINISHERS** 37 (6 JWRC).
OVERALL LEADERS Duval stage 1, Martin 2-22.
JWRC LEADER Tirabassi stages 1-22.
S1600 LEADERS Tirabassi stage 1, Jean-Joseph 2-4, Tirabassi 5-9, Jean-Joseph 10-22.
WINNER'S AVERAGE SPEED OVER STAGES 81.54kph.
WORLD CHAMPIONSHIP FOR MANUFACTURERS
Peugeot 73 points, Citroen 62 , Ford 39, Subaru 37, Skoda 20, Hyundai 3.
WORLD CHAMPIONSHIP FOR DRIVERS
Burns 37 points, Sainz 32, Gronholm 30, Martin 23, Solberg 19, McRae 18, Loeb 17, Makinen 15, Duval & Gardemeister 9, etc.

RECENT WINNERS

1993	Miki Biasion/Tiziano Siviero Ford Escort RS Cosworth (78.93kph)
1994	Carlos Sainz/Luis Moya Subaru Impreza 555 (76.17kph)
1995 *	Aris Vovos/Kostas Stefanis Lancia HF Integrale (68.69kph)
1996	Colin McRae/Derek Ringer Subaru Impreza 555 (77.58kph)
1997	Carlos Sainz/Luis Moya Ford Escort WRC (78.75kph)
1998	Colin McRae/Nicky Grist Subaru Impreza WRC (82.87kph)
1999	Richard Burns/Robert Reid Subaru Impreza WRC (85.93kph)
2000	Colin McRae/Nicky Grist Ford Racing Focus WRC (78.54kph)
2001	Colin McRae/Nicky Grist Ford Focus RS WRC (82.46kph)
2002	Colin McRae/Nicky Grist Ford Focus RS WRC (83.84kph)

Note * =W2L-only event.

7

CYPRUS SPORT ORGANISATION

L.I PAULS TOURISM ORGANISATION

CYPRUS AA

FiA

2003 CYPRUS RALLY

LEG 1 Peugeot drivers led all the way, transmission trouble dropping Harri Rovanpera back, letting Marcus Gronholm ahead. Markko Martin delayed by gearshift trouble. Tommi Makinen stopped to change a broken wheel.
1 Gronholm 1h28m49.8s, 2 Rovanpera +6.8s,
3 Solberg +10.3s, 4 Panizzi +13.9s,
5 Loeb +40.4s, 6 McRae +55.7s,
7 Martin +1m22.3s, 8 Burns +1m31.2s.
PCWRC Arai (18th) 1h37m48.5s.

LEG 2 Rally leader Gronholm had a broken propshaft which led to clutch failure, Petter Solberg took over the lead, with Rovanpera close behind. In two stages two Fords, two Peugeots and one Hyundai retired. Makinen was also delayed too much to continue.
1 Solberg 3h55m21.6s, 2 Rovanpera +25.3s,
3 Loeb +2m44.6s, 4 McRae +3m29.0s,
5 Sainz +4m32.9s, 6 Hirvonen +6m49.4s,
7 Schwarz +10m03.3s, 8 Ginley +16m24.7s.
PCWRC Arai (9th) 4h18m35.5s.

LEG 3 Rovanpera suffered a broken driveshaft and gradually fell back, only just finishing ahead of third placed Sebastien Loeb.
1 Solberg 5h09m12.6s, 2 Rovanpera +4m14.0s,
3 Loeb +4m16.8s, 4 McRae +4m45.3s,
5 Sainz +5m42.2s, 6 Hirvonen +8m58.7s,
7 Schwarz +13m29.0s, 8 Ginley +23m57.3s.
PCWRC Arai (9th) 5h39m13.7s.

The never-ending twists and turns in the Troodos mountains make the Cyprus Rally quite distinct and contribute to this being by far the slowest rally in the championship. This, combined with the high ambient temperatures, makes the event itself very hard on the cars and almost as hard on the crews. Right from the start of action

Carlos Sainz up to second place in the championship.

on the Friday the rally became a remarkable test. By Saturday morning there had been a high rate of attrition among the top teams, which made the reliability and consistency of the Citroen team, which finished with Sebastien Loeb third, Colin McRae fourth and Carlos Sainz fifth, all the more impressive. In conditions where surface cleaning was

important, eventual winner Petter Solberg had been in the frame from the start. Running fifth on the road Solberg was initially headed only by 11th running Harri Rovanpera and briefly by third running Marcus Gronholm. The Norwegian had a small electrical problem on the second stage which delayed him a little, but by the first stage on the second day he was leading. The only driver then able to keep him in their sights was Rovanpera, who had been leading till the final stage on the Friday when he had a gearbox problem which let his teammate Marcus Gronholm in front. On Saturday morning, however,

What's New in 2003

● A new Service Park location inside Limassol port.
● The organisers implemented the FIA's spectator control recommendations by limiting attendance to specific areas. "Park and Ride" transport was provided to prevent them parking on the roads close to stages.
● Three completely new stages were run.
● The event was used as the basis for a major international tourist promotion.

Great team! Petter Solberg and Philip Mills and Subaru!

Tales of Two Englishmen

At the half way point in the championship the effect of the new points scoring rules was becoming clear. Richard Burns' consistent finishing record (this was the first time in 2003 he had retired) had kept him ahead in the Drivers' series, even though he had scored no wins. Four other drivers had one win each and Marcus Gronholm had three! Under the points scoring system of previous years, Burns would have been third in the series at this time. By the end of the event Richard's results on the stages was even more revealing. Until now he had only scored 11 fastest times all year, out of the 131 stages run. Richard's frustration was evident. At one point he exclaimed "This is the third rally I have had trouble, how can I ever win the championship?" He felt the problem was the 206 which after 18 months had

still not provided him with an outright win, but insofar as this was the car that continued to help him towards a second world title, why complain?

From an unhappy Englishman to a happy one; the Gentleman driver Alistair Ginley *(below)*. He is the first really private driver to score a world championship point since the days of Frederic Dor, and loved every moment. The smile was etched indelibly after an incident when Juuso Pykalisto was struggling with power steering failure and was baulking Alistair. Recalling Solberg's incident in Greece with Colin McRae, Alistair nudged the rear of the Peugeot with the front of his Focus, and was immediately let past. "Fancy that, me pushing a famous Flying Finn out of the way. My broken bumper cost £1000, but it was well worthwhile just for the memory!"

Gronholm had a propshaft failure and he was out of the rally.

With the evident high degree of elimination of top competitors on the Saturday morning, Solberg resisted the temptation to drive too fast, and held an oscillating lead through the second day before he put on a spurt on the last stage on Saturday, and pulled another ten seconds further ahead. The Sunday saw Solberg tempted again to attack and kill off the hopes of the remaining Peugeot driver, but in fact he was able to control the event without needing to do this. When Rovanpera also had a driveshaft problem with three stages to go he was hard pressed to hold even second place in front of Loeb's Citroen. It had been a welcome change of fortune for Subaru, especially on account of their extra success in the PCWRC category.

For Citroen it was a strange event. Their cars were well off the pace (Sainz said his car was only handling the way he wanted on the final afternoon, McRae said he was very disappointed with the performance of his) but it did not matter. On this occasion it was much more important that the cars were reliable. For all three days there was no serious technical trouble on any of them, except for a suspension failure for McRae, which could have been caused by any of the impacts, and a last day misfire for Loeb. For Ford, Cyprus was a most unexpected disappointment. Since Argentina the team knew they had a problem with dust being ingested into the engine, and they worked hard and innovatively to overcome it. Things had gone so well in Greece they assumed the problem was cured. The first few kilometres of stage five proved otherwise. First Francois Duval then Markko Martin stopped within 500 metres of each other. Team chief Malcolm Wilson "I guess there can only be a half dozen stages in the whole championship where these problems could have happened. It all proves that cars must absolutely be good everywhere!"

The Hyundais were in deep problems immediately. On the first stage their number three driver Justin Dale had both radiator cooling fans fail and he reached the end of stage two with terminal overheating. Freddy Loix went out with engine failure after overheating trouble, while Armin Schwarz struggled on with differential, gearbox and shock absorber problems, but finished. The biggest shock, however, was the systematic

Long walk home for the Ford crews...

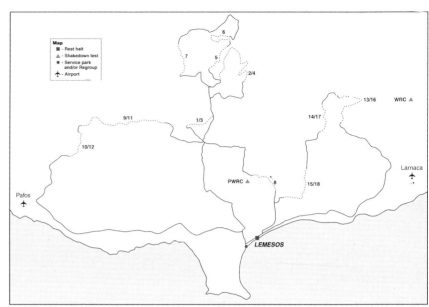

elimination of four of the five Peugeots. Gronholm's broken propshaft led to clutch failure and retirement. Burns, meanwhile, was suffering badly from being first car on the road but started to recover on day two despite gearshift difficulties. Engine overheating trouble finally stopped him on day two after he had recovered to sixth place. Gilles Panizzi's works - prepared car stopped with engine failure, Jusso Pykalisto's works - supported entry was withdrawn after damage from overheating, leaving only Rovanpera to support the marque. He then also had driveshaft failure on the final morning and just scraped home second.

This was the final world rally for the Skoda Octavia WRC. Didier Auriol finished the first stage magnificently in third place, but the glory did not last. Both he and Toni Gardemeister had fuel system trouble, probably because of the heat, though Auriol retired with an electrical problem on a road section and Gardemeister crashed. About Subaru, it was a familiar story with Tommi Makinen having a series of problems. On the first day he lost time stopping on a stage when he hit a rock, on the second when a tyre wrapped itself round the suspension and the delay made him too late to carry on. Solberg, however, continued with virtually no troubles all event.

Production Car Championship

There was a walkover for Subaru cars in the Group N category, led all the way by Toshihiro Arai chased initially by the Mitsubishis of Niall McShea and then Daniel Sola, but from the last stage of the first day the Japanese driver headed the two Imprezas of the David Sutton Cars team. Arai's only problem was a puncture on the first day but it did not cost him his position. For two stages Stig Blomqvist was second, but then on stage six he had brake trouble and dropped behind his teammate Martin Rowe *(below)*. Marcos Ligato lost a quarter hour on day one when his air box was dislodged. Many drivers had brake troubles, leading to the retirement of Ramon Ferreyros, and delays for others. Many others had suspension woes including the reigning champion Karamjit Singh, while transmission trouble ended the hopes of Sola and McShea. This event was a major breakthrough in upsetting the traditional Mitsubishi monopoly of the group and the PCWRC in particular, by far the biggest wake-up call they have ever suffered in this category.

Justin Dale retired with overheating when his radiator fans failed.

31ST CYPRUS RALLY

POSITION/ LAST STAGE COMPLETED	ENTRANT	DRIVER/CODRIVER	NAT.	COMP CAR NO.	CAR	CAT.	REG NO.	TOTAL PENALTY/ CAUSE
1	555 Subaru World R.T.	PETTER SOLBERG/Philip Mills	N/GB	7	Subaru Impreza	WRC	S80WRT (GB)	5h.09m.12.6s.
2	T. Marlboro Peugeot Total	HARRI ROVANPERA/Risto Pietilainen	FIN	3	Peugeot 206	WRC	290NNN75(F)	5h.13m.26.6s.
3	Citroen Total	SEBASTIEN LOEB/Daniel Elena	F/MC	18	Citroen Xsara	WRC	16DDM92 (F)	5h.13m.30.4s.
4	Citroen Total	COLIN McRAE/Derek Ringer	GB	17	Citroen Xsara	WRC	14DDM92 (F)	5h.13m.57.9s.
5	Citroen Total	CARLOS SAINZ/Marc Marti	E	19	Citroen Xsara	WRC	39CSP92 (F)	5h.14m.54.8s.
6	Ford Motor Company Ltd	MIKKO HIRVONEN/Jarmo Lehtinen	FIN	0	Ford Focus RS	WRC	EX02OBB (GB)	5h.18m.11.3s.
7	Hyundai World R.T.	ARMIN SCHWARZ/Manfred Hiemer	D	10	Hyundai Accent	WRC	X22HMC (GB)	5h.22m.41.6s.
8	-	Alistair Ginley/Rory Kennedy	GB/IRL	32	Ford Focus RS	WRC	EJ02KMO(GB)	5h.33m.09.9s.
9	Subaru Production R.T.	Toshihiro Arai/Tony Sircombe	J/NZ	54	Subaru Impreza WRX	PCWRC	GMG300NO9070(J)	5h.39m.13.7s.*
10	David Sutton (Cars) Ltd	Martin Rowe/Trevor Agnew	GB	55	Subaru Impreza WRX	PCWRC	X2DSC (GB)	5h.42m.56.7s.
LEADING RETIREMENTS								
2	Hyundai World R.T.	JUSTIN DALE/Andrew Bargery	GB	12	Hyundai Accent	WRC	X12HMC (GB)	engine
4	Ford Motor Company Ltd	MARKKO MARTIN/Michael Park	EE/GB	4	Ford Focus RS	WRC	EO03YWC (GB)	engine
4	Ford Motor Company Ltd.	FRANCOIS DUVAL/Stephane Prevot	B	5	Ford Focus RS	WRC	EJ02KMU (GB)	engine
5	T. Marlboro Peugeot Total	MARCUS GRONHOLM/Timo Rautiainen	FIN	1	Peugeot 206	WRC	943NVB75 (F)	clutch
5	Bozian Racing	Gilles + Herve Panizzi	F	20	Peugeot 206	WRC	948NVB75 (F)	oil pressure
5	Hyundai World R.T.	FREDDY LOIX/Sven Smeets	B	11	Hyundai Accent	WRC	X21HMC (GB)	engine
6	-	Antony Warmbold/Gemma Price	D/GB	21	Ford Focus RS	WRC	Y3FMC (GB)	fuel
8	Skoda Motorport	TONI GARDEMEISTER/Paavo Lukander	FIN	15	Skoda Octavia	WRC	MBO90-41(CZ)	engine damage
10	Bozian Racing	Juuso Pykalisto/Esko Mertsalmi	FIN	22	Peugeot 206	WRC	4852YW69(F)	engine
10	T. Marlboro Peugeot Total	RICHARD BURNS/Robert Reid	GB	2	Peugeot 206	WRC	950NVB75 (F)	engine
10	555 Subaru World R.T.	TOMMI MAKINEN/Kaj Lindstrom	FIN	8	Subaru Impreza	WRC	S60WRT (GB)	withdrawn
10	Skoda Motorsport	DIDIER AURIOL/Denis Giraudet	F	14	Skoda Octavia	WRC	MBN15-48 (CZ)	electrical

MANUFACTURER'S REGISTERED DRIVER. *PCWRC/Group N winner.

THE ROUTE

		SPECIAL STAGES	TOTAL DISTANCE	CREWS RUNNING
Leg 1 (1-4)	Lemesos (Friday 0800) - Lemesos - Lemesos (Friday 1807)	4 gravel-99.84km	329.63km	42
Leg 2 (5-12)	Lemesos (Saturday 0600) - Lemesos - Lemesos - Lemesos (Saturday 1935)	8 gravel-158.35km	549.61km	18
Leg 3 (13-18)	Lemesos (Sunday 0730) - Lemesos - Lemesos (Sunday 1520)	6 gravel-82.86km	305.30km	17
		18 stages-341.05km	1184.54km	

Ceremonial Start Thursday 2030. Weather: sunny and hot with a little rain.
No stages at night.

OVERALL LEADING SPECIAL STAGE POSITIONS

	1	2	3	4	5	6
Solberg	7	5	3	1	1	1
Rovanpera	5	6	4	-	-	-
Makinen	4	2	-	-	-	-
Sainz	1	3	1	1	5	2
Gronholm	1	1	-	1	-	-
Loeb	-	1	4	7	1	1
McRae	-	1	4	6	3	2
Panizzi	-	-	2	-	1	2
Auriol	-	-	1	-	-	-

PCWRC/GROUP N Arai & Ligato (Mitsubishi) won 8 stages each, Kulig (Mitsubishi) & Sola (Mitsubishi) 1 each.

STARTERS 51(20 PCWRC). **FINISHERS** 17 (6 PCWRC).
OVERALL LEADERS Rovanpera stages 1-3,Gronholm 4, Solberg 5-18.
PCWRC/GROUP N LEADER Arai stages 1-18.
WINNER'S AVERAGE SPEED OVER STAGES 66.18kph.
WORLD CHAMPIONSHIP FOR MANUFACTURERS
Peugeot 81 points, Citroen 73, Subaru 47, Ford 43, Skoda 20, Hyundai 6.
WORLD CHAMPIONSHIP FOR DRIVERS
Burns 37 points, Sainz 36, Gronholm 30, Solberg 29, Loeb, Martin & McRae 23, Rovanpera 16, Makinen 15, Duval & Gardemeister 9, etc.

RECENT WINNERS
1993	*	Alex Fiorio/Vittorio Brambilla Lancia HF Integrale
1994	*	Alex Fiorio/Vittorio Brambilla Lancia HF Integrale
1995	*	'Bagheera'/Naji Stephan Lancia HF Integrale
1996	*	Armin Schwarz/Denis Giraudet Toyota Celica GT-Four
1997	*	Krzysztof Holowczyc/Maciej Wislawski Subaru Impreza 555
1998	*	Andrea Navarra/Alexandra Materazzetti Subaru Impreza 555
1999	*	Jean-Pierre Richelmi/Stephane Prevot Subaru Impreza WRC
2000		Carlos Sainz/Luis Moya Ford Racing Focus WRC (64.11kph)
2001		Colin McRae/Nicky Grist Ford Focus RS WRC (66.60kph)
2002		Marcus Gronholm/Timo Rautiainen Peugeot 206 (67.54kph)
Note	*	=ECR-only event.

24. - 27. Juli 2003

ADAC RALLYE DEUTSCHLAND

8

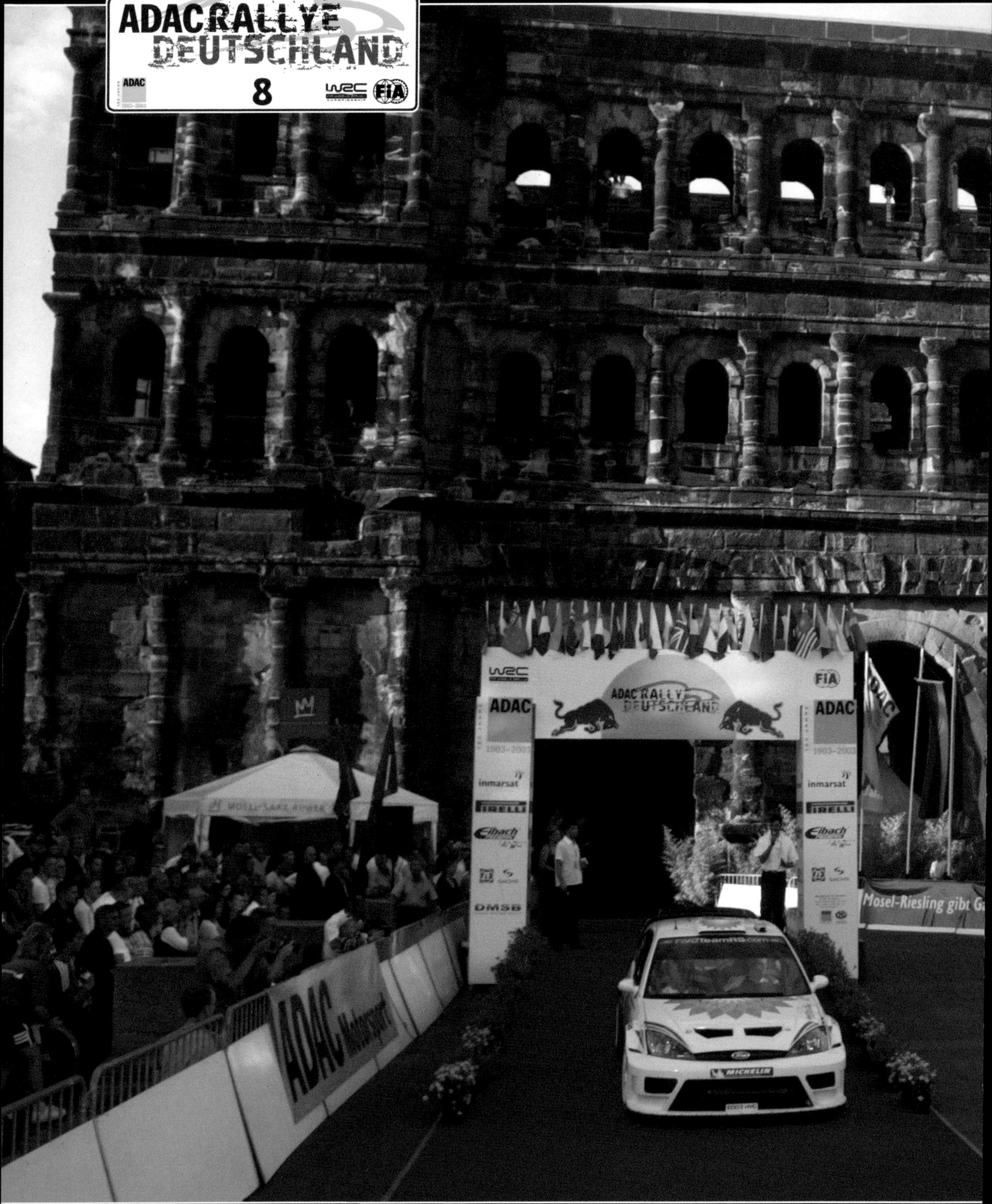

Amazing fight for victory on the final stage, eventually resolved in Sebastien Loeb's favour.

Loeb's second successive Deutschland win.

Peugeot, Ford and Citroen all led but Markko Martin (Ford) was easily the fastest driver.

Debut for Skoda Fabia World Rally Car.

LEG 1 Richard Burns and Markko Martin vied for the lead until Martin had transmission trouble. Subarus and Hyundais off the pace. Unexpectedly dry conditions. Retirements for Tommi Makinen and Didier Auriol.
1 Burns 1h08m45.1s, 2 Gronholm +9.4s,
3 Loeb +10.3s, 4 McRae +29.0s,
5 Panizzi +43.1s, 6 Sainz +47.0s,
7 Duval +49.9s, 8 Robert +55.6s.
PCWRC Sola (27th) 1h14m42.1s.

LEG 2 Frequent but scattered showers played havoc with tyre choices. End for Toni Gardemeister and Philippe Bugalski. Marcus Gronholm passed Burns and then Loeb took the lead. Good restart position order favoured Martin who climbed from 10th to third. More troubles for Hyundai. Jani Paasonen crashed.
1 Loeb 2h46m20.8s, 2 Gronholm +5.5s,
3 Martin +34.8s, 4 McRae +45.3s,
5 Burns +48.8s, 6 Sainz +1m54.6s,
7 Duval +1m59.4s, 8 Panizzi +2m19.2s.
PCWRC Sola (21st) 3h02m04.5s.

LEG 3 Martin had more transmission trouble and fell back. Showers followed the rally round again. Gronholm slid into a wall and fought hard to catch time back on Loeb, which finally he just failed to do.
1 Loeb 3h46m50.4s, 2 Gronholm +3.6s,
3 Burns +19.7s, 4 McRae +31.4s,
5 Martin +57.9s, 6 Sainz +1m38.6s,
7 Duval +1m48.1s, 8 Solberg +2m30.2s.
PCWRC Sola (22nd) 4h11m45.9s.

Until the last few yards of the final stage there was no assurance of victory for Sebastien Loeb and Citroen. Indeed halfway through the stage it seemed World Champion Marcus Gronholm would snatch a last-gasp win in his Peugeot, but finally Loeb came home the winner by 3.6 seconds. It had been one of the most treacherous events in memory, intermittent rain making the asphalt and concrete roads like skating rinks, though it was a miracle how few cars actually crashed during the event. Before the final showdown, there had been a three cornered fight between Ford, Citroen and Peugeot, each taking turns leading the event and setting fastest times. Markko Martin had been easily the fastest driver, but was badly delayed on the first day with transmission trouble. On the second day he fought back from tenth place to third, but finally had to settle for fifth.

Deutschland's rally roads could never be called normal. Driving in the dry was bad enough, however, words cannot *Exciting new shape on the championship scene. Toni Gardemeister showes off the lines of the Skoda Fabia WRC.*

describe the horrors of driving on the slippery surfaces in the rain. A large proportion are run on concrete, a surface that is characterised by steps which jar the suspensions, and ripples which create high speed vibrations. On the military grounds, many roads have deteriorated and cause extra damage to passing cars. In the rain there is more trouble where earlier cars have cut corners and scattered loose gravel on the track. The effect of all this was to create some of the most demanding driving conditions in the championships.

What's New in 2003

● New philosophy of route management, visiting each of the three main regions each day.
● New Shakedown location.
● Same Service Park for all four days (still Bostalsee).
● All except one stage changed, though usually only in small details.
● Special marshal training scheme and increased spectator marshals.
● Clerk of the Course Armin Kohl returned to this position, replacing Friedhelm Kissel.

Looks familiar? Sebastien Loeb won the same rally two years running - in the same car! Only the competition number had changed.

Battle of the Youngsters

Only just over half the entries eventually reached the finish, but amongst them were all five under-23 year old competitors who were driving World Rally Cars. Highest placed was 22 year old Francois Duval, ahead of his Ford teammates Mikko Hirvonen (22) and Jari-Matti Latvala (18), but within the next six places were two drivers in a battle of their own in privately run cars. These were 21 year old Jan Kopecky *(right)*

from the Czech Republic and Tibor Cserhalmi from Slovakia, respectively in an Octavia and a Focus, and both were on their second Deutschland Rally and finished within three minutes of each other. After the first day they had been only 8.5 seconds apart!

The first day had been dry, against predictions, and Richard Burns, once again starting first car on the road, as befits the Drivers' series leader, felt his chance of running ahead of the opposition might just suit him. For a while it did. The dirty stages did not clean with the passage of rally cars, as on other events. Was this going to be his first win for Peugeot, was his two year drought of victories about to end, was he about to win his first asphalt world championship rally? Sadly, no. He took an early lead but a tyre mousse broke. Burns then found it difficult to hold a competitive speed on the military ranges and was honest enough to say he did not know why. Martin then led for Ford, but only for one stage until he had transmission problems allowing Burns to regain the lead. On the second day Burns suffered from the weather on the military stages. From holding the lead on leg one he had, within 24 hours, slid down to fifth. Gronholm, the Finn who excels in slippery conditions, took over the lead from his teammate, but was slowed by a double

puncture on stage 12. The mousses kept the tyres inflated. One tyre could be changed but under the 'only one spare wheel' rule he had to start the following stage without air in the other. Loeb took the lead and, although Gronholm fought back, held this to the finish.

One Citroen (that of the former full team driver Philippe Bugalski) had an engine failure due to a turbo problem. For Subaru Tommi Makinen suffered a flat battery after having power steering failure, while his teamate Petter Solberg, who had felt ill for the first two days, was off the pace. All the Hyundais reached the finish, Freddy Loix's in the championship points. A surprising star was the Czech driver Roman Kresta, who eventually retired when a hub collapsed on his Peugeot. He had two claims to fame. Firstly he rolled his car at Shakedown but happily with little damage. Then he scored fastest time

Richard Burns could handle the concrete on the vineyard stages, but hated the concrete on the military ranges.

on the final stage on the second day. "As we lined up for the stage we were third car in line and we had dry weather tyres fitted. Then the rain started. It was a nightmare. But I realised that however much I would be disadvantaged, drivers following after me (all the leading drivers) would suffer far more." The next day came a suspension problem and he was out of the event. On only the second appearance of the Mitsubishi team in 2003 Kristian Sohlberg finished while Jani Paasonen crashed heavily, putting codriver Arto Kapanen in hospital.

The rally marked the debut of the Skoda Fabia WRC. Team director Dr. Petr Kohoutek, "We planned to start Fabia competition at the end of the season, but

Bad start for Roman Kresta. A fastest stage time on day two, however, was to come. No Czech driver had achieved that honour before.

A messy rally for an off-form Petter Solberg.

An oil pressure problem for Freddy Loix.

the 2002 event, and indeed it was not until two months beforehand did the FIA signify its approval for the 2003 event to qualify for the championship.

With the start of the second half of the 2003 season the next seven rallies to be faced would have quite a different character to those in the first half. The roughest roads were now gone, in fact four of the remaining seven would be on asphalt roads. Smoother rallies were coming.

found we were already quite as fast as with our existing Octavia, so we decided to start now." Problems which never appeared in testing soon manifested themselves. Brakes too soft, hydraulic weakness, and then for Didier Auriol a broken camshaft belt as well. Teammate Toni Gardemeister lasted longer but then suffered suspension collapses and finally a seized gearbox. Both Skodas were out by half way.

This was the second year the world championship had included Rallye Deutschland, and the organisers faced a far harder task in running an event to sufficient standard than they envisaged. Many issues remained outstanding since

Production Car Championship

Championship leader Toshihiro Arai elected to miss this event. Reigning JWRC champion Daniel Sola *(below)*, now a PCWRC contender, led from start to finish, but there were a lot of struggles behind. Firstly Niall McShea gave chase but had transmission troubles, which delayed him and promoted Martin Rowe. Gradually Marcos Ligato, a driver new to this event, gained confidence and chased Rowe. Despite a broken handbrake on the first day Ligato passed Rowe at half distance into second place, but was then slowed on the third day when the turbo pressure fell. This let Rowe pull ahead again. Ligato held a safe third place until the clutch failed on the final day and he was out. Janusz Kulig rose to third in front of reigning champion Karamjit Singh, who was bravely tackling his first ever all-asphalt event. Stig Blomqvist fell back badly when he had two punctures. There was, however, an extraordinary battle for the last place. Nine PCWRC contenders were still running but only the first eight would score points. The closest battle of the rally was that on the final stage between Gentleman drivers Stefano Marrini and Riccardo Errani. In the end Stefano beat Riccardo by 0.4 seconds and took the final remaining championship point!

Map

- ■ - Rest halt
- ▲ - Shakedown test
- ● - Service park and/or Regroup
- ✈ - Airport

■ Start/Finish
TRIER
Night Halt

22ND ADAC RALLYE DEUTSCHLAND
24/27.07.2003

POSITION/ LAST STAGE COMPLETED	ENTRANT	DRIVER/CODRIVER	NAT.	COMP NO.	CAR	CAT.	REG NO.	TOTAL PENALTY/ CAUSE
1	Citroen Total	SEBASTIEN LOEB/Daniel Elena	F/MC	18	Citroen Xsara	WRC	27CSP92 (F)	3h.46m.50.4s.
2	T. Marlboro Peugeot Total	MARCUS GRONHOLM/Timo Rautiainen	FIN	1	Peugeot 206	WRC	283NNN75 (F)	3h.46m.54.0s.
3	T. Marlboro Peugeot Total	RICHARD BURNS/Robert Reid	GB	2	Peugeot 206	WRC	952NVB75 (F)	3h.47m 10.1o.
4	Citroen Total	COLIN McRAE/Derek Ringer	GB	17	Citroen Xsara	WRC	2003P92 (F)	3h.47m.21.8s.
5	Ford Motor Company Ltd	MARKKO MARTIN/Michael Park	EE/GB	4	Ford Focus RS	WRC	R55OTH (GB)	3h.47m.48.3s.
6	Citroen Total	CARLOS SAINZ/Marc Marti	E	19	Citroen Xsara	WRC	19DDM92 (F)	3h.48m.29.0s.
7	Ford Motor Company Ltd	FRANCOIS DUVAL/Stephane Prevot	B	5	Ford Focus RS	WRC	EO03XYG (GB)	3h.48m.38.5s.
0	555 Subaru World R.T.	PETTER SOLBERG/Philip Mills	N/GB	7	Subaru Impreza	WRC	S400WRT (GB)	3h.49m.20.6s.
9	Equipe de France FFSA	Cedric Robert/Gerald Bedon	F	21	Peugeot 206	WRC	290NNN75 (F)	3h.50m.03.2s.
10	T. Marlboro Peugeot Total	GILLES PANIZZI/Herve Panizzi	F	3	Peugeot 206	WRC	286NNN75 (F)	3h.50m.30.0s.
11	Hyundai World R.T.	FREDDY LOIX/Sven Smeets	B	11	Hyundai Accent	WRC	X26HMC (GB)	3h.51m.46.0s.
12	Hyundai World R.T.	ARMIN SCHWARZ/Manfred Hiemer	D	10	Hyundai Accent	WRC	X27HMC (GB)	3h.54m.05.6s.
13	Ford Motor Company Ltd.	MIKKO HIRVONEN/Jarmo Lehtinen	FIN	6	Ford Focus RS	WRC	EX02OBC (GB)	3h.54m.24.7s.
14	Mitsubishi Motor Sports	Kristian Sohlberg/Jakke Honkanen	FIN	34	Mitsubishi Lancer Evo.	WRC	KN52XBC (GB)	3h.58m.39.8s.
15	Skoda Auto Deutschland	Matthias Kahle/Peter Gobel	D	22	Skoda Octavia	WRC	MBO82-74 (CZ)	3h.59m.22.3s.
17	Ford Motor Company Ltd	Jari-Matti Latvala/Miikka Anttila	FIN	24	Ford Focus RS	WRC	Y6FMC (GB)	4h.01m.49.0s.
18	Hyundai World R.T.	MANFRED STOHL/Ilka Minor	A	12	Hyundai Accent	WRC	X18HMC (GB)	4h.02m.58.3s.
22	-	Daniel Sola/Alex Romani	E	52	Mitsubishi Lancer Evo VII	PCWRC	BZ721KW (I)	4h.11m.45.9s.*
28	Hyundai World R.T.	JUSTIN DALE/Andrew Bargery	GB	25	Hyundai Accent	WRC	X12HMC (GB)	4h.22m.38.7s.

LEADING RETIREMENTS

6	555 Subaru World R.T.	TOMMI MAKINEN/Kaj Lindstrom	FIN	8	Subaru Impreza	WRC	S30WRT (GB)	powersteering belt
6	Skoda Motorsport	DIDIER AURIOL/Denis Giraudet	F	14	Skoda Fabia	WRC	3S3 1942 (CZ)	cambelt
12	Skoda Motorsport	TONI GARDEMEISTER/Paavo Lukander	FIN	15	Skoda Fabia	WRC	3S3 1943 (CZ)	gearbox
10	Citroen Total	Philippe Bugalski/Jean-Paul Chiaroni	F	20	Citroen Xsara	WRC	27DDM92 (F)	turbo
10	-	Jani Paasonen/Arto Kapanen	FIN	32	Mitsubishi Lancer Evo.	WRC	KN52XBB (GB)	accident
20	Bozian Racing	Roman Kresta/Jan Tomanek	CZ	23	Peugeot 206	WRC	4854YW69 (F)	hub

MANUFACTURER'S REGISTERED DRIVER. *PCWRC/Group N winner.

THE ROUTE

		SPECIAL STAGES	TOTAL DISTANCE	CREWS RUNNING
Leg 1 (1-7)	Trier (Friday 0800) - Bostalsee - Bostalsee - Trier (Friday 2125)	7 asphalt-117.31km	606.74km	65
Leg 2 (8-16)	Trier (Saturday 0630) - Bostalsee - Bostalsee - Trier (Saturday 2016)	9 asphalt-169.38km	573.01km	56
Leg 3 (17-22)	Trier (Sunday 0500) - Bostalsee - Trier (Sunday 1550)	6 asphalt-101.54km	557.83km	44
		22 stages-388.23km	1737.58km	

Ceremonial start on Thursday 2000. Weather: changeable. No stages in darkness.

OVERALL LEADING SPECIAL STAGE POSITIONS

	1	2	3	4	5	6
Martin	10	2	1	2	1	2
Burns	4	2	1	5	3	2
Loeb	2	7	5	2	-	-
Gronholm	2	3	5	3	1	2
McRae	2	2	4	3	6	1
Kresta	1	1	-	2	-	-
Sainz	1	-	-	1	-	7
Duval	-	3	1	2	4	-
Solberg	-	1	1	4	1	3

PCWRC Sola won 11 stages, McShea (Mitsubishi) 4, Ligato (Mitsubishi) 3, Kulig (Mitsubishi) 2, Rowe (Subaru) & de Dominicis (Mitsubishi) 1 each.
GROUP N Sola won 10 stages, McShea 4, Ligato 3, Kulig 2, Rowe, Vossen (Mitsubishi) & Solowow (Mitsubishi) 1 each.

STARTERS 79 (20 PCWRC). **FINISHERS** 44 (9 PCWRC).
OVERALL LEADERS Burns stages 1-3, Martin 4, Burns 5-8, Gronholm 9-12, Loeb 13-22.
PCWRC/GROUP N LEADER Sola stages 1-22.
WINNER'S AVERAGE SPEED OVER STAGES 102.69kph
WORLD CHAMPIONSHIP FOR MANUFACTURERS
Peugeot 95 points, Citroen 88, Ford 50, Subaru 49, Skoda 20, Hyundai 7.
WORLD CHAMPIONSHIP FOR DRIVERS Burns 43 points, Sainz 39, Gronholm 38, Loeb 33, Solberg 30, McRae 28, Martin 27, Rovanpera 16, Makinen 15, Duval 11, etc.

RECENT WINNERS

1993 * Patrick Snyers/Dany Colebunders Ford Escort RS Cosworth
1994 * Dieter Depping/Peter Thul Ford Escort RS Cosworth
1995 * Enrico Bertone/Massimo Chiapponi Toyota Celica Turbo 4WD
1996 * Dieter Depping/Fred Berssen Ford Escort RS Cosworth
1997 * Dieter Depping/Dieter Hawranke Ford Escort RS Cosworth
1998 * Matthias Kahle/Dieter Schneppenheim Toyota Corolla WRC
1999 * Armin Kremer/Fred Berssen Subaru Impreza WRC
2000 * Henrik Lundgaard/Jens Christian Anker Toyota Corolla WRC
2001 * Philippe Bugalski/Jean-Paul Chiaroni Citroen Xsara WRC
2002 Sebastien Loeb/Daniel Elena Citroen Xsara WRC (103.67kph)
Note * =ECR-only event.

Emotive victory for Estonian Markko
Martin. Top five finishers were non-Finns.

❖

Great battle for second place, won
by Petter Solberg from Richard Burns
by 1.2 seconds.

❖

First win for a Suzuki driver in the
JWRC category.

❖

Peugeot blighted by wheel
bearing failures.

LEG 1 All day the gap between Markko Martin
and Marcus Gronholm never exceeded 4.1
seconds. Frequently damp conditions helped
first-running Burns. Colin McRae was the
top running Citroen driver. Didier Auriol
withdrew due to a shoulder injury.
1 Martin 1h08m16.5s, 2 Gronholm +2.6s,
3 Burns +24.2s, 4 McRae +49.3s,
5 Solberg +50.2s, 6 Sainz +56.7s,
7 Loeb +1m21.9s, 8 Makinen +1m39.5s.
JWRC Tirabassi (29th) 1h18m55.3s.

LEG 2 Gronholm drove flat out on (and off)
the road, but by the afternoon he was out with
wheel bearing failure and Burns was delayed by
a similar problem. Martin survived electronic
troubles. The race was on for second place with
a half-second separating three drivers. Mikko
Hirvonen retired after a turbocharger fire.
McRae and Harri Rovanpera both crashed.
1 Martin 2h30m59.0s, 2 Burns +1m13.0s,
3 Sainz +1m13.3s, 4 Solberg +1m13.5s,
5 Loeb +2m02.6s, 6 Makinen +2m37.4s,
7 Tuohino +3m25.0s, 8 Lindholm +3m35.6s.
JWRC Carlsson (22nd) 2h54m06.3s.

LEG 3 Carlos Sainz dropped back after
breaking a shock absorber. The battle for
second place was intense. Ari Vatanen
finished a superb 11th on his first World
rally for nearly five years.
1 Martin 3h21m51.7s, 2 Solberg +58.9s,
3 Burns +1m00.1s, 4 Sainz +1m59.0s,
5 Loeb +2m48.7s, 6 Makinen +3m25.2s,
7 Tuohino +4m22.9s, 8 Lindholm +4m39.5s.
JWRC Carlsson (19th) 3h52m22.9s.

M arkko Martin achieved a lifetime dream, winning the '1000 Lakes' Rally in Finland, the country which is the great cultural and sporting rival of his native Estonia. Competitive right from the start, his 2003 model Ford Focus had to resist a challenge from hattrick winner Marcus Gronholm. However, Gronholm's Peugeot retired with wheel bearing failure when in the lead, and his teammate Richard Burns was slowed for the same reason. It was a fight where tenths of seconds mattered all the time. In the first half of the rally the greatest gap between Martin and Gronholm was never more than five

What's New in 2003

● There was a separate Shakedown for Priority 2 and 3 drivers on the Wednesday evening 20km west of Jyvaskyla.
● Several stages were rescheduled to improve spectator movement control.
● Return to Urria (stage13) for the first time since 1987, which traditionally has had the most dramatic jump on the event. The special feature of the jump is the vertical distance the cars must drop after the crest, rather than the speed or the distance the cars fly through the air.

seconds, but the excitement increased when the Peugeots struck trouble and Martin had a panic caused by an electrical failure at the same time. Only when Ford solved this could Martin cautiously relax, as much as one can at an average of over 120kph! But behind him there was a frantic battle for second place between Richard Burns, Petter Solberg and Carlos

Worth the trip. Estonia's Prime Minister, Juhan Parts, enjoys the celebrations.

Sainz. As Sainz was slowed by a broken shock absorber, Solberg snatched second place from Burns on the final stage.

The result of the rally, however, was a major embarrassment for the pride of the the Finnish enthusiasts. Never had there

Markko Martin in full flight!

Junior Championship

Favourite on the fourth round of the 2003 series was Daniel Carlsson but he fell back on the first day, with a puncture, letting Brice Tirabassi into the lead. The Swede, however, recovered as the rally progressed and he regained the lead when the Frenchman was delayed by a broken shock absorber. So it was Suzuki's turn to win, their first JWRC victory. The two Finns in the category (Kosti Katajamaki and Ville-Pertti Teuronen) both went off the road! All except two of the top placed championship contenders were among the eight finishers, but delays through punctures on the first day took a heavy toll. Despite going off the road on the first day for three minutes the Puma driver Guy Wilks finished third, while the three Suzukis (of Carlsson, Urmo Aava and Salvador Canellas) which finished, were all in the top five places. Denied a chance to test before the event the Top Run Fiats suffered badly, and Marcos Ligato *(below)* struggled even to finish

seventh after puncture problems while Abdo Feghali *(below)* did not even finish the first stage.

been such a poor performance by their star drivers. Hopes were high while Gronholm was fighting for the lead, but when he disappeared the only Finn left in the top six was Tommi Makinen, and he was having a disappointing event starting with a broken wheel and continuing with many minor troubles.

Fastest Citroen driver until he crashed was Colin McRae.

It was difficult to know whether Gronholm would be able to score a fourth successive win. His determination was there, but was his car good enough for another success? Starved of development for many months, the 206 World Rally Car was now starting to show its age and it had been four events since its last win. What was not expected was the loss of Gronholm for a technical failure, after which the team immediately changed the failed unit on the car of teammate Burns. Unfortunately it seems they replaced it with a piece from the same faulty batch. The effect of this disaster for Burns was not only to gift the event to Martin but also to launch Richard into a frantic race for second place with Solberg's Subaru. Solberg took time getting up to pace but in the second half he saw his chances of a top placing emerge. This was only decided in the Norwegian's favour on the final stage of the rally, where both drivers nearly crashed on the first corner.

Citroen came to the rally conscious their car lacked the necessary pace to succeed on the fastest event of the season. The reliability which had earned them an impressive points score on the rougher events in the series would not be so essential here. They finished with two cars in the points. Colin McRae drove hard to make the car competitive and scored one best time before he ultimately crashed off the road.

Finnish rivals racing for seventh place Sebastian Lindholm, Janne Tuohino and Jusso Pykalisto.

Petter Solberg won a hard battle for second place, passing Richard Burns on the final stage.

Ford's victory was not completely euphoric as they did not all have a great time. Francois Duval went off the road on the final day when out of the top ten, Mikko Hirvonen's car retired because of delays caused by a fire and Jari-Matti Latvala survived after suffering a water leak.

This was Skoda's second outing with the Fabia, but Didier Auriol had to withdraw after the opening superspecial because of a painful problem with his shoulder. Toni Gardemeister continued until half distance when the engine broke. Hyundai, however, continued with all three cars until guest driver Jussi Valimaki went off the road alongside Duval, while both Freddy Loix and Armin Schwarz finished in the points for the team.

Close behind the top team cars, and well ahead of the Hyundais, was a trio of non-championship Finns, anxious to gain the kudos for being the best local competitor. Their private race was won by Janne Tuohino in a 2002 Focus in front of the Peugeots of Sebastian Lindholm and Jusso Pykalisto. Splitting the Hyundais came Ari Vatanen's 206WRC.

There were many happy faces at the finish. Michelin announced they had won their 200th world championship rally, Ari Vatanen returned to a World rally after nearly five years, using the event as part of his electioneering campaign for the 2004 Euro parliament. When the competition began he was in fine form waving at fans and driving well. Vatanen scored a remarkable 11th place overall. The biggest smile, however, came from the winner. For years Markko had held his Finnish neighbours in awe. This was a victory that ignited a passion in his fellow countrymen, a win which was far more emotive than his

Low Technology Wins

Colin McRae had been a little surprised near the end of the Cyprus Rally when his car misfired and he asked his team (Citroen) how to overcome the problem. He was told to pour some water on the ECU. He did, and the misfiring disappeared. Markko Martin was similarly surprised during the Neste Rally when he also had electronic trouble and was told by his team (Ford) to hold the ECU out of the window to let it cool down. For Markko this did not achieve a permanent solution, so the team resorted to the other time honoured alternative, change everything in sight, and just hope you replace the bit that is faulty. Once again the panic solutions, in these days of high technology, seem to work best! Martin was asked after the rally how come he risked everything just to achieve his record leap, 57 metres, at Ouninpohja. "Well, two reasons. I was really very upset at the car (because of the electronic problem) and felt it was already broken so if I landed badly things could not be any worse than they were. And secondly, going flat-out over the jumps is, we have found with the new car, the only way to make it fly level!"

inaugural victory two months earlier in Greece, and which even brought his country's Prime Minister across the Gulf of Finland to shake his hand.

It was a fight to the finish in the best '1000 Lakes' tradition. When asked what it had been like behind the wheel at these speeds, Markko admitted it was scary. "I knew that I was driving far faster than ever before when I noticed that my codriver Michael Park was not looking out of the windscreen like he normally does! To win this rally you have to drive over your personal limit, and you cannot keep that up for three whole days! When Marcus retired it was a relief not to have to drive so fast any more."

The Burns enigma continued. He pulled even further ahead in the lead of the Drivers series, while once again he felt frustrated that the car had again let him down and denied him the chance to win. For Peugeot the writing on the wall was clear. Now was the time for mechanical change.

POSITION/ LAST STAGE COMPLETED	ENTRANT	DRIVER/CODRIVER	NAT.	COMP NO.	CAR	CAT.	REG NO.	TOTAL PENALTY/ CAUSE
1	Ford Motor Company Ltd	MARKKO MARTIN/Michael Park	EE/GB	4	Ford Focus RS	WRC	EO03YRJ (GB)	3h.21m.51.7s.
2	555 Subaru World R.T.	PETTER SOLBERG/Philip Mills	N/GB	7	Subaru Impreza	WRC	S500WRT (GB)	3h.22m.50.6s.
3	T. Marlboro Peugeot Total	RICHARD BURNS/Robert Reid	GB	2	Peugeot 206	WRC	334NQZ75 (F)	3h.22m.51.8s.
4	Citroen Total	CARLOS SAINZ/Marc Marti	E	19	Citroën Xsara	WRC	36CSP92 (F)	3h.23m.50.7s.
5	Citroen Total	SEBASTIEN LOEB/Daniel Elena	F/MC	18	Citroen Xsara	WRC	17DDM92 (F)	3h.24m.40.4s.
6	555 Subaru World R.T.	TOMMI MAKINEN/Kaj Lindstrom	FIN	8	Subaru Impreza	WRC	S90WRT (GB)	3h.25m.16.9s.
7	LPM Racing	Janne Tuohino/Jukka Aho	FIN	23	Ford Focus RS	WRC	CL187 (FIN)	3h.26m.14.6s.
8	Peugeot Sport Finland	Sebastian Lindholm/Timo Hantunen	FIN	24	Peugeot 206	WRC	BQ483 (FIN)	3h.26m.31.2s.
9	Bozian Racing	Juuso Pykalisto/Esko Mertsalmi	FIN	22	Peugeot 206	WRC	341NQZ75 (F)	3h.28m.15.1s.
10	Hyundai World R.T.	FREDDY LOIX/Sven Smeets	B	11	Hyundai Accent	WRC	X21HMC (GB)	3h.30m.11.6s.
11	Bozian Racing	Ari Vatanen/Juha Repo	FIN	26	Peugeot 206	WRC	4852YW69 (F)	3h.33m.41.0s.
12	Hyundai World R.T.	ARMIN SCHWARZ/Manfred Hiemer	D	10	Hyundai Accent	WRC	X22HMC (GB)	3h.34m.43.2s.
19	-	Daniel Carlsson/Mattias Andersson	S	52	Suzuki Ignis	JWRC	ITA852 (H)	3h.52m.22.9s.*

LEADING RETIREMENTS

1	Skoda Motorsport	DIDIER AURIOL/Denis Giraudet	F	14	Skoda Fabia	WRC	3S3 1942 (CZ)	withdrawn
11	T. Marlboro Peugeot Total	HARRI ROVANPERA/Risto Pietilainen	FIN	3	Peugeot 206	WRC	BQ481 (FIN)	accident
11	Ford Motor Company Ltd	MIKKO HIRVONEN/Jarmo Lehtinen	FIN	6	Ford Focus RS	WRC	AE209 (FIN)	fire damage
12	Skoda Motorsport	TONI GARDEMEISTER/Paavo Lukander	FIN	15	Skoda Fabia	WRC	3S3 1943 (CZ)	engine
14	T. Marlboro Peugeot Total	MARCUS GRONHOLM/Timo Rautiainen	FIN	1	Peugeot 206	WRC	BQ480 (FIN)	wheel bearing
15	Citroen Total	COLIN McRAE/Derek Ringer	GB	17	Citroen Xsara	WRC	22DDM92 (F)	accident
18	Ford Motor Company Ltd	FRANCOIS DUVAL/Stephane Prevot	B	5	Ford Focus RS	WRC	EJ02KMU (GB)	accident
18	Hyundai World R.T.	JUSSI VALIMAKI/Jakke Honkanen	FIN	12	Hyundai Accent	WRC	CH536 (FIN)	accident

MANUFACTURER'S REGISTERED DRIVER. *JWRC/S1600 winner.

THE ROUTE

		SPECIAL STAGES	TOTAL DISTANCE	CREWS RUNNING
Leg 1 (1-10)	Jyvaskyla (Thursday 1800) - Jyvaskyla - Jyvaskyla - Jyvaskyla - Jyvaskyla (Friday 2102)	10 gravel-140.36km	623.05km	59
Leg 2 (11-17)	Jyvaskyla (Saturday 0600) - Jyvaskyla - Jyvaskyla - Jyvaskyla (Saturday 1948)	7 gravel-167.92km	745.52km	42
Leg 3 (18-23)	Jyvaskyla (Sunday 0800) - Jyvaskyla - Jyvaskyla (Sunday 1545)	6 gravel-100.90km	359.03km	35
		23 stages-409.18km	1727.60km	

Weather: Mixed, but mostly dry. No stages in darkness.

OVERALL LEADING SPECIAL STAGE POSITIONS

	1	2	3	4	5	6
Martin	8	5	6	2	1	1
Gronholm	6	7	-	-	-	-
Burns	6	6	3	5	1	1
Solberg	3	4	4	1	4	6
McRae	1	1	5	1	2	2
Sainz	-	1	1	7	7	-
Loeb	-	-	1	3	3	3
Rovanpera	-	-	1	1	-	2
Makinen	-	-	-	1	2	2

JWRC Carlsson won 15 stages, Wilks (Ford) 4, Teuronen (Suzuki) & Tirabassi 2 each, Katajamaki (VW) & Svedlund (VW) 1 each.
S1600 Carlsson won 11 stages, Jean-Joseph, Wilks & Andersson 3 each, Tirabassi 2, Teuronen & Svedlund 1 each.

STARTERS 71 (17 JWRC). **FINISHERS** 35 (8 JWRC).
OVERALL LEADERS Martin stages 1-4, Gronholm 5-8, Martin 9-11, Gronholm 12+13, Martin 14-23.
JWRC LEADERS Carlsson stages 1-7, Tirabassi (Renault) 8-13, Carlsson 14-23.
S1600 LEADERS Carlsson stage 1, Jean-Joseph (Renault) 2-5, Carlsson 6+7, Andersson (Renault) 8-14, Carlsson 15-23.
WINNER'S AVERAGE SPEED OVER STAGES 121.62kph.
WORLD CHAMPIONSHIP FOR MANUFACTURERS
Peugeot 101 points, Citroen 97, Ford & Subaru 60, Skoda 20, Hyundai 10.
WORLD CHAMPIONSHIP FOR DRIVERS Burns 49 points, Sainz 44, Gronholm & Solberg 38, Loeb & Martin 37, C.McRae 28, Makinen 18, Rovanpera 16, Duval 11, etc.

RECENT WINNERS

1993		Juha Kankkunen/Denis Giraudet Toyota Celica Turbo 4WD (115.45kph)
1994		Tommi Makinen/Seppo Harjanne Ford Escort RS Cosworth (114.58kph)
1995	*	Tommi Makinen/Seppo Harjanne Mitsubishi Lancer Evolution (114.12kph)
1996		Tommi Makinen/Seppo Harjanne Mitsubishi Lancer Evolution (117.05kph)
1997		Tommi Makinen/Seppo Harjanne Mitsubishi Lancer Evolution (116.62kph)
1998		Tommi Makinen/Risto Mannisenmaki Mitsubishi Lancer Evolution (116.87kph)
1999		Juha Kankkunen/Juha Repo Subaru Impreza WRC (119.83kph)
2000		Marcus Gronholm/Timo Rautiainen Peugeot 206 WRC (122.46kph)
2001		Marcus Gronholm/Timo Rautiainen Peugeot 206 WRC (119.99kph)
2002		Marcus Gronholm/Timo Rautiainen Peugeot 206 WRC (121.80kph)
Note	*	=W2L-only event.

Long and close battle for the lead between Petter Solberg and Sebastien Loeb, finally resolved on the last two stages in the rain in favour of the Norwegian.

❖

Richard Burns extends his championship lead after yet another podium finish, otherwise a disappointing event for Peugeot.

❖

Another reliable performance by Citroen, although brake trouble for Colin McRae.

❖

Martin Rowe favourite for PCWRC title after his victory in the category. Toshihiro Arai retired.

LEG 1 Damp conditions obviated cleaning surface dramas. Marcus Gronholm led then slid off at a tight bend, later withdrawing from the rally. Solberg suffered a scare when an oil pressure warning light sensor failed. Carlos Sainz went off, blinded by low sunlight.
1 Loeb 1h23m52.4s, 2 Solberg +4.1s,
3 Burns +39.1s, 4 Makinen +1m00.2s,
5 Martin +1m05.0s, 6 Sainz +1m12.6s,
7 McRae +1m25.0s, 8 Rovanpera +1m53.1s.
PCWRC Rowe (17th) 1h32m29.0s.

LEG 2 Race for the lead hotted up. Big off road excursion for Sainz. Markko Martin excluded. Group N leader Ed Ordynski (Mitsubishi) rolled and retired at the superspecial. Tommi Makinen slightly damaged his suspension which cost two places.
1 Loeb 2h32m04.6s, 2 Solberg +5.1s,
3 Burns +1m25.8s, 4 Martin +1m53.0s,
5 McRae +2m19.4s, 6 Makinen +2m20.8s,
7 Sainz +2m26.7s, 8 Rovanpera +2m54.2s.
PCWRC Rowe (17th) 2h47m53.9s,

LEG 3 Solberg attacked and when the rains descended won the rally. Punctures afflicted PCWRC drivers Niall McShea (Mitsubishi) and Stig Blomqvist (Subaru).
1 Solberg 3h32m07.1s, 2 Loeb +26.6s.
3 Burns +1m53.0s, 4 McRae +2m30.7s,
5 Sainz +2m37.2s, 6 Makinen +3m01.5s,
7 Rovanpera +4m03.9s, 8 Loix +7m00.7s.
PCWRC Rowe (15th) 3h54m17.1s.

Petter Solberg (right) and Philip Mills once again at the top.

What's New in 2003

● A new Clerk of the Course and Chairman of Organising Committee. Adrian Stafford, previously Deputy Clerk, assumed the position held by the event's founder Garry Connelly.
● Rally headquarters at Gloucester Park, instead of at the Sheraton Hotel.
● Held the first weekend in September.
● The Superspecial stage was sited at Gloucester Park, not Langley Park, run once on the Thursday and Friday and then twice on the Saturday evening.
● Every stage but one was either new, changed or in the opposite direction.
● A single Service Park location for the first time, therefore no more servicing in Perth.
● The route was more contained, not going east to Muresk or south to the Wellington stages.
● There was a new "Shire Road" stage (stage 4), a change to the usual forest road.
● Stage 7 (Turner Hill), had previously been used as a road for private pre-event testing.

Dampness on the ground took away much of the traditional road cleaning handicap, and soon the championship leader Richard Burns settled into a fast and regular routine in his Peugeot. Petter Solberg's Subaru was fastest on the Superspecial but Marcus Gronholm took an immediate lead on the second stage which he held through most of the first leg. This was until he took an uphill hairpin too tightly and his Peugeot was firmly stuck inside the corner. He eventually regained the road and finished the stage but with a delay of 17 minutes he decided to withdraw. Loeb, in his Citroen, now went ahead of Solberg, Martin and Burns, but Markko Martin was struggling. "It is all down to the difficulty on this event of making good pacenotes. Only after you have checked these at high speed can you drive with confidence. Nearly all our instructions are graded too slow, and the one time the notes were right we went off the road!" The Acropolis and Finland winner finished the first day in fifth place, Loeb on only his second time in Australia was leading by 4.1 seconds.

When the running order was reversed on the second day Burns found himself going flat out - but still not catching up. "People keep saying how steadily I drive. I can tell you I am going flat out!" The closeness and the length of the Loeb-Solberg fight was stunning. For well over a day there was less than five seconds between them. Solberg was surprised at Loeb's progress. "Sebastien is supposed to be a tarmac expert, his consistency and speed on these roads is incredible!" It was Solberg who was making the occasional little mistakes, not Loeb. Behind them Tommi Makinen was back in form in his Subaru and fought hard with the other two Citroen drivers, Colin McRae and Carlos Sainz, who it appeared seemed to be fighting for the chance to stay in the team in 2004. Although McRae had been badly hampered by brake troubles for the first two days, as the trouble was progressively eased he showed glimpses of his old speed. The

Farewell friends. Australia turned out to be Hyundai's final rally. This is Freddy Loix.

reliability of all the world championship cars was impressive. Not since New Zealand two years ago had there been such a display of top car finishing.

At the end of the second leg Loeb led by 5.1 seconds, but there were dark clouds of various forms in the air. Firstly there was an extraordinary happening with Ford. FIA observers reported that there was something strange going on at Martin's service. It seemed that a heavy

rock was removed from the car. The Stewards came to the conclusion that the team had feared, wrongly as it transpired, that they might be running underweight, and added extra ballast as a precaution.

Late into the night the issue was discussed. Officials dismissed Ford's assertion a rock had been put into the car because the spare wheel securing ratchet had failed, and the car was excluded for running with unauthorised and unsecured ballast (a safety issue) rather than for doing anything underhand. With Martin out of the event, the two battling Citroen drivers were promoted to fourth and fifth.

Then came developments in the sky. There was a lot of rain in the air on the final day. For the first two stages in the traditional "Bunnings" forest the surfaces were dry and dusty. Could the teams guarantee this would continue for the remaining two stages? What tyres to choose? Make an error if you have chosen a wet tyre and the effect on times would be disastrous. Other way round and the mistake would not be so serious. Well, it rained, so nearly everyone had the wrong tyres. The precipitation made the tracks more slippery than anyone imagined. With every minute the conditions got worse. Petter was running 14th car on the road and Sebastien Loeb 15th, so even that two minute gap gave Petter a decided advantage, which he took in full measure. Loeb settled for second place. It was a classic victory for the Norwegian.

People on Edge

The atmosphere in Perth had been charged even before the rally began. News about proposed late and unexpected changes to the future championship regulations for 2004 left drivers on edge about the security for their future careers and created anger between team managers. Peugeot team chief Corrado Provera described the work of the FIA's World Rally Championship Commission as "useless", then the WRCC President Shekhar Mehta compounded confusion when he told journalists the only reason for the proposed changes was to enable the Hokkaido Rally to be in the championship in 2004. It was a welcome relief when this event got underway!

Mikko Hirvonen learned more and more as the season progressed.

Production Car Championship

The race for the Production Car championship was nearing a climax. This was the penultimate round in the series, and although only Toshihiro Arai or Martin Rowe, both driving Subarus, could now be champion, the competition was strong. Seven of the 11 PCWRC starters scored fastest stage times. Top Run driver Marcos Ligato was easily the fastest driver in the early stages but then his Mitsubishi suffered transmission troubles and delays at service which forced his retirement. This let Rowe *(right)* into the lead which he kept to gain his first ever PCWRC category win. Daniel Sola's Nocentini team Mitsubishi had similar transmission troubles to Ligato, which eventually were resolved but only after losing a lot of time. This was Karamjit Singh's final qualifying event of the season and a steady drive in his Proton brought him into second place after Niall McShea (Mitsubishi) stopped on the final day to change a flat tyre. Rowe's David Sutton Cars teammate Stig Blomqvist lost a lot of time with brake problems and came

home fourth of the six finishers. The series leader Arai had a disappointing event. His Subaru lacked top-end power, and on the second day the car stopped with clutch failure when he was third. Arai will go to the final round, Corsica, with a seven points deficit behind Rowe, so after a good placing there last year Rowe is now the favourite for the title. Causes for non-appearance were varied: Bob Colsoul ligament injuries suffered playing football, Krzysztof Holowczyc sinus trouble, Giovanni Manfrinato a heart ailment! Janusz Kulig and Riccardo Errani did not appear.

This was the second win in 2003 for Subaru and Solberg, and was another

sign of the arrival of a new generation of top rally men. Once Gronholm had withdrawn, Peugeot were uncomfortable. The 206 had started to show its age. Ford's problem was that all the cars had been off the pace. Of the team's four fastest times, three of them were gained on the superspecial stages! Freddy Loix, for Hyundai, collected more points but Armin Schwarz had constant handling difficulties. The two Skoda Fabias went reliably but with some handling troubles. It was the first rally both Fabias had finished, their drivers both having recovered from injury scares since Finland, Didier Auriol from the shoulder injury which had caused his withdrawal on that occasion and Toni Gardemeister from an injury to his wrist playing in an ice hockey match.

(top to bottom) Sebastien Loeb, Richard Burns and Toni Gardemeister.

POSITION/ LAST STAGE COMPLETED	ENTRANT	DRIVER/CODRIVER	NAT.	COMP NO.	CAR	CAT.	REG NO.	TOTAL PENALTY/ CAUSE
1	555 Subaru World R.T.	PETTER SOLBERG/Philip Mills	N/GB	7	Subaru Impreza	WRC	S600WRT (GB)	3h.32m.07.1s.
2	Citroen Total	SEBASTIEN LOEB/Daniel Elena	F/MC	18	Citroen Xsara	WRC	30CSP92 (F)	3h.32m.33.7s.
3	T.Marlboro Peugeot Total	RICHARD BURNS/Robert Reid	GB	2	Peugeot 206	WRC	810NVT75 (F)	3h.34m 00 1s.
4	Citroen Total	COLIN McRAE/Derek Ringer	GB	17	Citroen Xsara	WRC	19DDM92 (F)	3h.34m.37.8s.
5	Citroen Total	CARLOS SAINZ/Marc Marti	E	19	Citroen Xsara	WRC	29CSP92 (F)	3h.34m.44.3s.
6	555 Subaru World R.T.	TOMMI MAKINEN/Kaj Lindstrom	FIN	8	Subaru Impreza	WRC	S200WRT (GB)	3h.35m.08.6s.
7	T.Marlboro Peugeot Total	HARRI ROVANPERA/Risto Pietilainen	FIN	3	Peugeot 206	WRC	814NVT75 (F)	3h.36m.11.0s.
8	Hyundai World R.T.	FREDDY LOIX/Sven Smeets	B	11	Hyundai Accent	WRC	X26HMC (GB)	3h.39m.07.8s.
9	Ford Motor Company Ltd	MIKKO HIRVONEN/Jarmo Lehtinen	FIN	6	Ford Focus RS	WRC	EX02OBC (GB)	3h.39m.17.7s.
10	Ford Motor Company Ltd	FRANCOIS DUVAL/Stephane Prevot	B	5	Ford Focus RS	WRC	EO03YWC (GB)	3h.39m.53.3s.
11	Skoda Motorsport	TONI GARDEMEISTER/Paavo Lukander	FIN	15	Skoda Fabia	WRC	3S3 1947 (CZ)	3h.42m.17.3s.
12	Skoda Motorsport	DIDIER AURIOL/Denis Giraudet	F	14	Skoda Fabia	WRC	3S3 1946 (CZ)	3h.43m.15.2s.
13	Hyundai World R.T.	ARMIN SCHWARZ/Manfred Hiemer	D	10	Hyundai Accent	WRC	X27HMC (GB)	3h.46m.21.5s.
15	David Sutton Cars	Martin Rowe/Trevor Agnew	GB	55	Subaru Impreza WRX	PCWRC	X2DSC (GB)	3h.54m.17.1s.*

LEADING RETIREMENTS

2	Best Racing T.	Balazs Benik/Bence Racz	H	23	Ford Focus RS	WRC	1Z4 4600 (CZ)	accident
9	T.Marlboro Peugeot Total	MARCUS GRONHOLM/Timo Rautiainen	FIN	1	Peugeot 206	WRC	624NZT75 (F)	withdrawn
20	Ford Motor Company Ltd	MARKKO MARTIN/Michael Park	EE/GB	4	Ford Focus RS	WRC	R55OTH (GB)	excluded

MANUFACTURER'S REGISTERED DRIVER. *1st PCWRC/Group N.

THE ROUTE

		SPECIAL STAGES	TOTAL DISTANCE	CREWS RUNNING
Leg 1 (1-10)	Perth (Thursday 1830) - Perth - Jarrahdale - Perth - Perth (Friday 2040)	10 gravel-145.20km	805.42km	39
Leg 2 (11-20)	Perth (Saturday 0730) - Jarrahdale - Perth - Perth (Saturday 1958)	10 gravel-124.00km	515.13km	34
Leg 3 (21-24)	Perth (Sunday 0700) - Jarrahdale - Perth - Perth (Sunday 1630)	4 gravel-117.11km	474.61km	32
		24 stages-386.31km	1795.16km	

Weather: Mostly cool with a little rain. Four stages in darkness.

OVERALL LEADING SPECIAL STAGE POSITIONS

	1	2	3	4	5	6
Solberg	9	9	4	2	-	-
Loeb	9	5	-	5	2	2
Martin	3	1	7	3	1	-
Gronholm	2	2	1	1	1	-
McRae	1	2	2	1	5	6
Duval	1	-	-	-	-	-
Sainz	-	3	2	2	4	2
Makinen	-	2	-	3	5	6
Burns	-	-	6	5	3	5

PCWRC Ligato & Rowe won 5 stages each, Sola (Mitsubishi) 4, Arai (Subaru), McShea (Mitsubishi) & Blomqvist (Subaru) 3 each, Singh (Proton) 1.
GROUP N Ordynski won 11 stages, Ligato & McShea 3 each, D.Herridge, Blomqvist & Rowe 2 each, Singh & Sola 1 each.

STARTERS 49 (11 PCWRC). **FINISHERS** 32 (6 PCWRC).
OVERALL LEADERS Solberg stage 1, Gronholm 2-7, Loeb 8-20, Solberg 21, Loeb 22, Solberg 23+24.
PCWRC LEADERS Ligato (Mitsubishi) stages 1-7, Rowe 8- 24.
GROUP N LEADERS D.Herridge (Subaru) stage 1, Ligato 2-5, Ordynski (Mitsubishi) 6-18, D.Herridge 19+20, Rowe 21-24.
WINNER'S AVERAGE SPEED OVER STAGES 109.27kph (record)
WORLD CHAMPIONSHIP FOR MANUFACTURERS
Peugeot & Citroen 110 points, Subaru 74, Ford 61, Skoda 20, Hyundai 12.
WORLD CHAMPIONSHIP FOR DRIVERS
Burns 55 points, Solberg & Sainz 48, Loeb 45, Gronholm 38, Martin 37, McRae 33, Makinen 21, Rovanpera 18, Duval 11, etc.

RECENT WINNERS

1993		Juha Kankkunen/Nicky Grist Toyota Celica Turbo 4WD (103.24kph)
1994	*	Colin McRae/Derek Ringer Subaru Impreza 555 (103.08kph)
1995		Kenneth Eriksson/Staffan Parmander Mitsubishi Lancer Evolution (102.84kph)
1996		Tommi Makinen/Seppo Harjanne Mitsubishi Lancer Evolution (99.88kph)
1997		Colin McRae/Nicky Grist Subaru Impreza WRC (102.99kph)
1998		Tommi Makinen/Risto Mannisenmaki Mitsubishi Lancer Evolution (104.30kph)
1999		Richard Burns/Robert Reid Subaru Impreza WRC (105.79kph)
2000		Marcus Gronholm/Timo Rautianen Peugeot 206 WRC (104.80kph)
2001		Marcus Gronholm/Timo Rautianen Peugeot 206 WRC (107.00kph)
2002		Marcus Gronholm/Timo Rautianen Peugeot 206 WRC (107.98kph)
Note	*	=W2L-only event.

Sebastien Loeb won his third rally of 2003, although Markko Martin's Ford was the fastest car on the event.

The first of three successive asphalt rallies, all run in the month of October. The final time Sanremo Rally is to be run as a world championship event.

Remarkable personal triumph for Carlos Sainz, recovering from a hospital operation just before the event.

Hyundai withdrew from the Championship and did not start.

LEG 1 The Hyundai team did not come to Sanremo. Sebastien Loeb shot into a strong lead. Markko Martin's Ford overheated, lost power and time but recovered to second. Toni Gardemeister's Skoda lost its brakes and he crashed. Mikko Hirvonen's engine failed. Petter Solberg's active suspension Subaru ran out of fuel.
1 Loeb 1h30m15.7s, 2 Martin +32.4s, 3 Gronholm +49.6s, 4 Sainz +1m14.8s, 5 Duval +1m19.0s, 6 Panizzi +1m29.6s, 7 McRae +1m41.9s, 8 Makinen +2m50.2s.
JWRC Baldacci (16th) 1h40m28.9s.

LEG 2 The 52km stage was run twice, won both times by Martin who earlier incurred a 30 second penalty through a delay with an electronic problem. Philippe Bugalski gradually gained confidence.
1 Loeb 3h07m00.7s, 2 Martin +43.2s, 3 Gronholm +1m10.5s, 4 Sainz +1m42.3s, 5 Panizzi +1m59.1s, 6 Duval +2m23.8s, 7 McRae +3m07.3s, 8 Bugalski +4m06.6s.
JWRC Baldacci (16th) 3h28m37.9s.

LEG 3 Two fastest times in the rain elevated Gilles Panizzi from fifth to second. Marcus Gronholm crashed and retired. Richard Burns only jumped into the points zone on the final stage.
1 Loeb 4h16m33.7s, 2 Panizzi +28.3s, 3 Martin +54.6s, 4 Sainz +2m33.2s, 5 Duval +3m58.9s, 6 McRae +4m23.8s, 7 Burns +7m09.5s, 8 Bugalski +7m12.6s.
JWRC Baldacci (16th) 4h43m22.6s.

Unstoppable on tarmac, so far...Sebastien Loeb in action.

Citroen and Sebastien Loeb had now won the first three asphalt events in 2003, and with Corsica and Catalunya to come they had high hopes of two championship titles. With several new technical improvements the Ford of Markko Martin was highly competitive and was the fastest car on the event, but the Estonian's result was tempered by three delays. All the Peugeots were off the pace although Gilles Panizzi made two best times in the rain on the final day.

What's New in 2003

● This was the final Sanremo Rally in the form we knew it! If Italy is to stay in the world championship in 2004, the event must be run on gravel roads, and through the organisation of the national federation CSAI, not the private AC Sanremo club. This meant the end of the career for Adolfo Rava. Rava had been Clerk of the Course from the days of the Flowers Rally, named after the Costa Fiori (Flowers Coast), through to Sanremo Rally until 1986, then as the event's general manager.

● One last dream came true, the longest stage ever held on the event.

Championship leader Richard Burns had a poor event, but eventually gained two points. Subaru joined Peugeot in using active suspension, just on Petter Solberg's car, but both the old and the new systems were off the pace and Solberg retired when his car ran out of fuel.

From the start to the finish Loeb's Citroen was the car to beat. After only two stages he was a quarter minute ahead, by the end of the first day it was a half minute, one stage more and his lead was more than a minute! All four works Xsaras finished in the top eight. Fourth placed Carlos Sainz had a remarkable week. Two days before recce started he had an operation for kidney stones in Madrid. He felt so ill on arrival for the event an Italian hospital warned him they would prevent him competing unless he improved. He did! He struggled with brake problems on the first day, and gradually he felt weaker but was happy to finish. Philippe Bugalski in the fourth, non-nominated, works Xsara, gradually found his confidence, "I haven't rallied since Deutschland and really noticed my lack of recent experience". Meanwhile Colin McRae was a strong sixth.

It was a surprise that Peugeot were off the pace and uncompetitive in the dry, particularly surprising that Gronholm (who still had not won an asphalt World rally) was the fastest Peugeot driver for most of the event, that Burns could not find any confidence in the car at all, while Panizzi only started to believe in his car on the final day. Panizzi: "I drove just as well as last year but this year everyone else is better".

There was no mystery about Ford. There were many changes on the cars since Australia and Martin won seven out of the 14 stages, against five for Loeb. On the first stage Martin's engine overheated, because of leaves blocking the radiator grill, causing the engine to revert to

Missing magic for Makinen. The event which has bought the best out in Tommi before was not a happy experience this time.

Leaves blocking the grill badly delayed Markko Martin on the first leg.

"safe-mode" and lose power. Then on the second day he incurred a 30 second penalty for a delay at service when the engine would not fire up, and on the final day he was not ready for the sudden rains and had the wrong tyres. Martin's teammate Francois Duval started strongly but gradually slid down the field, finishing fifth. Mikko Hirvonen, in a 2002 car, was settling into another reliable experience-gaining event, when his car suddenly stopped and he retired.

There were high hopes for Subaru but they flattered only to deceive. Neither car was competitive, at all. Solberg's active suspension car had the front suspension mounting fail before it then ran out of fuel on a road section while Tommi Makinen's orthodox car was driven steadily to tenth

place, just inside the Makes' points.

Skoda lost Toni Gardemeister off the road on the second stage when the brakes overheated after a long spell of left foot braking, while Didier Auriol drove to the finish, with relatively few problems but he was again off the pace.

The 52km stage, the longest stage ever held in the history of the event, turned out to be a test for the concentration of the drivers rather than for stress on the cars or tyres. The autumn weather kept temperatures down and the relatively smooth surfaces spared wear. Martin was quickest on both these stages, in fact on all four stages that day. There was a nostalgia about the event. Although Sanremo has become an increasingly difficult rally for spectators to follow, every

Didier Auriol's 12th place bought Skoda their first points for the Fabia.

SANREMO

Thanks for the memories! Sanremo rally promoter Adolfo Rava (left) and President Sergio Maiga.

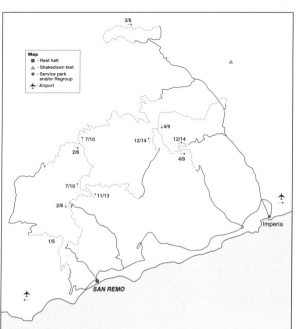

Map
■ - Rest halt
▲ - Shakedown test
● - Service park and/or Regroup
✈ - Airport

3/8
4/9
12/14
12/14
7/10
2/6
4/9
7/10
2/6
11/13
Imperia
1/5
SAN REMO

Last day reversal of form for Gilles Panizzi. Suddenly the car worked well and he rose to second.

aspect of the organisation this year worked well. It was a high note on which to bow out. Adolfo Rava, for 35 years the man at the helm of the event, was wistful. "If we had really done a bad job I could understand losing the championship status, but people worked so hard and things went so well, it feels a little sad..."

Once again the curious way the championship points system was affecting the title was noticeable. Under last year's rules Solberg would have come to Italy jointly leading the Drivers series with Burns and with Gronholm one point behind. Peugeot would have been four points ahead of Citroen. Under 2004 rules, Peugeot would be 16 points in front! Under the rules which apply this year, Sebastien Loeb has suddenly come into the spotlight. Burns had hoped for another safe points-

Junior Championship

Both the top favourites in the JWRC failed to finish. Series leader Brice Tirabassi (Renault) had electrical trouble at the end of the first day, having initially led before sliding off the road, and had trouble restarting his stalled engine. Daniel Carlsson (Suzuki) settled into second place but threw away a great points opportunity by going off the road on the second day when driving on a flat tyre. His crash caused stages 11 and 12 to be neutralised for JWRC cars. Instead it was Mirco Baldacci (*below*, Fiat) who was ahead and scored his first win in the category. Sixteen JWRC crews started the event and nine retired.

Brakes caused a lot of difficulty, especially for the Suzukis, but in the rain at the end of the event their asphalt specialist Salvador Canellas was able to rise to second in front of Dimitar Iliev (Peugeot). Marcos Ligato (Fiat) damaged the chassis when the steering arm broke and his car was withdrawn. Kris Meeke (Opel) was second for a long time but crashed on the last morning. The VW drivers were told the company had withdrawn from rallying and they could not have their cars for this or the subsequent rallies. Eventually Kosti Katajamaki's car was released, but he retired near the finish with a broken driveshaft after earlier delays with electrical trouble, while Oscar Svedlund and 'V-man' were excused a penalty for not starting.

enhancing event but it did not happen that way. Until the final stage he was not even in the points zone, then suddenly he jumped from tenth to seventh!

POSITION/ LAST STAGE COMPLETED	ENTRANT	DRIVER/CODRIVER	NAT.	COMP NO.	CAR	CAT.	REG NO.	TOTAL PENALTY/ CAUSE
1	Citroen Total	SEBASTIEN LOEB/Daniel Elena	F/MC	18	Citroen Xsara	WRC	32CSP92 (F)	4h.16m.33.7s.
2	T. Marlboro Peugeot Total	GILLES PANIZZI/Herve Panizzi	F	3	Peugeot 206	WRC	206NLL75 (F)	4h.17m.02.0s.
3	Ford Motor Company Ltd	MARKKO MARTIN/Michael Park	EE/GB	4	Ford Focus RS	WRC	EK52LNP (GB)	4h.17m.28.3s.
4	Citroen Total	CARLOS SAINZ/Marc Marti	E	19	Citroen Xsara	WRC	31CSP92 (F)	4h.19m.06.9s.
5	Ford Motor Company Ltd	FRANCOIS DUVAL/Stephane Prevot	B	5	Ford Focus RS	WRC	EO03XYG (GB)	4h.20m.32.6s.
6	Citroen Total	COLIN McRAE/Derek Ringer	GB	17	Citroen Xsara	WRC	15DDM92 (F)	4h.20m.57.5s.
7	I. Marlboro Peugeot Total	RICHARD BURNS/Robert Reid	GB	2	Peugeot 206	WRC	206NLM75 (F)	4h.23m.43.2s.
8	Citroen Total	Philippe Bugalski/Jean-Paul Chiaroni	F	20	Citroen Xsara	WRC	27DDM92 (F)	4h.23m.46.3s.
9	Equipe De France FFSA	Cedric Robert/Gerald Bedon	F	23	Peugeot 206	WRC	4852YW69 (F)	4h.23m.59.4s.
10	555 Subaru World R.T.	TOMMI MAKINEN/Kaj Lindstrom	FIN	8	Subaru Impreza	WRC	S30WRT (GB)	4h.24m.05.9s.
12	Skoda Motorsport	DIDIER AURIOL/Denis Giraudet	F	14	Skoda Fabia	WRC	3S3 1946 (CZ)	4h.31m.22.8s.
13	-	Nicolas Bernardi/Bruno Brissart	F	106	Renault Clio	S1600	938AQJ83 (F)	4h.37m.27.9s.**
16	-	Mirco Baldacci/Giovanni Bernacchini	RSM/I	51	Fiat Punto	JWRC	BS099GJ (I)	4h.43m.22.6s.*

LEADING RETIREMENTS

1	Skoda Motorsport	TONI GARDEMEISTER/Paavo Lukander	FIN	15	Skoda Fabia	WRC	3S3 1947 (CZ)	accident
3	Ford Motor Company Ltd	MIKKO HIRVONEN/Jarmo Lehtinen	FIN	6	Ford Focus RS	WRC	EX02OBE (GB)	camshaft belt
6	555 Subaru World R.T.	PETTER SOLBERG/Philip Mills	N/GB	7	Subaru Impreza	WRC	S300WRT (GB)	no fuel
13	T. Marlboro Peugeot Total	MARCUS GRONHOLM/Timo Rautiainen	FIN	1	Peugeot 206	WRC	206NDQ75 (F)	accident

MANUFACTURER'S REGISTERED DRIVER. *JWRC winner. **S1600 winner.

THE ROUTE

		SPECIAL STAGES	TOTAL DISTANCE	CREWS RUNNING
Leg 1 (1-6)	Sanremo (Friday 0630) - Imperia - Sanremo (Friday 2013)	6 asphalt-142.14km	551.24km	43
Leg 2 (7-10)	Sanremo (Saturday 0700) - Imperia - Sanremo (Saturday 1920)	4 asphalt-149.10km	491.06km	39
Leg 3 (11-14)	Sanremo (Sunday 0700) - Imperia - Sanremo (Sunday 1530)	4 asphalt-96.12km	333.56km	36
		14 stages-387.36km	1375.86km	

Ceremonial Start: Thursday 2030. Weather: dry except for Leg 3, a little fog on Leg 1. No stages in darkness.

STARTERS 54 (16 PCWRC) **FINISHERS** 36 (7 PCWRC).
OVERALL LEADER Loeb stages 1-14.
JWRC LEADERS Tirabassi (Renault) stage 1, Baldacci 2-14.
S1600 LEADERS Bernardi stage 1, Jean-Joseph (Renault) 2-5, Bernardi 6-14.
WINNER'S AVERAGE SPEED OVER STAGES 90.59kph.
WORLD CHAMPIONSHIP FOR MANUFACTURERS
Citroen 125 points, Peugeot 121, Subaru 76, Ford 71, Skoda 21, Hyundai 12.
WORLD CHAMPIONSHIP FOR DRIVERS
Burns 57 points, Loeb 55, Sainz 53, Solberg 48, Martin 43, Gronholm 38, C.McRae 36, Makinen 21, Rovanpera 18, Duval 15, etc.

OVERALL LEADING SPECIAL STAGE POSITIONS

	1	2	3	4	5	6
Martin	7	3	-	2	-	-
Loeb	5	5	1	1	1	-
Panizzi	2	1	2	4	1	2
Gronholm	-	3	6	2	2	-
Duval	-	1	3	1	2	4
Tarantino	-	1	-	-	-	-
Sainz	-	-	2	2	6	1
Bernardi	-	-	1	-	1	-
M.Higgins	-	-	-	1	-	-

Tarantino 20th (Renault Clio, GpA). M.Higgins 17th (Subaru Impreza GpN).
JWRC Baldacci won 6 stages, Tirabassi & Canellas (Suzuki) 2 each, Feghali (Ford) & Ceccato (Fiat) 1 each.
S1600 Bernardi & Jean-Joseph won 6 stages each.
Note: S1600 cars did not contest stages 11+12.

RECENT WINNERS

CORSICA

12

PlayStation.2

RALLYE DE FRANCE

TOUR DE CORSE

2003

Five different leaders, including the 22 years old Francois Duval. Finally Petter Solberg won despite a major crash in Shakedown.

❖

Changeable weather again! As in Australia the bonoficiary was Solberg.

❖

For the first time in seven months, a new Drivers' championship leader. Carlos Sainz's second place gave him a three point lead in the series.

❖

Martin Rowe becomes Production Car World Champion.

LEG 1 Three different leaders on one day: Carlos Sainz, Markko Martin then Sebastien Loeb. Didier Auriol retired before the first stage. Martin led but then went off the road and hit a rock face, losing 20 seconds.
1 Loeb 1h01m24.7s, 2 Duval +3.9s,
3 Gronholm +5.3s, 4 Sainz +10.2s,
5 Martin +18.5s, 6 Burns +19.5s,
7 McRae +29.4s, 8 Solberg +43.8s.
PCWRC Sola (20th) 1h06m47.6s.

LEG 2 The day the rains came, a very long day! On stage eight both Loeb (for the first time) and Martin (again!) went off the road. Mikko Hirvonen, alone of the top drivers, drove stage eight in the dry - and was quickest. Duval led for most of the day until Solberg pulled ahead on the final stage.
1 Solberg 3h09m13.6s, 2 Duval +17.9s,
3 Sainz +22.4s, 4 McRae +1m15.5s,
5 Gronholm +1m23.6s, 6 Panizzi +1m26.5s,
7 Makinen +2m10.3s, 8 Burns +2m22.0s.
PCWRC Sola (16th) 3h29m09.0s.

LEG 3 Martin had his third and final crash. Sainz snatched second place on the final stage. Gilles Panizzi was angry at almost constant errors of tyre choice. Emotional victory for Solberg.
1 Solberg 4h20m15.3s, 2 Sainz +36.6s,
3 Duval +41.7s, 4 Gronholm +1m09.2s,
5 McRae +1m26.0s, 6 Panizzi +1m58.7s,
7 Makinen +2m25.8s, 8 Burns +2m36.7s.
PCWRC McShea (16th) 4h49m47.8s.

What a race! Five different leaders, a winner whose car had been extensively damaged before the start and repaired, weather that changed every stage and often several times within the same stage, a driver who jumped from third place to the lead in the World Drivers' Championship, and the first World Champion of the 2003 season, in the Production Car series. The Tour de Corse exceeded its mercurial reputation! Certainly Petter Solberg will never forget the stress of those days on the

Second podium finish for Francois Duval.

Mediterranean island. "I started off by being so upset that I had crashed the car. So upset when I realised just how hard and long the team had to work to bring the car back to life, and I was so nervous about wanting to make things up to them. I hardly slept at all!" It was Solberg's third win this year, a total which puts him equal with Sebastien Loeb and Marcus Gronholm, but it was the canny old Carlos Sainz who pushed his way up to second place by the end of the event and now led the Drivers' series.

Crews who two weeks earlier in

What's New in 2003

● New Shakedown location, to the west of Ajaccio, with a special Service Park nearby used on the Thursday.
● Characteristically rougher and bumpier stages than in recent years.
● A change of date, 19 months since the last Tour de Corse, made transportation between successive world championship rallies easier. The event had only once been held so late in the year since 1980.

Fastest of the Peugeots was Marcus Gronholm.

Solberg in Style

Petter Solberg's accident at Shakedown led to a major effort to make his car ready in time for the start the next morning. It seemed that bringing another car down from Banbury, England would be the easiest solution, as had been done for Hamed Al-Wahaibi in Portugal in 2001, but the Stewards refused to allow this. A late night lay

ahead for the 13 technicians assigned to the task of bringing chassis 03017 back to life. "I have never seen such large hammers and such strong chains being used to straighten a car before in my time", said Prodrive competition chief David Lapworth. Just in case you think this was an exaggeration, this is the job list for Prodrive: Repair damage to left rear body, wheel arch and sills, straighten front chassis. Replace damaged engine. Replace rear door, two bumpers, front wing, boot lid and spoiler and all the radiator package. In recognition of their efforts, Inmarsat presented the Star of the Rally award to Petter's No 1 Technician John McLean and the 555 Subaru World Rally Team.

would have gone down a 200 metre drop." That did not assist his mental turmoil as mechanics worked through the night to repair the damage. They were needing something to go right.

Citroen came with a team of four cars, two of them leading the event, three of them finishing in the top ten, and Sainz thinking hard what to do. The weather was classic Sainz territory. Although he was a lot slower than Loeb, the veteran stayed on the road and attacked when it mattered. Peugeot, however, were all at sea. As in Sanremo the fastest driver of the team was usually the Finn, Marcus Gronholm, but Gilles Panizzi, twice previous winner in Corsica, was in despair. "Every time I get bad information from the team, this rally is terrible for me." Richard Burns had a better time than in Sanremo, but in the end could only finish eighth. The feared French cars' asphalt domination was not to happen this time.

Ford hoped for much but Markko Martin's mistake on the Friday was unfortunate and when he went off the road for good on Sunday nothing was changed. Duval drove with a new maturity, leading in extremely tricky conditions. He lost his second place on the final stage in a no-win tyre choice decision, while Mikko Hirvonen scored a fastest time in pure

Sanremo found weather predictions unreliable had not experienced anything compared with what they faced this time. Predictions of rain on Friday evening were well documented and it duly arrived, but that was only one small part of the equation. It was the way that extreme contrasts occurred on opposite sides of ranges of hills all the time. Often tyre selections had to be made over two hours before the cars started a stage, time for anything to happen.

Sebastien Loeb was widely regarded as favourite, with Markko Martin as the outsider. In fact it was Sainz who took an initial lead before Martin took over for a couple of stages. Markko was comfortably the pacemaker until he spun and hit a rock face and had trouble to restart. Loeb did not hesitate to take over and inched ahead of his rivals until sliding into a bank of gravel beside the road. The car was beached and the wheels spun helplessly. Eventually, but ten minutes later, he set off again. This incident brought the 22 year old Ford driver Francois Duval into the picture and he held the lead for four stages. On the second run through the 40km stage, however, there was every conceivable condition and surface, which had all the elements that Solberg, Subaru and Pirelli tyres love. Solberg won the stage (his teammate Tommi Makinen second) and took the lead which he held to the finish.

Subaru needed this success. It had been a hard time deciding how they

should tackle this event. They decided not to use the active suspension system, tried at Sanremo, and made a last minute car swop in consequence. Then came the pre-event crash for Solberg. "It was my fourth run through shakedown and I slid wide on a patch of unexpected gravel. Luckily there was a telegraph pole just there." Luckily? "Yes. Otherwise the car

Petter Solberg at his brilliant best.

Toni Gardemeister finished a troubled 11th.

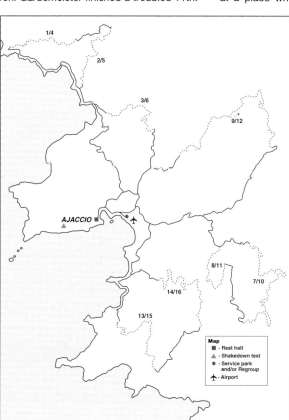

Map
- ■ - Rest halt
- ▲ - Shakedown test
- ● - Service park and/or Regroup
- ✈ - Airport

Second World Rally Group N victory for Mark Higgins in three weekends.

Corsican magical conditions. Rain was only in the air when he started stage eight, the instant the second car was about to start the stage it started to rain very heavily!

Skoda had a bad start when Didier Auriol found water had leaked on to an ECU, which prevented him selecting gear at a place where he was not permitted to open the bonnet and personally select manual gearshift mode. He was out before he had started a stage. Toni Gardemeister drove steadily to finish 11th but suffered curious problems, probably hydraulic, which affected the rear suspension and the steering generally.

At the end of the rally Peugeot were trying not to look sad at being eight points behind Citroen, while in the Drivers' series there were still six drivers in with the chance of the title, including Burns and Gronholm. The vagaries of the weather apart, the general expectation was that Catalunya

Production Car Championship

This was showdown time for the PCWRC drivers. Toshihiro Arai *(right)*

hoped Martin Rowe *(left)* would have a bad event, but Rowe was careful, made no errors and trailed the Japanese driver to the finish to take the title. There were various winners in Group N on this event. Overall, non-championship Group N was won by Mark Higgins, for the second world championship rally running, in the private R-E-D Subaru.

Fastest driver early on was Gianluigi Galli, and then the PCWRC driver Daniel Sola. Galli went off the road; Sola had a succession of troubles including a broken alternator cable, a puncture, then a detached turbo pipe and finally a differential which broke the clutch. When Sola went out the Group N leader was another Spaniard Xavier Pons but his car suddenly broke its engine, and Higgins was through. Sola impressively led the PCWRC category for the first two days in an Evo VII converted to Evo VIII specification, but then it all went wrong. McShea took over the lead and went on to gain his first win in the category this season. Rowe therefore won the title, Arai came second. Although Stig Blomqvist and Karamjit Singh (not competing here) were tied on equal points Blomqvist took third place under the tie-deciding rules. So it was Subaru's 1-2-3 and the first time a driver using this make of car had won a Group N World title.

would produce nothing very different to Sanremo or Corsica, but one wondered how powerful the Sainz-factor would be in his home country.

RALLYE DE FRANCE 47TH TOUR DE CORSE

POSITION/ LAST STAGE COMPLETED	ENTRANT	DRIVER/CODRIVER	NAT.	COMP NO.	CAR	CAT.	REG NO.	TOTAL PENALTY/ CAUSE
1	555 Subaru World R.T.	PETTER SOLBERG/Philip Mills	N/GB	7	Subaru Impreza	WRC	S700WRT (GB)	4h.20m.15.3s.
2	Citroen Total	CARLOS SAINZ/Marc Marti	E	19	Citroen Xsara	WRC	19DDM92 (F)	4h.20m.51.9s.
3	Ford Motor Company Ltd	FRANCOIS DUVAL/Stephane Prevot	B	5	Ford Focus RS	WRC	EJ02KMU (GB)	4h.20m.57.0s.
4	T. Marlboro Peugeot Total	MARCUS GRONHOLM/Timo Rautiainen	FIN	1	Peugeot 206	WRC	952NVB75 (F)	4h.21m.24.5s.
5	Citroen Total	COLIN McRAE/Derek Ringer	GB	17	Citroen Xsara	WRC	26CSP92 (F)	4h.21m.41.3s.
6	T. Marlboro Peugeot Total	GILLES PANIZZI/Herve Panizzi	F	3	Peugeot 206	WRC	283NNN92 (F)	4h.22m.14.0s.
7	555 Subaru World R.T.	TOMMI MAKINEN/Kaj Lindstrom	FIN	8	Subaru Impreza	WRC	S90WRT (GB)	4h.22m.41.1s.
8	T. Marlboro Peugeot Total	RICHARD BURNS/Robert Reid	GB	2	Peugeot 206	WRC	286NNN75 (F)	4h.22m.52.0s.
9	Citroen Total	Philippe Bugalski/Jean-Paul Chiaroni	F	20	Citroen Xsara	WRC	36CSP92 (F)	4h.23m.02.1s.
10	Ford Motor Company Ltd	MIKKO HIRVONEN/Jarmo Lehtinen	FIN	6	Ford Focus RS	WRC	EX02OBC (GB)	4h.24m.10.7s.
11	Skoda Motorsport	TONI GARDEMEISTER/Paavo Lukander	FIN	15	Skoda Fabia	WRC	3S3 1949 (CZ)	4h.25m.25.2s.
13	Citroen Total	SEBASTIEN LOEB/Daniel Elena	F/MC	18	Citroen Xsara	WRC	27CSP92 (F)	4h.29m.49.3s.
15	-	Mark Higgins/Michael Gibson	GB	100	Subaru Impreza	N	WX03RED (GB)	4h.49m.09.7s.**
16	-	Niall McShea/Chris Patterson	GB	60	Mitsubishi Lancer Evo VI	PCWRC	X566YBD (GB)	4h.49m.47.8s.*
LEADING RETIREMENTS								
0	Skoda Motorsport	DIDIER AURIOL/Denis Giraudet	F	14	Skoda Fabia	WRC	3S3 1948 (CZ)	electrical
6	Team BSA	Alexandre Bengue/Caroline Escudero	F	21	Peugeot 206	WRC	337PPZ75 (F)	accident
6	-	Alistair Ginley/Rory Kennedy	GB/IRL	35	Ford Focus	WRC	EJ02KMO (GB)	engine
9	-	Benoit Rousselot/Gilles Mondesir	F	34	Subaru Impreza	WRC	S80WRT (GB)	accident
10	Stohl Racing	Manfred Stohl/Ilka Minor	A	32	Peugeot 206	WRC	206MWP75 (F)	accident
14	Ford Motor Company Ltd	MARKKO MARTIN/Michael Park	EE/GB	4	Ford Focus RS	WRC	EO03YRJ (GB)	accident

MANUFACTURER REGISTERED DRIVER. *PCWRC winner. **Group N winner.

THE ROUTE

		SPECIAL STAGES	TOTAL DISTANCE	CREWS RUNNING
Leg 1	Ajaccio (Friday 0905) - Ajaccio -	6 asphalt-95.30km	283.03km	
(1-6)	Ajaccio (Friday 1714)			55
Leg 2	Ajaccio (Saturday 0715) - Campo dell'Oro - Campo dell'Oro - Campo dell'Oro -	6 asphalt-190.00km	447.80km	
(7-12)	Ajaccio (Saturday 1928)			39
Leg 3	Ajaccio (Sunday 0700) - Campo dell'Oro - Campo dell'Oro -	4 asphalt-112.10km	240.92km	
(13-16)	Ajaccio (Sunday 1430)			34
		16 stages-397.40km	971.75km	

Ceremonial Start: Thursday 1930. Weather: Very changeable. No stages in darkness.

OVERALL LEADING SPECIAL STAGE POSITIONS

	1	2	3	4	5	6
Loeb	5	3	3	-	1	-
Martin	4	3	2	-	-	-
Solberg	3	3	-	1	-	3
Duval	1	1	4	1	2	2
Sainz	1	-	4	5	1	2
Panizzi	1	-	-	2	2	1
Hirvonen	1	-	-	-	-	-
Gronholm	-	3	2	1	5	-
Burns	-	1	-	1	1	4

PCWRC Sola won 11 stages, Arai (Subaru) & Kulig (Mitsubishi) 2 each, McShea 1.
GROUP N Sola won 6 stages, Galli 4, M.Higgins 3, McShea, Pons & Kulig 1 each.

STARTERS 62 (15 PCWRC). **FINISHERS** 34 (10 PCWRC).
OVERALL LEADERS Sainz stage 1, Martin 2+3, Loeb 4-7, Duval 8-11, Solberg 12-16.
PCWRC LEADERS Sola (Mitsubishi) stages 1-12, McShea 13-16.
GROUP N LEADERS Sola stage 1, Galli (Mitsubishi) 2-6, Sola 7-12, Pons (Mitsubishi) 13, M.Higgins 14-16.
WINNER'S AVERAGE SPEED OVER STAGES 91.62kph. .
WORLD CHAMPIONSHIP FOR MANUFACTURERS
Citroen 137 points, Peugeot 129, Subaru 88, Ford 78, Skoda 21, Hyundai 12.
WORLD CHAMPIONSHIP FOR DRIVERS
Sainz 61 points, Solberg & Burns 58, Loeb 55, Gronholm & Martin 43, C.McRae 40, Makinen 23, Duval 21, Rovanpera 18, etc.

RECENT WINNERS
1993   Francois Delecour/Daniel Grataloup Ford Escort RS Cosworth (89.12kph)
1994   Didier Auriol/Bernard Occelli Toyota Celica Turbo 4WD (91.32kph)
1995   Didier Auriol/Denis Giraudet Toyota Celica GT-Four (91.58kph)
1996 * Philippe Bugalski/Jean-Paul Chiaroni Renault Maxi Megane (90.48kph)
1997   Colin McRae/Nicky Grist Subaru Impreza WRC (90.29kph)
1998   Colin McRae/Nicky Grist Subaru Impreza WRC (93.06kph)
1999   Philippe Bugalski/Jean-Paul Chiaroni Citroen Xsara KC (94.32kph)
2000   Gilles + Herve Panizzi Peugeot 206 WRC (90.70kph)
2001   Jesus Puras/Marc Marti Citroen Xsara WRC (92.14kph)
2002   Gilles + Herve Panizzi Peugeot 206 WRC (91.10kph)
Note * =W2L-only event.

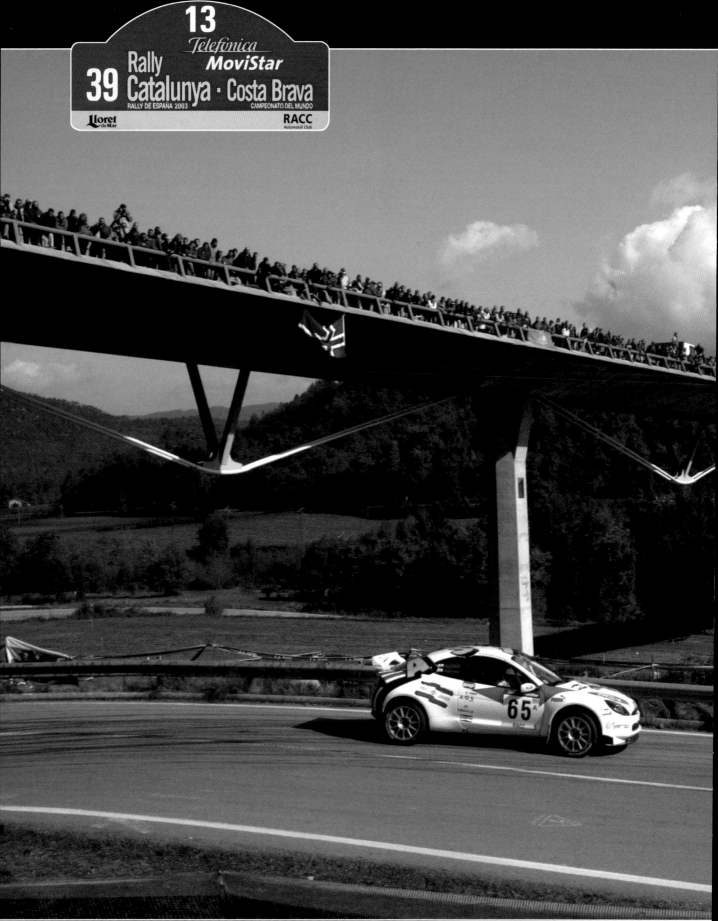

Fourth rally running when rain on the
last day upset the results.
❖
Gilles Panizzi's win on his final
full works Peugeot drive!
❖
Sebastien Loob led for 20 out of
22 stages.
❖
Four drivers and three manufacturers
could win the 2003 Drivers title, two
drivers the Junior title.

LEG 1 Petter Solberg led while other teams
misjudged the early dampness, Loeb then
went ahead. First off-road excursion for
Markko Martin. Francois Duval had a
slipping clutch, alternator problem caused
time control penalty for Solberg.
1 Loeb 1h31m37.8s, 2 Sainz +26.2s,
3 Martin +31.2s, 4 Panizzi +33.5s,
5 Duval +55.0s, 6 Burns +1m14.0s,
7 McRae +1m22.9s, 8 Bugalski +1m39.3s.
JWRC Tirabassi (21st) 1h41m09.8s.

LEG 2 Didier Auriol, on his 150th world
rally, retired. Carlos Sainz fell back with
handling trouble all day. Martin locked
in second place battle with Panizzi.
Marcus Gronholm went off the road and
stalled his engine in a field.
1 Loeb 2h46m28.6s, 2 Martin +20.8s,
3 Panizzi +36.7s, 4 Sainz +1m05.2s,
5 Duval +1m08.8s, 6 Burns +1m40.4s,
7 McRae +2m12.2s, 8 Gronholm +2m16.8s.
JWRC Tirabassi (20th) 3h03m27.3s.

LEG 3 The rains came. Martin first had brake
then hydraulic troubles, Loeb made
a tyre choice error. Richard Burns crashed.
Sainz had engine cut out trouble and finally
Panizzi came through to win.
1 Panizzi 3h55m09.4s, 2 Loeb +13.0s,
3 Martin +13.6s, 4 Duval +55.4s,
5 Solberg +1m10.8s, 6 Gronholm +1m29.1s,
7 Sainz +1m43.0s, 8 Makinen +1m55.1s.
JWRC Tirabassi (17th) 4h16m33.7s.

Gilles Panizzi crowned his five years with Peugeot by winning the Catalunya Rally in style. After a rally in which he was plagued with poor tyre choice, it all came good on the last day. On the final stage he took advantage of the misfortunes of Carlos Sainz and Markko Martin, and the bad tyre choice of the long time leader Sebastien Loeb, to come through to win. In Sanremo Panizzi had jumped from fourth to second at the end of the event, now in Spain the Frenchman leapt from second to first. Rain earlier in the day had catapulted Petter Solberg from tenth to sixth. All down to rain. This time it wasn't only just the placings which changed, the bias of the whole championship was shifted. Three drivers now had only one point between them as the series headed to the final round, and expectations that Citroen would pull well ahead of Peugeot were suddenly dashed. What a day it was in the rain in the hills behind the Costa Brava!

Catalunya was the last of three successive asphalt rallies, all run in October and all in the western Mediterranean region. This was the fastest of the three, on roads which are generally the smoothest and the widest of the three, and it was the penultimate round of the world series. In the damp conditions on the event's first morning many teams made poor tyre choices, fooled by unexpectedly fast rising temperatures which quickly dried out the road. After Solberg led initially, Loeb went into a lead he thought he was going to keep for the rest the event - and almost did! Various drivers gave chase during the rally, starting with Markko Martin before he began to suffer neck pains after his crash five days earlier in Corsica. "I found I lost concentration on the longer stages," he confessed. Then came Sainz, motivated by his home crowd and sensing a third world title was well within his grasp. Things started to go wrong for the Spaniard on the second day when he tried to improve the handling of the Xsara by adjusting the anti roll bar but made things worse,

(above and below) Happy ending for the Panizzi brothers after a frustrating season.

What's New in 2003

● The entire route of the rally was run in the region north or north-east of Barcelona, not going to the Tarragona area at all.

● New date, back again in October, the traditional fixture for the event, 18 months since the last Catalunya Rally.

● Some stages were used in both directions. Three stages (in the region between Ripoll and Berga) were completely new. Stages 3/6 were run past La Pobla de Lillet, at high altitude (1174 metres) and passed a ski centre.

● A new Service Area on the west side of Vic, operated on the three days of the rally. There was a different Shakedown Service Park for the Thursday, at the usual location beneath the famous viaduct on the C25 road.

● Further attention had been paid to spectator movements. This year there were strict controls as to the areas where spectators could stand, and their advanced access to stages.

and he slipped back to fourth. Martin again took up the chase, and found himself in a close tussle with Panizzi. This went on till the final day when Martin firstly had brake problems then worse still he lost his hydraulics for the final two stages. "That was

serious, it meant that I had to change gear manually all the time, as well as affecting the differentials. It made the difference between winning and eventually coming third."

Ford dearly wanted one asphalt victory this year but it was not to happen. Their pace was undeniable. Nobody scored more fastest stage times than Martin. Teammate Francois Duval had many problems, mostly none of his making, and pulled through to finish fourth. The Fords were running their revolutionary air accumulator system on their two 2003 cars, which the FIA vowed they would ban before the final rally. It was Citroen, however, who genuinely expected to win. They all had various brake problems, Sainz his handling troubles as well, but till that final stage it still looked good, not only to

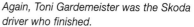

Again, Toni Gardemeister was the Skoda driver who finished.

win the rally but to pull impressively far ahead in the manufacturers' championship.

The joker in the world championship pack was Panizzi and his Peugeot, their "asphalt expert". When he did not suffer from wrong tyre choices

Too Many Rallies in October!

For the first time ever, two world championship rallies followed on consecutive weekends. The reason was to pursue the "roll-on, roll-off" cost-saving objective for the teams, to avoid the need for a second set of service equipment (vans, recce cars, etc) by being able to have one set and transport that set to every rally in the world, without resorting to air freight. Having Sanremo, Corsica then Catalunya all together helped the work of arranging the rest of the calendar, but was it individually a good idea? Markko Martin summed it up: "It could have worked if they were different types of rally. Think about the TV viewers, they want variety. When they switched on to watch the Catalunya Rally, it would have looked like a repeat of the Corsica or Sanremo programmes. They were all similar events, asphalt stages, mountainous scenery and so on". The confusion was not helped by always having rain on the final day and a last stage shuffle of position, either!

Another mature drive for 22 year-old Francois Duval.

CATALUNYA

Petter Solberg lost ground in dry conditions.

Panizzi's car went well but his teammate Gronholm had mysterious handling troubles for nearly two days, while Burns had mixed fortunes before he went off the road on the final day when holding a safe sixth

So near yet so far away for Sebastien Loeb.

place. Their chief Corrado Provera captured the team's emotion when he said afterwards "People have said many things about the 206WRC being dead but we never give up, we concentrated on our job, and we are not going to stop in our efforts to win our fourth (manufacturers') title with this car."

Subaru had a rally linked inextricably with the weather and their tyres. Their progress was linked to the climate. Once again they used passive suspension. Skoda was the only team to come to Spain with the same cars used a week ago in Corsica, and once again Auriol, (celebrating his 150th championship rally) retired, while Gardemeister finished, albeit again just outside the top ten.

Catalunya was a memorable event. No fewer than nine different drivers won stages including, for the second time this year, the Czech driver Roman Kresta (Peugeot), who had the advantage of changeable weather conditions. The red cars from France once again won the rally, but it was experience that counted. Citroen's problems in fact had their silver lining. Loeb: "Sure I was disappointed not to win, but things are not all that bad for

Junior Championship

Brice Tirabassi *(below)* led the JWRC category from start to finish. This third win of 2003 kept him ahead in the series, now by seven points. Second in the category (the first time all season he had scored points in the JWRC) on this event was Kris Meeke, the 2003 British Super 1600 champion. There were several non championship Super 1600 cars, notably Clios, and at the start of the event Clios were holding the top five Super. 1600 places. In the end three retired, leaving the non championship driver Simon Jean-Joseph ahead of Tirabassi in overall classification. Suzukis then took the next four JWRC places, led by the asphalt specialist Salvador Canellas now the only driver able to challenge Tirabassi for the title. Guy Wilks challenged hard at the beginning of the event in his Puma but then lost a lot of time off the road and finally finished the event in absolutely last position! After their pre-Sanremo crisis, the two usual VW drivers (Kosti Katajamaki and Oscar Svedlund) both made the start but both retired (Svedlund on the final stage) while curiously the two drivers from San Marino, Mirco Baldacci Fiat and Alex Broccoli (now back with Opel) both had to retire with engine failure.

me, because my rival Carlos had more problems." Panizzi's position in the championship was like a joker. His win did not upset the battle at the head of the field while Loeb's championship's chances were in fact strengthened rather than weakened. So Panizzi walked away from the Velizy team at the end of the season for Mitsubishi who were willing to give him a full championship programme in 2004.

Map
- ■ - Rest halt
- ▲ - Shakedown test
- ● - Service park and/or Regroup
- ✈ - Airport
- ○ - Other towns

3/8
2/7
10/15
11/16
1/6
17/20
9/14
Vic
19/22
18/21
4/12
5/13
19/22
LLORET DE MAR
Barcelona

39TH RALLY CATALUNYA-COSTA BRAVA

23/26.10.2003

POSITION/ LAST STAGE COMPLETED	ENTRANT	DRIVER/CODRIVER	NAT.	COMP NO.	CAR	CAT.	REG NO.	TOTAL PENALTY/ CAUSE
1	T. Marlboro Peugeot Total	GILLES PANIZZI/Herve Panizzi	F	3	Peugeot 206	WRC	945NVB75 (F)	3h.55m.09.4s.
2	Citroen Total	SEBASTIEN LOEB/Daniel Elena	F/MC	18	Citroen Xsara	WRC	16DDM92 (F)	3h.55m.22.4s.
3	Ford Motor Company Ltd	MARKKO MARTIN/Michael Park	EE/GB	4	Ford Focus RS	WRC	EK52NWN (GB)	3h.55m.23.0s.
4	Ford Motor Company Ltd	FRANCOIS DUVAL/Stephane Prevot	B	5	Ford Focus RS	WRC	FO03XYQ (GB)	3h.56m.04.8s.
5	555 Subaru World R.T.	PETTER SOLBERG/Philip Mills	N/GB	7	Subaru Impreza	WRC	S400WRT (GB)	3h.56m.20.2s.
6	T. Marlboro Peugeot Total	MARCUS GRONHOLM/Timo Rautiainen	FIN	1	Peugeot 206	WRC	334NQZ75 (F)	3h.56m.38.5s.
7	Citroen Total	CARLOS SAINZ/Marc Marti	E	19	Citroen Xsara	WRC	39CSP92 (F)	3h.56m.52.4s.
8	555 Subaru World R.T.	TOMMI MAKINEN/Kaj Lindstrom	FIN	8	Subaru Impreza	WRC	S30WRT (GB)	3h.57m.04.5s.
9	Citroen Total	COLIN McRAE/Derek Ringer	GB	17	Citroen Xsara	WRC	14DDM92 (F)	3h.58m.24.6s.
10	Citroen Total	Philippe Bugalski/Jean-Paul Chiaroni	F	20	Citroen Xsara	WRC	27DDM92 F()	4h.00m.23.0s.
12	Skoda Motorsport	TONI GARDEMEISTER/Paavo Lukander	FIN	15	Skoda Fabia	WRC	3S3 1949 (CZ)	4h.01m.07.6s.
13	Bozian Racing	Roman Kresta/Jan Tomanek	CZ	22	Peugeot 206	WRC	3976XR69 (F)	4h.01m.18.9s.
14	Ford Motor Company Ltd	MIKKO HIRVONEN/Jarmo Lehtinen	FIN	6	Ford Focus RS	WRC	EX02OBE (GB)	4h.04m.15.3s.
16	-	Simon Jean-Joseph/Jacques Boyere	F	101	Renault Clio	S1600	872AMC83 (F)	4h.14m.38.6s.**
17	-	Brice Tirabassi/Jacques-Julien Renucci	F	61	Renault Clio	JWRC	871AMC83 (F)	4h.16m.33.7s.*

LEADING RETIREMENTS

8	Skoda Motorsport	DIDIER AURIOL/Denis Giraudet	F	14	Skoda Fabia	WRC	3S3 1948 (CZ)	clutch
18	T. Marlboro Peugeot Total	RICHARD BURNS/Robert Reid	GB	2	Peugeot 206	WRC	950NVB75 (F)	accident

MANUFACTURER'S REGISTERED DRIVER. *JWRC winner. **S1600 winner.

THE ROUTE

		SPECIAL STAGES	TOTAL DISTANCE	CREWS RUNNING
Leg 1 (1-8)	Lloret de Mar (Friday 0645) - Lloret de Mar - Vic - Vic - Lloret de Mar (Friday 2103)	8 asphalt-146.36km	654.07km	45
Leg 2 (9-16)	Lloret de Mar (Saturday 0700) - Vic - Lloret de Mar (Saturday 1808)	8 asphalt-131.26km	429.69km	39
Leg 3 (17-22)	Lloret de Mar (Sunday 0530) - Vic - Lloret de Mar (Sunday 1509)	6 asphalt-103.56km	469.96km	34
		22 stages-381.18km	1553.72km	

Weather: Legs 1 and 2 essentially dry, Leg 3 wet. No stages in darkness.

OVERALL LEADING SPECIAL STAGE POSITIONS

	1	2	3	4	5	6
Martin	5	5	2	1	2	1
Panizzi	5	4	2	4	3	-
Loeb	5	2	2	3	4	1
Solberg	2	2	2	1	1	3
Duval	1	5	3	3	3	1
Makinen	1	2	-	1	1	-
Gronholm	1	1	3	1	2	-
Burns	1	-	2	3	3	3
Kresta	1	-	-	-	1	-

JWRC Tirabassi won 14 stages, Meeke (Opel) 4, Canellas (Suzuki) 3, Teuronen (Suzuki) 1.
S1600 Bernardi won 8 stages, Jean-Joseph 7, Tirabassi 4, Membrado (Renault), Meeke & Canellas 1 each.

STARTERS 47 (16 JWRC). **FINISHERS** 33 (11 JWRC).
OVERALL LEADERS Solberg stage 1, Loeb stages 2-21, Panizzi 22.
JWRC LEADER Tirabassi stage 1-22.
S1600 LEADERS Bernardi (Renault) stages 1-7, Jean-Joseph 8-22.
WINNER'S AVERAGE SPEED OVER STAGES 97.26kph.
WORLD CHAMPIONSHIP FOR MANUFACTURERS
Citroen 147 points, Peugeot 142, Subaru 93, Ford 89, Skoda 21, Hyundai 12.
WORLD CHAMPIONSHIP FOR DRIVERS
Loeb & Sainz 63 points, Solberg 62, Burns 58, Martin 49, Gronholm 46, McRae 40, Panizzi 27, Duval 26, Makinen 24, etc.

RECENT WINNERS

1993		Francois Delecour/Daniel Grataloup Ford Escort RS Cosworth (91.63kph)
1994	*	Enrico Bertone/Massimo Chiapponi Toyota Celica Turbo 4WD (89.27kph)
1995		Carlos Sainz/Luis Moya Subaru Impreza 555 (93.02kph)
1996		Colin McRae/Derek Ringer Subaru Impreza 555 (92.77kph)
1997		Tommi Makinen/Seppo Harjanne Mitsubishi Lancer Evolution (93.51kph)
1998		Didier Auriol/Denis Giraudet Toyota Corolla WRC (92.97kph)
1999		Philippe Bugalski/Jean-Paul Chiaroni Citroen Xsara KC (89.93kph)
2000		Colin McRae/Nicky Grist Ford Racing Focus WRC (92.98kph)
2001		Didier Auriol/Denis Giraudet Peugeot 206 WRC (94.32kph)
2002		Gilles + Herve Panizzi Peugeot 206 WRC (97.54kph)
Note	*	=W2L-only event.

14

WRC   FIA

WALES RALLY GB

6-9 NOVEMBER 2003

Petter Solberg, Citroen and Brice Tirabassi
are the new 2003 world champions.
❖
Championship contender Richard Burns
withdrew before the event through illness.
❖
Fastest over 'RAC' Rally.
❖
Last rallies for Tommi Makinen
and Colin McRae.

LEG 1 Carlos crashed, Gronholm stopped
by the police, Martin's engine failed after
a water leak, Hirvonen slid off the road. Tyre
choice errors slowed Loeb. Oldtimers Makinen
and McRae joined battle for third place.
1 Solberg 1h32m37.2s, 2 Loeb +8.0s,
3 Makinen +1m32.2s, 4 McRae +1m43.6s,
5 Rovanpera +2m41.2s, 6 Panizzi +2m49.3s,
7 Duval +3m35.2s, 8 Kresta +4m05.2s.
JWRC Carlsson (20th) 1h46m25.3s.

LEG 2 Solberg fastest on every stage,
edging ahead of Loeb, other drivers
far behind. Loix progressively improved
as he learned the 206WRC. Stohl and
Kresta close behind.
1 Solberg 2h48m55.4s, 2 Loeb +41.2s,
3 Makinen +2m25.2s, 4 McRae +2m31.4s,
5 Rovanpera +4m33.9s, 6 Duval +5m53.7s,
7 Loix +6m29.2s, 8 Stohl +7m35.8s.
JWRC Carlsson (17th) 3h12m47.8s.

LEG 3 Rovanpera and Gardemister
retired. JWRC management dilemma
for Suzuki regarding team orders.
1 Solberg 3h28m58.1s, 2 Loeb +43.6s,
3 Makinen +2m58.8s, 4 McRae +5m28.1s,
5 Duval +7m16.1s, 6 Loix +8m06.5s,
7 Stohl +8m48.4s, 8 Kresta +9m02.6s.
JWRC Carlsson (14th) 3h57m29.8s.

Citroen's first full year in the championship brought them success when they won the Manufacturers' title. Perhaps the most exciting world championship season in memory ended with the Drivers' championship title, and victory on the event going to Petter Solberg, bringing a title success to Subaru and Pirelli, while Citroen proved to be the most consistent manufacturer. As it became clear that Solberg was going to beat Loeb, however hard the Frenchman tried, the emphasis swung on to the shoot-out in the Junior championship. Eventual champion Brice Tirabassi retired at half distance, and the

drama was whether the four-car Suzuki team would have the chance to manipulate their drivers' positions to bring the JWRC title to Salvador Canellas. In the end the Suzuki team declined to impose orders, letting Daniel Carlsson win the category by sacrificing his teammates chance of the World title.

Held for perhaps the final time as a season finale, the British round of the series was non-stop drama for a week. First headline was the withdrawal of Richard Burns, the man Peugeot entrusted to help them leap-frog Citroen to the Manufacturers' title. Burns was also one of four drivers able to win the World Drivers'

Second successive 'RAC Rally' win for Petter Solberg, a popular victory and championship success.

title on his own account, though the strength of his personal chances depended on misfortunes for Carlos Sainz, Petter Solberg and Sebastien Loeb. Burns' withdrawal was due to a collapse which manifested itself when twice he fainted on the evening before reconnaissance began. Immediately it was clear that he could not drive on the rally, but when promised medical explanations did

What's New in 2003

● After 17 years of Lombard, then ten years of Network Q Rally GB, a new sponsor, the Welsh Development Agency. Support also came from the Welsh Assembly Government.

● Scrutineering was located outside the official headquarters in the Cardiff City Hall. This area (called the 'Rally Village') was the site for parc ferme, the trade and display areas, and the official start and ceremonial finish.

● The official finish of the event was at Margam Park (after stage 18) and the cars were then led in convoy to a ceremonial finish at Cardiff.

● New personnel. 'Chairman' of the organising committee (effectively the Sporting Manager) and deputy Clerk of the Course was the Australian Claire Parker.

Did he actually slow down on team orders, or was that a publicity explanation for defeat? Whatever, Sebastien Loeb was the only driver to match Solberg's speed and his second place on the event, and in the Championship, was brilliant!

Watch this space. Freddy Loix had never expected to compete in Britain this year and the first time he drove a 206WRC on gravel was the day before the start.

End of an Era

So ended the 2003 season, but was this the start of a new way of rally life or more the end of an old one? It was goodbye to friends like Tommi Makinen and Colin McRae, goodbye to gravel crews, goodbye to three car teams, goodbye to the already small amount of time to breathe during each event with looo time to recover from injuries (physical or financial!), goodbye for organisers to capitalise on the promotional opportunities during events. People went away from Cardiff wondering if things will be as enjoyable again. Just normal evolutionary changes, or changes with a message behind them? A pronoucement from Skoda that 16 rallies in 2004 were too many for a company developing a new car to enter must have alarmed the FIA. They confirmed they would pull out of the full championship rather than continue with an underdeveloped car as they were. But that was nothing compared with the explanation by Suzuki that it was better for them that one of their drivers should win his second qualifying round of the JWRC of the season, rather than another driver should win the world title. Is the FIA's dream of an expanded championship too much to achieve?

not materialise, there were increasing worries about the 2001 champion's opportunities to continue as a competitor in the sport. Freddy Loix was nominated as the replacement driver for Peugeot.

On the first morning there was a series of shocks. Firstly Sainz retired in bizarre circumstances. Wiring to the official in-car camera was faulty and led to an internal fire. This in turn led to a continuing smell of burning which distracted the twice former world champion to such an extent that he lost concentration and crashed, his first and only retirement of the year. The outgoing world champion Marcus Gronholm clipped a pile of logs which damaged the steering, and the police ordered that he retire from the rally and not drive to the Service Park. Markko Martin's engine overheated due to a water leak and failed, and teammate Mikko Hirvonen slid off the road. The race for the world title settled down into a head-to-head battle between Solberg and Loeb, then Citroen

confirmed extraordinary rumours that the company had ordered Loeb not to take risks, better that he take second place, because fighting for the lead could damage their prospects of beating Peugeot to the manufacturers' title. Solberg enjoyed the scene. He had already learned 12 months ago the technique of winning this event, now he was engaged in learning how to become a world champion. By the final day it was clear he was going to be a popular hero for the sport.

Solberg's title came as an unexpected turnaround in the fortunes of Subaru this year. It had taken so long to make the 2003 model reliable, it was only in the second half of the season it had become a winner at all. From there on things went Solberg's way, this was his fourth win in the final seven events of the series.

Citroen, who started the season on form, with wins in Monte-Carlo and Turkey, gradually improved the performance of the car so it was one of the best all-rounders in the sport. Peugeot were the last remaining team able to beat Citroen to the Manufacturers' title but when Burns had to withdraw and Gronholm retired, they imagined they could only rely on Harri Rovanpera for any points. Coming up fast as the rally progressed however was Loix, and on his debut for the team finished a superb sixth when Rovanpera retired. Overall this had to be a disappointing end to the career of the remarkable 206WRC.

Ford and Skoda came to Wales with no chance of winning a title this year. The Focus was no longer able to use the revolutionary air accumulation system, but

Those were the days! On the final chance to compete with a 'classic' Mini on a world championship rally, Neil Burgess and Jim Holder won their class in a private car first time out. Back in the late '50s and early '60s it took the officially entered Minis five attempts before they could win their class on this event!

Daniel Carlsson finished his dramatic 2003 season with his second JWRC category win of 2003.

they had not intended to use this on gravel events, and anyway Markko Martin's speed while he was still in the event suggested the car was fast enough as it was! Skoda were still learning about the Fabia. While Didier Auriol reached the finish and scored championship points, Toni Gardemeister went off the road on the

Carlos Sainz, Petter Solberg and Sebastien Loeb before the start.

final day and retired. Skoda announced the day before the rally that they would run a reduced programme in 2004, to give themselves time to develop the car ready for a full attack again in 2005.

While Solberg battled away, a lot of attention focussed on Tommi Makinen on his final rally before retirement. It was to be one of his best rallies all year. For a long time he was locked in battle with Colin McRae, who also announced his withdrawal from championship rallying. It was wonderful to see these two oldtimers fighting for third place all through the rally, ahead of everybody except the championship contenders! Makinen had been given some gold shoes in which to drive. It was smiles all the way for the man who has so frequently in his recent career been seen looking unhappy.

Junior Championship

Tirabassi started the final event as odds on favourite for the Junior title. Both he and his non-championship teammate Simon Jean-Joseph suffered a lot of shock absorber troubles and it took all of Brice's efforts to hold on to fourth place in the category before he retired. Racing for the lead were Daniel Carlsson, Kris Meeke and Mirco Baldacci, but things did not go well for Suzuki. All four of their cars suffered gearbox troubles, for no evident reason. It was a struggle to keep the cars going. At one point Canellas had no gears left and needed to be pushed into the Service Park, he settled in seventh place *(below)*. Then

came Tirabassi's retirement and suddenly the championship fight livened up. If Canellas finished second, he would be champion. It seemed an impossible task, but gradually things seemed clear. With three Suzuki drivers ahead, team orders could elevate Canellas into third place. This meant that if something happened to either Meeke or Baldacci, a title for Canellas was within reach. The pressure became acute when Meeke swerved to avoid some rocks and went off the road on the final morning. Suzuki could not avoid the facts. The company was consulted and they said that if it would make a difference Teuronen could be ordered to slow down, and gamble on Baldacci striking trouble. In the end the driver from San Marino survived the event, Carlsson won the category, Tirabassi took the title.

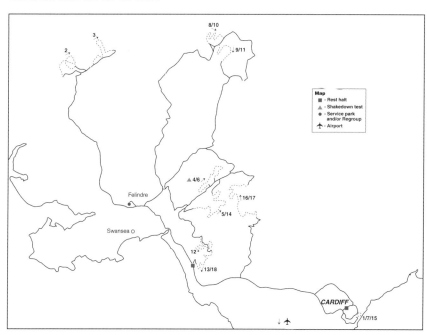

POSITION/ LAST STAGE COMPLETED	ENTRANT	DRIVER/CODRIVER	NAT.	COMP NO.	CAR	CAT.	REG NO.	TOTAL PENALTY/ CAUSE
1	555 Subaru World R.T.	PETTER SOLBERG/Philip Mills	N/GB	7	Subaru Impreza	WRC	S600WRT (GB)	3h.28m.58.1s.
2	Citroen Total	SEBASTIEN LOEB/Daniel Elena	F/MC	18	Citroen Xsara	WRC	20DDM92 (F)	3h.29m.41.7s.
3	555 Subaru World R.T.	TOMMI MAKINEN/Kaj Lindstrom	FIN	8	Subaru Impreza	WRC	S200WRT (GB)	3h.31m.56.9s.
4	Citroen Total	COLIN McRAE/Derek Ringer	GB	17	Citroen Xsara	WRC	21DDM92 (F)	3h.34m.26.2s.
5	Ford Motor Company Ltd	FRANCOIS DUVAL/Stephane Prevot	B	5	Ford Focus RS	WRC	EJ02KMU (GB)	3h.36m.14.2s.
6	T.Marlboro Peugeot Total	FREDDY LOIX/Sven Smeets	B	2	Peugeot 206	WRC	206NLM75 (F)	3h.37m.04.6s.
7	-	Manfred Stohl/Ilka Minor	A	34	Peugeot 206	WRC	206MWP75 (F)	3h.37m.46.5s.
8	Bozian Racing	Roman Kresta/Jan Tomanek	CZ	22	Peugeot 206	WRC	3976XR69 (F)	3h.38m.00.7s.
9	Bozian Racing	Juuso Pykalisto/Risto Mannisenmaki	FIN	24	Peugeot 206	WRC	4854YW69 (F)	3h.38m.51.7s.
10	Ford Motor Company Ltd	Jari-Matti Latvala/Miikka Anttila	FIN	20	Ford Focus RS	WRC	X7FMC (GB)	3h.41m.23.4s.
11	Skoda Motorsport	DIDIER AURIOL/Denis Giraudet	F	14	Skoda Fabia	WRC	3S3 1946 (CZ)	3h.44m.44.0s.
14	-	Daniel Carlsson/Mattias Andersson	S	52	Suzuki Ignis	JWRC	ITA852 (H)	3h.57m.29.8s.*

LEADING RETIREMENTS

2	Ford Motor Company Ltd	MIKKO HIRVONEN/Jarmo Lehtinen	FIN	6	Ford Focus RS	WRC	EX02OBE (GB)	accident
2	Citroen Total	CARLOS SAINZ/Marc Marti	E	19	Citroen Xsara	WRC	18DDM92 (F)	accident
3	T.Marlboro Peugeot Total	MARCUS GRONHOLM/Timo Rautiainen	FIN	1	Peugeot 206	WRC	943NVB75 (F)	suspension
3	Ford Motor Company Ltd	MARKKO MARTIN/Michael Park	EE/GB	4	Ford Focus RS	WRC	EO03YWC (GB)	engine
7	Bozian Racing	Gilles + Herve Panizzi	F	21	Peugeot 206	WRC	341NQZ75 (F)	transmission
13	Citroen Sport	Daniel Sola/Alex Romani	E	25	Citroen Xsara	WRC	20CSP92 (F)	turbocharger
15	T.Marlboro Peugeot Total	HARRI ROVANPERA/Risto Pietilainen	FIN	3	Peugeot 206	WRC	624NZT75 (F)	transmission
15	Skoda Motorsport	TONI GARDEMEISTER/Paavo Lukander	FIN	15	Skoda Fabia	WRC	3S3 1943 (CZ)	accident
15	Skoda Matador Team	Jan Kopecky/Filip Schovanec	CZ	26	Skoda Octavia	WRC	MBO72-74 (CZ)	alternator

MANUFACTURER'S REGISTERED DRIVER. *JWRC/S1600 winner.

THE ROUTE

		SPECIAL STAGES	TOTAL DISTANCE	CREWS RUNNING
Leg 1 (1-7)	Cardiff (Thursday 1900) - Cardiff - Felindre - Felindre - Cardiff (Friday 2007)	7 gravel-164.24km	628.28km	55
Leg 2 (8-15)	Cardiff (Saturday 0500) - Felindre - Felindre - Cardiff (Saturday 2013)	7 gravel-138.71km	582.62km	47
Leg 3 (16-18)	Cardiff (Sunday 0520) - Felindre - Felindre - Margam Park (Sunday 1324)	4 gravel-73.86km	363.62km	39
		18 stages-376.81km	1574.52km	

Weather: Dry but with damp surfaces. Three stages in darkness.

OVERALL LEADING SPECIAL STAGE POSITIONS

	1	2	3	4	5	6
Solberg	13	5	-	-	-	-
Loeb	5	9	1	2	-	1
Makinen	-	2	7	7	1	1
McRae	-	1	7	6	1	-
Martin	-	1	2	-	-	-
Duval	-	-	1	-	4	3
Gronholm	-	-	1	1	-	-
Stohl	-	-	-	1	2	-
Rovanpera	-	-	-	-	6	4

JWRC Carlsson won 10 stages, Meeke 6, Baldacci 2, Tirabassi 1.
S1600 Carlsson won 9 stages, Meeke 6, Baldacci, Tirabassi, Jean-Joseph & Andersson 1 each.

STARTERS 75 (14 JWRC). **FINISHERS** 39 (6 JWRC).
OVERALL LEADERS Solberg stage 1, Loeb 2+3, Solberg 4-18.
JWRC/S1600 LEADERS Meeke & Baldacci stage 1, Meeke 2-4, Carlsson 5-18.
WINNER'S AVERAGE SPEED OVER STAGES 108.19kph (record).
WORLD CHAMPIONSHIP FOR MANUFACTURERS Citroen 160 points, Peugeot 145, Subaru 109, Ford 93, Skoda 23, Hyundai 12. **Citroen now Champion**.
WORLD CHAMPIONSHIP FOR DRIVERS
Solberg 72 points, Loeb 71, Sainz 63, Burns 58, Martin 49, Gronholm 46, McRae 45, Makinen & Duval 30, Panizzi 27, etc. **Solberg now Champion**.

RECENT WINNERS

1993	Juha Kankkunen/Nicky Grist Toyota Celica Turbo 4WD (86.04kph)
1994	Colin McRae/Derek Ringer Subaru Impreza 555 (98.37kph)
1995	Colin McRae/Derek Ringer Subaru Impreza 555 (99.10kph)
1996 *	Armin Schwarz/Denis Giraudet Toyota Celica GT-Four (82.07kph)
1997	Colin McRae/Nicky Grist Subaru Impreza WRC (99.36kph)
1998	Richard Burns/Robert Reid Mitsubishi Lancer Evolutin (98.98kph)
1999	Richard Burns/Robert Reid Subaru Impreza WRC (99.97kph)
2000	Richard Burns/Robert Reid Subaru Impreza WRC (102.44kph)
2001	Marcus Gronholm/Timo Rautiainen Peugeot 206 WRC (104.42kph)
2002	Petter Solberg/Philip Mills Subaru Impreza WRC (104.68kph)
Note *	=W2L-only event.

IMPREZA
WRX *STi*

Past success.
Future glory.

World Championship Charts

In 2003 (as in 2002) there were four main series, as follows:

A World Rally Championship for Manufacturers (WCR)
C Junior World Rally Championship (JWRC)
B World Championship for Drivers (WCD)
D Production Car World Rally Championship (PCWRC)

As before, each round of the main series also counted as a round for either the Junior or the Production Car series, but this year the 14 rounds were equally divided between both series. In all four series there was a change to the points scoring system whereby, rather than the first six finishers, points were allocated to the first eight finishers in each series on the basis of 10, 8, 6, 5, 4, 3, 2, 1, and in each series all points counted.

A Points could only be scored by the six registered manufacturers. Before the season teams had to nominate two drivers who would contest each event, and at a specific time before each event teams could also nominate one extra driver to be eligible to score points on that event. All the points gained by the best two were counted. Results gained by a third entry or by drivers not nominated by the manufacturer were considered 'invisible' for points purposes. In these instances, lower placed competitors were bunched up for points scoring purposes. Results gained by Hyundai, who eventually only officially contested ten of the 14 events before withdrawing from the series, were retained.
B Points based on top eight positions overall. No minimum number of entries needed. No registration required.
C Points based on the final top eight positions of registered drivers. Drivers had to register for the series and compete on all seven rounds to be classified in the final championship standings.
D Points based on the final top eight positions of registered drivers. Drivers had to register and nominate which six of the seven qualifying events they wished to be counted. All six nominated events had to be contested to be classified in the final championship standings.
C+D Failure to give acceptable explanation for failure to compete could attract financial and other penalties and any unapproved absence led to exclusion from the series. Where a competitor was subsequently excluded, their points were annulled but the drivers finishing behind them on previous events were not 'bunched up'.

Final positions in 2003 FIA World Championship for Manufacturers (WCR)

		Total	Monte-Carlo	Sweden	Turkey	New Zealand	Argentina	Acropolis	Cyprus	Germany	Finland	Australia	Sanremo	Corsica	Catalunya	Great Britain
		Total	MC	S	TR	NZ	RA	GR	CY	D	FIN	AUS	I	F	E	GB
1	Citroen	**160**	18	6	15	5	8	10	11	15	9	13	15	12	10	13
2	Peugeot	**145**	6	16	9	18	16	8	8	14	6	9	11	8	13	3
3	Subaru	**109**	0	11	2	9	5	10	10	2	11	14	2	12	5	16
4	Ford	**93**	10	5	10	1	3	10	4	7	10	1	10	7	11	4
5	Skoda	**23**	2	1	3	6	7	1	0	0	0	0	1	0	0	2
6	Hyundai	**12**	3	0	0	0	0	0	3	1	3	2	X	X	X	X

Final positions in 2003 FIA World Championship for Drivers (WCD)

		Total	MC	S	TR	NZ	RA	GR	CY	D	FIN	AUS	I	F	E	GB
1	Petter Solberg (N)	**72**	R	3	R	6	4	6	10	1	8	10	R	10	4	10
2	Sebastien Loeb (F)	**71**	10	2	R	5	R	R	6	10	4	8	10	R	8	8
3	Carlos Sainz (E)	**63**	6	0	10	0	8	8	4	3	5	4	5	8	2	R
4	Richard Burns (GB)	**58**	4	6	8	8	6	5	R	6	6	6	2	1	R	W
5	Markko Martin (EE)	**49**	5	5	3	R	R	10	R	4	10	R	6	0	6	R
6	Marcus Gronholm (FIN)	**46**	0	10	0	10	10	R	R	8	R	R	R	5	3	R
7	Colin McRae (GB)	**45**	8	4	5	R	R	1	5	5	R	5	3	4	0	5
8	Tommi Makinen (FIN)	**30**	R	8	1	2	R	4	R	R	3	3	0	2	1	6
9	Francois Duval (B)	**30**	2	R	6	0	1	R	R	2	R	0	4	6	5	4
10	Gilles Panizzi (F)	**27**	R	0	4	0	0	2	R	0	0	0	8	3	10	R

Other points scorers Harri Rovenpera (FIN) 18, Toni Gardemeister (FIN) 9, Didier Auriol (F) & Freddy Loix (B) 4, Mikko Hirronen (FIN), Alister McRae (GB), Cedric Robert (F) & Armin Schwarz (D) 3, Janne Tuohino (FIN) & Manfred Stohl (A) 2, Philippe Bugalski (F), Alister Ginley (GB) & Sebastian Lindholm (FIN) 1.

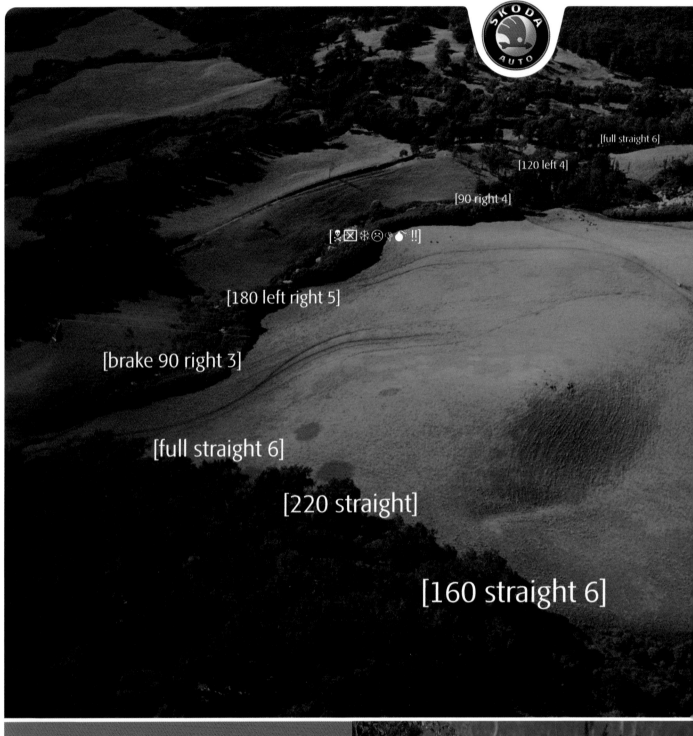

[full straight 6]

[120 left 4]

[90 right 4]

[180 left right 5]

[brake 90 right 3]

[full straight 6]

[220 straight]

[160 straight 6]

ŠKODA FABIA WRC, THE NEW REPRESENTATIVE OF THE ŠKODA AUTO MOTORSPORT TEAM, WAS INTRODUCED IN THE LAST 7 RACES OF THE 2003 FIA WORLD RALLY CHAMPIONSHIP.

www.skoda-auto.com

World Class Drivers

The following list gives details of every entry made on full world rally championship events by the drivers included, specifying: event, the type of car, codriver and final result or reason for retirement.

Appearances on World 2-litre-only events have been included within these records, indicated by a (2) by the event name.

#100 denotes the occassion of a drivers 100th WRC start.

COUNTRY/EVENT KEY: AUS=Australia, B=Belgium; CN=China; CY=Cyprus; CZ=Czech Republic; D=Germany; E=Spain; EAK=Safari; EE=Estonia; F=France/Corsica; F2=Formula 2; FIN=Finland; GB=Great Britain; GR=Greece/Acropolis; I=Italy/Sanremo; KC=Kit Car; MC=Monte-Carlo; N=Norway; NZ=New Zealand; P=Portugal; RA=Argentina; RI=Indonesia; S=Sweden; TR=Turkey; WRC=World Rally Car.

Didier Auriol (F)

Born 18/08/1958 at Montpellier
First rally car Simca Rallye 2 in 1979
BO = Bernard Occelli
DG = Denis Giraudet
JA = Jean-Marc Andrie
JB = Jack Boyere

1984
Event	Car	Codriver	Result
F	Renault 5 Turbo	BO	turbo/fire

1985
Event	Car	Codriver	Result
F	Renault Maxi 5 T.	BO	electrics

1986
Event	Car	Codriver	Result
F	MG Metro 6R4	BO	oil loss

1987
Event	Car	Codriver	Result
F	Ford Sierra RS Cos.	BO	8
I	Ford Sierra RS Cos.	BO	4

1988
Event	Car	Codriver	Result
P	Ford Sierra RS Cos.	BO	rear axle
F	Ford Sierra RS Cos.	BO	1
FIN	Ford Sierra RS Cos.	BO	3
I	Ford Sierra RS Cos.	BO	accident

6th World Championship for Drivers

1989
Event	Car	Codriver	Result
MC	Lancia D.Integrale	BO	2
P	Lancia D.Integrale	BO	clutch
F	Lancia D.Integrale	BO	1
GR	Lancia D.Integrale	BO	2
FIN	Lancia D.Integrale	BO	acc. damage
I	Lancia D.Integrale	BO	accident

Equal 4th World Championship for Drivers

1990
Event	Car	Codriver	Result
MC	Lancia D.Integrale	BO	1
P	Lancia D.Integrale	BO	2
F	Lancia D.Integrale	BO	1
GR	Lancia D.Integrale	BO	holed sump
RA	Lancia D.Integrale	BO	3
FIN	Lancia D.Integrale	BO	accident
AUS	Lancia D.Integrale	BO	accident
I	Lancia D.Integrale	BO	1
GB	Lancia D.Integrale	BO	5

2nd World Championship for Drivers

1991
Event	Car	Codriver	Result
MC	Lancia D.Integrale	BO	engine
S	Lancia D.Integrale	BO	9
P	Lancia D.Integrale	BO	2
F	Lancia D.Integrale	BO	2
GR	Lancia D.Integrale	BO	4
NZ	Lancia D.Integrale	BO	3
RA	Lancia D.Integrale	BO	3
FIN	Lancia D.Integrale	BO	2
AUS	Lancia D.Integrale	BO	engine
I	Lancia D.Integrale	BO	1
GB	Lancia D.Integrale	BO	12

3rd World Championship for Drivers

1992
Event	Car	Codriver	Result
MC	Lancia HF Integrale	BO	1
P	Lancia HF Integrale	BO	engine
F	Lancia HF Integrale	BO	1
GR	Lancia HF Integrale	BO	1
RA	Lancia HF Integrale	BO	1
FIN	Lancia HF Integrale	BO	1
AUS	Lancia HF Integrale	BO	1
I	Lancia HF Integrale	BO	broken wheel
E	Lancia HF Integrale	BO	10
GB	Lancia HF Integrale	BO	plug leads

3rd World Championship for Drivers

1993
Event	Car	Codriver	Result
MC	Toyota Celica T.4WD	BO	1
S	Toyota Celica T.4WD	BO	withdrawn
F	Toyota Celica T.4WD	BO	2
GR	Toyota Celica T.4WD	BO	overheating
RA	Toyota Celica T.4WD	BO	3
NZ	Toyota Celica T.4WD	BO	3
FIN	Toyota Celica T.4WD	BO	3
AUS	Toyota Celica T.4WD	BO	engine
E	Toyota Celica T.4WD	BO	2
GB	Toyota Celica T.4WD	BO	6

3rd World Championship for Drivers

1994
Event	Car	Codriver	Result
MC	Toyota Celica T.4WD	BO	accident
P	Toyota Celica T.4WD	BO	2
EAK	Toyota Celica T.4WD	BO	3
F	Toyota Celica T.4WD	BO	1
GR	Toyota Celica T.4WD	BO	engine
RA	Toyota Celica T.4WD	BO	1
NZ	Toyota Celica T.4WD	BO	5
FIN	Toyota Celica T.4WD	BO	2
I	Toyota Celica T.4WD	BO	1
GB	Toyota Celica T.4WD	BO	6

World Champion

1995
Event	Car	Codriver	Result
MC	Toyota Celica GT-4	BO	accident
S	Toyota Celica GT-4	BO	5
P	Toyota Celica GT-4	BO	5
F	Toyota Celica GT-4	DG	1
NZ	Toyota Celica GT-4	DG	2
AUS	Toyota Celica GT-4	DG	alternator belt
E	Toyota Celica GT-4	DG	excluded

Excluded from 1995 Championship

1996
Event	Car	Codriver	Result
S	Subaru Impreza 555	BO	10
I	Mit. Lancer Ev. III	DG	8

1997
Event	Car	Codriver	Result
MC	Ford Escort RS Cos.	JA	transmission
RA	Toyota Celica GT-4	DG	5
FIN	Toyota Corolla WRC	DG	8
RI	Toyota Corolla WRC	DG	electrical
I	Toyota Corolla WRC	DG	8
AUS	Toyota Corolla WRC	DG	3
GB	Toyota Corolla WRC	DG	accident

1998
Event	Car	Codriver	Result
MC	Toyota Corolla WRC	DG	14
S	Toyota Corolla WRC	DG	6
EAK	Toyota Corolla WRC	DG	4
P	Toyota Corolla WRC	DG	gearbox
E	Toyota Corolla WRC	DG	1
F	Toyota Corolla WRC	DG	6
RA	Toyota Corolla WRC	DG	engine
GR	Toyota Corolla WRC	DG	2
NZ	Toyota Corolla WRC	DG	2
FIN	Toyota Corolla WRC	DG	4
I	Toyota Corolla WRC	DG	suspension
AUS	Toyota Corolla WRC	DG	3
GB	Toyota Corolla WRC	DG	transmission

6th World Championship for Drivers

1999
Event	Car	Codriver	Result
MC	Toyota Corolla WRC	DG	3
S	Toyota Corolla WRC	DG	4
EAK	Toyota Corolla WRC	DG	2
P	Toyota Corolla WRC	DG	3
E	Toyota Corolla WRC	DG	2
F	Toyota Corolla WRC #100	DG	5
RA	Toyota Corolla WRC	DG	3
GR	Toyota Corolla WRC	DG	suspension
NZ	Toyota Corolla WRC	DG	4
FIN	Toyota Corolla WRC	DG	withdrawn
CN	Toyota Corolla WRC	DG	1
I	Toyota Corolla WRC	DG	3
AUS	Toyota Corolla WRC	DG	accident
GB	Toyota Corolla WRC	DG	suspension

3rd World Championship for Drivers

2000
Event	Car	Codriver	Result
MC	SEAT Cordoba WRC	DG	engine
S	SEAT Cordoba WRC	DG	10
EAK	SEAT Cordoba WRC	DG	3
P	SEAT Cordoba WRC	DG	10
E	SEAT Cordoba WRC	DG	13
RA	SEAT Cordoba WRC	DG	clutch
GR	SEAT Cordoba WRC	DG	suspension
NZ	SEAT Cordoba WRC	DG	accident
FIN	SEAT Cordoba WRC	DG	11
CY	SEAT Cordoba WRC	DG	wheel bearing
F	SEAT Cordoba WRC	DG	8
I	SEAT Cordoba WRC	DG	17
AUS	SEAT Cordoba WRC	DG	8
GB	SEAT Cordoba WRC	DG	9

2001
Event	Car	Codriver	Result
MC	Peugeot 206 WRC	DG	accident
S	Peugeot 206 WRC	DG	transmission
P	Peugeot 206 WRC	DG	8
E	Peugeot 206 WRC	DG	1
RA	Peugeot 206 WRC	DG	accident
CY	Peugeot 206 WRC	DG	overheating
GR	Peugeot 206 WRC	DG	clutch
EAK	Peugeot 206 WRC	DG	accident

FIN	Peugeot 206 WRC	DG	suspension
NZ	Peugeot 206 WRC	DG	6
I	Peugeot 206 WRC	DG	3
F	Peugeot 206 WRC	DG	3
AUS	Peugeot 206 WRC	DG	3
GB	Peugeot 206 WRC	DG	7

7th World Championship for Drivers

2002

MC	Toyota Corolla WRC	JB	engine

2003

MC	Skoda Octavia WRC	DG	9
S	Skoda Octavia WRC	DG	18
TR	Skoda Octavia WRC	DG	engine
NZ	Skoda Octavia WRC	DG	8
RA	Skoda Octavia WRC	DG	6
GR	Skoda Octavia WRC	DG	9
CY	Skoda Octavia WRC	DG	electrical
D	Skoda Fabia WRC	DG	cambelt
FIN	Skoda Fabia WRC	DG	withdrawn
AUS	Skoda Fabia WRC	DG	12
I	Skoda Fabia WRC	DG	12
F	Skoda Fabia WRC	DG	electrical
E	Skoda Fabia WRC	DG	clutch
GB	Skoda Fabia WRC	DG	11

Richard Burns (GB)

Born 17/01/1971 at Reading
First rally car Talbot Sunbeam in 1988
WG = Wayne Coble
RR = Robert Reid

1990

GB	Peugeot 309 GTI	WG	28/3rd GpN

1991

GB	Peugeot 309 GTI	RR	16/2nd F2

1992

GB	Peugeot 309 GTI	RR	lost wheel

1993

GB	Subaru Leg. 4WD Turbo	RR	7

1994

EAK	Subaru Impreza WRX-RA	RR	5/2nd GpN
NZ	Subaru Impreza 555	RR	accident
AUS²	Subaru Impreza 555	RR	5
GB	Subaru Impreza 555	RR	suspension

1995

P	Subaru Impreza 555	RR	7
EAK²	Subaru Impreza WRX-RA	RR	accident
NZ	Subaru Impreza 555	RR	engine
GB	Subaru Impreza 555	RR	3

9th World Championship for Drivers

1996

RI	Mit. Lancer Ev. III	RR	engine
RA	Mit. Lancer Ev. III	RR	4
NZ²	Mit. Lancer Ev. III	RR	1
AUS	Mit. Lancer Ev. III	RR	5
E	Mit. Lancer Ev. III	RR	accident

9th World Championship for Drivers

1997

EAK	Mit. Carisma GT	RR	2
P	Mit. Carisma GT	RR	gearbox
RA	Mit. Carisma GT	RR	rear suspension
GR	Mit. Carisma GT	RR	4
NZ	Mit. Carisma GT	RR	4
RI	Mit. Carisma GT	RR	4
AUS	Mit. Carisma GT	RR	4
GB	Mit. Carisma GT	RR	4

7th World Championship for Drivers

1998

MC	Mit. Carisma GT	RR	5
S	Mit. Carisma GT	RR	15
EAK	Mit. Carisma GT	RR	1
P	Mit. Carisma GT	RR	4
E	Mit. Carisma GT	RR	4
F	Mit. Carisma GT	RR	acc. damage
RA	Mit. Carisma GT	RR	4
GR	Mit. Carisma GT	RR	rear suspension
NZ	Mit. Carisma GT	RR	9
FIN	Mit. Carisma GT	RR	5
I	Mit. Carisma GT	RR	7
AUS	Mit. Carisma GT	RR	engine
GB	Mit. Carisma GT	RR	1

6th World Championship for Drivers

1999

MC	Subaru Impreza WRC	RR	8
S	Subaru Impreza WRC	RR	5
EAK	Subaru Impreza WRC	RR	front suspension
P	Subaru Impreza WRC	RR	4
E	Subaru Impreza WRC	RR	5
F	Subaru Impreza WRC	RR	7
RA	Subaru Impreza WRC	RR	2
GR	Subaru Impreza WRC	RR	1
NZ	Subaru Impreza WRC	RR	transmission
FIN	Subaru Impreza WRC	RR	2
CN	Subaru Impreza WRC	RR	2
I	Subaru Impreza WRC	RR	gearbox
AUS	Subaru Impreza WRC	RR	1
GB	Subaru Impreza WRC	RR	1

2nd World Championship for Drivers

2000

MC	Subaru Impreza WRC	RR	unable restart
S	Subaru Impreza WRC	RR	5
EAK	Subaru Impreza WRC	RR	1
P	Subaru Impreza WRC	RR	1
E	Subaru Impreza WRC	RR	2
RA	Subaru Impreza WRC	RR	1
GR	Subaru Impreza WRC	RR	turbo
NZ	Subaru Impreza WRC	RR	flywheel
FIN	Subaru Impreza WRC	RR	accident
CY	Subaru Impreza WRC	RR	4
F	Subaru Impreza WRC	RR	4
I	Subaru Impreza WRC	RR	engine
AUS	Subaru Impreza WRC	RR	2
GB	Subaru Impreza WRC	RR	1

2nd World Championship for Drivers

2001

MC	Subaru Impreza WRC	RR	withdrawn
S	Subaru Impreza WRC	RR	16
P	Subaru Impreza WRC	RR	4
E	Subaru Impreza WRC	RR	7
RA	Subaru Impreza WRC	RR	2
CY	Subaru Impreza WRC	RR	2
GR	Subaru Impreza WRC	RR	propshaft
EAK	Subaru Impreza WRC	RR	suspension
FIN	Subaru Impreza WRC	RR	2
NZ	Subaru Impreza WRC	RR	1
I	Subaru Impreza WRC	RR	accident
F	Subaru Impreza WRC	RR	4
AUS	Subaru Impreza WRC	RR	2
GB	Subaru Impreza WRC	RR	3

World Champion

2002

MC	Peugeot 206 WRC	RR	8
S	Peugeot 206 WRC	RR	4
F	Peugeot 206 WRC	RR	3
E	Peugeot 206 WRC	RR	2
CY	Peugeot 206 WRC	RR	2
RA	Peugeot 206 WRC	RR	excluded
GR	Peugeot 206 WRC	RR	suspension
EAK	Peugeot 206 WRC	RR	accident
FIN	Peugeot 206 WRC	RR	2
D	Peugeot 206 WRC	RR	2
I	Peugeot 206 WRC	RR	4
NZ	Peugeot 206 WRC	RR	accident
AUS	Peugeot 206 WRC	RR	clutch
GB	Peugeot 206 WRC	RR	accident

5th World Championship for Drivers

2003

MC	Peugeot 206 WRC	RR	5
S	Peugeot 206 WRC	RR	3
TR	Peugeot 206 WRC	RR	2
NZ	Peugeot 206 WRC	RR	2
RA	Peugeot 206 WRC	RR	3
GR	Peugeot 206 WRC	RR	4
CY	Peugeot 206 WRC	RR	engine
D	Peugeot 206 WRC	RR	3
FIN	Peugeot 206 WRC #100	RR	3
AUS	Peugeot 206 WRC	RR	3
I	Peugeot 206 WRC	RR	7
F	Peugeot 206 WRC	RR	8
E	Peugeot 206 WRC	RR	accident

4th World Championship for Drivers

Daniel Carlsson (S)

Born 29/06/1976 at Saffle
First rally car Volvo 240 in 1996
KS = Kent-Ake Stenback
BM = Benny Melander
PK = Per Karlsson
MA = Mattias Andersson

1999

S	Opel Astra GSi	KS	40
FIN	Mit. Lancer Evo.	KS	suspension

2000

S	Toyota Corolla WRC	BM	23

2001

S	Toyota Corolla WRC	BM	7
P	Toyota Corolla WRC	BM	suspension
FIN	Toyota Corolla WRC	BM	alternator
I	Toyota Corolla WRC	BM	accident

2002

MC	Ford Puma S1600	PK	20/4th JWRC
S	Mit. Lancer Evo.	MA	20/1st GpN
E	Ford Puma S1600	MA	engine
GR	Ford Puma S1600	MA	oil pressure
D	Ford Puma S1600	MA	engine
I	Ford Puma S1600	MA	lost wheel
GB	Ford Puma S1600	MA	oil leak

2003

MC	Suzuki Ignis S1600	MA	too late
TR	Suzuki Ignis S1600	MA	suspension
GR	Suzuki Ignis S1600	MA	18/2nd JWRC
FIN	Suzuki Ignis S1600	MA	19/1st JWRC
I	Suzuki Ignis S1600	MA	accident
E	Suzuki Ignis S1600	MA	22/4th JWRC
GB	Suzuki Ignis S1600	MA	14/1st JWRC

3rd Junior WRC

Francois Duval (B)

Born 18/11/1980 at Chimay
First rally car Citroen Saxo VTS in 1999
JF = Jean-Marc Fortin
SP = Stephane Prevot

2001

P	Mit. Lancer Evo.	JF	turbo
E	Ford Puma S1600	JF	accident
CY	Mit. Lancer Evo.	JF	engine
GR	Ford Puma S1600	JF	suspension
FIN	Ford Puma S1600	JF	alternator belt
I	Ford Puma S1600	JF	18/2nd S1600
F	Ford Puma S1600	JF	water pump
AUS	Mit. Lancer Evo.	JF	19/3rd GpN
GB	Ford Puma S1600	JF	accident

2002

MC	Ford Puma S1600	JF	17/1st JWRC
S	Ford Focus RS WRC	JF	10
F	Ford Focus WRC	JF	accident
E	Ford Puma S1600	JF	25/6th JWRC
CY	Ford Focus WRC	JF	engine
GR	Ford Puma S1600	JF	accident
FIN	Ford Focus WRC	JF	accident
D	Ford Puma S1600	JF	engine
I	Ford Puma S1600	JF	20/6th JWRC
AUS	Ford Focus WRC	JF	accident
GB	Ford Puma S1600	JF	gearbox

2003

MC	Ford Focus RS WRC	JF	7
S	Ford Focus RS WRC	JF	accident
TR	Ford Focus RS WRC	SP	3
NZ	Ford Focus RS WRC	SP	9
RA	Ford Focus RS WRC	SP	8
GR	Ford Focus RS WRC	SP	accident
CY	Ford Focus RS WRC	SP	engine
D	Ford Focus RS WRC	SP	7
FIN	Ford Focus RS WRC	SP	accident
AUS	Ford Focus RS WRC	SP	10
I	Ford Focus RS WRC	SP	5
F	Ford Focus RS WRC	SP	3
E	Ford Focus RS WRC	SP	4
GB	Ford Focus RS WRC	SP	5

9th World Championship for Drivers

Gianluigi Galli (I)

Born 13/01/1973 at Milan
First rally car Peugeot 309 in 1994
DA = Guido d'Amore
NA = Nicola Arena
FZ = Flavio Zanelli
MM = Maurizio Messina
GB = Giovanni Bernacchini
RP = Rudy Pollet

Gianluigi Galli

1998

I	Mit. Carisma GT	GD	19

1999

S	Mit. Carisma GT	GD	23
P	Mit. Carisma GT	GD	accident
E	Mit. Carisma GT	GD	punctures
F	Mit. Carisma GT	GD	suspension
FIN	Mit. Lancer Evo.	GD	25
I	Mit. Carisma GT	GD	22

2000

MC	Mit. Lancer Evo.	GD	12
S	Mit. Lancer Evo.	GD	26
P	Mit. Lancer Evo.	NA	accident
FIN	Mit. Lancer Evo.	FZ	27
F	Mit. Lancer Evo.	FZ	accident
I	Mit. Lancer Evo.	MM	22

2001

MC	Mit. Lancer Evo.	GB	transmission
FIN	Mit. Lancer Evo.	RP	accident

2002

MC	Fiat Punto S1600	GD	accident
E	Fiat Punto S1600	GD	23/4th JWRC
GR	Fiat Punto S1600	GD	power steering
D	Fiat Punto S1600	GD	withdrawn
I	Fiat Punto S1600	GD	9/5th JWRC

2003

S	Mit. Lancer Evo.	GD	22
FIN	Mit. Lancer Evo.	GD	21
F	Mit. Lancer Evo.	GD	accident

Toni Gardemeister (FIN)

Born 31/03/1975 at Kouvola
First rally car Opel Ascona in 1993
PL = Paavo Lukander

1996

FIN	Opel Astra	PL	retired
GB[2]	Nissan Sunny GTI	PL	16/7th W2L

1997

S	Nissan Sunny GTI	PL	engine
FIN	Nissan Sunny GTI	PL	12

1998

S	Nissan Sunny GTI	PL	21
NZ	SEAT Ibiza KC	PL	15
FIN	SEAT Ibiza KC	PL	14
I	SEAT Ibiza KC	PL	clutch
AUS	SEAT Ibiza KC	PL	transmission
GB	SEAT Ibiza KC	PL	16/2nd W2L

1999

MC	SEAT Ibiza KC	PL	14/1st F2
S	SEAT Ibiza KC	PL	33/5th F2
P	SEAT Ibiza KC	PL	transmission
NZ	SEAT Cordoba WRC	PL	3
FIN	SEAT Cordoba WRC	PL	6
I	SEAT Cordoba WRC	PL	engine
AUS	SEAT Cordoba WRC	PL	16
GB	SEAT Cordoba WRC	PL	clutch

2000

MC	SEAT Cordoba WRC	PL	4
S	SEAT Cordoba WRC	PL	engine
EAK	SEAT Cordoba WRC	PL	codriver ill
P	SEAT Cordoba WRC	PL	9
E	SEAT Cordoba WRC	PL	accident
RA	SEAT Cordoba WRC	PL	clutch
GR	SEAT Cordoba WRC	PL	steering
NZ	SEAT Cordoba WRC	PL	accident
FIN	SEAT Cordoba WRC	PL	fuel
CY	SEAT Cordoba WRC	PL	accident
F	SEAT Cordoba WRC	PL	11
I	SEAT Cordoba WRC	PL	turbocharger
AUS	SEAT Cordoba WRC	PL	6
GB	SEAT Cordoba WRC	PL	12

2001

MC	Peugeot 206 WRC	PL	5
S	Peugeot 206 WRC	PL	4
FIN	Mit. Carisma GT	PL	accident
NZ	Mit. Carisma GT	PL	15

2002

MC	Skoda Octavia WRC	PL	10
S	Skoda Octavia WRC	PL	accident
F	Skoda Octavia WRC	PL	12
E	Skoda Octavia WRC	PL	11
CY	Skoda Octavia WRC	PL	15
RA	Skoda Octavia WRC	PL	5
GR	Skoda Octavia WRC	PL	10
EAK	Skoda Octavia WRC	PL	suspension
FIN	Skoda Octavia WRC	PL	12
D	Skoda Octavia WRC	PL	accident
I	Skoda Octavia WRC	PL	accident
NZ	Skoda Octavia WRC	PL	8
AUS	Skoda Octavia WRC	PL	6
GB	Skoda Octavia WRC	PL	10

2003

MC	Skoda Octavia WRC	PL	injector
S	Skoda Octavia WRC	PL	8
TR	Skoda Octavia WRC	PL	7
NZ	Skoda Octavia WRC	PL	5
RA	Skoda Octavia WRC	PL	7
GR	Skoda Octavia WRC	PL	engine
CY	Skoda Octavia WRC	PL	engine
D	Skoda Fabia WRC	PL	gearbox
FIN	Skoda Fabia WRC	PL	engine
AUS	Skoda Fabia WRC	PL	11
I	Skoda Fabia WRC	PL	accident
F	Skoda Fabia WRC	PL	11
E	Skoda Fabia WRC	PL	12
GB	Skoda Fabia WRC	PL	accident

Toni Gardemeister

WORLD CLASS DRIVERS

Marcus Gronholm (FIN)

Born 5/02/1968 at Espoo
First rally car Ford Escort 1300 in 1987
IR = Ilkka Riipinen
TR = Timo Rautiainen
JR = Juha Repo
VS = Voitto Silander

1989
FIN	Lancia HF Integrale	IR	23

1990
FIN	Toyota Celica GT-4	TR	accident

1991
FIN	Toyota Celica GT-4	JR	13

1992
S	Toyota Celica GT-4	IR	accident
FIN	Toyota Celica Turbo 4WD	IR	withdrawn

1993
FIN	Toyota Celica Turbo 4WD	VS	10

1994
S²	Toyota Celica Turbo 4WD	VS	accident
FIN	Toyota Celica Turbo 4WD	VS	5

1995
S	Toyota Celica Turbo 4WD	VS	gearbox
P	Toyota Celica Turbo 4WD	VS	accident
NZ	Toyota Celica Turbo 4WD	TR	engine
FIN²	Toyota Celica Turbo 4WD	TR	2

1996
S	Toyota Celica Turbo 4WD	TR	7
FIN	Toyota Celica GT-4	TR	4

1997
S	Toyota Celica GT-4	TR	8
P	Toyota Celica GT-4	TR	accident
RA	Toyota Celica GT-4	TR	4
FIN	Toyota Corolla WRC	TR	fuel pressure
GB	Toyota Corolla WRC	TR	5

1998
S	Toyota Celica GT-4	TR	5
P	Toyota Corolla WRC	TR	suspension
E	Toyota Corolla WRC	TR	accident
NZ	Toyota Corolla WRC	TR	engine
FIN	Toyota Corolla WRC	TR	7
GB	Toyota Corolla WRC	TR	engine

1999
S	SEAT WRC	TR	engine
P	Mit. Carisma GT	TR	clutch
GR	Peugeot 206 WRC	TR	clutch
FIN	Peugeot 206 WRC	TR	4
I	Peugeot 206 WRC	TR	8
AUS	Peugeot 206 WRC	TR	5
GB	Peugeot 206 WRC	TR	accident

2000
MC	Peugeot 206 WRC	TR	unable restart
S	Peugeot 206 WRC	TR	1
EAK	Peugeot 206 WRC	TR	clutch
P	Peugeot 206 WRC	TR	2
E	Peugeot 206 WRC	TR	5
RA	Peugeot 206 WRC	TR	2
GR	Peugeot 206 WRC	TR	turbo
NZ	Peugeot 206 WRC	TR	1
FIN	Peugeot 206 WRC	TR	1
CY	Peugeot 206 WRC	TR	electrics
F	Peugeot 206 WRC	TR	5
I	Peugeot 206 WRC	TR	4
AUS	Peugeot 206 WRC	TR	1
GB	Peugeot 206 WRC	TH	2

World Champion

2001
MC	Peugeot 206 WRC	TR	water pump
S	Peugeot 206 WRC	TR	engine
P	Peugeot 206 WRC	TR	3
E	Peugeot 206 WRC	TR	accident
RA	Peugeot 206 WRC	TR	accident
CY	Peugeot 206 WRC	TR	engine
GR	Peugeot 206 WRC	TR	sump
EAK	Peugeot 206 WRC	TR	steering
FIN	Peugeot 206 WRC	TR	1
NZ	Peugeot 206 WRC	TR	5
I	Peugeot 206 WRC	TR	7
F	Peugeot 206 WRC	TR	lost wheel
AUS	Peugeot 206 WRC	TR	1
GB	Peugeot 206 WRC	TR	1

4th World Championship for Drivers

2002
MC	Peugeot 206 WRC	TR	5
S	Peugeot 206 WRC	TR	1
F	Peugeot 206 WRC	TR	2
E	Peugeot 206 WRC	TR	4
CY	Peugeot 206 WRC	TR	1
RA	Peugeot 206 WRC	TR	excluded
GR	Peugeot 206 WRC	TR	2
EAK	Peugeot 206 WRC	TR	engine
FIN	Peugeot 206 WRC	TR	1
D	Peugeot 206 WRC	TR	3
I	Peugeot 206 WRC	TR	2
NZ	Peugeot 206 WRC	TR	1
AUS	Peugeot 206 WRC	TR	1
GB	Peugeot 206 WRC	TR	accident

World Champion

2003
MC	Peugeot 206 WRC	TR	13
S	Peugeot 206 WRC	TR	1
TR	Peugeot 206 WRC	TR	9
NZ	Peugeot 206 WRC	TR	1
RA	Peugeot 206 WRC	TR	1
GR	Peugeot 206 WRC	TR	fuel feed
CY	Peugeot 206 WRC	TR	clutch
D	Peugeot 206 WRC	TR	2
FIN	Peugeot 206 WRC	TR	wheel bearing
AUS	Peugeot 206 WRC	TR	withdrawn
I	Peugeot 206 WRC	TR	accident
F	Peugeot 206 WRC	TR	4
E	Peugeot 206 WRC	TR	6
GB	Peugeot 206 WRC	TR	suspension

6th World Championship for Drivers

Mikko Hirvonen

Mikko Hirvonen (FIN)

Born 31 July 1980 at Jyvaskyla
First rally car Opel Kadett in 1998
MA = Miikka Antilla
JL = Jarmo Lehtinen

2002
FIN	Renault Clio	MA	21st/1st in class
I	Renault Clio	MA	rear axle
GB	Subaru Impreza WRC	JL	engine

2003
MC	Ford Focus RS WRC	JL	accident
S	Ford Focus RS WRC	JL	11
TR	Ford Focus RS WRC	JL	steering
NZ	Ford Focus RS WRC	JL	10
RA	Ford Focus RS WRC	JL	16
GR	Ford Focus RS WRC	JL	suspension
CY	Ford Focus RS WRC	JL	6
D	Ford Focus RS WRC	JL	13
FIN	Ford Focus RS WRC	JL	fire damage
AUS	Ford Focus RS WRC	JL	9
I	Ford Focus RS WRC	JL	camshaft belt
F	Ford Focus RS WRC	JL	10
E	Ford Focus RS WRC	JL	14
GB	Ford Focus RS WRC	JL	accident

Roman Kresta (CZ)

Born 24/04/1976 at Zlin
First rally car Skoda Favorit in 1994
JT = Jan Tomanek
MII – Milos Hulka

2001
GR	Ford Focus WRC	JT	brakes
EAK	Skoda Octavia WRC	JT	suspension
I	Skoda Octavia WRC	JT	engine
GB	Skoda Octavia WRC	JT	accident

2002
MC	Skoda Octavia WRC	JT	accident
F	Skoda Octavia WRC	JT	14
CY	Skoda Octavia WRC	JT	accident
EAK	Skoda Octavia WRC	JT	7
I	Skoda Octavia WRC	JT	12
GB	Skoda Octavia WRC	MH	15

2003
MC	Peugeot 206 WRC	MH	10
S	Peugeot 206 WRC	MH	13
GR	Peugeot 206 WRC	MH	water loss
D	Peugeot 206 WRC	JT	hub
I	Peugeot 206 WRC	JT	11
E	Peugeot 206 WRC	JT	13
GB	Peugeot 206 WRC	JT	8

Sebastien Loeb (F)

Born 26/02/1974 at Haguenau
First rally car Peugeot 106 in 1995
DE = Daniel Elena

1999

F	Citroen Saxo KC	DE	19
E	Citroen Saxo KC	DE	accident
I	Citroen Saxo KC	DE	21

2000

FIN	Citroen Saxo VTS	DE	flywheel
F	Toyota Corolla WRC	DE	9
I	Toyota Corolla WRC	DE	10
GB	Citroen Saxo VTS	DE	38

2001

MC	Citroen Saxo S1600	DE	15/1st S1600
S	Citroen Saxo VTS	DE	engine
E	Citroen Saxo S1600	DE	15/1st S1600
GR	Citroen Saxo S1600	DE	19/1st S1600
FIN	Citroen Saxo S1600	DE	28/1st S1600
I	Citroen Xsara WRC	DE	2
F	Citroen Saxo S1600	DE	13/1st S1600
GB	Citroen Saxo S1600	DE	15/1st S1600

Super 1600 Champion

2002

MC	Citroen Xsara WRC	DE	2
S	Citroen Xsara WRC	DE	17
E	Citroen Xsara WRC	DE	accident damage
GR	Citroen Xsara WRC	DE	7
EAK	Citroen Xsara WRC	DE	5
FIN	Citroen Xsara WRC	DE	10
D	Citroen Xsara WRC	DE	1
AUS	Citroen Xsara WRC	DE	7
GB	Citroen Xsara WRC	DE	suspension

10th World Championship for Drivers

2003

MC	Citroen Xsara WRC	DE	1
S	Citroen Xsara WRC	DE	7
TR	Citroen Xsara WRC	DE	no fuel
NZ	Citroen Xsara WRC	DE	4
RA	Citroen Xsara WRC	DE	accident
GR	Citroen Xsara WRC	DE	engine
CY	Citroen Xsara WRC	DE	3
D	Citroen Xsara WRC	DE	1
FIN	Citroen Xsara WRC	DE	5
AUS	Citroen Xsara WRC	DE	2
I	Citroen Xsara WRC	DE	1
F	Citroen Xsara WRC	DE	13
E	Citroen Xsara WRC	DE	2
GB	Citroen Xsara WRC	DE	2

2nd World Championship for Drivers

Freddy Loix (B)

Born 10/11/1970 at Tongeren
First rally car Lancia HF Integrale in 1989
JV = Johnny Vranken
AM = Andre Malais
SS = Sven Smeets

1993

I	Opel Astra GSi	JV	9/3rd F2

1994

FIN	Opel Astra GSi	AM	21/5th F2
I	Opel Astra GSi	AM	14/3rd F2
E[2]	Opel Astra GSi	JV	accident

1995

P	Opel Astra GSi	SS	transmission
F	Opel Astra GSi	SS	14/5th W2L
GR[2]	Opel Astra GSi	SS	9/5th W2L
I[2]	Opel Astra GSi	SS	8/1st W2L

1996

P[2]	Toyota Celica GT-4	SS	2
GR	Toyota Celica GT-4	SS	7
I	Toyota Celica GT-4	SS	4
E	Toyota Celica GT-4	SS	4

8th World Championship for Drivers

1997

MC	Toyota Celica GT-4	SS	16
P	Toyota Celica GT-4	SS	2
GR	Toyota Celica GT-4	SS	accident
FIN	Toyota Celica GT-4	SS	37
I	Toyota Corolla WRC	SS	5
AUS	Toyota Celica GT-4	SS	7

9th World Championship for Drivers

1998

P	Toyota Corolla WRC	SS	3
E	Toyota Corolla WRC	SS	2
GR	Toyota Corolla WRC	SS	5
AUS	Toyota Corolla WRC	SS	6

8th World Championship for Drivers

1999

MC	Mit. Carisma GT	SS	accident
S	Mit. Carisma GT	SS	9
EAK	Mit. Carisma GT	SS	accident
E	Mit. Carisma GT	SS	4
F	Mit. Carisma GT	SS	8
RA	Mit. Carisma GT	SS	lost wheel
GR	Mit. Carisma GT	SS	4
NZ	Mit. Carisma GT	SS	8
FIN	Mit. Carisma GT	SS	10
CN	Mit. Carisma GT	SS	accident
I	Mit. Carisma GT	SS	4
AUS	Mit. Carisma GT	SS	4
GB	Mit. Carisma GT	SS	5

8th World Championship for Drivers

2000

MC	Mit. Carisma GT	SS	6
S	Mit. Carisma GT	SS	8
EAK	Mit. Carisma GT	SS	engine
P	Mit. Carisma GT	SS	6
E	Mit. Carisma GT	SS	8
RA	Mit. Carisma GT	SS	5
GR	Mit. Carisma GT	SS	suspension
NZ	Mit. Carisma GT	SS	withdrawn
FIN	Mit. Carisma GT	SS	radiator
CY	Mit. Carisma GT	SS	8
F	Mit. Carisma GT	SS	accident
I	Mit. Carisma GT	SS	8
AUS	Mit. Carisma GT	SS	transmission
GB	Mit. Carisma GT	SS	accident

2001

MC	Mit. Carisma GT	SS	6
S	Mit. Carisma GT	SS	13
P	Mit. Carisma GT	SS	transmission
E	Mit. Carisma GT	SS	4
RA	Mit. Carisma GT	SS	6
CY	Mit. Carisma GT	SS	5
GR	Mit. Carisma GT	SS	9
FAK	Mit. Carisma GT	SS	5
FIN	Mit. Carisma GT	SS	10
NZ	Mit. Carisma GT	SS	11
I	Mit. Lancer Evo. WRC	SS	12
F	Mit. Lancer Evo. WRC	SS	12
AUS	Mit. Lancer Evo. WRC	SS	11
GB	Mit. Lancer Evo. WRC	SS	transmission

2002

MC	Hyundai Accent WRC	SS	accident
S	Hyundai Accent WRC	SS	suspension
F	Hyundai Accent WRC	SS	9
E	Hyundai Accent WRC	SS	10
CY	Hyundai Accent WRC	SS	transmission
RA	Hyundai Accent WRC	SS	electrical
GR	Hyundai Accent WRC	SS	engine
EAK	Hyundai Accent WRC	SS	clutch
FIN	Hyundai Accent WRC	SS	9
D	Hyundai Accent WRC	SS	engine
I	Hyundai Accent WRC	SS	28
NZ	Hyundai Accent WRC	SS	6
AUS	Hyundai Accent WRC	SS	accident
GB	Hyundai Accent WRC	SS	8

2003

MC	Hyundai Accent WRC	SS	accident
S	Hyundai Accent WRC	SS	10
TR	Hyundai Accent WRC	SS	10
NZ	Hyundai Accent WRC	SS	accident
RA	Hyundai Accent WRC	SS	withdrawn
GR	Hyundai Accent WRC	SS	suspension
CY	Hyundai Accent WRC	SS	engine
D	Hyundai Accent WRC	SS	11
FIN	Hyundai Accent WRC	SS	10
AUS	Hyundai Accent WRC	SS	8
GB	Peugeot 206 WRC	SS	6

Tommi Makinen (FIN)

Born 26/06/1964 at Puuppola
First rally car Ford Escort RS2000 in 1985
JN = Jari Nieminen
RM = Risto Mannisenmaki
RS = Rodney Spokes
TH = Timo Hantunen
SH = Seppo Harjanne
JR = Juha Repo
KL = Kaj Lindstrom

Tommi Makinen (FIN)

1987

FIN	Lancia D. HF 4WD	JN	accident

1988

FIN	Lancia D. HF 4WD	RM	front susp'n
GB	Lancia D. Integrale	RS	no fuel

1989

S	Lancia D. Integrale	TH	transmission
FIN	Lancia D. Integrale	TH	central diff.

1990

NZ	Mit.Galant VR-4	SH	6/1st GpN
FIN	Mit.Galant VR-4	SH	11/1st GpN
AUS	Mit.Galant VR-4	SH	7/1st GpN
I	Mit.Galant VR-4	SH	13/3rd GpN
GB	Mit.Galant VR-4	SH	gearbox

3rd Group N Cup

1991

S	Ford Sierra Cos.4x4	SH	13/2nd GpN
P	Ford Sierra Cos.4x4	SH	gearbox
NZ	Mit. Galant VR-4	SH	head gasket
FIN	Mazda 323 GTX	SH	5
GB	Mazda 323 GTX	SH	gearbox

1992

MC	Nissan Pulsar GTI-R	SH	9
P	Nissan Pulsar GTI-R	SH	accident
FIN	Nissan Pulsar GTI-R	SH	gearbox
GB	Nissan Pulsar GTI-R	SH	8

1993

S	Lancia HF Integrale	SH	4
GR	Lancia HF Integrale	SH	6
FIN	Lancia HF Integrale	SH	4

10th World Championship for Drivers

1994

S[2]	Nissan Sunny GTI	SH	transmission
P	Nissan Sunny GTI	SH	engine
FIN	Ford Escort RS Cos.	SH	1
I	Mit. Lancer Evo. II	SH	suspension
E[2]	Nissan Sunny GTI	SH	gearbox
GB	Nissan Sunny GTI	SH	9

10th World Championship for Drivers

1995

MC	Mit. Lancer Evo. II	SH	4
S	Mit. Lancer Evo. II	SH	2
F	Mit. Lancer Evo. III	SH	8
NZ	Mit. Lancer Evo. III	SH	accident
FIN[2]	Mit. Lancer Evo. III	SH	1
AUS	Mit. Lancer Evo. III	SH	4
E	Mit. Lancer Evo. III	SH	accident
GB	Mit. Lancer Evo. III	SH	transmission

5th World Championship for Drivers

1996

S	Mit. Lancer Evo. III	SH	1
EAK	Mit. Lancer Evo. III	SH	1
RI	Mit. Lancer Evo. III	SH	engine
GR	Mit. Lancer Evo. III	SH	2
RA	Mit. Lancer Evo. III	SH	1
NZ[2]	Mit. Lancer Evo. III	SH	accident
FIN	Mit. Lancer Evo. III	SH	1
AUS	Mit. Lancer Evo. III	SH	1
I	Mit. Lancer Evo. III	SH	accident
E	Mit. Lancer Evo. III	JR	5

World Champion

1997

MC	Mit. Lancer Evo. IV	SH	3
S	Mit. Lancer Evo. IV	SH	3
EAK	Mit. Lancer Evo. IV	SH	front diff'l
P	Mit. Lancer Evo. IV	SH	1
E	Mit. Lancer Evo. IV	SH	1
F	Mit. Lancer Evo. IV	SH	accident
RA	Mit. Lancer Evo. IV	SH	1
GR	Mit. Lancer Evo. IV	SH	3
NZ	Mit. Lancer Evo. IV	SH	accident
FIN	Mit. Lancer Evo. IV	SH	1
RI	Mit. Lancer Evo. IV	SH	engine
I	Mit. Lancer Evo. IV	SH	3
AUS	Mit. Lancer Evo. IV	SH	2
GB	Mit. Lancer Evo. IV	SH	6

World Champion

1998

MC	Mit. Lancer Evo.IV	RM	accident
S	Mit. Lancer Evo.IV	RM	1
EAK	Mit. Lancer Evo.IV	RM	engine
P	Mit. Lancer Evo.IV	RM	suspension
E	Mit. Lancer Evo.V	RM	3
F	Mit. Lancer Evo.V	RM	electrics
RA	Mit. Lancer Evo.V	RM	1
GR	Mit. Lancer Evo.V	RM	withdrawn
NZ	Mit. Lancer Evo.V	RM	3
FIN	Mit. Lancer Evo.V	RM	1
I	Mit. Lancer Evo.V	RM	1
AUS	Mit. Lancer Evo.V	RM	1
GB	Mit. Lancer Evo.V	RM	lost wheel

World Champion

1999

MC	Mit. Lancer Evo.	RM	1
S	Mit. Lancer Evo.	RM	1
EAK	Mit. Lancer Evo.	RM	excluded
P	Mit. Lancer Evo.	RM	5
E	Mit. Lancer Evo.	RM	3
F	Mit. Lancer Evo.	RM	6
RA	Mit. Lancer Evo.	RM	4
GR	Mit. Lancer Evo.	RM	3
NZ	Mit. Lancer Evo.	RM	1
FIN	Mit. Lancer Evo.	RM	clutch
CN	Mit. Lancer Evo.	RM	suspension
I	Mit. Lancer Evo.	RM	1
AUS	Mit. Lancer Evo.	RM	3
GB	Mit. Lancer Evo.	RM	engine

World Champion

2000

MC	Mit. Lancer Evo.	RM	1
S	Mit. Lancer Evo.	RM	2
EAK	Mit. Lancer Evo.	RM	electrics
P	Mit. Lancer Evo.	RM	steering
E	Mit. Lancer Evo.	RM	4
RA	Mit. Lancer Evo.	RM	3
GR	Mit. Lancer Evo.	RM	suspension
NZ	Mit. Lancer Evo.	RM	accident
FIN	Mit. Lancer Evo.	RM	4
CY	Mit. Lancer Evo.	RM	5
F	Mit. Lancer Evo.	RM	accident
I	Mit. Lancer Evo.	RM	3
AUS	Mit. Lancer Evo.	RM	excluded
GB	Mit. Lancer Evo.	RM	3

5th World Championship for Drivers

2001

MC	Mit. Lancer Evo.	RM	1
S	Mit. Lancer Evo.	RM	accident
P	Mit. Lancer Evo. #100	RM	1
E	Mit. Lancer Evo.	RM	3
RA	Mit. Lancer Evo.	RM	4
CY	Mit. Lancer Evo.	RM	accident
GR	Mit. Lancer Evo.	RM	4
EAK	Mit. Lancer Evo.	RM	1
FIN	Mit. Lancer Evo.	RM	accident
NZ	Mit. Lancer Evo.	RM	8
I	Mit. Lancer Evo. WRC	RM	accident
F	Mit. Lancer Evo. WRC	RM	accident
AUS	Mit. Lancer Evo. WRC	TH	6
GB	Mit. Lancer Evo. WRC	KL	suspension

3rd World Championship for Drivers

2002

MC	Subaru Impreza WRC	KL	1
S	Subaru Impreza WRC	KL	engine
F	Subaru Impreza WRC	KL	accident
E	Subaru Impreza WRC	KL	engine
CY	Subaru Impreza WRC	KL	3
RA	Subaru Impreza WRC	KL	accident
GR	Subaru Impreza WRC	KL	lost wheel
EAK	Subaru Impreza WRC	KL	suspension
FIN	Subaru Impreza WRC	KL	6
D	Subaru Impreza WRC	KL	7
I	Subaru Impreza WRC	KL	transmission
NZ	Subaru Impreza WRC	KL	3
AUS	Subaru Impreza WRC	KL	excluded
GB	Subaru Impreza WRC	KL	4

8th World Championship for Drivers

2003

MC	Subaru Impreza WRC	KL	accident
S	Subaru Impreza WRC	KL	2
TR	Subaru Impreza WRC	KL	8
NZ	Subaru Impreza WRC	KL	7
RA	Subaru Impreza WRC	KL	withdrawn
GR	Subaru Impreza WRC	KL	5
CY	Subaru Impreza WRC	KL	withdrawn
D	Subaru Impreza WRC	KL	powersteering belt
FIN	Subaru Impreza WRC	KL	6
AUS	Subaru Impreza WRC	KL	6
I	Subaru Impreza WRC	KL	10
F	Subaru Impreza WRC	KL	7
E	Subaru Impreza WRC	KL	8
GB	Subaru Impreza WRC	KL	3

8th World Championship for Drivers

Markko Martin (EE)

Born 10/11/1975 at Tartu
First rally car Lada Samara in 1994
TK = Toomas Kitsing
MP = Michael Park

1997

FIN	Toyota Celica Turbo 4WD	TK	gearbox

1998

P	Toyota Celica GT-4	TK	fire
FIN	Toyota Celica GT-4	TK	12
I	Toyota Celica GT-4	TK	suspension
GB	Toyota Celica GT-4	TK	9

1999

S	Ford Escort WRC	TK	8
P	Ford Escort WRC	TK	transmission
GR	Toyota Corolla WRC	TK	5
FIN	Toyota Corolla WRC	TK	turbo
I	Toyota Corolla WRC	TK	suspension
GB	Toyota Corolla WRC	TK	8

2000

S	Toyota Corolla WRC	MP	9
P	Toyota Corolla WRC	MP	7
E	Toyota Corolla WRC	MP	10
GR	Toyota Corolla WRC	MP	holed sump
FIN	Toyota Corolla WRC	MP	10
CY	Toyota Corolla WRC	MP	6
I	Toyota Corolla WRC	MP	accident
AUS	Subaru Impreza WRC	MP	fire
GB	Toyota Corolla WRC	MP	7

2001

MC	Subaru Impreza WRC	MP	electronics
S	Subaru Impreza WRC	MP	12
P	Subaru Impreza WRC	MP	accident
E	Subaru Impreza WRC	MP	electronics
GR	Subaru Impreza WRC	MP	suspension
FIN	Subaru Impreza WRC	MP	5
I	Subaru Impreza WRC	MP	accident
F	Subaru Impreza WRC	MP	6
GB	Subaru Impreza WRC	MP	engine

2002

MC	Ford Focus RS WRC	MP	12
S	Ford Focus RS WRC	MP	non start
F	Ford Focus RS WRC	MP	8
E	Ford Focus RS WRC	MP	8
CY	Ford Focus RS WRC	MP	8
RA	Ford Focus RS WRC	MP	4
GR	Ford Focus RS WRC	MP	6
EAK	Ford Focus RS WRC	MP	4
FIN	Ford Focus RS WRC	MP	5
D	Ford Focus RS WRC	MP	6
I	Ford Focus RS WRC	MP	5
NZ	Ford Focus RS WRC	MP	accident
AUS	Ford Focus RS WRC	MP	5
GB	Ford Focus RS WRC	MP	2

9th World Championship for Drivers

2003

MC	Ford Focus RS WRC 02	MP	4
S	Ford Focus RS WRC 02	MP	4
TR	Ford Focus RS WRC 02	MP	6
NZ	Ford Focus RS WRC 03	MP	engine

RA	Ford Focus RS WRC 03	MP	engine
GR	Ford Focus RS WRC 03	MP	1
CY	Ford Focus RS WRC 03	MP	engine
D	Ford Focus RS WRC 03	MP	5
FIN	Ford Focus RS WRC 03	MP	1
AUS	Ford Focus RS WRC 03	MP	excluded
I	Ford Focus RS WRC 03	MP	3
F	Ford Focus RS WRC 03	MP	accident
E	Ford Focus RS WRC 03	MP	3
GB	Ford Focus RS WRC 03	MP	engine

5th World Championship for Drivers

Colin McRae (GB)

Born 5/08/1968 at Lanark
First rally car Talbot Avenger in 1986
MB = Mike Broad
DR = Derek Ringer
NG = Nicky Grist

1987

S	Vauxhall Nova	MB	36
GB	Vauxhall Nova	DR	accident

1988

GB	Peugeot 205GTI	DR	engine

1989

S	Ford Sierra XR4x4	DR	15
NZ	Ford Sierra RS Cos.	DR	5
GB	Ford Sierra RS Cos.	DR	accident

1990

GB	Ford Sierra Cos. 4x4	DR	6

1991

GB	Subaru Leg. 4WD T.	DR	accident

1992

S	Subaru Leg; 4WD T.	DR	2
GR	Subaru Leg. 4WD T.	DR	4
NZ	Subaru Leg. 4WD T.	DR	engine
FIN	Subaru Leg. 4WD T.	DR	8
GB	Subaru Leg. 4WD T.	DR	6

8th World Championship for Drivers

1993

S	Subaru Leg. 4WD T.	DR	3
P	Subaru Leg. 4WD T.	DR	7
EAK	Subaru Vivio	DR	suspension
F	Subaru Leg. 4WD T.	DR	5
GR	Subaru Leg. 4WD T.	DR	suspension
NZ	Subaru Leg. 4WD T.	DR	1
AUS	Subaru Leg. 4WD T.	DR	6
GB	Subaru Impreza 555	DR	overheating

Equal 5th World Championship for Drivers

1994

MC	Subaru Impreza 555	DR	10
P	Subaru Impreza 555	DR	fire
F	Subaru Impreza 555	DR	acc. damage
GR	Subaru Impreza 555	DR	excluded
RA	Subaru Impreza 555	DR	accident
NZ	Subaru Impreza 555	DR	1
AUS²	Subaru Impreza 555	DR	1
I	Subaru Impreza 555	DR	5
GB	Subaru Impreza 555	DR	1

4th World Championship for Drivers

1995

MC	Subaru Impreza 555	DR	accident
S	Subaru Impreza 555	DR	engine
P	Subaru Impreza 555	DR	3
F	Subaru Impreza 555	DR	5
NZ	Subaru Impreza 555	DR	1
AUS	Subaru Impreza 555	DR	2
E	Subaru Impreza 555	DR	2
GB	Subaru Impreza 555	DR	1

World Champion

1996

3	Subaru Impreza 555	DR	3
EAK	Subaru Impreza 555	DR	4
RI	Subaru Impreza 555	DR	accident
GR	Subaru Impreza 555	DR	1
RA	Subaru Impreza 555	DR	engine
FIN	Subaru Impreza 555	DR	accident
AUS	Subaru Impreza 555	DR	4
I	Subaru Impreza 555	DR	1
E	Subaru Impreza 555	DR	1

2nd World Championship for Drivers

1997

MC	Subaru Impreza WRC	NG	acc. damage
S	Subaru Impreza WRC	NG	4
EAK	Subaru Impreza WRC	NG	1
P	Subaru Impreza WRC	NG	cambelt
E	Subaru Impreza WRC	NG	4
F	Subaru Impreza WRC	NG	1
RA	Subaru Impreza WRC	NG	2
GR	Subaru Impreza WRC	NG	steering
NZ	Subaru Impreza WRC	NG	cambelt
FIN	Subaru Impreza WRC	NG	cambelt
RI	Subaru Impreza WRC	NG	acc. damage
I	Subaru Impreza WRC	NG	1
AUS	Subaru Impreza WRC	NG	1
GB	Subaru Impreza WRC	NG	1

2nd World Championship for Drivers

1998

MC	Subaru Impreza WRC	NG	3
S	Subaru Impreza WRC	NG	electrical
EAK	Subaru Impreza WRC	NG	engine
P	Subaru Impreza WRC	NG	1
E	Subaru Impreza WRC	NG	withdrawn
F	Subaru Impreza WRC	NG	1
RA	Subaru Impreza WRC	NG	5
GR	Subaru Impreza WRC	NG	1
NZ	Subaru Impreza WRC	NG	5
FIN	Subaru Impreza WRC	NG	acc. damage
I	Subaru Impreza WRC	NG	3
AUS	Subaru Impreza WRC	NG	4
GB	Subaru Impreza WRC	NG	engine

3rd World Championship for Drivers

1999

MC	Ford Focus WRC	NG	excluded
S	Ford Focus WRC	NG	engine
EAK	Ford Focus WRC	NG	1
P	Ford Focus WRC	NG	1
E	Ford Focus WRC	NG	withdrawn
F	Ford Focus WRC	NG	4
RA	Ford Focus WRC	NG	suspension
GR	Ford Focus WRC	NG	gearbox
NZ	Ford Focus WRC	NG	electrics
FIN	Ford Focus WRC	NG	engine
CN	Ford Focus WRC	NG	suspension
I	Ford Focus WRC	NG	accident
AUS	Ford Focus WRC	NG	accident
GB	Ford Focus WRC	NG	accident

6th World Championship for Drivers

2000

MC	Ford Racing Focus WRC	NG	engine
S	Ford Racing Focus WRC	NG	3
EAK	Ford Racing Focus WRC	NG	flooded
P	Ford Racing Focus WRC	NG	engine
E	Ford Racing Focus WRC	NG	1
RA	Ford Racing Focus WRC	NG	engine
GR	Ford Racing Focus WRC	NG	1
NZ	Ford Racing Focus WRC	NG	2
FIN	Ford Racing Focus WRC	NG	2
CY	Ford Racing Focus WRC	NG	2
F	Ford Racing Focus WRC	NG	accident
I	Ford Racing Focus WRC	NG	6
AUS	Ford Racing Focus WRC #100	NG	engine
GB	Ford Racing Focus WRC	NG	accident

4th World Championship for Drivers

2001

MC	Ford Focus WRC	NG	throttle
S	Ford Focus WRC	NG	9
P	Ford Focus WRC	NG	engine
E	Ford Focus WRC	NG	fuel
RA	Ford Focus WRC	NG	1
CY	Ford Focus WRC	NG	1
GR	Ford Focus WRC	NG	1
EAK	Ford Focus WRC	NG	clutch
FIN	Ford Focus WRC	NG	3
NZ	Ford Focus WRC	NG	£
I	Ford Focus WRC	NG	8
F	Ford Focus WRC	NG	11
AUS	Ford Focus WRC	NG	5
GB	Ford Focus WRC	NG	accident

2nd World Championship for Drivers

2002

MC	Ford Focus RS WRC	NG	4
S	Ford Focus RS WRC	NG	6
F	Ford Focus RS WRC	NG	accident
E	Ford Focus RS WRC	NG	6
CY	Ford Focus RS WRC	NG	6
RA	Ford Focus RS WRC	NG	3
GR	Ford Focus RS WRC	NG	1
EAK	Ford Focus RS WRC	NG	1
FIN	Ford Focus RS WRC	NG	fire
D	Ford Focus RS WRC	NG	4
I	Ford Focus RS WRC	NG	8
NZ	Ford Focus RS WRC	NG	accident
AUS	Ford Focus RS WRC	DR	water Leak
GB	Ford Focus RS WRC	DR	5

4th World Championship for Drivers

2003

MC	Citroen Xsara WRC	DR	2
S	Citroen Xsara WRC	DR	5
TR	Citroen Xsara WRC	DR	4
NZ	Citroen Xsara WRC	DR	accident damage
RA	Citroen Xsara WRC	DR	fire
GR	Citroen Xsara WRC	DR	8
CY	Citroen Xsara WRC	DR	4
D	Citroen Xsara WRC	DR	4
FIN	Citroen Xsara WRC	DR	accident
AUS	Citroen Xsara WRC	DR	4
I	Citroen Xsara WRC	DR	6
F	Citroen Xsara WRC	DR	5
E	Citroen Xsara WRC	DR	9
GB	Citroen Xsara WRC	DR	4

7th World Championship for Drivers

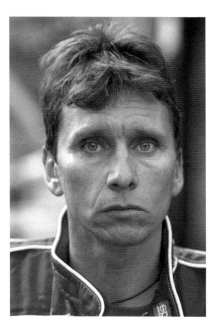

Gilles Panizzi (F)

Born 19/09/1965 at Menton
First rally car Opel Manta GT/E in 1988
HP = Herve Panizzi

Gilles Panizzi (F)

1990

MC	Lancia HF Integrale	HP	16/4th GpN

1993

F	Peugeot 106 XSi	HP	accident

1995

F	Peugeot 306 16v	HP	12/3rd W2L

1996

F²	Peugeot 306 Maxi	HP	2/2nd W2L

1997

E	Peugeot 306 Maxi	HP	3/1st W2L
F	Peugeot 306 Maxi	HP	3/1st W2L

1998

MC	Peugeot 306 Maxi	HP	9/1st W2L
E	Peugeot 306 Maxi	HP	6/1st W2L
F	Peugeot 306 Maxi	HP	4/1st 2nd W2L
FIN	Peugeot 106 Rallye	HP	35/10thGpN/5th W2L
I	Peugeot 306 Maxi	HP	5/1st W2L
GB	Subaru Impreza WRX	HP	gearbox

1999

MC	Subaru Impreza WRC	HP	accident
F	Peugeot 206 WRC	HP	fuel feed
FIN	Peugeot 206 WRC	HP	33
I	Peugeot 206 WRC	HP	2
GB	Peugeot 206 WRC	HP	7

2000

MC	Peugeot 206 WRC	HP	unable restart
EAK	Peugeot 206 WRC	HP	suspension
E	Peugeot 206 WRC	HP	6
F	Peugeoet 206 WRC	HP	1
I	Peugeot 206 WRC	HP	1
AUS	Peugeot 206 WRC	HP	transmission
GB	Peugeot 206 WRC	HP	8

7th World Championship for Drivers

2001

MC	Peugeot 206 WRC	HP	accident
P	Peugeot 206 WRC	HP	12
E	Peugeot 206 WRC	HP	2
CY	Peugeot 206 WRC	HP	punctures
GR	Peugeot 206 WRC	HP	front suspension
FIN	Peugeot 206 WRC	HP	14
I	Peugeot 206 WRC	HP	1
F	Peugeot 206 WRC	HP	2
AUS	Peugeot 206 WRC	HP	9
GB	Peugeot 206 WRC	HP	withdrawn

8th World Championship for Drivers

2002

MC	Peugeot 206 WRC	HP	7
S	Peugeot 206 WRC	HP	16
F	Peugeot 206 WRC	HP	1
E	Peugeot 206 WRC	HP	1
CY	Peugeot 206 WRC	HP	10
RA	Peugeot 206 WRC	HP	fuel
GR	Peugeot 206 WRC	HP	gearbox
EAK	Peugeot 206 WRC	HP	6
I	Peugeot 206 WRC	HP	1
NZ	Peugeot 206 WRC	HP	7
GB	Peugeot 206 WRC	HP	11

6th World Championship for Drivers

2003

MC	Peugeot 206 WRC	HP	driver ill
TR	Peugeot 206 WRC	HP	5
GR	Peugeot 206 WRC	HP	7
CY	Peugeot 206 WRC	HP	oil pressure
D	Peugeot 206 WRC	HP	10
I	Peugeot 206 WRC	HP	2
F	Peugeot 206 WRC	HP	6
E	Peugeot 206 WRC	HP	1
GB	Peugeot 206 WRC	HP	transmission

10th World Championship for Drivers

Harri Rovanpera (FIN)

Born 8/04/1966 at Jyvaskyla
First rally car Sunbeam Avenger in 1989
RP = Risto Pietilainen
JR = Juha Repo
VS = Voitto Silander

1993

FIN	Opel Manta 2.0E	RP	differential

1994

FIN	Mit. Galant VR-4	RP	12

1995

FIN²	Opel Astra GSi	RP	engine

Harri Rovanpera

1996

FIN	Ford Escort RS Cos.	JR	transmission
GB²	SEAT Ibiza KC	JR	8/4th W2L

1997

MC	SEAT Ibiza KC	VS	14/3rd W2L
P	SEAT Ibiza KC	VS	engine
E	SEAT Ibiza KC	VS	accident
RA	SEAT Ibiza KC	VS	8/1st W2L
NZ	SEAT Ibiza KC	VS	accident
FIN	SEAT Ibiza KC	VS	10/1st W2L
RI	SEAT Ibiza KC	VS	7/1st W2L
I	SEAT Ibiza KC	VS	10/1st W2L
AUS	SEAT Ibiza KC	VS	10/1st W2L
GB	SEAT Ibiza KC	VS	9/1st W2L

1998

MC	SEAT Ibiza KC	VS	11/3rd W2L
S	SEAT Ibiza KC	VS	engine
EAK	SEAT Ibiza KC	VS	5/1st W2L
P	SEAT Ibiza KC	RP	engine
E	SEAT Ibiza KC	RP	engine
RA	SEAT Ibiza KC	RP	engine
GR	SEAT Ibiza KC	RP	15/1st W2L
NZ	SEAT Ibiza KC	RP	13/1st W2L
FIN	SEAT WRC	RP	11
I	SEAT WRC	RP	accident
AUS	SEAT WRC	RP	11
GB	SEAT WRC	RP	6

1999

MC	SEAT WRC	RP	7
S	SEAT WRC	RP	16
EAK	SEAT WRC	RP	6
P	SEAT WRC	RP	accident
E	SEAT Cordoba WRC	RP	14
F	SEAT Cordoba WRC	RP	13
RA	SEAT Cordoba WRC	RP	engine
GR	SEAT Cordoba WRC	RP	accident
NZ	SEAT Cordoba WRC	RP	engine
FIN	SEAT Cordoba WRC	RP	5
CN	SEAT Cordoba WRC	RP	5
I	SEAT Cordoba WRC	RP	16
AUS	SEAT Cordoba WRC	RP	6
GB	SEAT Cordoba WRC	RP	3

2000

S	SEAT Cordoba WRC	RP	12
P	Toyota Corolla WRC	RP	4
FIN	Toyota Corolla WRC	RP	3
GB	SEAT Cordoba WRC	RP	10

9th World Championship for Drivers

2001

S	Peugeot 206 WRC	RP	1
P	Peugeot 206 WRC	RP	engine
RA	Peugeot 206 WRC	RP	suspension
CY	Peugeot 206 WRC	RP	suspension
GR	Peugeot 206 WRC	RP	3
EAK	Peugeot 206 WRC	RP	2

FIN	Peugeot 206 WRC	RP	4
NZ	Peugeot 206 WRC	RP	3
I	Peugeot 206 WRC	RP	11
F	Peugeot 206 WRC	RP	7
AUS	Peugeot 206 WRC	RP	6
GB	Peugeot 206 WRC	RP	2

5th World Championship for Drivers

2002

MC	Peugeot 206 WRC	RP	accident
S	Peugeot 206 WRC	RP	2
F	Peugeot 206 WRC	RP	11
E	Peugeot 206 WRC	RP	7
CY	Peugeot 206 WRC	RP	4
RA	Peugeot 206 WRC	RP	engine
GR	Peugeot 206 WRC	RP	4
EAK	Peugeot 206 WRC	RP	2
FIN	Peugeot 206 WRC	VS	accident
D	Peugeot 206 WRC	VS	accident delay
I	Peugeot 206 WRC	VS	9
NZ	Peugeot 206 WRC	VS	2
AUS	Peugeot 206 WRC	VS	2
GB	Peugeot 206 WRC	RP	7

7th World Championship for Drivers

2003

S	Peugeot 206 WRC	RP	accident
TR	Peugeot 206 WRC	RP	accident damage
NZ	Peugeot 206 WRC	RP	accident
RA	Peugeot 206 WRC	RP	4
GR	Peugeot 206 WRC	RP	6
CY	Peugeot 206 WRC	RP	2
FIN	Peugeot 206 WRC	RP	accident
AUS	Peugeot 206 WRC	RP	7
GB	Peugeot 206 WRC	RP	transmission

Carlos Sainz (E)

Born 12/04/1962 at Madrid
First rally car Renault 5 TS in 1980
AB = Antonio Boto
LM = Luis Moya
MM = Marc Marti

1987

P	Ford Sierra RS Cos.	AB	turbocharger
F	Ford Sierra RS Cos.	AB	7
GB	Ford Sierra RS Cos.	AB	8

1988

P	Ford Sierra RS Cos.	LM	engine
F	Ford Sierra RS Cos.	LM	5
FIN	Ford Sierra RS Cos.	LM	6
I	Ford Sierra RS Cos.	LM	5
GB	Ford Sierra RS Cos.	LM	7

1989

MC	Toyota Celica GT-4	LM	accident
P	Toyota Celica GT-4	LM	accident

F	Toyota Celica GT-4	LM	engine
GR	Toyota Celica GT-4	LM	bodywork
FIN	Toyota Celica GT-4	LM	3
I	Toyota Celica GT-4	LM	3
GB	Toyota Celica GT-4	LM	2

8th World Championship for Drivers

1990

MC	Toyota Celica GT-4	LM	2
P	Toyota Celica GT-4	LM	transmission
EAK	Toyota Celica GT-4	LM	4
F	Toyota Celica GT-4	LM	2
GR	Toyota Celica GT-4	LM	1
NZ	Toyota Celica GT-4	LM	1
RA	Toyota Celica GT-4	LM	2
FIN	Toyota Celica GT-4	LM	1
AUS	Toyota Celica GT-4	LM	2
I	Toyota Celica GT-4	LM	3
GB	Toyota Celica GT-4	LM	1

World Champion

1991

MC	Toyota Celica GT-4	LM	1
P	Toyota Celica GT-4	LM	1
EAK	Toyota Celica GT-4	LM	engine
F	Toyota Celica GT-4	LM	1
GR	Toyota Celica GT-4	LM	2
NZ	Toyota Celica GT-4	LM	1
RA	Toyota Celica GT-4	LM	1
FIN	Toyota Celica GT-4	LM	4
AUS	Toyota Celica GT-4	LM	accident
I	Toyota Celica GT-4	LM	6
E	Toyota Celica GT-4	LM	electrical
GB	Toyota Celica GT-4	LM	3

2nd World Championship for Drivers

1992

MC	Toyota Celica T. 4WD	LM	2
P	Toyota Celica T. 4WD	LM	3
EAK	Toyota Celica T. 4WD	LM	1
F	Toyota Celica T. 4WD	LM	4
GR	Toyota Celica T. 4WD	LM	accident
NZ	Toyota Celica T. 4WD	LM	1
RA	Toyota Celica T. 4WD	LM	2
AUS	Toyota Celica T. 4WD	LM	3
E	Toyota Celica T. 4WD	LM	1
GB	Toyota Celica T. 4WD	LM	1

World Champion

1993

MC	Lancia HF Integrale	LM	14
P	Lancia HF Integrale	LM	accident
F	Lancia HF Integrale	LM	4
GR	Lancia HF Integrale	LM	2
RA	Lancia HF Integrale	LM	engine
NZ	Lancia HF Integrale	LM	4
AUS	Lancia HF Integrale	LM	accident
I	Lancia HF Integrale	LM	excluded
E	Lancia HF Integrale	LM	electronics

8th World Championship for Drivers

1994

MC	Subaru Impreza 555	LM	3
P	Subaru Impreza 555	LM	4
F	Subaru Impreza 555	LM	2
GR	Subaru Impreza 555	LM	1
RA	Subaru Impreza 555	LM	2
NZ	Subaru Impreza 555	LM	engine
FIN	Subaru Impreza 555	LM	3
I	Subaru Impreza 555	LM	2
GB	Subaru Impreza 555	LM	accident

2nd World Championship for Drivers

1995

MC	Subaru Impreza 555	LM	1
S	Subaru Impreza 555	LM	engine
P	Subaru Impreza 555	LM	1
F	Subaru Impreza 555	LM	4
AUS	Subaru Impreza 555	LM	engine
E	Subaru Impreza 555	LM	1
GB	Subaru Impreza 555	LM	2

2nd World Championship for Drivers

1996

S	Ford Escort RS Cos.	LM	2
EAK	Ford Escort RS Cos.	LM	rear susp'n
RI	Ford Escort RS Cos.	LM	1
GR	Ford Escort RS Cos.	LM	3
RA	Ford Escort RS Cos.	LM	2
FIN	Ford Escort RS Cos.	LM	transmission
AUS	Ford Escort RS Cos.	LM	3
I	Ford Escort RS Cos.	LM	2
E	Ford Escort RS Cos.	LM	accident

3rd World Championship for Drivers

1997

MC	Ford Escort WRC	LM	2
S	Ford Escort WRC	LM	2
EAK	Ford Escort WRC	LM	wheel studs
P	Ford Escort WRC	LM	transmission
E	Ford Escort WRC	LM	10
F	Ford Escort WRC	LM	2
RA	Ford Escort WRC	LM	engine
GR	Ford Escort WRC	LM	1
NZ	Ford Escort WRC	LM	2
FIN	Ford Escort WRC	LM	transmission
RI	Ford Escort WRC	LM	1
I	Ford Escort WRC	LM	4
AUS	Ford Escort WRC	LM	engine
GB	Ford Escort WRC	LM	3

3rd World Championship for Drivers

1998

MC	Toyota Corolla WRC	LM	1
S	Toyota Corolla WRC	LM	2
EAK	Toyota Corolla WRC	LM	shock absorber
P	Toyota Corolla WRC #100	LM	2
E	Toyota Corolla WRC	LM	7
F	Toyota Corolla WRC	LM	8
RA	Toyota Corolla WRC	LM	2
GR	Toyota Corolla WRC	LM	4
NZ	Toyota Corolla WRC	LM	1
FIN	Toyota Corolla WRC	LM	2
I	Toyota Corolla WRC	LM	4
AUS	Toyota Corolla WRC	LM	2
GB	Toyota Corolla WRC	LM	engine

2nd World Championship for Drivers

1999

MC	Toyota Corolla WRC	LM	accident
S	Toyota Corolla WRC	LM	2
EAK	Toyota Corolla WRC	LM	3
P	Toyota Corolla WRC	LM	2
E	Toyota Corolla WRC	LM	electrics
F	Toyota Corolla WRC	LM	3
RA	Toyota Corolla WRC	LM	5
GR	Toyota Corolla WRC	LM	2
NZ	Toyota Corolla WRC	LM	6
FIN	Toyota Corolla WRC	LM	3
CN	Toyota Corolla WRC	LM	3
I	Toyota Corolla WRC	LM	accident
AUS	Toyota Corolla WRC	LM	2
GB	Toyota Corolla WRC	LM	suspension

5th World Championship for Drivers

2000

MC	Ford Racing Focus WRC	LM	2
S	Ford Racing Focus WRC	LM	oil pump
EAK	Ford Racing Focus WRC	LM	4
P	Ford Racing Focus WRC	LM	3
E	Ford Racing Focus WRC	LM	3
RA	Ford Racing Focus WRC	LM	accident
GR	Ford Racing Focus WRC	LM	2
NZ	Ford Racing Focus WRC	LM	3
FIN	Ford Racing Focus WRC	LM	14
CY	Ford Racing Focus WRC	LM	1
F	Ford Racing Focus WRC	LM	3
I	Ford Racing Focus WRC	LM	5
AUS	Ford Racing Focus WRC	LM	excluded
GB	Ford Racing Focus WRC	LM	4

3rd World Championship for Drivers

2001

MC	Ford Focus WRC	LM	2
S	Ford Focus WRC	LM	3
P	Ford Focus WRC	LM	2
E	Ford Focus WRC	LM	5
RA	Ford Focus WRC	LM	3
CY	Ford Focus WRC	LM	3
GR	Ford Focus WRC	LM	engine
EAK	Ford Focus WRC	LM	engine
FIN	Ford Focus WRC	LM	6
NZ	Ford Focus WRC	LM	4
I	Ford Focus WRC	LM	4
F	Ford Focus WRC	LM	oil leak
AUS	Ford Focus WRC	LM	8
GB	Ford Focus WRC	LM	withdrawn

6th World Championship for Drivers

2002

MC	Ford Focus RS WRC	LM	3
S	Ford Focus RS WRC	LM	3
F	Ford Focus RS WRC	LM	6
E	Ford Focus RS WRC	MM	accident
CY	Ford Focus RS WRC	LM	11
RA	Ford Focus RS WRC	LM	1
GR	Ford Focus RS WRC	LM	3
EAK	Ford Focus RS WRC	LM	engine
FIN	Ford Focus RS WRC	LM	4
D	Ford Focus RS WRC	LM	8
I	Ford Focus RS WRC	LM	hydraulic leak
NZ	Ford Focus RS WRC	LM	4
AUS	Ford Focus RS WRC	LM	4
GB	Ford Focus RS WRC	LM	3

3rd World Championship for Drivers

2003

MC	Citroen Xsara WRC	MM	3
S	Citroen Xsara WRC	MM	9
TR	Citroen Xsara WRC	MM	1
NZ	Citroen Xsara WRC	MM	12
RA	Citroen Xsara WRC	MM	2
GR	Citroen Xsara WRC	MM	2
CY	Citroen Xsara WRC	MM	5
D	Citroen Xsara WRC	MM	6
FIN	Citroen Xsara WRC	MM	4
AUS	Citroen Xsara WRC	MM	5
I	Citroen Xsara WRC	MM	4
F	Citroen Xsara WRC	MM	2
E	Citroen Xsara WRC	MM	7
GB	Citroen Xsara WRC	MM	accident

3rd World Championship for Drivers

Kristian Sohlberg (FIN)

Born 15/02/1978 at
First rally car Ford Escort in 1997
JA1 = Jussi Aariainen
JA2 = Jukka Aho
JH = Jakke Honkanen
AK = Arto Kapanen

2000

FIN	Carisma GT	JA1	punctures

2001

S	Carisma GT	JA2	clutch
FIN	Carisma GT	JA2	withdrew

2002

S	Mit. Lancer Evo.	JA2	24/1st PCWRC
F	Mit. Lancer Evo.	JA2	accident
CY	Mit. Lancer Evo.	JA2	suspension
FIN	Mit. Lancer Evo.	JH	20/2nd PCWRC
D	Mit. Lancer Evo.	AK	16
NZ	Mit. Lancer Evo.	JH	14/1st PCWRC
AUS	Mit. Lancer Evo.	JH	suspension

2nd Production Car WRC

2003

S	Mit. Lancer Evo. WRC	JH	12
NZ	Mit. Lancer Evo. WRC	JH	accident
D	Mit. Lancer Evo. WRC	JH	14

Petter Solberg (N)

Daniel Sola (E)

Born 3/01/1975 at Vic Barcelona
First rally car Peugeot 205 Rallye in 1996
AR = Alex Romani
DM = David Moreno
JM = Josep Martinez

1999

E	Peugeot 106 Rallye	JM	40

2001

GB	SEAT Ibiza GTi	DM	34

2002

MC	Citroen Saxo S1600	AR	transmission
E	Citroen Saxo S1600	AR	19/1st JWRC
GR	Citroen Saxo S1600	AR	23/4th JWRC
D	Citroen Saxo S1600	AR	12/1st JWRC
I	Citroen Saxo S1600	AR	17/3rd JWRC
GB	Citroen Saxo S1600	AR	21/1st JWRC

Junior World Champion

2003

NZ	Mitsubishi Lancer Evo	AR	44/15th PCWRC
RA	Mitsubishi Lancer Evo	AR	12/2nd PCWRC
GR	Citroen Xsara WRC	AR	12
CY	Mitsubishi Lancer Evo	AR	transmission
D	Mitsubishi Lancer Evo	AR	22/1st PCWRC
AUS	Mitsubishi Lancer Evo	AR	20/5th PCWRC
F	Mitsubishi Lancer Evo	AR	differential
GB	Citroen Xsara WRC	AR	turbocharger

5th Production Car WRC

Petter Solberg (N)

Born 18/11/1974 at Spydeberg
First rally car Toyota Celica in 1996
ES = Egil Solstad
CM = Cato Menkerud
PM = Philip Mills
FG = Fred Gallagher

1998

S	Toyota Celica GT-4	ES	16
GB	Toyota Celica GT-4	CM	accident

1999

S	Ford Escort WRC	PM	11
EAK	Ford Focus WRC	FG	5
P	Ford Focus WRC	PM	11
FIN	Ford Focus WRC	PM	12
I	Ford Focus WRC	PM	27
GB	Ford Focus WRC	PM	9

2000

EAK	Ford Focus WRC	PM	5
P	Ford Focus WRC	PM	clutch
RA	Ford Focus WRC	PM	6
GR	Ford Focus WRC	PM	differential
NZ	Ford Focus WRC	PM	4
FIN	Ford Focus WRC	PM	accident
F	Subaru Impreza WRC	PM	gear selection
I	Subaru Impreza WRC	PM	9
AUS	Subaru Impreza WRC	PM	accident
GB	Subaru Impreza WRC	PM	accident

10th World Championship for Drivers

2001

MC	Subaru Impreza WRC	PM	accident
S	Subaru Impreza WRC	PM	6
P	Subaru Impreza WRC	PM	suspension
E	Subaru Impreza WRC	PM	accident
RA	Subaru Impreza WRC	PM	5
CY	Subaru Impreza WRC	PM	fire
GR	Subaru Impreza WRC	PM	2
EAK	Subaru Impreza WRC	PM	wheel bearing
FIN	Subaru Impreza WRC	PM	7
NZ	Subaru Impreza WRC	PM	7
I	Subaru Impreza WRC	PM	9
F	Subaru Impreza WRC	PM	5
AUS	Subaru Impreza WRC	PM	7
GB	Subaru Impreza WRC	PM	no fuel

10th World Championship for Drivers

2002

MC	Subaru Impreza WRC	PM	6
S	Subaru Impreza WRC	PM	engine
F	Subaru Impreza WRC	PM	5
E	Subaru Impreza WRC	PM	5
CY	Subaru Impreza WRC	PM	5
RA	Subaru Impreza WRC	PM	2
GR	Subaru Impreza WRC	PM	5
EAK	Subaru Impreza WRC	PM	engine
FIN	Subaru Impreza WRC	PM	3
D	Subaru Impreza WRC	PM	lost wheel
I	Subaru Impreza WRC	PM	3
NZ	Subaru Impreza WRC	PM	engine
AUS	Subaru Impreza WRC	PM	3
GB	Subaru Impreza WRC	PM	1

2nd World Championship for Drivers

2003

MC	Subaru Impreza WRC	PM	accident
S	Subaru Impreza WRC	PM	6
TR	Subaru Impreza WRC	PM	steering
NZ	Subaru Impreza WRC	PM	3
RA	Subaru Impreza WRC	PM	5
GR	Subaru Impreza WRC	PM	3
CY	Subaru Impreza WRC	PM	1
D	Subaru Impreza WRC	PM	8
FIN	Subaru Impreza WRC	PM	2
AUS	Subaru Impreza WRC	PM	1
I	Subaru Impreza WRC	PM	fuel
F	Subaru Impreza WRC	PM	1
E	Subaru Impreza WRC	PM	5
GB	Subaru Impreza WRC	PM	1

World Champion

Diary

November 2002

No sooner had the Network Q Rally of GB come to a close than the Welsh Development Agency announced they would take over sponsorship of the world championship event from 2003. It was henceforth to be known as Wales Rally GB.

A series of developments surrounding the future of the Mitsubishi world championship team began to unravel.

Many difficulties became evident in the organisation of Telstra Rally Australia and there started a series of meetings, the initial results of which made it seem the FIA's likelihood of sanctioning the event in the 2003 season unlikely.

December

The FIA World Council confirmed that the FIA sanctioned championship rallying, like Formula 1 and other series, would have points for the top eight, not the top six finishers. This was seen as a U-turn after the FIA declared that as from 1997 the top six placings would replace the previous top ten. At that time it was explained that the top six would give a more suitable points reward to successful competitors. This latest decision seemed to have been a reaction arising from the dominations of Ferrari and Peugeot in their respective fields of motorsport activities.

MSD, running the Hyundai World championship team, announced job reductions at their Milton Keynes headquarters and that the team would only run two not three fully works-prepared cars in the 2003 WCR, with guest drivers invited to participate on an event-to-event basis.

Ford 1: After deciding earlier that Ford could only finance a two car team (Martin and Duval) in their 2003 world championship programme, the team then added a third guest driver, 22 year old Mikko Hirvonen sponsored by business interests in Finland, who would be eligible for scoring manufacturers' points. Hirvonen had only entered three world rallies previously.

Ford 2: After carrying out a lot of pre-Monte Carlo, then pre-Swedish, tests with Pirelli tyres it was decided that the team would compete on rallies with Michelin tyres instead, leaving only Subaru among the registered teams running Pirellis.

Luis Moya announced his retirement from active rallying. As the world's most successful and the most experienced world championship codriver. Moya cited the growing levels of physical danger for competitors in the sport, coupled with a down-turn of financial rewards, as reasons to pursue other activities in life. His driver of 15 years Carlos Sainz announced he

would compete the 2003 season with Marc Marti, with whom he had previously contested the 2002 Catalunya Rally, ironically because Moya was unfit after of a testing crash. There were two special memories relating to Moya in rally action. Firstly an uncharacteristic display of emotion when the 1998 Drivers' championship was lost on the final stage of the season, in which the rear window of his Corolla was mysteriously smashed. Secondly in-car television coverage had made a superstar out of Moya. Viewers heard the incredible pace at which he was able to read out the notes!

Carlos Sainz finally concluded negotiations to become the third team Citroen driver, so Ford's two top drivers in 2002 were back together again with another team. This came after the FIA received nominations that Colin McRae and Sebastien Loeb were the permanent registered drivers. Later rule changes by the FIA designed to encourage teams to

Changes that Happened in 2003

● Points changes, top eight to score instead of six.
● Turkey replaced Safari, therefore more percentage on asphalt and half the events were in Mediterranean countries.
● Three asphalt events in October.
● Citroen replaced Mitsubishi as the sixth regular team in the championship. Mitsubishi entered only two events (New Zealand and Germany).
● Much more concentration on central service parks.
● Shekhar Mehta replaced Kari Sohlberg as President of WRCC in addition to his ongoing role as President of the Rallies Commission, which deals with non WCR matters.

employ younger and less successful drivers made it seem that Carlos would not be allowed to continue in the role as third team driver in 2004. In the end, however, it was Sainz who stayed with Loeb and, one of the world's two most successful rally drivers, Colin McRae who left *(seen here with Citroen team manager Guy Frequelin).*

Peugeot announced their world rally championship sponsorship agreement with Philip Morris (Marlboro), thus having their cars painted in a similar shade of red to those of their colleagues at Citroen.

Interestingly the agreement was for a term which extended one year longer than the period allowed under European law for tobacco sponsorship. Peugeot's Sporting Director Corrado Provera explained that Philip Morris also produces Toblerone, a confectionery item to which he was particularly partial!

The JWRC Suzuki team moved their premises from Esztergom in Hungary to a new base at Milton Keynes in England.

January 2003

While Mitsubishi were debating their future world championship rally activities, the Lancer Evo VIII model was being prepared for its rally debut - in the USA.

The Hyundai rally team's financial troubles continued to deteriorate, and rumours of an imminent withdrawal, or at least a programme of "starting line specials" was mooted.

February

At the start of the Swedish Rally came news that the Hyundai parent company in Korea had given a positive commitment to its continued presence in the world rally championship.

Plans to run roll-on, roll-off boats to transport all the rally teams' equipment to the non-European events went wrong and it was announced that all the teams had to make their own plans to travel to New Zealand. This was a bad blow as virtually all the dates in the 2003 calendar were based on the availability of this service, as part of a global cost saving project in the sport. In the expectation that this plan would work teams had already begun to dispose of all their secondary kit of equipment (vans, recce cars, etc), because the same kit could be taken to every event.

For Sale, all with one careful owner...

At short notice Ford works driver Francois Duval ended his work with

codriver Jean-Marc Fortin *(left)* and invited Stephane Prevot to accompany him. Their first event together was Turkey, in which the new pairing came third overall. Prevot had twice worked with Ford previously, the final time being in the 1998 season with Bruno Thiry. On the last occasion (Network Q 1998, with Thiry) he had finished third overall. "You see, I have taken over where I left off", Prevot declared!

Hopes arose that the world championship could return to Kenya, should the problems in Australia not be resolved. Plans were taken to pay the FIA the 65,000 Swiss francs fees due to them from the country's previous federation, and help was sought from the newly elected Kenyan government (which had pledged to use international sport as a promotional platform) for funding to run the 2004 event to world standards. Any expectations of the event returning in time for the 2003 season, however, were just too premature. It was essential for Kenya to remain in the limelight however, because the rally teams were now designing and building future cars without the engineering compromises necessary for running in Kenya. The FIA rules allow teams to run only one type of car at one time, so one-off special designs to cater for the extended distances in Africa are forbidden. A lot of teams had sympathy for the Safari, the scene of many happy and successful past memories, but in practical terms the chance of returning there as a world championship event was fast receding. Hoping that the the event would not disappear from the mind, the name of the Mombasa based Equator Rally changed its name to Safari Rally.

March

The organisers of the former world championship Rally of Portugal, ACP, celebrated their 100th anniversary by holding a special rally! This was called the Centenario Rally, with just four invited

drivers. In a Peugeot 206WRC was five times Portugal Rally winner Markku Alen, in Toyota Corolla WRCs were four times world champion Juha Kankkunen and Thomas Radstrom, while in a Ford Focus WRC was Alister McRae. Alen retired with turbo trouble, McRae fell back with transmission problems, Kankkunen won and Radstrom was second. Kankkunen, meanwhile, had just embarked on an exciting new venture, a business interest in the new Finnish airline, Flying Finn. He had the first plane (an MD83) publicly launched with his name on the side.

(left to right) Juha Kankkunen, Markku Alen, Thomas Radstrom and Alister McRae.

Niall McShea was finally admitted to the PCWRC after the first round (Sweden) had been held, after other drivers had cancelled their entries. He would have liked to contest the JWRC again, on account he was born on 1st January 1974, the very day specified as the earliest possible date to be accepted into that series but a Super 1600 programme could not be arranged!

April

No sooner than Australia's problems were finally solved and the event's inclusion in the 2003 calendar was confirmed, other trouble arose with Rallye Deutschland! Already included in the 2003 WRC Calendar under proviso following concerns about safety issues, the FIA inspectors were disappointed with apparently unfinished business. The FIA declared that if matters were not resolved within one month, the event would be removed from the 2003 calendar.

Sad news was the death of Possum Bourne as a result of a freak accident at the Race to the Sky HillClimb course, South Island, New Zealand. A few days earlier Belgian champion Rocco Theunissen also died, of natural causes.

Nic Gullino *(below left)* competition manager of HF Grifone and Step 2, accepted the post of Team Manager of Peugeot Sport in their world championship programme. Francois Chatriot *(right)* meanwhile moved from that position to an equivalent position at Citroen.

May

Owners of the PCWRC cars being flown from New Zealand to Argentina had a nasty surprise when they found the loaders were demanding the cars be shortened in order to fit into the aircraft. An acceptable price for the carriage had been agreed, but then there had been a misunderstanding. The plane now operating this route was no longer a Boeing 747 but the smaller Airbus 340! Pat Richard was mortified. "For 48 hours the people in New Zealand, encouraged by our friend Possum Bourne, had completely rebuilt my car after its accident. Every panel had been replaced. We then went to the airport and found they were cutting bits off it to make it fit in the plane!"

Martin Whitaker left Ford and was replaced by Jost Capito. Seen in happier days, Capito *(left)* with Whitaker.

It was farewell time for one of Argentina's most amazing and best loved motor sport stars, Gabriel Raies. He had decided to hang up his helmet at the end of the 2002 season, but viewers of his motorsport TV programme were so upset they campaigned him to enter Rally Argentina, as his one great finale. He received 474 e-mails begging him to make one last appearance! He finished tenth overall, best Argentina driver, in his Toyota Corolla WRC.

Petter Solberg agreed a three year contract with Prodrive and will stay at Subaru until the end of 2006.

Christina Lundqvist was appointed Clerk of the Course of the Swedish Rally, her predecessor Bertil Klarin remained on the organising team as Operations Manager.

On 20th May the FIA finally confirmed that Rallye Deutschland would qualify for the 2003 world championship.

There was an extraordinary accident on the Matador Tatry Rally in Slovakia when the Skoda Octavia WRC of Jan Kopecky was almost literally rolled into a ball. The FIA officials were relieved to notice how much the cockpit retained its shape despite the impact.

FRYBA

June

The FIA's World Council announced far-reaching plans for restructuring world championship events, so as to save money, time and also allow more events into the annual calendar. These were to be discussed in detail by the World Rally Championship Commission for later

Mitsubishi's Manoeuvres

As soon as some of the control over the Mitsubishi Corporation passed from Japan to Germany attention was paid to the viability of the Ralliart Europe rally team, particularly in view of disappointing results after Tommi Makinen left the team at the end of the 2001 season. Under the guidance of Sven Quandt *(below)* a series

of decisions was taken. ① The team withdrew from the 2003 FIA World Championship, under a promise to return in strength in 2004. This was accepted without penalty by the FIA, ② A new company to be known as MMSP was formed, notably with a proviso that this was to be a trading, rather than a non-profit organisation. The Ralliart name was retained for customer and special formulae work, ③ In the long term there was to be a new European base at Trebur (near Frankfurt), but for the present the organisation at Rugby England would continue to operate, ④ A new competition technical director, Mario Fornaris (for ten years working with Peugeot as test and development manager) was appointed, ⑤ Andrew Cowan's commercial interests were bought out by MMSP, but personal contracts with staff in Rugby were to be secure for the following 30 months.

Meanwhile there was a long wait to discover who would be the official team drivers in 2004. Believing that his services would still be required, Francois Delecour announced that his former lady codriver Anne-Chantal Pauwels would replace Daniel Grataloup, still recovering from his 2002 Rally Australia injuries, but within two weeks it was announced that Francois Delecour was released from his contract, so the only regular driver in the team was Alister McRae, himself recuperating after his mountain bike injuries which caused him to withdraw from Sanremo 2002. Then when it was announced that Panizzi would be the team's lead driver in 2004, McRae was released from his agreement as well.

ratification. They also confirmed that the "three driver rule" would go ahead in any case. (The third driver of a team had to be someone who had not scored a podium placing on a world championship rally within the past three years.) This rule was intended to help bring young talent into top teams, but raised criticism that this denied the sport of proven top level talent.

18 year old Jari-Matti Latvala made his world championship debut, as a works driver!

How many can you recognise? The old boys' and girls' outing at the Acropolis Rally. *(Answers on page 207)*

Roggia starts his last world championship rally, the Swedish Rally alongside Fabio Frisiero.

The veteran codriver Loris Roggia died in an accident on the Salento Rally, a national championship event in Southern Italy, in a Peugeot 206 S1600 car.

Inmarsat experimented with satellite timing communication systems at the Acropolis.

Hamed Al-Wahaibi discovered the price for his decision to retire from motor sport in mid season. He was fined USD20,000 by the Stewards of the Cyprus Rally.

Vic Elford, one of motorsport's legendary drivers, who had succeeded in Formula 1, long distance racing and rallies, was guest of honour at the 30th anniversary Cyprus Rally. He had helped prepare the route for the very first Cyprus Rally.

July

After considerable rallying experience abroad Jari-Matti Latvala had his first rally in his native Finland, at the Exide Rally, where he finished fourth. "I had no idea how fast or slowly I should drive, but I

quickly found out how fast the other Finnish drivers are!"

Made it at last! By being nominated for the Deutschland Rally by Hyundai, Manfred Stohl had eventually became an official works driver, after 70 prior entries in world championship rallies, stretching back to Ivory Coast in 1991.

New fast-line Jani Paasonen. The Finnish driver appeared almost unrecognisable at Deutschland Rally. He had recently lost 30kg in weight. Check picture on page 140 of Pirelli WR25.

Marcus Gronholm arrived at Deutschland Rally with his elbow heavily bandaged, after treatment following a mysterious infection which needed hospital attention.

Australia Crisis

The problems only became evident through omission. It was when Garry Connelly, Clerk of the Course of Telstra Rally Australia and founder of the event, did not appear in Finland 2002 that it was clear something was wrong. The Neste Rally Finland was the venue for critical planning meetings of the World Rally Championship Commission. Connelly was uncharacteristically absent. Then other strange things emerged. Journalists found he and other staff members of TRA's organisation had been barred from speaking to them. Then came reports that Australia had refused to fit into the planned 2003 calendar in a way which would have facilitated the "roll-on, roll-off" system and in so doing made a major threat to the smooth running of plans for the season. Come the event in November 2002 there was a noticeable coolness in the air. The rally lacked much of the vibrancy for which it had been noted in the past. Immediately after the event there were two resignations among leading members of the WATC (West Australia Tourist Commission) and then came the resignation of Connelly himself. The balloon was going up.

At this point, the FIA became alarmed at what was happening and made their own enquiries. They discovered the rally was locked into complex contractual agreements which the FIA felt were negative to the interests of the championship. Max Mosley, FIA President, explained there were two major problems. Firstly there was insufficient separation between the interests of the promoters and the operation of the sporting organisation. There had already been reports that promotional people had been asked to undertake sporting work for which they were not experienced. Secondly there were confidentiality clauses between the promoters and CAMS (the Australian federation) which forbade CAMS from telling even the FIA, whom they represented, the details of the agreements. Negotiations ensued but then came another sticking point. One of WATC's most cherished contractual powers was that world championship status could not be taken away from WATC for another 65 years. This was unacceptable in any form to the FIA. The FIA asked for a "performance related" clause allowing CAMS the power to offer the event to another rally in Australia if organisational standards were found to be unacceptable. Eventually this was resolved. In March WA's Minister for Tourism met with Mosley then, at the FIA's World Council meeting, in April it was announced that the problems were over. Fresh working systems were agreed, Adrian Stafford *(right)* took over the work of Clerk of the Course in place of Connelly and it was almost like back in the old days when the WRC came back to Perth in 2003. An eight-months hiatus was over. Connelly meanwhile directed his rallying attention to helping Rally Hokkaido's successful progress in its world championship challenge.

Consultation with the World Rally Championship Commission (WRCC) after the World Council's plans for 2004 raised a hornets' nest of discontent. In the absence of its President Shekhar Mehta on business abroad, David Richards prepared a letter of complaint on behalf of the majority of the teams, mostly against increasing the number of world rallies at this time. The teams, however, had only a minority voice in the WRCC and this had no effect.

August

As the confusing pressures from interested parties mounted, the WRCC found it difficult to rationalise its recommendations to the World Council and delays ensued. The organisers of the opening rounds of the 2004 series became desperate. They did not know what style of event to organise. Eventually Monte Carlo and Sweden were told they could run to a pre-2004 format.

Number competition plate changes

again! The Neste Rally Finland again dispensed with the traditional bonnet plate, using the miniature door plates but added large competition numbers on the rear side windows.

Neste Rally Finland witnessed a definite 100th rally for Richard Burns and an arguable 100th for Ari Vatanen. Vatanen had been given his congratulations cake at the Network Q Rally in 1998. The debate centred on whether his non-start in Acropolis 1977 counted or not. It had been three years between Vatanen's last World rally win and Burns' first, and to date both had scored ten World rally wins.

Another celebration. The Impreza rally car's career began in Finland, ten years previously. The Finnish Pirelli distributor produced postage stamp souvenirs.

DIARY

Possum Bourne

A most bizarre accident ended the life of one of motorsport's most popular and charismatic drivers. New Zealander Peter "Possum" Bourne died on 30th April 2003 as a result of injuries suffered in a collision on the course of Race to the Sky HillClimb near Queenstown, South Island, New Zealand. While he was transiting down to the bottom of the course, his vehicle was struck by an oncoming car travelling up the hill, driven by a competitor making his reconnaissance.

Possum (born 13 April 1956) had been at the top level of New Zealand rallying for 20 years, and was FIA Asia-Pacific Champion three times and national Australian champion seven times, but these were not his greatest achievements. The lasting memory of Bourne will be his joy of friendship for everyone who had been lucky and privileged enough to know him. He was a guy who commanded your respect whatever your level of contact.

The remarkable presence of Subaru at world level rallying owes a lot to the determination of Bourne, which began many years ago and continued until the day he died. He drove their four-wheel drive cars in Kenya and the USA as well as the antipodes, and his first national win, in 1985 in the South Island, was on account of the traction opportunities of his underpowered car. Soon successes were undeniably attributed to his driving talents! He dreamed of representing Subaru on world championship rallies on a regular basis, but this chance ebbed away when Prodrive was given the chance to run the cars. It was the chance to contest the 2003 FIA Production Car World Rally Championship that finally gave Possum the realisation of achieving that ambition.

Rallying brought tragedy to Possum on two particular occasions. Firstly when Subaru's tyre chief Odama Kobayasgi died in a road accident in the 1986 Rally NZ and Possum's team withdrew from the rally out of respect. Then even more personally when his codriver and life long friend Rodger Freeth died from internal injuries suffered on the 1993 Rally Australia, in an accident in which Possum himself was unhurt. Possum died leaving a loving family behind. While he was rallying in Kenya he met his wife Peggy, the mother of their three children Taylor, Spencer and Jazlin.

Mark Lovell and Roger Freeman

British competitors Mark Lovell (born 27 March 1960) and codriver Roger Freeman (born 9 October 1951) died on 12 July 2003 in an unusual accident at the Oregon Trails Rally in the USA. Their Subaru left the road, hit a tree and violently ricocheted into a bank on the other side of the road, the almost instantaneous double impact causing fatal injuries. Mark had been a remarkable driver, a Champion in four different countries (Britain, the Netherlands, Ireland and the USA). In 1986, and at the wheels of a Ford RS200, he was the youngest driver ever to win the British title. He had enjoyed two careers in rallying, firstly in the '80s, driving mainly for Ford but also for Citroen and Nissan, then later when he returned to the sport in 2001 when he joined the Subaru USA team. He had been concentrating in the meantime on business affairs. It was a fitting tribute that his final success was winning the rally car division at the Pikes Peak International Hill Climb, in Colorado.

Mark had been closely associated with Roger all the time he had been rallying, but Roger's other main achievement was to be codriver for Toshihiro Arai in 2000 when they won the FIA Teams' Cup with Subaru. He was an epitome of someone who enjoyed his sport, happy to compete anywhere in the world, on events of every possible significance and with drivers of every conceivable range of talent.

In the weeks leading up to Telstra Rally Australia, the Skoda team were worried that neither of their drivers would be fit to start the event. Didier Auriol had an operation on his shoulder muscles which had caused so much pain in Finland, while Toni Gardemeister broke a bone in his wrist after an accident in a charity ice hockey match. Finally all ended well. Both drivers started the event and it was the first time a Fabia WRC had finished a rally.

Doug Stewart, celebrating his 50th year in Australian motorsport, missed the Telstra Rally Australia. He was on his honeymoon instead!

Tommi Makinen announced he would retire from world rally championship competition at the end of 2003. Within moments, it was announced that Burns would return to Subaru and become teammate to Petter Solberg.

Howard Marsden died. Best known for his work with Ford Australia in circuit racing, he was instrumental as project manager in 1990 at getting the Nissan Pulsar/Sunny GTI-R Group N rally car project off the ground. Howard had fought a long battle with cancer.

Mitsubishi announced Gilles Panizzi would head their 2004 driver line up and that Alister McRae had been dropped. Gilles had been an official driver with Peugeot for ten years, nearly all the time working with Mario Fornaris, who joined Mitsubishi earlier in 2003 as Technical Director.

Peugeot announced their line-up for 2004 was to be Gronholm, Rovanpera, Freddy Loix (below) and Daniel Carlsson while Cedric Robert was to be a guest

driver for occasional events. The team was selected on the basis that the rules confirmed at the June World Council ("third-driver rule") was definitive. A few days later they discovered the FIA had replaced the "three-driver rule" by the "two-driver rule".

It is believed Citroen had offered an attractive opportunity under the "third-driver rule" to Simon Jean-Joseph, only to discover not only about the two-driver rule, but that the two-driver rule was the inspiration of ... Citroen! Within a few days Citroen announced their team would consist of just Loeb and Sainz, that McRae had been "freed" with no mention of the agreement with Jean-Joseph at all.

September

Urgent calls located the New Zealand codriver Rob Scott, summoned to Australia to replace Ana Goni as codriver for Stig Blomqvist. "It was deja vue. My father Jim had the ride of a lifetime with Ari Vatanen on our rally in 1977. Twenty six years later I had the ride of a lifetime with another rally legend, Stig. Now we both have memories we will always treasure."

WRCC President, Shekhar Mehta, confessed that the reason for the rule changes for 2004 had been to enable Hokkaido Rally to be included in the world championship.

The FIA's World Council agreed by fax vote to proceed with a package of changes, including a new measure by which only two permanent drivers should be nominated per event, not three as in 2003, and also approval for the full 16

round calendar including Mexico and Japan. Changes to the original plan included two, not one, passes in reconnaissance.

The WRCC met two days after Hokkaido and recommended to the World Council two alterations to the proposals laid out by the World Council. That the new "two-driver" rule should be amended, now only one driver should be permanent. Also, drivers should have two, not one, pre-event passes in reconnaissance. Also there were date changes for New Zealand and Argentina.

MSD struck more accounting problems in relation to Hyundai Motor Company (HMC). The team declared that if promised funds were not received from Korea they would have to send their staff home. The next day HMC in Korea announced that the Accent WRC programme would stop at the end of the 2003 season, and that the company would come back to the world championship in the later part of 2006 with a new model, based in Germany. Poor results and financial misunderstanding were not the only reason for ending the Accent programme, matters were made worse by delays in obtaining a replacement engine.

VW Racing director Kris Nissen announced he wanted to stop all rally activities forthwith, notwithstanding the obligations of their drivers to contest the JWRC.

The man is back! Luis Moya ended ten months of exile from the sport by accepting the position of Sporting Director at Prodrive, starting in time for Sanremo.

The Elpa Rally (ECR coefficient 20) was stopped after only three stages following a fatal accident for a local driver in a one-make Toyota Yaris car. All the Greek drivers retired out of sympathy, leaving only three foreign drivers in the competition. FIA rules for the ECR (unlike the WRC) say that maximum points are awarded in these circumstances.

The Rallye Charleroix in Canada, a candidate event for the world championship, was cancelled for want of an overall sponsor.

October

There was a sensation when information was leaked from Australia. After the Telstra Rally, the Stewards declared that

the absentees Holowczyc, Kulig and Colsoul were to be not only fined but also they would be suspended from FIA championship rallying until 2004. In the end the FIA announced that the penalties would not be enforced.

November

Richard Burns *(seen right before the start of his final rally for Peugeot, with Robert Reid)* suffered a black out when driving from London to the Wales Rally GB. Markko Martin was a passenger and steered their car to safety on to the hard shoulder of the motorway. Richard was hospitalized immediately given tests to discover the trouble and withdrew from the rally, thereby relinquishing his chance of regaining his world title.

Another absentee from the Wales Rally GB, and indeed Corsica and Catalunya before, was Marcos Ligato who broke his wrist in a mountain bike accident.

On the eve of Wales Rally GB, the Chairman of the Board of Skoda Auto Vratislav Kulhanek gave an internet interview in which he outlined the team's plans for 2004. Unless a major sponsor was acquired, the team would only enter European based rounds of the World Rally Championship. With the time and funds saved, they will continue testing and development of the Fabia WRC, ready for a big attack in 2005.

The FIA considered how to react to Skoda's withdrawal from the World Championship and the effect of the rule that homologations cannot be granted to companies who do not contest the series. It was decided that the homologations of parts which can be made every three months (Variant Options) could continue, but not those which could only be made every year.

Richard Burns' absence from the Wales Rally GB gave Freddy Loix an earlier first outing in a Peugeot than expected. This was to have taken place one week later at the Condroz Rally.

Mitsubishi in Japan announced their plans for 2004 for entering all 16 rounds of the WCR with two World Rally Cars and two Group N cars, for the drivers Gilles Panizzi, Kristian Sohlberg, Daniel Sola and Gianluigi Galli, leaving out Jani Paasonen. No more details were announced, except that Panizzi would be driving the WRC on every rally.

On Monday 10th November, one day after the end of Wales Rally GB, rally drivers with various speeding offences arising from the 2002 Network Q Rally GB had their cases heard. These offences were committed during pre-rally Shakedown, when drivers used the same stretch of road in order to return to the Service Park or en route to make another run. Neath Magistrates Court agreed to hold the proceedings on this day in order to minimise the effect on the drivers' professional careers, considering that six-month bans were likely to be imposed. Three drivers were banned from driving in Britain for the six month period, on account of being caught more than three times. The financial penalties also imposed were: Loix (for seven offences) £1725, Schwarz (5, £1000) and Carlsson (4, £800). Other drivers caught in this multiple speed trap were both Hirvonen and Paasonen (3, £600 each), both Makinen and Sainz (2, £400 each), and for Jaio, Martin, Colin McRae, Rowe, Stohl, Burns and Delecour (one time and £150 each). For other offences, Kris Meeke was banned from driving for one year and fined £300.

Changes to come for 2004.

- 16 rallies instead of 14. Mexico and Japan join the series.
- The Italian WRC round will be run on gravel in Sardinia instead of asphalt in Sanremo, therefore there will be a much reduced percentage of the championship on asphalt.
- Shorter total time span for every event: Wednesday morning through to Sunday afternoon.
- Only two drivers can be nominated for World Manufacturers' points. One (permanent) for all the year, the other from event to event. Limits on the previous successes of drivers nominated as a third driver (ordered by the June 2003 World Council) were therefore superfluous.
- No more recce or gravel cars: all recce has to be made in actual rally car or in a completely standard car.
- There were to be two alternative reconnaissance programmes. Drivers are always to be allowed two passes. First option is to have one pass on Wednesday (and maybe Thursday morning), the other on the morning when the rally will use those stages. The second pass would also serve the role previously carried out by gravel note crews. This is called the '1000 Pistes' system. The alternative rule (called the '2+3' system) is to have two passes before the start with reliance on organisers' supplied danger notes made earlier on the day the stage is run.
- When the '1000 Pistes' system is used, the competitive part of the events will start each day around 1130. It is planned to have two service halts each day, one after recce and the other at the end of each leg. With the '2+3' system, there will be reliance on fuel and tyre halts during the day.
- Expectation of changes to testing regulations faded away, while flexi-service systems are to be used so as to reduce the number of technical staff and equipment attending events.

World Championship

World Rally Cars (all turbocharged, four-wheel drive)

Team	Citroen Total	Ford Motor Company Ltd	Hyundai World Rally Team	
Model	Xsara WRC	Focus RS WRC03	Accent WRC[3]	
Engine				
No. Cylinders	4 in line	4 in line	4 in line	
cc (x 1.7 if turbocharged)	1998 (3397)	1988 (3380)	1998 (3397)	
Bore/Stroke (mm)	86/86	84.8/88	85/88	
Compression ratio	n/a	n/a	9.2:1	
Stated Max. Power (bhp)	315	300	300	
@ Revs.	5500	6500	n/a	
Max. Torque (kg/m)	58	56	55	
@ Revs.	2750	4000	n/a	
Induction	Magneti-Marelli	Pi	Pectel	
Turbo	-	Garrett	Garrett	
No. and Position of Cams	2 ohc	2 ohc	2 ohc	
Location	Front-Transverse	Front-Transverse	Front-Transverse	
Transmission				
Clutch (Manufacturer)	Carbon (AP)	Carbon (Sachs)	Carbon (AP)	
No. of plates	3	3	2	
Gearbox	6 speed s/q	6 speed s/q	6 speed s/q	
Location	Transverse	Longitudinal	Longitudinal	
Manufacturer	Xtrac	Xtrac	Xtrac	
Brakes (Ø=mm)				
Manufacturer	Alcon	Brembo	Alcon	
Front gravel	DV310	DV300	DV304	
asphalt	DV376	DV370	DV370	
Rear gravel	DV318	DV300	DV304	
asphalt	DV318 OR 376	DV370	DV355	
Suspension (shock absorbers)				
Manufacturer	Extremetech	Reiger	Proflex	
Dimensions				
Length (mm)	4167	4442	4200	
Width (mm)	1770	1770	1770	
Wheelbase (mm)	2555	2615	2440	
Weight (kg)	1230	1230	1230	
General Sponsor	Total/MoviStar	BP/Castrol	-	
Tyre supplier	Michelin	Michelin	Michelin	
Oil Lubricant supplier	Total	BP/Castrol	-	
Date of Homologation				
First basic model	1.03.2001	1.01.1999	1.01.2000	
First Major Rally for WRC	Lyon-Charbonnieres 2000 (T4)	Monte-Carlo 1999	Swedish 2000	
Debut for current version	New Zealand 2003	New Zealand 2003	Corsica 2002	

NOTE: All the above have:
    (1) Front located, 16-valve engines (except the Skoda which has 20 valves) fitted with 34mm turbo restrictors.
    (2) Rack and pinion steering.
    (3) MacPherson-type suspension front and rear (except Ford with a trailing arm strut rear suspension).

Rally Car Specifications

	Team Marlboro Peugeot Total	Skoda Motorsport	555 Subaru World Rally Team
	206 WRC	Fabia WRC	Impreza WRC2003
	4 in line	4 in line	4 flat
	1997 (3395)	1999 (3398)	1994 (3390)
	85/88	82.5/93.5	92/75
	n/a	8.7:1	9.0:1
	300	298	300
	5250	5500	5500
	54	52	60
	3500	3500	4000
	Magneti-Marelli	Bosch	STI
	Garrett	Garrett	IHI
	2 ohc	2 ohc	2x2 ohc
	Front-Transverse	Front-Transverse	Front-Longitudinal
	Carbon (AP)	Carbon (AP)	Carbon (Alcon)
	3	3	various
	5 speed s/q	6 speed s/q	6 speed s/q
	Longitudinal	Transverse	Longitudinal
	Xtrac	Xtrac/Unic	Prodrive
	Brembo	AP	Alcon
	DV300	DV304	DV304
	DV370	DV378	DV366
	DV300	DV304	DV304
	DV370	DV355	DV304
	Peugeot	Reiger	Prodrive/Sachs
	4005	4002	4340
	1770	1770	1770
	2468	2462	2520
	1230	1230	1230
	Marlboro/Total	Allianz	555
	Michelin	Michelin	Pirelli
	Total	Shell	Motul
	1.05.1999	1.07.2003	1.01.1997
	Corsica 1999	Germany 2003	Monte-Carlo 1997
	Acropolis 2002	Germany 2003	Monte-Carlo 2003

Key: **DV** = Disc Vented
n/a = not available,
ohc = overhead cam,
s/q. = sequential.

(4) Semi-automatic gearshift systems (except for Hyundai).

(5) Triple-active differentials (front, central, rear).

(6) Homologated with 18" wheels as standard. In competition, teams usually fit 15" for gravel, 16" for winter rallies and 18" for asphalt.

Rally Car Developments
World Rally Cars

Citroen Xsara

The team started their first full season in world championship competition using 2002 version cars. The main novelty starting at Monte Carlo was a revolutionary system of connecting the front and rear anti roll bars by an hydraulic system. A revised air inlet system was used in the hope that ingress of snow could be averted in Sweden: unfortunately this system was not fully used and led to McRae still suffering this problem. The 2003 version cars first appeared in New Zealand and externally they were unchanged. Main changes were: new crankshaft, exhaust manifold, turbocharger housing and intercooler, all aimed at providing greater power. Initial testing was delayed when McRae crashed in Spain. High braking temperatures experienced in New Zealand led to changes in brake pad material. When the FIA announced the intention to ban telemetry in rallying in the future, Citroen had a revised Magneti Marelli datalog system to download information by normal flash card system, starting in Finland. For the first time Citroen used asphalt-specification large diameter rear brake discs on some cars starting at Deutschland.

Ford Focus

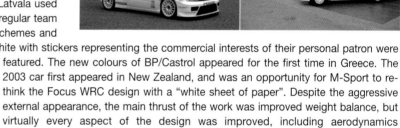

One of the early unexpected events faced by Ford was the late decision to use Michelin rather than Pirelli tyres this season, which was made after the initial testing for Monte Carlo and Sweden had been carried out. Martin and Duval used 2002 version cars through to Turkey and Hirvonen and Latvala used older cars for all the season. The cars for the two regular team drivers started the season in a variety of design schemes and for Hirvonen and Latvala the cars were basically white with stickers representing the commercial interests of their personal patron were

featured. The new colours of BP/Castrol appeared for the first time in Greece. The 2003 car first appeared in New Zealand, and was an opportunity for M-Sport to re-think the Focus WRC design with a "white sheet of paper". Despite the aggressive external appearance, the main thrust of the work was improved weight balance, but virtually every aspect of the design was improved, including aerodynamics particularly for faster rallies, notably by moving the rear wing backwards. Regulations forbid the rear wing extending beyond the

bumper, so the homologation was based on the American SVT170, in which the rear bumpers are situated further back, not the European ST170 version. Like on other teams' cars, vertical fences were built into the design of the wing. Other changes were seemingly endless. The underbonnet cooling package was changed, the engine block was substantially reworked to remove metal that was not required. There was a new hydraulic system, a revolutionary triple piece propshaft so as to allow the transmission tunnel to be narrower, which gave more room inside the cockpit for moving the crew's seats closer together and lower down. There were secret changes to the rear suspension aimed at improving kinematics, a floor mounted pedal box. An ingenious system of combining the reserve

Original.

Hyundai Accent

Since the fire problems from the exhaust on the Network Q Rally, the cars appeared in Monte Carlo with a revised exhaust design. Also, following the end of their contractual agreement with Castrol cars appeared with a new colour scheme, awaiting the announcement (which never came) of their commercial partnership with Shell. Cars in 2002 specification continued to be used until Turkey. MSD removed the roof scoops on the cars of Schwarz and Loix for Sweden. Small evolution changes were carried out in time for New Zealand. The model they called their "Evo 3.5" included new turbocharger housing, boost pressure sensor, aimed

at improving response through better management of exhaust gasses, and giving better bottom end

performance. MSD began using in-house developed shock absorbers as from New Zealand. There were changes to air inlet systems aimed at avoiding water ingress in Argentina. And that sadly was all. The programme came to a premature end.

Later.

manual gearlever with the handbrake seemed a good idea until this led to Martin having long delays on the Deutschland Rally! This car was a

model of original thought, surely a classic!. Certain details of the car were subsequently changed at the request of the FIA, notably the design of the rear differential guard and of the front corner panels, to remove inherent aerodynamic benefits. Gradually experience with the car led to improvements. For Cyprus stronger anti roll bar arms were fitted. Following ingress of dust into the engine in Argentina, various changes were made to the air inlet, notably a full length splitter across the grill intended to prevent dust from becoming scooped up from hitting the ground. Following ongoing troubles with the hydraulic contamination, a new oil, stronger pump was designed, which used higher viscosity fluid, was first used on the non-championship Estonian EOS Rally entry for Martin. A completely new airbox design was designed for Finland. For Italy there were more changes, notably a lightweight bell housing, new hydraulic transmission systems and a new engine ECU system. The front grill splitter system was discontinued later in 2003. When leaves blocked the front grill and led to overheating on Martin's car in Sanremo, holes were drilled in a front panel behind the grill and in front of the radiators so that air could still reach the radiator. Despite all this, the car won on its third rally (Acropolis), gained the second fastest stage time on its first ever competitive special stage in New Zealand. For the three end of season

asphalt rallies, the 2003 cars featured an ingenious air accumulation system, described later.

Mitsubishi

Ralliart (later called MMSP) used their existing "Step 2" cars for a small number of events, also their 2000 version "Evo 6.5" for British championship events, but carried out no development. All such work was being focussed on the new model due to be launched at the end of 2003. During the year the whole world championship programme for 2004 was being planned, of which the design of the car to be used for the next three seasons was only one aspect. The project began in February 2003, and it was apparent that the current "Step 2" car had been developed in a way which was too highly focussed to enable a longer term developed programme to be undertaken. It was decided that a fresh design was necessary, based on the Evo VIII (in material ways, similar to Evo VII), but with full WRC possibilities (full body modifications and aerodynamical aids, without close reference to the appearance of production road cars) and with straightforward systems which could be evolved over the next few seasons.

Peugeot 206 and 307

The team started the season with 2002 cars, their new red Marlboro colour scheme being the most striking change. The controlled anti roll bar system was only used this season on asphalt road rallies. Main purpose of this work was to improve traction, therefore the general available grip, so that the tyres could wear less and in turn softer compounds could be used. The method was to control the degree of bodywork roll of the car by noting the grip available at any particular moment and the speed at which the car was cornering. This in turn would ensure the biggest possible tyre "footprint" was in contact with the road surface. Cockpit air conditioning was provided in Greece and used by Burns and Rovanpera. This featured a radiator mounted in front of the intercooler with a water spray nozzle mounted just in front of the radiator. At the request of the FIA, the cooling spray was disconnected before Cyprus. Gearbox troubles experienced in Greece were solved before Cyprus by fitting clutches which were less aggressive in operation. Wheel bearing failures in Finland were found to be due to faulty assembly.

Tantalising glimpses of the 307WRC were issued during the season but full details were not to be released until the car was homologated in January 2004. From information initially released, various pointers were evident. Firstly the car was evidently at the other end of the scale, among the biggest as opposed to the smallest in the field, wheelbase now 2610mm, was 2468. Secondly it was the second successive WRC design which carried a revolutionary element. With the 206WRC, means needed to be found to bring the size of the car up to the minimum car length for homologation. With the 307WRC it was the problem of the roof became evident. Based for homologation purposes on the 307CC cabriolet, there was no existing provision for a soft top car to be homologated. This was overcome by the team agreeing to weld a roof permanently in place! Other special characteristics to note: the transmission is by five speed transverse unit, not a five or six speed longitudinal system, and the rake of the windscreen is quite the flattest seen on a rally car. The first prototype ran at the end of December 2002, seven months after plans were first made. The engine used in competition is virtually identical to that used currently in the Citroen Xsara WRC, a more recent version of the power unit used in the 206WRC.

Skoda Octavia and Fabia

Skoda started the season with modified 2002 Octavia WRC cars, principally with attention being paid to improved weight balance, notably by relocating the fuel tank to a position under the floor pan. The big moment came in Germany with the debut of the Fabia WRC, which had been first shown in public at the Geneva motor show in March. Permission to produce this car was confirmed in late 2001 and work started middle 2002. The Fabia WRC was homologated out of the Fabia RS turbocharged 1.9 litre diesel, which has a standard length of 4002mm (other models are 3960mm long). The Fabia basis gave a chance to optimise weight management and distribution. The engine is inclined further rearwards than possible on the Octavia, and the transmission units were now designed by Xtrac. Locating ancillaries under the bonnet was critical as the available space is less. The engine was similar to the Octavia, modified as necessary and with a lighter crankshaft. The hydraulic systems were split, with one system for the gearbox and another for the differentials, to overcome problems with lubrication and hydraulic unified system experienced in earlier viscous of the Octavia. Originally the Fabia was not due to appear in competition until

the last quarter of 2003, but when early tests showed the car was very soon as quick as the Octavia, the debut was brought forward. One surprise on the debut was that the team were also experimenting with an alternative transmission system by Unic in Sweden. This system was used in Germany on Gardemeister's car and the orthodox Xtrac for Auriol, but afterwards always with Xtrac. Other changes from the car first seen in Geneva included new air orifices in bumpers, changes to under bonnet cooling and a new rear wing design with fences. For gravel rallies various changes were made, with larger

rear top suspension mounting plates, a new circular gearshift "paddles" in place of the buttons for use on asphalt events, so as to be operated at greater angles of steering wheel movement and these were then also used for asphalt as well. Stronger rear top suspension mounts were fitted after failures in Germany. New for Italy was a revised airbox, designed to create better airflow. Watercooled brakes used in Corsica.

Subaru Impreza

Entering their tenth season with the Impreza, the only team to launch their new 2003 version cars at Monte Carlo was Subaru. This model was conceived to a far greater degree alongside the work of the company's central design office, and with detailed designs being evolved through

simulation rather than testing. Much of the car's improvement was aerodynamic, with smaller changes to engine including a new turbocharger, exhaust manifold and it was intended to have new camshafts, but this was deferred. Structurally there was a 15mm increase in wheelbase achieved by changes in suspension geometry. As the car was capable of running under the minimum weight, the lower mounted ancillaries were deliberately over-engineered. Main external difference was the large box

shaped rear wing with vertical fences. There were many detailed changes in the bodywork. Sachs shock absorbers were used for the first time in Argentina. Roof scoops were normally removed but fitted just for Greece and Cyprus. When the basic version had established reliability, enhanced engine settings for improved performance were introduced for Germany. Most important change came on Solberg's car in Italy when a form of active suspension based on spring control was introduced.

New Technical Rules for 2004

New minimum weights for Group A (which means World Rally Cars) have been ordered to prevent an increasing unfairness in favour of smaller cars. The minimum weight of bodyshells had to be 320kg while the basic minimum weights already existing would continue. In order to retain the overall minimum weights, various bodywork panels can now be lightened. Like in JWRC, the total minimum weight is to be increased by 150kg and the cars weighed with crew on board. Boot and bonnet material can be replaced by metallic pieces, fenders with plastic. Springs could no longer be constructed out of titanium, bumpers and windscreens had to be heavier. Twin-clutch gearboxes were to be banned. In addition, it is planned to introduce a ban on electronics in steering (to prevent work on 'steer-by-wire') and in new areas of transmission work for 2004, with plans to limit electronic work with suspensions in 2005. New regulations also gave stability to key elements in rally car designs till the end of 2006. World Rally Cars will be banned from FIA or WCR events and eligible for national events only.

Group N developments

2003 saw Subaru become, for the first time, a regular winner in Group N, especially at world championship level. The only major technical changes were internal changes in the gearbox, designed to strengthen the life of 3rd gear, but more particularly the cars used in PCWRC events were built initially at Prodrive, and careful attention was taken to controlling how the cars were used, lifing the various accessories and so on. The new version (coded N9) was

otherwise a facelifted version of the previous model. For Corsica Arai appeared with a new car, fitted with a roll cage that was substantially modified. Mitsubishi still numerically dominated the Group N scene, though there were few appearances of Evo VIII cars. Some converted Evo VII cars appeared. MMSP meanwhile were developing a '8.5" version, featuring many changes including lighter bodywork, and revised electronics aimed at increasing power output.

SUPER 1600 CHAMPION

**CONGRATULATIONS TO
KRIS MEEKE THE BRITISH
SUPER 1600 CHAMPION
IN THE 2003 PIRELLI BRITISH
RALLY CHAMPIONSHIP**

Team PALMER

**Team Palmer, Hill Parke, Trusham, Devon, TQ13 0NL. Tel: (44) 01626 854404, Fax: (44) 01626 854414
Email: rob@teampalmer.co.uk Web: www.teampalmer.co.uk**

Super 1600 Cars

Citroen C2

First shown at the Geneva Motor Show was a concept for a new generation entry-level competition car, based on the C2. This project was aimed at different lower level disciplines, the top level being a Super 1600. Due for homologation in April 2004 the car is to have a shorter bodywork (by 80mm) and wheelbase (by 75mm) than the Saxo model which it is to replace, with an engine in Super 1600, it should produce 225bhp.

Ford Fiesta

Due to compete during the course of 2004 is the Fiesta, a replacement for the Puma programme. Designed as a project with strong links with the central design office of the car, the Fiesta is aimed to project Ford's future designs through present day motor sport, as a taster for mass produced cars due to be launched later on. The Puma had been aimed as a joint one-make series and a Super 1600 car, with compromises that were appropriate to the combined project, but as a competition car it is developed as a stand-alone project. To this extent the Fiesta has a purpose designed transmission unit from Hewland, the engine although based on the same Sigma family in fact has a longer stroke with smaller valves and the induction designed from scratch with the mandatory single plenum chamber throttle. Wheel travel is considerably greater, so ride height can be a lot lower than the Puma. More details of the design are expected to be released nearer homologation time.

Philip Dunabin

Opel Corsa

During the course of the season, Opel applied for their 'joker' homologation parts, comprising of engine induction and exhaust manifold and these were fitted in the cars used by Meeke in the British and JWRC series

Suzuki Ignis

Shown at the Frankfurt Motor Show in September was the 2004 Ignis. This car is based on a new five-door bodyshell instead of the current three-door. Dimensions of wheelbase are unchanged, but the car is 175mm longer and the width is now increased by 30mm. There is a revised rear wing. Engine is more powerful. Suspension geometry has been altered, and a new roll cage has increased body stiffness.

Alfa 147

A car that defied categorisation! Enthusiasts in Britain were given consent by the British federation to run an Alfa 147 in the Pirelli British Rally championship, on the expectation that the manufacturing company hoped to apply for homologation in the future. This project had its roots in an earlier circuit racing team. The engine was a 1600cc version derived from the production 1800cc unit, transmission had been prepared by Hewland with a specially designed bell housing and a six speed sequential gearshift.

"WE'RE JUST DOING IT"

RALLY CAR RENTAL ROUND THE WORLD IN 2004

For details contact:
Kevin Sanderson
General Manager
kevin@possumbourne.co.nz

Unit C, 159 Manukau Road,
Pukekohe, New Zealand
Tel: 64-9-2385732
Fax: 64-9-2385737

Read all about Possum in his autobiography *Bourne to Rally*
ISDN No: 0-9582388-1-2 Published by Phantom House Books Ltd www.phantomhouse.com

World Rally Car Countdown

Chassis	Reg No.	Notes/Drivers
Citroen Xsara		
06	26CSP92	McRae: S, D, F
07	27CSP92	Loeb: S, **D**
08	28CSP92	McRae: RA
09	29CSP92	Sainz: S, GR, AUS
10	30CSP92	Loeb: NZ, AUS
11	31CSP92	Sainz: MC, I
12	32CSP92	Loeb: **MC, I**
16	36CSP92	Sainz: RA, FIN. Bugalski: F
19	39CSP92	Sainz: **TR**, CY, E
20	20CSP92	Sola: GR, GB
21	27DDM92	Bugalski: D, I. Loeb: F. Bugalski: E
22	14DDM92	McRae: TR, CY, E
23	15DDM92	McRae: MC, I
24	16DDM92	Loeb: TR, CY, E
25	17DDM92	Loeb: RA, FIN
26	18DDM92	McRae: NZ, AUS. Sainz: GB
27	19DDM92	Sainz: NZ, D, F
28	20DDM92	Loeb: GR, GB
29	21DDM92	McRae: GR, GB
30	22DDM92	McRae: FIN
Ford Focus (versions interchangeable)		
	P10FMC	Roux: MC
	S10FMC	Cserhalmi: D
	V3FMC	Yazici: TR
	V4FMC	A.Eriksson: S, GB
	V9FMC	Viita: FIN
	X7FMC	Latvala: GB
	X8FMC	Tuohino: S
	X493YOO=*IZ4 4600	(CZ) Benik: TR, *AUS
	Y3FMC	Warmbold: MC, S, RA, CY, D, FIN, AUS, F, GB
	Y6FMC=*AE208	Latvala: GR, D, *FIN
	Y129XEV	Kuchar: S, GR
	EJ02KMO	Ginley: TR, CY, D, FIN, F, GB
	EK51UAB=*CC804	Kuistila: *FIN
	EK51HXZ	Hirvonen: MC
	EK51HYA	Hirvonen: S
	EX02OBB	Martin: S. Hirvonen: NZ, GR, CY Perez: GB
	EX02OBC	Duval: S. Hirvonen: TR, RA, D, AUS, F
	EX02OBD=*CL187	Martin: MC, TR. Tuohino: *FIN
	EX02OBE=*AE209	Duval: MC, TR. Vovos: GR Hirvonen: *FIN, I, E, GB
Ford Focus 2003 version		
	EJ02OBF	Test car
	EJ02KMU	Martin: NZ, Duval: RA, CY, FIN, F, GB
	EJ02KMV	Duval: NZ, GR
	EO03XYG	Duval: D, I, E
	R55OTH	Martin: D, AUS
	EO03YWC	Martin: RA, CY. Duval: AUS

Chassis	Reg No.	Notes/Drivers
		Martin: GB
	EO03YRJ	Martin: **GR, FIN**, F
	EK52LNP	Martin: I
	EK52NWN	Martin: E
Hyundai Accent 2/3		
12	X12HMC	Dale: CY, D
14	X14HMC	Valimaki: S, NZ, GR, FIN
Hyundai Accent 3		
18	X18HMC	Schwarz: MC, TR. Stohl: D
19	X19HMC	Loix: MC, TR. Schwarz: GR
20	not allocated	
21	X21HMC	Loix: RA, CY, FIN
22	X22HMC	Schwarz: RA, CY, FIN
23	X23HMC	Loix: S, NZ
24	X24HMC	Schwarz: S, NZ
26	X26HMC	Loix: GR, D, AUS
27	X27HMC	Schwarz: D, AUS
Mitsubishi Lancer Evolution WRC2		
06	KP51RWL	McRae: NZ
08	KP51RWN	Sohlberg: NZ
16	KN52XBB	Paasonen: D
17	KN52XBC	Sohlberg: D
Peugeot 206 (first used as versions 1 or 2)		
3	206MWP75 (previously 206MTC75)	Stohl: NZ, F
9	206MWJ75	Pykalisto: S
14	3976XR69 (previously 206NHW75)	Robert: MC Pykalisto: TR, GR. Kresta: E, GB
16	BQ483 (previously 206NAK75)	Lindholm: FIN
17	4852YW69 (previously 206NAP75)	Kresta: MC, S Pykalisto: CY. Vatanen: FIN Robert: E
20	337PPZ75 (previously 206NAN75)	Bengue: F
24	4854YW69 (previously 206NDP75)	Kresta: GR, D, F Pykalisto: GB
Peugeot 206 (first used as version 3)		
26	206NLN75	gravel test car: crashed by Burns in Scotland
34	290NNN75	Gronholm: TR. Rovanpera: CY Robert: D
35	286NNN75	Gronholm: **NZ**. Panizzi: D. Burns: F
38	344NQZ75 (*BQ481)	Rovanpera: TR, *FIN
40	341NQZ75	Panizzi: TR, GR. Pykalisto: FIN Panizzi: GB
41	334NQZ75	Burns: TR, FIN
42	943NVB75	Gronholm: CY, GB
43	945NVB75 (*BQ480)	Gronholm: *FIN. Panizzi: **E**
44	950NVB75	Burns: CY

Chassis	Reg No.	Notes/Drivers
45	938NVB75	Rovanpera: NZ
46	948NVB75	Panizzi: CY
47	952NVB75	Burns: NZ, D. Gronholm: F
Peugeot 206 (first used as version 4)		
48	206NLM75	Burns: MC, RA, I, GB
49	206NLL75	Gronholm: MC Rovanpera: RA. Panizzi: I
50	624NZT75	Burns: S, Rovanpera: GR Gronholm: AUS. Rovanpera: GB
51	810NVT75	Gronholm: **S**, Burns: GR, AUS
52	814NVT75	Rovanpera: S, Gronholm: GR Rovanpera: AUS
53	206NDQ75	Panizzi: MC. Gronholm: **RA**, I
54		Spare car
55	283NNN75	Gronholm: D. Panizzi: F
Skoda Octavia WRC		
10	MBO82-74	Kahle: D
11	MBN44-30	Pozzo: RA. Errani: I
21	MBO72-24	Gardemeister: TR. Kopecky: D
23	MBN15-48	Auriol: S, RA, CY
24	MBO90-42	Auriol: TR
25	MBO90-41	Gardemeister: S, RA, CY
26	2S5 1190	Gardemeister: MC, NZ, GR
27	2S5 1180	Auriol: MC, NZ, GR
Skoda Fabia WRC		
1	3S3 1941	Test car
2	3S3 1944	Test car
3	3S3 1945	Test car
4	3S3 1943	Gardemeister: D, FIN
5	3S3 1942	Auriol: D, FIN
6	3S3 1947	Auriol: AUS. Gardemeister: I, GB
7	3S3 1946	Gardemeister: AUS. Auriol: I, GB
8	3S3 1948	Auriol: F, E
9	3S3 1949	Gardemeister: F, D
Subaru Impreza (chassis number indicates version)		
03001 + 03002		Show cars
03003	S30WRT	Makinen: MC, TR, D, I, E
03004	S40WRT	Solberg: MC
03005	S50WRT	Makinen: S, Solberg: NZ
03006	S60WRT	Solberg: S, Makinen: CY
03007	S70WRT	Makinen: RA
03008	S80WRT	Solberg: TR, Makinen: NZ
		Solberg: **CY**. Rousselot: F
03009	S90WRT	Solberg: RA. Makinen: FIN, F
03010	S100WRT	Solberg: GR
03011	S200WRT	Makinen: GR, AUS, GB
03012	S300WRT	Solberg: I
03014	S400WRT	Solberg: D, E
03015	S500WRT	Solberg: FIN
03016	S600WRT	Solberg: **AUS, GB**
03017	S700WRT	Solberg: **F**

It's time for a fresh challenge.

During its first season in the Junior World Rally Championship, the Suzuki Ignis more than proved its worth. It won 56 out of the 124 stages, and fought its way to two rally wins and two second places, with driver Daniel Carlsson achieving most of the fastest times. After these initial successes, we're well prepared for the 2004 season. And by successfully testing the Suzuki Ignis on some of the world's most demanding terrain, we can apply the knowledge gained to our continued search for excellence and enhanced customer satisfaction.

www.suzuki-swt.com

Alessandro Broccoli tests the strength of the Opel Corsa in Finland.

Junior

World Rally Championship

Held for the third year (and for the second year with an official world championship status), there were two major changes in the Junior series in 2003. Firstly that the series covered seven rather than six rounds. Turkey was the extra event, while Finland was brought in to replace Deutschland. Secondly, there was a maximum age limit for the drivers, who had to be born on or after 1st January 1974.

There was a change of cars this year. After Citroen Saxo drivers had won the first two championships, it was surprising that only two of these cars were entered for the 2003 series, and after the first two rounds both had disappeared. Fiats were the most popular cars chosen by the contenders this year, six being initially entered, but the team which was the most impressive was the four Suzuki Ignis cars, one more than last year. The championship continued to be for drivers not makes, always for private entries, but the professionalism of the Ignis cars again

set impressive standards, looking exactly like any works rally team except in name. These little square yellow boxes on wheels won hearts wherever they went, and gained podium positions on every event except Monte Carlo. Among the other popular marques were Ford, in which four drivers started the season and in which Guy Wilks made an international name for himself, and Peugeot and VW which each attracted three drivers

In 2003 there were almost all new winners. Except for the Sanremo when the San Marino driver Mirco Baldacci scored a popular win with his ageing Fiat Punto, every event in the 2003 championship was won by a type of car which had never been successful before, namely VW Polo, Renault Clio and Suzuki Ignis. The most important arrivals on the scene were the Renault Clio cars, two years after they were first developed. Two were entered originally but only the car of Brice Tirabassi, the French Super 1600 champion in 2002, saw out the series. With cars prepared by Oreca, Brice often had a teammate Simon Jean-Joseph who drove a similar car outside the championship, but in conditions that replicated those of championship contenders except for the age of the driver...

Two drivers rose to be stars of the season. Clearly Tirabassi proved to be a good all-rounder. About the only times he struggled were in Finland where Daniel Carlsson was clearly faster, and in Britain where the car was not working well and then let him down for other reasons. Carlsson was the other star, showing driving and other qualities that outstripped his rivals, but with an inconsistency which matched his speed! The man who was

World Champions Brice Tirabassi and Jacques-Julien Renucci (Renault Clio).

2003 FIA Junior World Rally Championship (JWRC)

Event listing: position in category (overall result), retirement, car registration. NS = did not start.

Comp No	Driver Codriver	Nat	Car	Monte-Carlo	Turkey	Acropolis	Finland	Sanremo	Catalunya	Great Britain
51	Mirco Baldacci / Giovanni Bernacchini	RSM / I	Fiat Punto	7th (23rd) BS096GJ (I)	front suspension BS096GJ (I)	oil cooler BS096GJ (I)	driveshaft BS096GJ (I)	1st (16th) BS096GJ (I)	engine BS096GJ (I)	2nd (15th) BS096GJ (I)
52	Daniel Carlsson / Mattias Andersson	S / S	Suzuki Ignis	too late IBE200 (H)	suspension IBE200 (H)	2nd (18th) IIM719 (H)	1st (19th) ITA852 (H)	accident IVG648 (H)	4th (22nd) IIM720 (H)	1st (14th) ITA852 (H)
53	David Doppelreiter / Ola Floene	A / N	Peugeot 206	NS (A)	-	-	-	-	-	-
54	Kosti Katajamaki / (a) Miikka Anttila / (b) Jani Laaksonen	FIN / FIN / FIN	VW Polo	(a) excluded H-RM388 (D)	(a) 1st (15th) H-RM388 (D)	(a) gearbox H-RM388 (D)	(b) accident BV091 (FIN)	(b) driveshaft H-RM495 (D)	(b) alternator belt H-RM388 (D)	(b) steering HRM388 (D)
55	Martin Stenshorne / Clive Jenkins	N / GB	Ford Puma	accident EK51HXY (GB)	codriver ill EK51HXY (GB)	alternator belt EK51HXY (GB)	NS (B) USD2500	-	-	-
57	Dimitar Iliev / (a) Peter Sivov / (b) Yanaki Yanakiev	BG / BG	Peugeot 206	(a) accident 2877MK70 (F)	(a) 7th (27th) 2877MK70 (F)	(b) engine 2877MK70 (F)	(b) driveshaft 2877MK70 (F)	(b) 3rd (21st) 2877MK70 (F)	(b) accident 2877MK70 (F)	NS excused
58	Marcos Ligato / Ruben Garcia	RA / RA	Fiat Punto	2nd (18th) BY593NX (I)	gearbox BY579NX (I)	steering BY579NX (I)	7th (30th) BY579NX (I)	withdrawn BY579NX (I)	NS medical	NS medical
59	Beppo Harrach / Michael Kolbach	A / D	Ford Puma	8th (24th) Y36NNO (GB)	lost oil Y36NNO (GB)	lost wheel Y36NNO (GB)	NS excused	-	-	-
60	Pavel Valousek / Pierangelo Scalvini	CZ / I	Citroen Saxo	withdrawn before start 8892NA52 (F)	(C)	-	-	-	-	-
61	Brice Tirabassi / Jacques-Julien Renucci	F / F	Renault Clio	1st (17th) 871AMC83 (F)	accident 871AMC83 (F)	1st (17th) 871AMC83 (F)	2nd (20th) 871AMC83 (F)	electrical 871AMC83 (F)	1st (17th) 871AMC83 (F)	electrical 871AMC83 (F
62	Oscar Svedlund / Bjorn Nilsson	S / S	VW Polo	accident H-RM495 (D)	steering H-RM495 (D)	5th (27th) H-RM495 (D)	8th (33rd) H-RM495 (D)	NS excused	differential H-RM495 (D)	electrics H-RM495 (D)
63	Massimo Ceccato / Mitia Dotta	I / I	Fiat Punto	5th (21st) BS100GJ (I)	transmission BS100GJ (I)	engine BS099GJ (I)	accident BS099GJ (I)	accident CE078WE (I)	8th (29th) CE078WE (I)	6th (30th) CE078WE (I)
64	Ville-Pertti Teuronen / (a) Harri Kaapro / (b) Mikko Markkula	FIN / FIN / FIN	Suzuki Ignis	(a) accident IKM730 (H)	(a) 4th (19th) IKM730 (H)	(a) driveshaft IIM720 (H)	(a) accident ITA853 (H)	(a) 4th (23rd) IVG649 (H)	(b) 6th (25th) IVG649 (H)	(b) 3rd (23rd) ITA853 (H)

Suspension penalties: (A) all world championship rallies until end of 2004, (B) all JWRC events until end of 2004, (C) all FIA, ebents until end of 2004.

Kosti Katajamaki (right) celebrates victory in Turkey with Miikka Antilla and manager Risto Burri.

Salvador Canellas Junior.

Comp No	Driver / Codriver	Nat	Car	Monte-Carlo	Turkey	Acropolis	Finland	Sanremo	Catalunya	Great Britain
65	Abdo Feghali / Joseph Matar	RL / RL	Ford Puma	10th (26th) EX02PXL (GB)	6th (25th) EX02PXL (GB)	engine X881YOO (GB)	accident Y36NNO (GB)	7th (32nd) EX02PXL (GB)	7th (27th) EX02PXL (GB)	gearbox Y36NND (GB)
66	Sebastien Ceccone / Julien Giroux	F / F	Citroen Saxo	accident 8036NA52 (F)	clutch 8036NA52 (F)	NS (B) USD2500	-	-	-	-
67	Alessandro Broccoli (a) Simona Girelli (b) Giovanni Agnese	RSM I I	(i) Opel Corsa (ii) Renault Clio	(a) 3rd (19th) (i) BW930PS (I)	(a) suspension (i) BW930PS (I)	(a) driveshaft (i) BW930PS (I)	(a) 6th (27th) (i) BW930PS (I)	(b) steering (ii) BW326KT (I)	(b) engine (i) BW930PS (I)	(b) 5th (29th) (i) BW930PS (I)
68	Juraj Sebalj / Toni Klinc	HR / HR	Renault Clio	6th (22nd) CB599VF (I)	rear suspension CB599VF (I)	NS (C)	-	-	-	-
69	Salvador Canellas / Xavier Amigo	E / E	Suzuki Ignis	driveshaft IKM729 (H)	2nd (16th) IKM729 (H)	4th (22nd) IKM729 (H)	5th (26th) IEK314 (H)	2nd (18th) IVG650 (H)	3rd (21st) IVG650 (H)	4th (28th) IEK314 (H)
70	Guy Wilks / Phil Pugh	GB / GB	Ford Puma	wheelstuds EX02PXM (GB)	3rd (18th) EX02PXM (GB)	6th (32nd) EX02PXM (GB)	3rd (24th) EX02PXM (GB)	6th (28th) EX02PXM (GB)	11th (33rd) EX02PXM (GB)	crankshaft pulley EX02PXM (GB)
71	Urmo Aava / Kuldar Sikk	EE / EE	Suzuki Ignis	4th (20th) IKM728 (H)	suspension IKM728 (H)	3rd (19th) IKM728 (H)	4th (25th) ITA854 (H)	driveshaft IVG651(H)	5th (24th) IVG651(H)	driveshaft ITA854 (H)
72	Jader Vagnini / Lorenzo Granai	RSM I	Fiat Punto	NS (A)	-	-	-	-	-	
73	Krum Donchev / Rumen Manolov	BG / YU	Peugeot 206	11th (27th) 6499MG70 (F)	suspension 6499MG70 (F)	lost wheel 6499MG70 (F)	NS medical reason	accident BM767AE (I)	9th (31st) BM767AE (I)	NS USD1000
74	Kris Meeke / Chris Patterson	GB / GB	Opel Corsa	12th (29th) GG-VP307 (D)	wheel studs GG-VP307 (D)	steering GG-VT506 (D)	electrics GG-VT506 (D)	accident GG-VT506 (D)	2nd (19th) GG-VT506 (D)	accident X10PEL(GB)
76	Luca Cecchettini / Marco Muzzarelli	I / I	Fiat Punto	9th (25th) BS099GJ (I)	5th (21st) BS099GJ (I)	engine BS100GJ (I)	accident BS100GJ (I)	5th (25th) BS100GJ (I)	10th (32nd) BS100GJ (I)	engine BS100GJ (I)
77	Filippo Suessli / Loris Pala	CH / CH	Fiat Punto	NS (A)	-	-	-	-	-	-
78	'V-Man' Vladan Vasiljevic / Sebastian Geipel	D / D	(i) VW Polo (ii) Peugeot 206	too late (i) H-VW880 (D)	engine (i) H-VW880 (D)	accident (i) H-VW880 (D)	withdrawn (ii) SWB247 (S)	NS excused	-	-

Salvador Canellas, the asphalt specialist of Suzuki's team, finished the highest placed in the series.

Line up in Monte Carlo.

Unlucky season in both JWRC and PCWRC for Marcos Ligato!

Tirabassi's last rival for the title, however, was Salvador Canellas from Spain, son of a works SEAT rally driver a generation ago. Canellas was Suzuki's 'asphalt expert', but like all the Suzukis suffered gearbox troubles on the final round of the series,

Super 1600 competition has increased at national level round the world with an international crossover of activities. The San Marino driver Mirco Baldacci for example twice entered British championship rallies and this gave him useful experience for the Wales Rally GB. Baldacci was one of the strengths of the JWRC, progressing in mid season to a World Rally Car in which he won a rally in Austria, on the first occasion he competed with a four-wheels drive vehicle. Notwithstanding that the JWRC events have been limited to Europe (Turkey included!) there continued to be a notable internationality of drivers; 17 countries were represented, including non-European countries such as Lebanon and Argentina.

There were few technical troubles this year, the biggest problem coming with the exclusion of Kosti Katajamaki after Monte Carlo Rally for using the wrong specification of rear brakes. Regarding the general specification of the formula, the cost factor seemed to be out of control. This was intended to be a core point of the formula. Ford, who had designed the Puma with cost limitations strongly in mind (they built in as much commonality as the one-make 1400cc cars as possible), went ahead with their Fiesta S1600 with quite different financial philosophies.

Cars eligible for Super 1600 continue to change. The demise of the Saxo in 2003 was largely connected with the impending arrival of the C2, while the decline in the fortune of the Puma is related to the wait for the Fiesta to come along. Both are expected to be ready in time for Acropolis, 2004. About the only unexpected turn of fortune came with VW, whose new competition director announced in mid season his wish to end the support of the factory. This led to Oscar Svedlund missing Sanremo, and nearly the same for Katajamaki, these two drivers saw out the season, but the prize drive winner 'V-Man' did not.

In 2001 the JWRC had a spectacular success when Sebastien Loeb was promoted in mid season to works World Rally Car drives with Citroen, and he then became the moral winner of Monte Carlo Rally. The 2002 champion Daniel Sola spent the following year in PCWRC, and then at the end of 2003 was given a place in the new MMSP (Mitsubishi) world rally team. Kristian Sohlberg had entered the 2003 season but withdrew from the series when he had the offer of a drive in a World Rally Car. Tirabassi has still not announced his plans for 2004, but it is possible he will seek to retain his JWRC title.

Considering the huge upheaval in the format of world championship rallying in 2004, there are few specific changes to

Guy Wilks enjoys Greek food...

JWRC. Perhaps the main change will be that Pirelli will be the control tyre supplier rather than Michelin. It is hoped that flexi-service will make it easier for teams to run multi-car teams. Perhaps the only unfortunate thing about the '04 season is the long gap between the opening round, Monte Carlo, and the second, which will be Acropolis. Gradually the JWRC concept is getting better known. Television exposure has increased, one of the top WRC manufacturers has been discussing ways in which one of their young World Rally Car drivers can downgrade his activities into JWRC, and benefit from learning a completely new aspect to rally sport. The constant flow of new ideas can only promise good things for the future.

Brice Tirabassi (left) and fans.

Final positions in 2003 FIA Junior World Rally Championship (JWRC)

		Total	Monte-Carlo	Turkey	Acropolis	Finland	Sanremo	Catalunya	Great Britain
1	Brice Tirabassi (F)	**38**	10	R	10	8	R	10	R
2	Salvador Canellas (E)	**36**	R	8	5	4	8	6	5
3	Daniel Carlsson (S)	**33**	R	R	8	10	R	5	10
4	Mirco Baldacci (RSM)	**20**	2	R	R	R	10	R	8
5	Urmo Aava (EE)	**20**	5	R	6	5	R	4	R
6	Ville-Pertti Teuronen (FIN)	**19**	R	5	R	R	5	3	6
7	Guy Wilks (GB)	**18**	R	6	3	6	3	0	R
8	Alessandro Broccoli (RSM)	**13**	6	R	R	3	R	R	4
9	Kosti Katajamaki (FIN)	**10**	Ex	10	R	R	R	R	R
10	Marcos Ligato (RA)	**10**	8	R	R	2	NS	NS	NS

Ex = excluded, **NS** = non start, **R** = retired.
Other points scorers Dimitar Iliev (BG), Kris Meeke (GB), Luca Cecchettini (I) 8, Massimo Ceccato (I) & Abdo Feghali (RL) 7, Oscar Svedlund (S) 5, Juraj Sebalj (HR) 3, Beppo Harrach (A) 1.

ASTRA

FIA Junior World Rally Championship Team

Astra Racing-B.go San Martino, 20
12060 Pocapaglia CN, Italy

T +39.0172.413174 F +39.0172.431850
info@astraracing.com www.astraracing.com

**Ford Fiesta and Ford Puma S1600 available for Junior World Rally Championship
and S1600 National Championship Programmes**

World Rally Champions

1981 and 2003 (Group N)

**Martin Rowe &
Trevor Agnew**

**Stig Blomqvist
& Ana Goni**

**Subaru Impreza
WRX-STI**

**2 Cars
6 Rallies
12 Results**

Special Thanks to: **BODEGA OTAZU**

*1981 Ford Escort RS
Ari Vatanen - David Richards*

*Daventry - England
Tel: 44 1327 300677
Fax: 44 1327 300683
Email: historicmotorsportltd@btinternet.com
Web: davidsuttoncars.com*

Production Car

Deja Vue. David Sutton wins another world rally title, this time with Martin Rowe (left) and codriver Trevor Agnew.

World Rally Championship

This was the second year of the PCWRC. The big change was the fact that Mitsubishi cars in 2003 did not dominate the series, in fact the Subaru Impreza won five of the seven qualifying rounds. In 2003 there were seven not eight qualifying rounds, competitors had to nominate one, instead of two, events on which they would not take part. All six scores from the six events actually entered would count. The arrival of a competitive and reliable Subaru was a marked change. Five drivers entered themselves with programmes based on Imprezas. Toshihiro Arai was the only Subaru user in 2002, this year his programme continued but there was now also a two-car team from David Sutton Cars in Britain while the New Zealander Possum Bourne had another programme as did Pat Richard from Canada. There were several faithful Mitsubishi teams represented in the championship, notably Top Run and Nocentini, while there was a new team from Spain, Calm Competicion. Manfred Stohl was also active on many events with a Mitsubishi run by customers. There was a lot of rivalry between the private Mitsubishi teams, with competitors often changing allegiance from event to event. Only one manufacturer was directly involved, this was Proton, who supported

the reigning PCWRC champion Karamjit Singh's Pert in a rebadged Evo VI, run by the British company Mellors Elliott Motorsport.

Car development through the year came to both Subaru and Mitsubishi. Subaru's latest model was not ready at the start of the season but from the second round, New Zealand, onwards it was used by Arai and the DSC drivers straightaway and later by Richard. Only Joakim Roman drove an Evo V, more and more Mitsubishi drivers progressed from Evo VI to Evo VII, but with the long delay before left-hand drive production Evo VIIIs were available, there was only one left-hand drive version Evo VIII seen in the series, a converted VII driven by Daniel Sola at Corsica.

In order to promote the Junior World Rally Championship as a lower cost formula, the PCWRC competitors again found they were given the long-haul events in the calendar. It was interesting that this led to teams from further afield being involved, notably two from New Zealand, not only Possum Bourne Motorsport but also Neil Allport Motorsport, who was running the Mitsubishi for Niall McShea. When the initial championship list of 27 drivers was announced, nine of them were from outside Europe, and a total of 18 different countries were represented. There soon became a very distinct division

between the top class drivers and the also rans. Reliability was an essential ingredient for success. Eventual champion Martin Rowe, with his David Sutton teammate Stig Blomqvist, were the only drivers in the series who finished all six rounds they were required to drive.

There were some hard moments during the season. The Polish driver Janusz Kulig was found with a flywheel of the wrong type, evidently obtained from an unauthorised source and which was not believed to give any performance advantage, but had to be excluded after winning the category on the Swedish. But that was nothing to the shock when Possum Bourse died after an accident only one week following the New Zealand

Discovering the world with the PCWRC. Karamjit Singh and Allen Oh meet snow!

2003 FIA Production Car World Championship (PCWRC)

Position in category, overall result/retirement, type of car, car registration (country)
NS = Nominated but did not start, X = elected not to start, - = withdrawn from series.

Comp No	Driver/Codriver	Car	Tyres	Swedish	New Zealand	Argentina	Cyprus	Germany	Australia	Corsica
51	Karamjit Singh (MAL) Allen Oh (MAL)	Proton Pert	P	2nd (27th) VI WU02XFA (GB)	6th (21st) VI WU02XFA (GB)	3rd (13th) VI WU02XFB (GB)	front suspension VI WU02XFA (GB)	4th (27th) VI WU02XFB (GB)	2nd (17th) VI WU02XFA (GB)	X
52	Daniel Sola (E) Alex Romani (E)	Mit. Lancer Evolution	P	X	15th (44th) VII BW655PS (I)	2nd (12th) VII BZ721KW (I)	transmission VII BW655PS (I)	1st (22nd) VII BZ721KW (I)	5th (20th) VII BW655PS (I)	differential VIII BZ928KY
53	Ramon Ferreyros (PER) (a) Javier Marin (MEX) (b) Guifre Pujol (E)	Mit. Lancer Evolution	P	X	(a) 5th (19th) VII BW654PS (I)	(a) radiator VII BW654PS (I)	(a) brakes VI BR350XX (I)	(a) electrical VII BW654PS (E)	(a) withdrawn VI BH121ZG (I)	(b) engine AZ458WC (I)
54	Toshihiro Arai (J) Tony Sircombe (NZ)	Subaru Impreza	P	engine GD Y10WRX (GB)	1st (11th) WRX GMG300NO9070 (J)	1st (9th) WRX GMG300NO9070 (J)	1st (9th) WRX GMG300NO9070(J)	X	clutch WRX GMG300NO9070 (J)	2nd (17th) WRX GMG300NO9071 (J)
55	Martin Rowe (GB) Trevor Agnew (GB)	Subaru Impreza	P	3rd (29th) GD OE52TEU (GB)	4th (18th) GD OE52TEU (GB)	X	2nd (10th) WRX X2DSC (GB)	2nd (24th) WRX X2DSC (GB)	1st (15th) WRX X2DSC (GB)	3rd (18th) WRX X2DSC (GB)
56	Gustavo Trelles (ROU) Jorge del Buono (RA)	Mit. Lancer Evolution	-	X	NS USD2,500	X	X	X	X	X
57	Giovanni Manfrinato (I) Claudio Condotto (I)	Mit. Lancer Evolution	P	X	9th (28th) VI AZ458WC (I)	4th (14th) VI BK633LY (I)	heavy landing VII CA814BV (I)	electrical VII BZ928KY (I)	NS illness	NS force majeure
58	Marcos Ligato (RA) Ruben Garcia (RA)	Mit. Lancer Evolution	P	X	2nd (16th) VII CA845BV (I)	engine VII CE49OCM (I)	4th (12th) VII CE491CM (I)	clutch VII CE490CM (I)	central differential VII CE491CM (I)	NS injury force majeure
59	Stefano Marrini (I) (a) Massimo Agostinelli (I) (b) Tiziana Sandroni (I)	Mit. Lancer Evolution	P	(a) engine VII BX168VW (I)	X	(a) engine VII BX168VW (I)	(a) heavy landing VI BH457ZG (I)	(a) 8th (38th) VII BX168VW (I)	(a) excluded VII BH457ZG (I)	(b) 10th (33rd) BX168VW (I)
60	Niall McShea (GB) Chris Patterson (GB)	Mit. Lancer Evolution	M	X	7th (22nd) VI X566YBD (GB)	oil cooler VI X564YBD (GB)	transmission VI X566YBD (GB)	driveshaft VI X566YBD (GB)	3rd (18th) VI X564YBD (GB)	1st (16th) X566YBD (GB)
61	Janusz Kulig (PL) (a) Jaroslaw Baran (PL) (b) Dariusz Burkat (PL) (c) Maciej Szczepaniak (PL)	Mit. Lancer Evolution	M	(a) excluded VI KBC.V034 (PL)	(a) fuel pump VII CE491CM (I)	X	(b) accident VII KBC.V035 (PL)	(c) 3rd (26th) VI KBC.V034 (PL)	NS procedural error	(c) 4th (19th) VII KBC.V035 (PL)
62	Possum Bourne (NZ) Mark Stacey (AUS)	Subaru Impreza	P	4th (31st) GD ROJ 1 (NZ)	engine WRX ROJ 2 (NZ)	-	X	-	-	-
63	Luca Baldini (I) (a) Roberto Vittori (I) (b) Alessandro Floris (I)	Mit. Lancer Evolution	P	(a) 11th (45th) VI AZ458WC (I)	(b) NS USD5,000	X	X	X	X	X

2002 Canadian champion Pat Richard sets off on the Rallye Deutschland.

Stig, still winning in Sweden. His first Swedish Rally win was in 1971.

Position in category, overall result/retirement, type of car, car registration (country)

NS = Nominated but did not start, X = elected not to start, - = withdrawn from series.

Comp No	Driver/Codriver	Car	Tyres	Swedish	New Zealand	Argentina	Cyprus	Germany	Australia	Corsica
64	Joakim Roman (S) (a) Tina Mitakidou (S) (b) Ragnar Spjuth (S)	Mit. Lancer Evolution	M/MRF	(a) 6th (36th) V REM523 (S)	(a) 12th (32nd) V REM523 (S)	X	(a) accident V REM523 (S)	(a) turbocharger V REM523 (S)	(b) 6th (26th) VI XLD973 (NSW,AUS)	(b) 9th (32nd) REM523 (S)
65	Stig Blomqvist (S) (a) Ana Goni (YV) (b) Rob Scott (NZ)	Subaru Impreza	P	(a) 1st (26th) GD OE52WXH (GB)	(a) 8th (24th) GD OE52WXH (GB)	X	(a) 3rd (11th) WRX X1DSC (GB)	(a) 5th (29th) WRX X1DSC (GB)	(b) 4th (19th) WRX X1DSC (GB)	(a) 5th (20th) WRX X1DSC (GB)
66	Hamed Al-Wahaibi (OM) Nicky Beech (GB)	Mit. Lancer Evolution	P	X	3rd (17th) VII GF.222BF (A)	withdrawn VII GF.222BF (A)	NS USD20,000	X	X	X
67	Krzysztof Holowczyc (PL) Lukasz Kurzeja (PL)	Mit. Lancer Evolution	M	5th (33rd) VII F4141 (FIN)	accident VII LKR.A494 (PL)	NS illness	NS illness	fuel pump VII NO35777 (PL)	NS procedural error	X force majeure
69	Bob Colsoul (B) Tom Colsoul (B)	Mit. Lancer Evolution	M	9th (42nd) VII CNC461 (B)	X	accident damage VII RCB877 (B)	5th (14th) VI KRS027 (B)	turbo pipe VII CLZ643 (B)	NS procedural error	6th (23rd) VII DTS430 (B)
70	Riccardo Errani (I) Stefano Casadio (I)	Mit. Lancer Evolution	P	X	road accident VI AFF898 (NZ)	7th (24th) VI not registered (RA)	6th (17th) VI AZ458WC (I)	9th (39th) VI 875ANZ06 (F)	NS illness	8th (29th) VI 875ANZ06 (F)
71	Georgi Geradzhiev (BG) Nikola Popov (BG)	Mit. Lancer Evolution	P	13th (53rd) VI 1646CDL (E)	14th (37th) VI 1646CDL (E)	engine VI 1646CDL (E)	electrical VI 1646CDL (E)	fuel pump VI S1.ALDA (PL)	X	NS force majeure
72	Constantin Aur (RO) (a) Silviu Moraru (RO) (b) Adrian Berghea (RO)	Mit. Lancer Evolution	P	(a) gearbox VII W.RAFO.10 (A)	(b) gearbox VII W.RAFO.10 (A)	X	(b) steering VII W.RAFO.10 (A)	(b) 7th (36th) VII W.RAFO.10 (A)	(b) rear suspension VI GF.222BF (A)	NS E2500
73	Stanislav Chovanec (CZ) Karel Holan (CZ)	Mit. Lancer Evolution	-	X	X	X	X	X	X	X
74	Fabio Frisiero (I) (a) Loris Roggia (I) (b) Giovanni Agnese (I)	Mit. Lancer Evolution	P	(a) 12th (46th) VI 1826CDM (E)	(b) 10th (30th) VII 9234BVK (E)	(b) rear suspension VII 9234BVK (E)	(b) withdrawn VII 9234BVK (E)	(b) transmission VII CA845BV (I)	X	(b) accident CA845BV (I)
76	Patrick Richard (CDN) (a) Mikael Johanson (S)	Subaru Impreza	P	(a) 8th (41st) GD WRX (BC,CDN)	(a) accident GD WRX (BC,CDN)	(a) transmission GD WRX (BC,CDN)	(b) front suspension GD WRX (BC,CDN)	(b) gearbox WRX KMT813 (B)	X	(b) transmission WRX KMT813 (B)
77	Alfredo de Dominicis (I) Giovanni Bernacchini (I)	Mit. Lancer Evolution	P	10th (44th) VI M3646ZT (E)	13th (34th) VI BH122ZG (I)	5th (18th) VII ACG900 (B) Michelin	engine VI BH122ZG (I)	engine VII 4631BVS (E)	X	gearbox 4631BVS (E)
78	Lukasz Sztuka (PL) (a) Per Carlsson (S) (b) Zbigniew Cieslar (PL)	Mit. Lancer Evolution	M	(a) 7th (38th) VII ONY.V881 (PL)	(b) withdrawn VI ZX2720 (NZ)	NS USD2,500	X	X	X	X
80	Ricardo Trivino (MEX) Jordi Barrabes (E)	Mit. Lancer Evolution	P	transmission VII T8996BBB (E)	11th (31st) VII T1683BBC (E)	6th (22nd) VII T1413BBK (E)	front suspension VII T1683BBC (F)	6th (34th) VII T1683BBC (E)	X	7th (25th) VII T3338BBC (F)

An unhappy season in the series for Marcos Ligato. This was his best result, second in New Zealand.

They came all ages. Bob Colsoul was 22 years old at the start of the season.

Rally. Another hard moment came to the Oman driver Hamed Al-Wahaibi. He had a crisis in his life in Argentina. Events which had recently happened in the sport, especially Possum's accident, had very much upset him on a personal level, and forced him to conclude that his considerable days away from home pursuing the sport were not what a man with his responsibilities should pursue. The FIA, however, declared his responsibilities were contractual and that if he left the championship this was a very serious breach of faith. For Hamed there was no choice. He followed his beliefs, incurred the costs and retired from the series.

There were some lighter moments, not the least when Alfredo de Dominicis successfully pleaded with the FIA to give him his favourite competition number, 77. The payback came when the Swedish organisers seeded the starting order for their event. Competition numbers had been allocated according to championship classification the year before. Alfredo had finished tenth so why couldn't he start tenth in order? Because he had asked for 77, not 60 was the reply. When he asked what if he had asked for 51 instead, would they have allowed him to start in front of the champion Singh, he was not happy with the anwser.

Economic problems led to a lot of altered plans. When competitors found they were unable to compete the FIA took varying attitudes, mostly based on whether the drivers were perceived to have been casual in their commercial plans or whether they were victims. The penalties had no evident pattern. Sometimes the drivers were excluded from the rest of the series, other times they were expected to appear the next time. There was an extraordinary incident post-Australia when the decisions of the Stewards (which this time included having competition licences suspended for a year or more) were never communicated

Janusz Kulig was denied victory in Sweden by the scrutineers.

to the drivers concerned, and in the end the FIA overruled the Stewards and declared the drivers could take advantage of 'procedural errors' and walk away with their licences and pockets intact.

The second year of the PCWRC saw a significant growth in the importance of Group N, a series which had begun in 1987, and had seldom attracted attention until now. New disciplines are constantly being evolved by the FIA, and as 2003 progressed more ideas were introduced. During the season a catering service was introduced, similar to that for the JWRC, which was a major step forward. Official films were produced, and offered to television networks. Whereas young drivers Niall McShea and Daniel Sola were present in PCWRC, they were not typical. The typical PCWRC competitor was emerging as a national rally champion looking for a new step forward in their sport. Drivers like Constantin Aur, seven times Romanian champion, were given a way to go forward in the sport. It was in many ways a Cup winners Cup.

Tour of Perth, Australia for the PCWRC drivers.

Final Positions in 2003 FIA Production Car World Rally Championship (PCWRC)

		Total	Sweden	New Zealand	Argentina	Cyprus	Germany	Australia	Corsica
1	Martin Rowe (GB)	**43**	6	5	X	8	8	10	6
2	Toshihiro Arai (J)	**38**	R	10	10	10	x	R	8
3	Stig Blomqvist (S)	**30**	10	1	X	6	4	5	4
4	Karamjit Singh (MAL)	**30**	8	3	6	R	5	8	X
5	Daniel Sola (E)	**22**	X	0	8	R	10	4	R
6	Niall McShea (GB)	**18**	X	2	R	R	R	6	10
7	Janusz Kulig (PL)	**11**	R	R	X	R	6	NS	5
8	Marcos Ligato (RA)	**13**	X	8	R	5	R	R	NS
9	Ricardo Trivino (MEX)	**8**	R	0	3	R	3	X	2
10	Bob Colsoul (B)	**7**	0	X	R	4	R	NS	3

Key: NS = did not start, R = retired, X = elected to miss.

Other point scorers: Hamed Al-Wahaibi (OM) 6, Joakim Roman (PL) 6, Giovanni Manfrinato (I) & Possum Bourne (NZ) 5, Alfredo de Dominicis (I) Ramon Ferryros (PER) & Krzysztof Holowczyc (PL) 4, Stefano Marrini (I) & Patrick Richard CDN) 1.

Live to feel the passion

Competition is like life. The challenge is to master the rules, lead the pace and create a sensation. Spare no effort and let it ride—success requires extreme dedication and boldness. The ultimate reward is in the effort of doing your best at all times, regardless of how challenging the road may be. Winning, after all, is more than a fleeting moment. It's an attitude that we live for, running deep in everything we do, inspiring performance on and off the track. Just ask the many motorists leading the way in their Mitsubishi. **Long may they run.**

British Rally Championship

www.brcweb.co.uk

Jonny Milner, Champion for the second year.

PIRELLI BRITISH RALLY CHAMPIONSHIP 2003

British Championships

The calendar for the 2003 Pirelli British Rally Championship originally consisted of eight events, due to start with the Rally of Wales, which had to be cancelled through lack of entries in the supporting classes. The Pirelli Rally therefore inherited the honour of being the opening event. In 2003 there were subtle changes in the series: all events counted for the Drivers' as well as the Manufacturers' series, the points system was simplified, so that drivers in the Overall or the Super 1600 did not receive added points for positions in their category. The Super 1600 category was expanded to include any 1600cc Kit Cars which had to carry extra ballast if they were homologated outside Super 1600 rules. In the overall scene, only World Rally Cars of versions up to and including 2001 spec were admitted, therefore not including cars to designs of the last two years. Peugeot was the only manufacturer officially to enter a car in the series, a Super 1600 206 for last year's 206 Challenge winner Garry Jennings, while M-Sport ran a Ford Focus for the 18 year old Finn Jari-Matti Latvala, as a career development exercise. The most competitive Super 1600 in the series

promised to be the Renault Clio run by R-E-D for Mark Higgins while Gwyndaf Evans drove an MG ZR prepared by the MG Sport and Racing department with a few improvements since the full works entry last year. There were two Fiat Puntos, one for the San Marino JWRC driver Mirco Baldacci and the other for the British driver Leon Pesticcio, the first time Puntos had been seen in action in British championship events. An interesting entry was an Alfa 147 driven by Steve Hill, in Super 1600 form and accepted as such a car by the championship organisers. World Rally Cars, notwithstanding their older specification, were expected to be the strongest contenders, headed by Jonny Milner in a Toyota Corolla, in which he won the title last year, while at the last moment Latvala's fellow Finn Tapio Laukkanen, who won the series in 1999, announced he would contest the series in a Subaru Impreza.

Round 1 Pirelli

Last minute entry Tapio Laukkanen snatched victory after taking the lead on the penultimate stage, after an extraordinary battle of catch-up by four-wheel drive cars after two-wheel drive cars were unbeatable

in the fog of the first evening. Leader for most of the event was Guy Wilks in a Puma, but after being overtaken by the World Rally Cars two stages before the finish he went off the road and retired on the final stage.

The Pirelli Rally was run once again in the Kielder stages in the border country

Tapio Laukkanen, Pirelli Rally winner.

between England and Scotland, based at Gateshead, where a couple of superspecial spectaculars were held immediately after the start. This stage was to have been run on roads in a condemned development zone, but at a late moment the route had to be changed. Then it began to rain, and it turned out to be a muddy and dark section of about 500 metres length. It was so slow that 50 seconds was a very good time! The heart of the rally, however, was the forest stages, three of which would round off the first leg of the event, all run in dusk and darkness, conditions which few drivers had encountered before. And more relevant still was the fog, and the surprising thing was that by the end of the first day Super 1600 cars were in the top three placings, headed by Wilks. On the first foggy stage Latvala went into the lead, but then slid off the road, and was badly delayed driving behind another competitor. "My lamps were completely covered by his mud. I will not make that mistake again." Latvala finished the first day 20th out of the 38 cars still running.

The performance of Wilks on the final stage of the evening, stage 5, is one of the unsolved mysteries of the event. Over 11.42 miles (18km) he finished 36 seconds faster than anyone else, and virtually a minute ahead of the next fastest S1600 driver, Mark Higgins. Wilks used his bumper mounted spotlights to good effect, and those spectators who could see through the weather reported how fast the Puma was going. This put Wilks almost a minute in front of Higgins in the lead of the event, with Evans third and then Laukkanen. The second day dawned clear and dry and now the WRCars planned their revenge. With two stages to go Laukkanen was second behind Wilks with 13.2s to make up. Wilks had a poor time on stage 10 and Laukkanen took the lead, then on stage 11 Wilks went off the road and Milner came up to second. The British Touring Car driver James Thompson, at the wheel of an ex-works Mitsubishi fought back from delays in the first event, finally jumping from ninth to sixth on the final stage of the rally. Six different types of cars were in the top six places at the finish.

Round 2 Scottish

Punctures decided the outcome of the three-car battle for the lead of the Scottish Rally, an event where rocky, and this year dusty dry conditions prevailed, in a series

A season of learning for Jari-Matti Latvala.

where deflation proof mousse inserts are forbidden. Initially Jari-Matti Latvala went ahead, but on the fourth stage he had a front wheel puncture on a nine mile stage, dropping to 17th overall. This allowed his fellow Finn Tapio Laukkanen to go ahead who at the end of the first day was 22 seconds in front. On the second stage of the second day, last year's winner Jonny Milner gradually caught up and by stage eight passed into the lead. Then he had not only a puncture but also brake trouble, letting Laukkanen back into the lead with one stage to go. There were now just 6.6 seconds between them, with the Finn in front. This time it was Laukkanen's turn to have problems, a puncture slowing him down and allowing the Toyota driver to win the event for the second year in succession, gaining revenge on his defeat on the opening round of the series. They finished the event as joint championship leaders.

Behind the leaders James Thompson settled into fourth place with his Mitsubishi, in front of a driver who had been a surprise at the Pirelli Rally, Barry Johnson. Austin McHale had his gearbox stick in third but managed to hold fourth place to the end. Latvala meanwhile had risen at the end of the first day to fourth, and was third overall on the second day all the way. He was lucky to finish, going off the road and keeping his position on the final stage of the event. Thompson withdrew after the first day with accident damage, after sliding off and on the road when the gearbox jumped into neutral.

Veteran driver Gwyndaf Evans (MG) faced strong opposition in the Super 1600

category from Kris Meeke's Opel, and also from Mirco Baldacci who had brought his Punto, urgently repaired after the Acropolis Rally. Higgins did not start. Evans ran as high as fourth place overall at the start of the event but a puncture dropped him down to ninth overall before finishing fifth, behind Meeke. Meeke got up to fifth before he also had a puncture. Baldacci had a flat tyre and his fellow Punto driver Leon Pesticcio had two, but only one spare wheel. Meeke struggled to the finish on three cylinders while Simon Hughes retired when he went off the road.

This year the rally made less second-usage of stages than the year before, and the Dumfries event used an airfield base at Baldoon, south of Newton Stewart as the permanent Service Park location.

Round 3 Jim Clark

The Irish Tarmac Champion driver Andrew Nesbitt won the Jim Clark Memorial Rally for the second year running, after leading most of the way. Having headed a strong supporting line of fellow Irish championship Subaru drivers in the early stages, he eventually finished in front of Jonny Milner (Toyota). Milner pulled well clear of his main championship rivals (Tapio Laukkanen and Jari-Matti Latvala) both of whom crashed in wet conditions on the first full day of rallying. Another Ulsterman Kris Meeke won the Super 1600 category after his closest rivals all retired.

The third round of the series was run this year as the first asphalt event. Held on closed public rounds in south-east Scotland around the town of Duns, home of the 1963 and 1965 Formula 1 World Champion, the event attracted a host of drivers from Ireland, whose national sport is based on this type of event, all in late model Subaru Impreza WRCs and nearly all of them running outside the championship. The headquarters of the event was in fact at Leith, Edinburgh's seaport town, where a superspecial was run round the docklands. The event was incredibly popular, some 250 entries overall accepted in various categories, and towards another 200 having entries refused.

With so many well driven ex-works World Rally Cars at the event and horrible conditions which made the roads treacherous, the opening stages of the event were very exciting. While Milner led after the intial two publicity stages, he lost a minute on the first orthodox stage (three) with a puncture and dropped to 25th. "I am not discouraged by the Irish drivers because only one of them (McHale) is eligible for championship points. My objective on this rally is to pay attention just to the two Finns Tapio Laukkanen and Jari-Matti Latvala." Laukkanen snatched the lead, but it was not to last. The older Finn was finding the handling of his '99 Impreza very unpredictable and on stage six he was off the road, the young Finn then crashing at the same place. In the case of Latvala the accident was serious as codriver Carl Williamson was taken to hospital with an injured pelvis. This put him out of action for the rest of the season. In one stage Milner's championship worries were eased, he was now tenth overall but with only McHale ahead of him in the race for points.

After the first morning, the Irish Imprezas were dominant. Nesbitt's '01 car was in front of McGarrity's '02 model, Donnelly's '97 car, Hurson's '00 version and Boland's '01 model. The only mainland driver who was able to match their pace was James Thompson's ex-works '00 Mitsubishi Lancer Evolution "6.5," but he had a lot of unexpected moments off and on the roads, and fell back as a result to finish eighth. At the end of Saturday Nesbitt led by almost a minute from McGarrity while Milner had climbed ahead of McHale (delayed by turbo pipe troubles, then a broken exhaust manifold) and was third overall in the rally. On the short final day (around 30 miles of stages) when conditions were fine and sunny again, Nesbitt held his lead despite hydraulic problems but Milner in his 1998 Toyota pulled in front of McGarrity and clinched

maximum championship points ahead of sixth place Austin McHale.

The Super 1600 championship event was disappointing. For the second event running Mark Higgins, entered in a Clio, did not appear, while Mirco Baldacci (Punto) from San Marino was also a non-starter. Gwyndaf Evans held the initial lead but went off the road twice, second time terminally, allowing Kris Meeke in a new Opel Corsa to go in front. In the early stages the Peugeot GB team driver Garry Jennings went off the road, then his 206's camshaft belt failed, while Simon Hughes (Clio) retired off the road. After missing the Scottish Rally due to a pre-event engine problem, the Alfa 147 of Steve Hill retired with fuel problems on the first morning. This left Kris Meeke under complete control, over a minute ahead of Leon Pesticcio (Punto) and Ryan Champion (Puma), who had been delayed by various problems earlier due to water damaging a fan. Barry Clark in another Puma retired on the final day, again with problems caused by the water crossing in the popular stage close to Duns, this time when the water radiator mounting shifted and broke the oil filter.

Round 4 Manx

Reigning British champion Jonny Milner scored his third successive maximum points on the British championship rally, this time on the asphalt roads of the Isle of Man. He led from start to finish, pacing himself to stay just ahead of his nearest rivals, but careful not to take risks especially on the wet first day. On the first stage his closest challenge came from

Welcome visitor, Mirco Baldacci.

James Thompson, but then for more than half the rally his Toyota was chased by the 2001 version works Focus of Jari-Matti Latvala. When the Finn went off the road, Milner found himself a half minute in front of Tapio Laukkanen who retired at the end of the second day when repairs to a broken exhaust took too long. The Yorkshire driver was therefore over four minutes in front of a series of Subaru Imprezas driven by Irish drivers, most of whom were not registered for the championship.

This was the 40th Manx Rally, an event which has progressed from being an open-road night event to the fastest British rally. On this island the authorities traditionally encourage the use of their public roads for sporting use and are happy this rally is the longest distance regular championship event in the series. Like on the Jim Clark Rally, the first day of the Manx was run over wet roads, but on the second and third days the conditions were clear and dry. Laukkanen had a different Impreza this time and began the event cautiously, but his fellow Finn Latvala's two year old Focus championship car scored fastest time on the second stage. On the first stage of the

James Thompson ran out of road too often in 2003!

second day, third placed Kenny McKinstry had two punctures on his Subaru and began a day long recovery back to second, not helped by a spin. In the afternoon Thompson crashed his Mitsubishi, going straight on at a right hand bend. He had been lying fourth behind Milner, Latvala and Laukkanen, and in front of Derek McGarrity when the latter punctured and fell back. As the retirements continued, so Milner's position strengthened and he cruised through the final day to victory.

The Super 1600 category promised to a good fight between Kris Meeke (Opel Corsa) and Gwyndaf Evans (MG ZR) but by early on the second day both were out of the running. Meeke had driveshaft failure, while Evans was delayed by gearbox trouble. By now the Puma of Ryan Champion was ahead, but then he retired with broken front suspension and Peugeot's prize-drive winner Garry Jennings was in front and cruising to the end. The only other registered S1600 driver to reach the finish was Leon Pesticcio (Fiat Punto). He lost four minutes with a broken wheel on the first day, then later had more troubles with clutch, engine mounting and gearbox problems. Missing from this event were the Clios of Simon Hughes and last year's overall winner Mark Higgins.

Round 5 Ulster

Despite predictions this event would be a walkover for local crews, Tapio Laukkanen avenged his disappointments on the last two championship rallies winning the Ulster Rally in Northern Ireland, the third and last all-asphalt round of the series. Taking over the lead at half distance after reigning Irish champion driver Andrew Nesbitt went off the road when driving with a puncture, Laukkanen won by nearly two minutes from Irish driver Derek McGarrity. Reigning British champion Jonny Milner strengthened his championship position by finishing in third place. With two more

Ryan Champion in his Super 1600 Puma.

Austin McHale, regular Irishman.

rallies to run, only three drivers remained in the race for the 2003 title, Milner, Austin McHale and Tapio Laukkanen.

Ireland is known for its changeable climate, and true to form the rally started on treacherously slippery wet roads in the region to the south of the province. Almost within sight of the start of the first stage Peadar Hurson crashed his Impreza. Laukkanen survived the stage, even though his intercom was not working. From then on he played a waiting game as Andrew Nesbitt pulled away, Laukkanen taking the lead on the eighth stage on Saturday morning when Nesbitt retired. The rally now moved to the western side of the province and the changeable conditions continued! This let Latvala up to second place behind Laukkanen. Latvala fell back to third when McGarrity overtook him, while further back Milner, despite his anxiety to avoid any errors, passed firstly Austin McHale then Latvala. Latvala then spun on the final stage at the same place and dropped a place. McGarrity held his second place. The wet roads coupled with muddy patches both from the proximity of farms and also the result of double usage of stages made the event treacherous, all of which earned considerable praise for the efforts of Latvala who finished fourth overall.

In Super 1600, Meeke led initially but then on the third stage punctured. For the next ten stages he drove hard to recover and with three stages to go went back into the lead. When Meeke was delayed, Pesticcio went ahead but he was caught and passed by Evans, in the dark foggy

stages on the Friday evening, and then also by Meeke, but with five stages to go Pesticcio crashed, blocking the stage for a while and retired. On the Saturday there was a big fight between Meeke and Evans. Evans retired after the final stage with engine failure, elevating Ryan Champion into second place in the category despite a driveshaft which broke, fortunately on a road section. Meeke safely reached the end of the final stage but on the way to the finish he had engine troubles, and eventually reached the finish. At last, a success for the Irishman! Third was Garry Jennings after gearbox trouble and then a puncture. Steve Hill finished 26th overall in his prototype Alfa 147.

There was a series of leaders in Group N, starting with 23 year old Michael Curran (Mitsubishi, turbocharger pipe problems), then Andrew Stewart (Mitsubishi), Seamus Leonard (who crashed his Subaru close to his home, near Omagh, on the second day) and finally Roy White (despite electric troubles after going off the road), just 1.1 seconds in front of Stewart.

Disappointing year for Gwyndaf Evans.

A cheeky interloper! Steve Hill brought extra interest.

Round 6 Trackrod

Britain's two major rally titles were won at the Trackrod Rally, Yorkshireman Jonny Milner took his second successive overall title on his home event and Northern Ireland driver Kris Meeke the Super 1600 title. Overall winner after leading virtually all the way was Tapio Laukkanen. World Rally Cars took the top seven positions followed by Meeke who was in front of a new name to British rallying, the Finnish driver Aki Teiskonen, who comes from Laukka and who is managed by Juha Kankkunen's brother Timo. At the wheel of a Saxo previously rallied by Niall McShea, Teiskonen was second in S1600. The Trackrod Rally, like the Jim Clark in its various categories attracted a huge entry. 230 crews, of which 53 were in the international championship category, and the two day event was held in splendid weather conditions. After a run of three asphalt rallies in the series, the two final events were to be back on gravel. There were some interesting foreign entries, including Jenni-Lee Hermansson from Sweden, a former VW Polo cup driver, and the Finn Sami Vatanen, a distant relative of Ari and who comes from the same region, in a Peugeot 206 cup car. After a variety of other locations in recent years, the event this time was based at Malton, the competitive sections were based on the North Yorkshire stages and with four stages at a superspecial run in the Pickering show grounds.

To clinch the title on this event Milner had to finish among the top nine registered championship drivers, while Meeke had to win the Super 1600 to clinch this series. After taking an initial lead on the superspecial which opened the event, Laukkanen pulled ahead with his fellow Finn Jari-Matti Latvala staying ahead of Milner. These three were comfortably ahead of a procession headed by Austin McHale's Subaru, Steve Petch's privately-run Hyundai

Kris Meeke, 2003 Super 1600 Champion.

Accent WRC, a Subaru of Scottish championship driver Barry Johnson and a veteran driver making his return. This was Chris Mellors, once a Yorkshire expert who had three times won this event, better known now as the preparation chief for Karamjit Singh's world championship Proton and David Higgins' US championship-winning Evo VIII. For the first time in over two years he was in action on his own account, at the wheel of an Escort WRC and finished seventh. The teenager Latvala had divided loyalties. He sensed this was an event he could win, but he knew he was tired after a very busy few weeks, firstly rallying in Italy, then taking school examinations in Finland. On top of these, he knew that he had suffered too many accidents already this season... Hermansson was an early retirement with gearbox problems with her rented Group N Subaru.

The second day began when Latvala got very close to Laukkanen but on the second stage he went off the road and the crew had to push the car off a fallen log. He dropped back to third place behind Milner, who was cruising along, making no mistakes and taking no risks. Laukkanen had no major problems. He stalled near the start of the first forest stage, and on Saturday evening let his lead over Latvala drop from a quarter-minute to a handful of seconds when he overshot a junction. Otherwise he finished strongly in the car previously rallied by Marcus Dodd in last year's BRC events. For Milner this was success in front of his local fans, for codriver Beech this was a happy conclusion after the disappointment earlier this season when his world championship ride was lost without warning

The Super 1600 category once again flattered only to deceive. Gwyndaf Evans struck a winning pace for most of the first

day but then his MG's gearbox broke, and this handed the lead to Meeke. There were disappointments early on. On the first stage the Alfa 147 of Steve Hill broke a driveshaft, while on stage three the Punto driver Leon Pesticcio, who for this event had entered a Puma, lost two minutes with a broken driveshaft as well, and then two stages later Ryan Champion had the same problem. Garry Jennings in his prize drive 206 hoped for better luck than on previous events but he lost four minutes in a ditch. Meeke spun on the final stage but made the finish just in time to drive to Liverpool to catch the plane to Sanremo. "This time I hope my luck will hold in the JWRC. I still have not scored any points in that series..." Champion survived a water leak and finished sixth in the category.

Round 7 Tempest

After a season of learning the various rally scenes round Britain, 18 year old Jari-Matti Latvala finally won an event outright, dominating the final round of the 2003 British series in his two-year old works Focus WRC. Austin McHale held second place in the early stages until he spun and lost time, ending up in fourth place, behind Ryan Champion, which was enough to clinch his second place in the series behind the absent Jonny Milner. Champion, previously known as a Puma driver, was fast learning the ways of four-wheel drive Group A rallying! Milner was absent but his car was now driven by Julian Reynolds, who finished third on the event. McHale was the only driver to finish all seven qualifying events.

In Super 1600 Garry Jennings in the prize-drive Peugeot 206 led away from the start but lost time when he hit a tree three stages from the finish, Leon Pesticcio won the category and came second in the series, having been slow in the early stages

with unsatisfactory set-up. Steve Hill had unhappy event in the Alfa, firstly when a driveshaft broke and then when he overturned and retired. S1600 champion driver Kris Meeke was away in Catalunya (finally opening his points score in the

Garry Jennings, Peugeot 206.

JWRC) so missed this event. In the end the top five S1600 drivers all drove different makes of car! The remaining title fight was for the Group N cars in which Roy White led throughout but with championship leader Neil Buckley needing only to finish to win the title, Buckley drove steadily and finished second in the category.

The Tempest is a one-off event in the series, held mostly on military land close to London for promotional reasons but consequently run with less than half the stage distance of most other events. Also, it is a one-day event. With all the major national titles settled at the Trackrod Rally, the penultimate round, except the Group N series, the entry list for the Tempest was lower level than usual. This year the event counted for all the

Moment of success for Buckley.

championship categories. The season ended with the same British champion, but the presence of Laukkanen and Latvala did much to create international interest, while the Irish driver Austin McHale's loyal presence gave a further depth to the series.

Round 1 PIRELLI INTERNATIONAL RALLY 2003 25/26.04.2003
Gateshead. 11 Stages, 11 gravel - 101.47 miles.

1	Tapio Laukkanen/Miika Antilla	Subaru Impreza	WRC	1h.38m.24.3s.
2	Jonny Milner/Nicky Beech	Toyota Corolla	WRC	1h.38m.33.6s.
3	Mark Higgins/Bryan Thomas	Renault Clio	S1600	1h.39m.31.4s.
4	Gwyndaf Evans/Howard Davies	MG ZR	S1600	1h.41m.34.0s.
5	Kris Meeke/Chris Patterson	Opel Corsa	S1600	1h.44m.38.7s.
6	James Thompson/Plug Pulleyn	Mitsubishi Lancer Evo 6.5	WRC	1h.45m.23.8s.
10	Jari-Matti Latvala/Carl Williamson	Ford Focus	WRC	1h.45m.56.4s.
14	Neil Buckley/Douglas Redpath	Mitsubishi Lancer Evo	N	1h.50m.37.0s.

43 starters. 28 finishers.

LEADING RETIREMENTS & LAST STAGE COMPLETED

Garry Jennings/Gordon Noble	Peugeot 206	S1600	accident	4
Steve Hill/Jim Kitson	Alfa Romeo 147	"S1600"	power steering	4
Julian Reynolds/Ieuan Thomas	Subaru Impreza	WRC	turbocharger	6
Barry Johnson/Stewart Merry	Subaru Impreza	WRC	gearbox	7
Guy Wilks/Phil Pugh	Ford Puma	S1600	accident	10

OVERALL SPRINTERS Milner & Laukkanen won 3 stages each, Wilks & Johnson 2 each, Latvala 1.
SUPER 1600 SPRINTERS Higgins won 6 stages, Evans & Wilks 2 each, Meeke 1.
OVERALL LEADERS Johnson stages 1+2, Latvala 3, Wilks 4-9, Laukkanen 10+11.
SUPER 1600 LEADERS Evans stages 1+2, Higgins 3, Wilks 4-9, Higgins 10+11.

Round 2 RSAC SCOTTISH RALLY 13/15.06.2003
Dumfries. 11 Stages, gravel - 106.45 miles

1	Jonny Milner/Nicky Beech	Toyota Corolla	WRC	1h.30m.11.1s.
2	Tapio Laukkanen/Miika Anttila	Subaru Impreza	WRC	1h.30m.39.1s.
3	Jari-Matti Latvala/Carl Williamson	Ford Focus	WRC	1h.33m.58.3s.
4	Austin McHale/Brian Murphy	Subaru Impreza	WRC	1h.35m.28.3s.
5	Gwyndaf Evans/Claire Mole	MG ZR	S1600	1h.35m.57.1s.
6	Julian Reynolds/Ieuan Thomas	Subaru Impreza	WRC	1h.36m.25.8s.
10	Neil Buckley/Douglas Redpath	Mitsubishi Lancer Evo	N	1h.39m.13.0s.

30 starters. 20 finishers.

LEADING RETIREMENTS & LAST STAGE COMPLETED

Natalie Barrett/Roger Freeman	Toyota Corolla	WRC	engine	1
James Thompson/Plug Pulleyn	Mitsubishi Lancer Evo 6.5	WRC	withdrawn	6
Simon Hughes/Calvin Cooledge	Renault Clio	S1600	accident	9

OVERALL SPRINTERS Laukkanen won 5 stages, Latvala 4, Milner 2.
SUPER 1600 SPRINTERS Evans won 7 stages, Meeke 4.
OVERALL LEADERS Latvala stages 1-3, Laukkanen 4-7, Milner 8+9, Laukkanen 10, Milner 11.
SUPER 1600 LEADERS Evans stages 1-4, Meeke 5, Evans 6-11.

ROUND 3 JIM CLARK MEMORIAL 4/6.07.2003
Duns. 23 Stages, asphalt - 141.49 miles.

1	Andrew Nesbitt/James O'Brien	Subaru Impreza	WRC	2h.03m.42.1s.
2	Jonny Milner/Nicky Beech	Toyota Corolla	WRC	2h.04m.25.8s.
3	Derek McGarrity/Dermot O'Gorman	Subaru Impreza	WRC	2h.04m.48.0s.
4	Peadar Hurson/Ian Porter	Subaru Impreza	WRC	2h.05m.17.2s.
5	Eugene Donnelly/Paul Kiely	Subaru Impreza	WRC	2h.05m.44.7s.
6	Austin McHale /Brian Murphy	Subaru Impreza	WRC	2h.07m.38.1s.
9	Kris Meeke/Chris Patterson	Opel Corsa	S1600	2h.12m.23.1s.
10	Seamus Leonard/Paul McLaughlin	Subaru Impreza	N	2h.12m.55.0s.

60 starters. 36 finishers.

LEADING RETIREMENTS & LAST STAGE COMPLETED

Simon Hughes/Calvin Cooledge	Renault Clio	S1600	accident	2
Steve Hill/Jim Kitson	Alfa 147	"S1600"	fuel system	4
Garry Jennings/Gordon Noble	Peugeot 206	S1600	camshaft belt	5
Gwyndaf Evans/Claire Mole	MG ZR	S1600	accident	5
Tapio Laukkanen/Mikka Anttila	Subaru Impreza	WRC	accident	5
Jari-Matti Latvala/Carl Williamson	Ford Focus	WRC	accident	5
Barry Clark/Neil Shanks	Ford Puma	S1600	oil filter	19

OVERALL SPRINTERS Milner won 12 stages, Nesbitt 6, Thompson (Mitsubishi) 3, Donnelly & Kearney (Peugeot) 1 each. 2 stages cancelled.
SUPER 1600 SPRINTERS Meeke won 13 stages, Evans & Champion (Ford) 4 each, Pesticcio (Fiat) 2.
OVERALL LEADERS Milner stages 1+2, Hurson 3, Laukkanen 4, Donnelly 5-8, Thompson 9, Nesbitt 10-25.
SUPER 1600 LEADERS Evans stages 1-5, Meeke 6-25.

Round 4 MANX INTERNATIONAL 1/3.08.2003
Castletown-Douglas. 26 stages, asphalt - 207.77 miles.

1	Jonny Milner/Nicky Beech	Toyota Corolla	WRC	3h.01m.03.5s.
2	Kenny McKinstry/Noel Orr	Subaru Impreza	WRC	3h.06m.01.0s.
3	Derek McGarrity/Dermot O'Gorman	Subaru Impreza	WRC	3h.07m.38.2s.
4	Austin McHale/Brian Murphy	Subaru Impreza	WRC	3h.08m.45.4s.
5	Eamonn Boland/Francis Regan	Subaru Impreza	WRC	3h.08m.58.4s.
6	Seamus Leonard/Paul McLaughlin	Subaru Impreza	N	3h.16m.18.7s.
7	Garry Jennings/Gordon Noble	Peugeot 206	S1600	3h.19m.11.4s.

58 starters. 31 finishers.

LEADING RETIREMENTS & LAST STAGE COMPELETED

Kris Meeke/Chris Patterson	Opel Corsa	S1600	driveshaft	7
Gwyndaf Evans/Claire Mole	MG ZR	S1600	gearbox	10
James Thompson/Plug Pulleyn	Mitsubishi Lancer Evo 6.5	WRC	accident	12
Jari-Matti Latvala/Miikka Anttila	Ford Focus	WRC	accident	14
Tapio Laukkanen/Ilkka Riipinen	Subaru Impreza	WRC	broken exhaust	19
Ryan Champion/Cliff Simmons	Ford Puma	S1600	suspension	20
Steve Hill/Joanne Lockwood	Alfa 147	"S1600"	engine	21

OVERALL SPRINTERS Milner won 11 stages, Laukkanen 5, Latvala & McKinstry 4 each, McGarrity 2, Boland 1.
SUPER 1600 SPRINTERS Pesticcio won 7 stages, Evans & Champion 6 each, Jennings 5, Meeke & Hill 1 each.
OVERALL LEADER Milner stages 1-26.
SUPER 1600 LEADERS Meeke stage 1, Evans 2-7, Champion 8-19, Jennings 20-26.

Round 5 ANSWERCALL DIRECT ULSTER RALLY 2003 5/6.09.2003 (ECR35)
Armagh. 16 Stages, asphalt - 124.91 miles

1	Tapio Laukkanen/Ilka Riipinen	Subaru Impreza	WRC	2h.06m.11.2s.
2	Derek McGarrity/Dermot O'Gorman	Subaru Impreza	WRC	2h.08m.01.8s.
3	Jonny Milner/Nicky Beech	Toyota Corolla	WRC	2h.08m.20.0s.
4	Jari-Matti Latvala/Miikka Anttila	Ford Focus	WRC	2h.08m.42.8s.
5	Austin McHale/Brian Murphy	Subaru Impreza	WRC	2h.08m.50.5s.
6	Kris Meeke/David Senior	Opel Corsa	S1600	2h.11m.00.3s.
9	Roy White/Greg Shinners	Mitsubishi Lancer Evo	N	2h.15m.02.8s.

86 starters. 52 finishers.

LEADING RETIREMENTS & LAST STAGE COMPLETED

Peadar Hurson/Ian Porter	Subaru Impreza	WRC	accident	0
Eamonn Boland/Damien Morrissey	Subaru Impreza	WRC	fire	3
Seamus Leonard/Paul McLaughlin	Subaru Impreza	N	accident	3
Andrew Nesbitt/James O'Brien	Subaru Impreza	WRC	accident	7
Leon Pesticcio/Tim Sturla	Fiat Punto	S1600	accident	11
Gwyndaf Evans/Claire Mole	MG ZR	S1600	engine	16

OVERALL SPRINTERS Nesbitt won 7 stages, Laukkanen & Milner 3 each, McGarrity 2, Latvala 1.
SUPER 1600 SPRINTERS Meeke won 12 stages, Evans 3, Pesticcio 1.
OVERALL LEADERS Nesbitt stages 1-7, Laukkanen 8-16.
SUPER 1600 LEADERS Meeke stages 1+2, Pesticcio 3+4, Evans 5-13, Meeke 14-16.

Round 6 TRACKROD RALLY YORKSHIRE 2003 27/28.09.2003
Malton. 14 Stages, gravel - 107.81 miles.

1	Tapio Laukkanen/Ilka Riipinen	Subaru Impreza	WRC	1h.38m.11.6s.
2	Jonny Milner/Nicky Beech	Toyota Corolla	WRC	1h.39m.00.2s.
3	Jari-Matti Latvala/Miikka Anttila	Ford Focus	WRC	1h.39m.38.6s.
4	Austin McHale/Brian Murphy	Subaru Impreza	WRC	1h.41m.30.9s.
5	Steve Petch/John Richardson	Hyundai Accent	WRC	1h.42m.51.5s.
6	Barry Johnson/Stewart Merry	Subaru Impreza	WRC	1h.43m.21.8s.
8	Kris Meeke/Chris Patterson	Opel Corsa	S1600	1h.47m.31.1s.
10	Neil Buckley/Doug Redpath	Mitsubishi Lancer Evo	N	1h.48m.33.5s.

53 starters. 36 finishers.

LEADING RETIREMENTS & LAST STAGE COMPLETED

Steve Hill/Joanne Lockwood	Alfa 147	"S1600"	driveshaft	1
Gwyndaf Evans/Claire Mole	MG ZR	S1600	gearbox	7
Julian Reynolds/Ieuan Thomas	Subaru Impreza	WRC	gear linkage	12

OVERALL SPRINTERS Laukkanen won 6 stages, Latvala 5, Milner 3.
SUPER 1600 SPRINTERS Champion & Meeke won 5 stages each, Evans 3, Teiskonen 1.
OVERALL LEADERS Milner stages 1+2, Laukkanen 3-15. 1 stage cancelled.
SUPER 1600 LEADERS Evans stages 1-6, Meeke 8-15.

2003 KUMHO TYRES NATIONAL RALLY CHAMPIONSHIP

Round 1 SUNSEEKER Bournemouth 22.02.2003 — 114s 75f

1	Dodd/McAuley	Subaru Impreza	WRC	1h.09m.36.4s.
2	Burton/Roberts	Peugeot Cosworth	B	1h.09m.55.4s.
3	Mann/Cook	Subaru Impreza	B	1h.10m.26.2s.
13	Nicholls/Broom	Subaru Impreza	N	1h.13m.57.8s.
32	Middleton/Parry	Hyundai Coupe KC	F2	1h.17m.51.8s.

Round 2 ASTRA STAGES Llangollen 12.04.2003 — 78s 46f

1	Burton/Roberts	Peugeot Cosworth	B	1h.04m.13s.
2	Ceen/Douglas	Subaru Impreza	B	1h.05m.04s.
3	Munro/Ewing	Subaru Impreza	WRC	1h.05m.07s.
7	Higgins/Thomas	Renault Clio	S1600	1h.05m.58s.
8	Crealey/Harris	Mitsubishi Lancer Evo	N	1h.06m.36s.
17	Middleton/Sankey	Hyundai Coupe KC	F2	1h.10m.09s.

Round 3 ROUSH MANX Douglas (IOM) 9/10.05.2003 — 136s 84f

1	Mann/Cook	Subaru Impreza	B	1h.45m.37.7s.
2	M.Evans/Jones	Subaru Impreza	WRC	1h.46m.04.3s.
3	Davies/Thomas	MG Metro 6R4	B	1h.47m.54.8s.
11	Fowden/Hynes	Mitsubishi Lancer Evo	N	1h.51m.16.9s.
14	Quine/Skinner	Ford Escort RS2000	F2	1h.51m.35.8s.

Round 4 MUTINY Llandrindod Wells 31.05.2003 — 61s 40f

1	Duckworth/Broomfield	Subaru Impreza	A	1h.20m.40.4s.
2	Petch/Richardson	Hyundai Accent	WRC	1h.21m.14.6s.
3	Mann/Cook	Subaru Impreza	A	1h.21m.28.1s.
4	Crealey/Beckett	Mitsubishi Lancer Evo	N	1h.22m.08.3s.
11	Middleton/Hernaman	Hyundai Coupe KC	F2	1h.24m.58.5s.

Round 7 SOUTH OF ENGLAND TEMPEST RALLY 26.10.2003
Aldershot. 14 Stages, mixed - 51.15 miles.

1	Jari-Matti Latvala/Miikka Anttila	Ford Focus	WRC	49m.40.7s.
2	Ryan Champion/Cliff Simmons	Subaru Impreza 555	A	50m.51.0s.
3	Julian Reynolds/Ieuan Thomas	Toyota Corolla	WRC	50m.56.4s.
4	Austin McHale/Brian Murphy	Subaru Impreza	WRC	51m.26.7s.
5	Phil Morgan/Martin Douglas	Subaru Impreza	WRC	53m.20.9s.
6	Will Nicholls/Nick Broom	Subaru Impreza	WRC	53m.57.6s.
7	Roy White/Greg Shinnors	Mitsubishi Lancer Evo	N	54m.16.5s.
11	Leon Pesticcio/Tim Sturla	Fiat Punto	S1600	55m.51.8s.

41 starters. 32 finishers.

LEADING RETIREMENTS & LAST STAGE COMPLETED

Steve Hill/Joanne Lockwood	Alfa 147	"S1600"	accident	6
Robert Swann/Philip Morgan	Mitsubishi Lancer Evo	N	differential	8

OVERALL SPRINTERS Latvala won 12 stages, Champion 2.
SUPER 1600 SPRINTERS Pesticcio won 6 stages, Jennings 5 Gareth Jones (Citroen) 2, Stuart Jones (Proton) 1.
OVERALL LEADERS Latvala stages 1-14.
SUPER 1600 LEADERS Jennings stages 1-10, Pesticcio 11-14.

FINAL LEADING POSITIONS IN 2003 PIRELLI BRITISH RALLY CHAMPIONSHIP

		Total (best 6 rounds)	Pirelli International Rally	RSAC Scottish Rally	Jim Clark Memorial Rally	Manx International Rally	Ulster International Rally	Trackrod Rally Yorkshire	Tempest South of England Rally
1	Jonny Milner	81	12	15	15	15	12	12	-
2	Austin McHale	62 (60)	(2)	9	12	12	9	9	9
3	Tapio Laukkanen (FIN)	57	15	12	0	0	15	15	-
4	Jari-Matti Latvala (FIN)	48	3	10	0	0	10	10	15
5	Kris Meeke	39	8	6	9	0	8	8	-
6	Roy White	26	-	-	8	0	5	5	8
7	Ryan Champion	24	-	0	6	0	6	0	12
8	Leon Pesticcio	23	0	0	7	9	0	3	4
9	Neil Buckley	21	1	4	3	-	-	7	6
10	Garry Jennings	20	0	2	0	10	4	1	3

Manufacturer Champion: Peugeot.
Production Cup winner: Neil Buckley (Mitsubishi Lancer Evolution)
Super 1600 & Junior winner: Kris Meeke (Opel Corsa)
Lady winner: Shelly Taunt (Nissan Micra)
Formula 2000 winner: Markus Foss (Nissan Almera)
Nations Cup winners: Ireland

Round 5 SWANSEA BAY Swansea 9.08.2003 — 59s 47f

1	Duckworth/Davies	Subaru Impreza	A	1h.07m.08.0s.
2	Mann/Cook	Subaru Impreza	A	1h.07m.29.3s.
3	Crealey/Harris	Mitsubishi Lancer Evo	N	1h.09m.01.6s.
12	Middleton/Hernaman	Hyundai Coupe KC	F2	1h.10m.53.3s.
30	Coomber/Pole	Proton Satria	S1600	1h.15m.50.5s.

Round 6 PARK SYSTEMS Newton Stewart 13.09.2003 — 31s 23f

1	Johnson/Merry	Subaru Impreza	WRC	54m.15.4s.
2	Duckworth/Broomfield	Subaru Impreza	WRC	54m.22.7s.
3	Wedgbury/Dashfield	Subaru Impreza	WRC	56m.16.9s.
9	Clark/Shanks	Ford Puma	S1600	57m.26.6s.
14	Gwynne/Robinson	Vauxhall Corsa	F2	1h.02m.22.4s.

Round 7 BULLDOG Shrewsbury 18.10.2003 — 68s 49f

1	Perrott/Hopewell	Ford Escort	WRC	1h.18m.42.1s.
2	Duckworth/Broomfield	Subaru Impreza	WRC	1h.18m.58.6s.
3	Burton/Roberts	Peugeot Cosworth	B	1h.20m.06.5s..
4	Reynolds/Thomas	Subaru Impreza	N	1h.20m.13.3s.
28	Coomber/Pole	Proton Satria	F2	1h.28m.43.1s.

2003 Kumho Tyres National Rally Champion: David Mann 123pts,
2 Roger Duckworth 115, 3 Brendan Crealey 96, 4 Martyn Harrison 84, 5 Andrew Burton 80, etc

David Mann, 2003 Kumho National Rally Champion

Brendon Crealey, 2003 Mitsubishi Evolution Challenge winner

Raymond Munro, 2003 New Pig Scottish Champion

Stephen Hendy, 2003 GB Tarmac Series winner

Jon Ballinger, 2003 Dunlop BTRDA Silver Star, (Opel Manta)

Shaun Woffinden, 2003 Silkolene BTRDA 1400 winner (Ford Puma

Clive Wheeler, 2003 Castrol Polo Challenge winner

Jonathan Wigmore, 2003 Ford rallyesport (Ford Ka)

Shaun Gallagher, 2003 Pug 206 Super Cup winner

Andy Burton, 2003 Dunlop BTRDA Gold Star winner

Steve Perez, 2003 Armajaro MSA British Historic

European Championship

KOMAROCK

ECR1

BACKMAN

ECR4

ECR7

VAINIO

ECR2

ECR5

JUGAS

ECR8

BACKMAN

ECR3

ECR6

PHOTO 4

ECR9

ECR1 JANNER (A) Pregarten 2/4.01.2003 coeff.2 — W

1	Wittmann/Feichtinger	Toyota Corolla	WRC	2h.20m.03.3s.
2	Baumschlager/Zeltner	Mitsubishi Carisma	A	2h.20m.42.7s.
3	Gassner/Thannhauser	Mitsubishi Carisma	N	2h.24m.51.2s.
4	Harrach/Kolbach	Mitsubishi Lancer Evo	N	2h.25m.11.3s.
5	Kovar/Kohlbacher	Mitsubishi Lancer Evo	N	2h.29m.29.0s.
6	Haneder/Gottlieb	Mitsubishi Lancer Evo	A	2h.36m.34.5s.
7	Holzmuller/Langthaler	Mitsubishi Lancer Evo	A	2h.41m.06.9s.
8	Egger/Konigshofer	Mitsubishi Lancer Evo	A	2h.43m.55.0s.

24 starters. 18 finishers.

ECR2 ARCTIC LAPLAND (FIN) Rovaniemi 24/25.01.2003 coeff.10 — N

1	Tuohino/Tuohino	Ford Focus	WRC	2h.16m.48.1s.
2	Ampuja/Ovaskainen	Toyota Corolla	WRC	2h.19m.50.4s.
3	Lindholm/Heinonen	Peugeot 206	WRC	2h.21m.40.0s.
4	Viita/Leino	Ford Focus	WRC	2h.22m.11.3s.
5	Hotanen/Rasanen	Mitsubishi Lancer Evo	N	2h.22m.22.4s.
6	Tiri/Haipus	Subaru Impreza	A	2h.23m.05.8s.
7	Salo/Stenberg	Mitsubishi Lancer Evo	N	2h.23m.05.8s.
8	Hulkkonen/Kovalainen	Ford Focus	WRC	2h.24m.28.8s.

110 starters. 55 finishers.

ECR3 FINNSKOG NORWAY (N) — N
Kongsvinger 21/22.02.2003 coeff.10

1	H.Solberg/Menkerud	Mitsubishi Lancer Evo	A	2h.26m.25.0s.
2	K.Kolberg/Pettersen	Hyundai Accent	WRC	2h.28m.17.1s.
3	Ostberg/Floene	Subaru Impreza	WRC	2h.29m.18.0s.
4	Linnerud/Isdal	Toyota Corolla	WRC	2h.30m.47.5s.
5	Jensen/Pedersen	Ford Focus	WRC	2h.32m.07.8s.
6	Schie/Engen	Toyota Corolla	WRC	2h.32m.15.8s.
7	Kongsrud/Bekkevold	Mitsubishi Lancer Evo	N	2h.34m.47.8s.
8	Stenshorne/Pashley	Mitsubishi Lancer Evo	N	2h.35m.38.4s.

68 starters. 42 finishers.

ECR4 SWEDISH SNOW (S) Ostersund 28.02/1.03.2003 coeff.2 — N

1	Horbing/Olsson	Ford Escort	WRC	1h.53m.45.0s.
2	Walfridsson/Backman	Mitsubishi Lancer Evo	N	1h.55m.31.9s.
3	Eriksson/Svensson	Ford Focus	WRC	1h.55m.36.5s.
4	Hermansson/Jansson	Mitsubishi Lancer Evo	N	1h.58m.19.4s.
5	Fredriksson/Andersson	Mitsubishi Lancer Evo	N	1h.58m.46.5s.
6	Hansson/Stahl	Subaru Impreza WRX	A	1h.58m.48.2s.
7	Larsson/Wessman	Toyota Celica	A	1h.59m.40.8s.
8	Lindqvist/Lindqvist	Ford Escort	WRC	2h.00m.28.6s.

69 starters. 42 finishers.

ECR5 SUMAVA MOGUL(CZ) Klatovy 14/15.03.2003 coeff.5 — E

1	Kresta/Hulka	Peugeot 206	WRC	1h.23m.49.9s.
2	Pech/Uhel	Ford Focus	WRC	1h.25m.01.8s.
3	Hrdinka/Gross	Subaru Impreza	WRC	1h.27m.59.9s.
4	Trojan/Nesvadba	Skoda Octavia	WRC	1h.29m.07.1s.
5	Trneny/Pritzl	Toyota Corolla	WRC	1h.29m.26.6s.
6	Beres/Stary	Toyota Corolla	WRC	1h.29m.49.0s.
7	Vojtech/Ernst	Toyota Corolla	WRC	1h.31m.02.4s.
8	Tucek/Tesar	Mitsubishi Lancer Evo	N	1h.32m.03.2s.

90 starters. 56 finishers.

ECR6 IL CIOCCO VALLE DEL SERCHIO (I) — S
Castelnuovo di Garfagnana 21/23.03.2003 coeff.5

1	Basso/Dotta	Fiat Punto	A	2h.15m.53.2s.
2	Travaglia/Zanella	Peugeot 206	A	2h.16m.18.1s.
3	Andreucci/Andreussi	Fiat Punto	A	2h.16m.45.8s.
4	Galli/d'Amore	Mitsubishi Lancer Evo	N	2h.17m.42.0s.
5	Aghini Lombardi/Roggia	Peugeot 206	A	2h.17m.46.4s.
6	Longhi/Fappani	Subaru Impreza	N	2h.18m.25.6s.
7	Caldani/d'Esposito	Fiat Punto	A	2h.18m.33.1s.
8	Dallavilla/Canton	Fiat Punto	A	2h.18m.33.4s.

76 starters. 46 finishers.

ECR7 MILLE MIGLIA (I) Desenzano del Garda 3/5.04.2003 coeff.20

1	Campos/Magalhaes	Peugeot 206	WRC	3h.35m.49.7s.
2	Pedersoli/Vernuccio	Peugeot 306 Maxi	A	3h.36m.12.1s.
3	Basso/Guglielmini	Fiat Punto	A	3h.38m.20.8s.
4	Longhi/Baggio	Subaru Impreza	N	3h.38m.24.4s.
5	Cunico/Pirollo	Mitsubishi Lancer Evo	N	3h.39m.14.0s.
6	Travaglia/Zanella	Peugeot 206	A	3h.39m.28.1s.
7	Aghini/Roggia	Peugeot 206	A	3h.39m.28.1s.
8	Andreucci/Andreussi	Fiat Punto	A	3h.40m.46.8s.

88 starters. 40 finishers.

ECR8 BOUCLES DE SPA (B) Spa 4/6.04.2003 coeff.5 — W

1	Tsjoen/Chevallier	Toyota Corolla	WRC	1h.35m.49s.
2	Snijers/Muth	Subaru Impreza	WRC	1h.36m.04s.
3	Munster/Leyh	Subaru Impreza	A	1h.39m.48s.
4	Theunissen/Genten	Toyota Celica	A	1h.40m.08s.
5	Radoux/Gregoire	Ford Escort	WRC	1h.41m.09s.
6	Bruyneel/Meert	Toyota Celica	A	1h.41m.20s.
7	Bouche/Pirotte	Mitsubishi Lancer Evo	N	1h.42m.46s.
8	Princen/Marteau	Mitsubishi Lancer Evo	N	1h.43m.21s.

107 starters. 74 finishers.

ECR9 CANARIAS (E) Maspalomas 11/12.04.2003 coeff.20

1	Campos/Magalhaes	Peugeot 206	WRC	3h.02m.31.0s.
2	Fuster/Medina	Citroen Saxo	A	3h.08m.35.6s.
3	A.Ponce/Gonzalez	Skoda Octavia	A	3h.10m.06.2s.
4	Vallejo/Vallejo	Fiat Punto	A	3h.12m.04.1s.
5	J.M.Ponce/Larrode	VW Polo	A	3h.12m.54.1s.
6	Garcia/Mujica	Citroen Saxo	A	3h.12m.55.6s.
7	Concepcion/Del Rosario	Mitsubishi Lancer Evo	N	3h.15m.12.9s.
8	Delgado/Perez	Mitsubishi Carisma	A	3h.16m.25.2s.

38 starters. 20 finishers.

WEISER

ECR10

BACKMAN

ECR13

DIMOV

ECR16

PHOTO 4

ECR11

JUGAS

ECR14

WEYENS

ECR17

WEYENS

ECR12

PHOTO 4

ECR15

WEYENS

ECR18

ECR10 MATADOR TATRY (SK) Puchov 2/3.05.2003 coeff.5 — E

1	Pech/Uhel	Ford Focus	WRC	1h.28m.58.0s.
2	Cserhalmi/Bodnar	Ford Focus	WRC	1h.30m.58.4s.
3	Beres/Stary	Subaru Impreza	WRC	1h.31m.06.2s.
4	Jandik/Chrastecky	Mitsubishi Lancer Evo	N	1h.34m.24.7s.
5	Cais/Ondrejcik	Mitsubishi Lancer Evo	N	1h.35m.44.9s.
6	Alexandrov/Tamrazov	Subaru Impreza	N	1h.35m.51.2s.
7	Trnovec/Karnik	Mitsubishi Lancer Evo	N	1h.36m.20.0s.
8	Palko/Muller	Mitsubishi Lancer Evo	N	1h.36m.32.7s.

54 starters. 25 finishers.

ECR11 TARGA FLORIO (I) Palermo 1/3.05.2003 coeff.2 — S

1	Andreucci/Andreussi	Fiat Punto	A	2h.04m.05.4s.
2	Basso/Guglielmini	Fiat Punto	A	2h.04m.22.9s.
3	Travaglia/Zanella	Peugeot 206	A	2h.04m.26.4s.
4	Longhi/Fappani	Subaru Impreza	A	2h.05m.00.1s.
5	Cantamessa/Capolongo	Renault Clio	A	2h.05m.36.5s.
6	Dallavilla/Canton	Fiat Punto	A	2h.05m.54.8s.
7	Rossetti/Chiarcossi	Citroen Saxo	A	2h.06m.54.8s.
8	Galli/d'Amore	Mitsubishi Lancer Evo	N	2h.06m.55.8s.

60 starters. 43 finishers.

ECR12 TURKEY (TR) Izmir 16/18.05.2003 coeff.20

1	Thiry/Fortin	Peugeot 206	WRC	3h.04m.28.7s.
2	Yazici/Okan	Ford Focus	WRC	3h.09m.49.5s.
3	Andreucci/Andreussi	Fiat Palio	A	3h.13m.57.3s.
4	Kazaz/Gur	Citroen Saxo	A	3h.14m.57.7s.
5	Isik/Guleren	Fiat Punto	A	3h.16m.38.5s.
6	Genim/Atilgan	Renault Megane	A	3h.19m.53.8s.
7	Gulerhan/Dincer	Mitsubishi Lancer Evo	N	3h.20m.51.8s.
8	Akdilek/Uluocak	Subaru Impreza	N	3h.21m.04.5s.

52 starters. 32 finishers.

ECR13 SOUTH SWEDISH (S) Vaxjo 23/24.05.2003 coeff.5 — N

1	Radstrom/Skallman	Toyota Corolla	WRC	1h.52m.01.1s.
2	Thorszelius/Thorszelius	Toyota Corolla	WRC	1h.52m.22.4s.
3	Eriksson/Svensson	Ford Focus	WRC	1h.52m.37.3s.
4	Kuchar/Szczepaniak	Ford Focus	WRC	1h.52m.37.9s.
5	Johansson/Carlsson	Toyota Corolla	WRC	1h.53m.07.1s.
6	Jonsson/Johansson	Ford Escort	WRC	1h.53m.12.5s.
7	Dale/Bargery	Hyundai Accent	WRC	1h.53m.45.6s.
8	Carlsson/Fredriksson	Mitsubishi Lancer Evo	N	1h.54m.48.3s.

68 starters. 31 finishers.

ECR14 FEHERVAR (H) Dunaujvaros 23/25.05.2003 coeff.2 — S

1	Szabo/Kerek	Skoda Octavia	WRC	1h.47m.19.2s.
2	Benik/Somogyi	Ford Focus	WRC	1h.47m.56.2s.
3	Angyalfi/Kazar	Subaru Impreza	WRC	1h.49m.27.9s.
4	'Asi'/Foldesi	Mitsubishi Lancer Evo	A	1h.51m.51.6s.
5	Turi/Kerek	Mitsubishi Lancer Evo	A	1h.54m.27.7s.
6	Butor/Toth	Citroen Saxo	A	1h.57m.25.7s.
7	Oroszlan/Oroszlan	Mitsubishi Lancer Evo	N	1h.58m.35.7s.
8	Schleider/Horvath	Mitsubishi Lancer Evo	N	1h.59m.35.7s.

76 starters. 44 finishers.

ECR15 SAN MARINO (RSM) Serravalle 30/31.05.2003 coeff.10 — S

1	Navarra/Fedeli	Subaru Impreza	WRC	3h.00m.35.9s.
2	Grossi/Pavesi	Ford Focus	WRC	3h.02m.18.0s.
3	Longhi/Imerito	Subaru Impreza	N	3h.03m.46.9s.
4	Fiorio/Brambilla	Subaru Impreza	N	3h.05m.20.1s.
5	Andreucci/Andreussi	Fiat Punto	A	3h.09m.03.2s.
6	Pianezzola/Zanatta	Mitsubishi Lancer Evo	N	3h.09m.12.6s.
7	Aghini/Cerrai	Peugeot 206	A	3h.09m.21.6s.
8	Bruschetta/Civiero	Mitsubishi Carisma	N	3h.09m.41.9s.

93 starters. 53 finishers.

ECR16 INTERSPEED (SCG) Budva 30.05/1.06.2003 coeff.5 — E

1	Jereb/Kacin	Seat Ibiza KC	A	2h.10m.56.2s.
2	Donchev/Manolov	Peugeot 306 Maxi	A	2h.13m.03.2s.
3	Avci/Yilmaz	Fiat Palio	A	2h.14m.47.1s.
4	Klemencic/Serles	Mitsubishi Lancer Evo	N	2h.15m.49.1s.
5	Brkic/Tomic	Mitsubishi Lancer Evo	N	2h.24m.32.6s.
6	Petrovic/Kondic	Citroen Xsara	N	2h.29m.21.7s.
7	Stoilov/Delev	Ford Escort	N	2h.31m.41.2s.
8	Gvozdeikov/Hristov	Peugeot 306	N	2h.31m.51.8s.

38 starters. 21 finishers.

ECR17 POLAND (PL) Klodzko 30/31.05.2003 coeff.20

1	Campos/Magalhaes	Peugeot 206	WRC	2h.24m.18.9s.
2	Thiry/Fortin	Peugeot 206	WRC	2h.26m.59.8s.
3	Vasin/Shchukin	Peugeot 206	WRC	2h.31m.12.1s.
4	Czopik/Wronski	Subaru Impreza	WRC	2h.32m.03.7s.
5	Frycz/Gieras	Mitsubishi Lancer Evo	N	2h.35m.11.7s.
6	Bebenek/Bebenek	Mitsubishi Lancer Evo	N	2h.35m.42.2s.
7	Lubiak/Wislawski	Mitsubishi Lancer Evo	N	2h.38m.13.9s.
8	Jurczak/Ciupka	Fiat Punto	A	2h.39m.52.7s.

69 starters. 42 finishers.

ECR18 BULGARIA (BG) Borovetz 13/15.06.2003 coeff.20

1	Thiry/Fortin	Peugeot 206	WRC	2h.46m.21.5s.
2	Popov/Popov	Skoda Octavia	WRC	2h.52m.23.8s.
3	Donchev/Manolov	Peugeot 306 Maxi	A	2h.57m.15.5s.
4	Tsarski/Tevekelov	Ford Escort	WRC	2h.58m.02.7s.
5	Kozlekov /Sivov	Mitsubishi Lancer Evo	N	2h.58m.23.9s.
6	Isik/Guleren	Fiat Punto	A	2h.58m.56.1s.
7	Geradzhiev/Popov	Mitsubishi Lancer Evo	N	2h.59m.13.3s.
8	Marinov/Cholakov	Mitsubishi Lancer Evo	N	2h.59m.22.5s.

53 starters. 26 finishers.

ECR19

ECR22

ECR25

ECR20

ECR23

ECR26

ECR21

ECR24

ECR27

ECR19 ADAC SAARLAND (D) Merzig 20/21.06.2003 *coeff.2* **N**

1	Gassner/Schrankl	Mitsubishi Carisma	N	2h.05m.14.4s.
2	Mohe/Uhlig	Renault Clio	A	2h.06m.52.3s.
3	Neuschafer-Rube/Seitz	Mitsubishi Lancer Evo	N	2h.08m.02.9s.
4	Olsson/Carlsson	Mitsubishi Lancer Evo	N	2h.08m.56.9s.
5	Holz/Limbach	VW Golf KC	A	2h.09m.23.4s.
6	Liska/Jugas	Proton Pert	N	2h.09m.52.4s.
7	Corazza/Rothe	Honda Civic	N	2h.10m.24.0s.
8	Weijs/Robbers	VW Golf KC	A	2h.10m.27.9s.

53 starters. 29 finishers.

ECR20 SALENTO (I) Lecce 19/21.06.2003 *coeff.10* **S**

1	Varnakiotis/Theodosioy	Honda Integra	N	1h.07m.08.4s.
2	Zumelli/Cicognini	Renault Clio	N	1h.07m.20.9s.
3	Portaluri/Provenzano	Honda Civic	N	1h.08m.08.4s.
4	Greco/Schipa	Citroen Saxo	N	1h.09m.19.2s.
5	Gorgoni/Rizzo	Peugeot 205	A	1h.10m.16.3s.
6	Di Salvo/Cintolo	Peugeot 106	N	1h.16m.57.6s.

55 starters. 6 finishers. Leg 2 Cancelled following the death of Loris Roggia.

ECR21 YPRES WESTHOEK (B) Ypres 27/29.06.2003 *coeff.20*

1	Thiry/Fortin	Peugeot 206	WRC	2h.51m.21.3s.
2	Tsjoen/Chevallier	Toyota Corolla	WRC	2h.53m.00.0s.
3	Campos/Magalhaes	Peugeot 206	WRC	2h.59m.30.1s.
4	Munster/Haghedooren	Subaru Impreza	A	3h.03m.41.0s.
5	Cols/Godde	Fiat Punto	A	3h.05m.35.1s.
6	De Winkel/Van Hoek	VW Golf	A	3h.06m.13.4s.
7	Colsoul/Colsoul	Mitsubishi Lancer Evo	N	3h.07m.05.3s.
8	Bouche/Pirotte	Mitsubishi Lancer Evo	N	3h.07m.59.9s.

111 starters. 52 finishers.

ECR22 SATA ACORES (P) Ponta Delgada 3/5.07.2003 *coeff.10* **W**

1	Peres/Silva	Ford Escort	A	3h.36m.42.1s.
2	Araujo/Ramalho	Citroen Saxo	A	3h.40m.01.6s.
3	Carmo/Braganca	Mitsubishi Lancer Evo	N	3h.40m.43.1s.
4	A.Lopes/Lisboa	Fiat Punto	A	3h.41m.01.6s.
5	V.Lopes/Henriques	Fiat Punto	A	3h.44m.32.4s.
6	Rego/Rodrigues	Mitsubishi Lancer Evo	N	3h.45m.17.3s.
7	Casanova/Tavares	Mitsubishi Lancer Evo	N	3h.48m.39.2s.
8	Moura/Eiro	Citroen Saxo	A	3h.52m.47.4s.

60 starters. 30 finishers.

ECR23 ROMANIA (RO) Brasov 4/6.07.2003 *coeff.5* **E**

1	Girtofan/Pulpea	Seat Cordoba	WRC	1h.44m.06.9s.
2	Leu/Solomon	Hyundai Accent	WRC	1h.48m.02.1s.
3	Mihalache/Colceriu	Mitsubishi Lancer Evo	A	1h.48m.31.8s.
4	Ilina/Cimpeanu	Mitsubishi Lancer Evo	N	1h.48m.34.6s.
5	Ungur/Jucan	Mitsubishi Lancer Evo	N	1h.50m.04.3s.
6	Preda/Hangu	Mitsubishi Lancer Evo	N	1h.50m.48.0s.
7	Graef/Hard	Mitsubishi Lancer Evo	N	1h.52m.08.6s.
8	Iliescu/Neagu	Mitsubishi Lancer Evo	N	1h.54m.49.4s.

40 starters. 20 finishers.

ECR24 KURZEME (LV) Liepaja 11/13.07.2003 *coeff.5* **N**

1	Grjazin/Troshkin	Mitsubishi Lancer Evo	N	1h.35m.05.2s.
2	Vorobjovs/Ervalds	Mitsubishi Lancer Evo	N	1h.35m.12.1s.
3	Egle/Vilmanis	Mitsubishi Lancer Evo	N	1h.36m.41.4s.
4	Zigunov/Ter-Oganesjanc	Mitsubishi Lancer Evo	N	1h.38m.16.6s.
5	Dorosinski/Balin	Subaru Impreza	N	1h.39m.16.8s.
6	Niimenae/Markus	Mitsubishi Lancer Evo	N	1h.39m.44.5s.
7	Laur/Kornilov	Citroen Saxo	A	1h.41m.26.9s.
8	Cirba/Pivoras	Renault Clio	N	1h.42m.44.6s.

48 starters. 27 finishers.

ECR25 BOHEMIA (CZ) Mlada Boleslav 11/13.07.2003 *coeff.5* **E**

1	Kresta/Tomanek	Peugeot 206	WRC	1h.54m.02.6s.
2	Valousek/Houst	Toyota Corolla	WRC	1h.57m.02.6s.
3	T.Vojtech/Palivec	Peugeot 206	WRC	1h.57m.26.2s.
4	Pech/Uhel	Ford Focus	WRC	1h.58m.13.4s.
5	Trneny/Pritzl	Skoda Octavia	WRC	1h.58m.13.5s.
6	Beres/Stary	Subaru Impreza	WRC	1h.58m.47.2s.
7	Stary/Slambora	Skoda Octavia	WRC	1h.58m.51.8s.
8	Kahle/Gobel	Skoda Octavia	WRC	1h.58m.58.3s.
11	Jandik/Chrastecky	Mitsubishi Lancer Evo	N	2h.04m.46.1s.

129 starters. 73 finishers.

ECR26 SAN MARTINO DI CASTROZZA (I) 17/19.07.2003 *coeff.5* **S**

1	De Cecco/Campeis	Peugeot 206	WRC	2h.19m.37.5s.
2	De Tisi/Pollet	Peugeot 206	WRC	2h.21m.08.0s.
3	Andreucci/Andreussi	Fiat Punto	A	2h.23m.05.5s.
4	Papadimitriou/Harryman	Ford Focus	WRC	2h.23m.20.9s.
5	Basso/Guglielmini	Fiat Punto	A	2h.23m.27.1s.
6	Travaglia/Zanella	Peugeot 206	A	2h.24m.19.4s.
7	Longhi/Fappani	Subaru Impreza	N	2h.24m.47.6s.
8	Dallavilla/Canton	Fiat Punto	A	2h.25m.49.6s.

53 starters. 34 finishers.

ECR27 HEBROS (BG) Plovdiv 26/27.07.2003 *coeff.5* **E**

1	Yazici/Okan	Ford Focus	WRC	2h.27m.14.4s.
2	Popov/Popov	Skoda Octavia	WRC	2h.28m.04.8s.
3	Donchev/Manolov	Peugeot 306 Maxi	A	2h.28m.43.9s.
4	Isik/Guleren	Fiat Punto	A	2h.31m.23.6s.
5	Avci/Yilmaz	Fiat Palio	A	2h.35m.42.5s.
6	Knajzl/Cernohorsky	Skoda Octavia	A	2h.36m.49.9s.
7	Cukurova/Alpay	Ford Puma	A	2h.39m.49.5s.
8	Yanakiev/Ignatov	Citroen Saxo	A	2h.40m.39.5s.
15	Stajkov/Stajkov	Renault Clio	N	2h.50m.54.1s.

51 starters. 32 finishers.

WEYENS

ECR28

TREJTNAR

ECR29

ECR30 as seen on Turkey WRC event.

WEISER

ECR31

DIMOV

ECR32

PHOTO 4

ECR33

WEYENS

ECR34

EBREY

ECR35

NENAD

ECR36

ECR28 VINHO DA MADEIRA (P) Funchal 31.07/2.08.2003 *coeff.20*

1	M.Campos/Magalhaes	Peugeot 206	WRC	3h.00m.42.9s.
2	Thiry/Fortin	Peugeot 206	WRC	3h.00m.47.7s.
3	Delecour/Pauwels	Peugeot 206	WRC	3h.04m.40.9s.
4	Sa/Camacho	Peugeot 306 Maxi	A	3h.07m.57.0s.
5	A.Campos/Camacho	Peugeot 306 Maxi	A	3h.08m.41.6s.
6	Camacho/Cabral	Peugeot 306 Maxi	A	3h.12m.27.7s.
7	Gomes/Rodrigues	VW Golf	A	3h.13m.07.0s.
8	Freitas/Figueiroa	Opel Astra	A	3h.15m.20.2s.
12	Spinola/Castro	Mitsubishi Lancer Evo	N	3h.17m.10.5s.

78 starters. 35 finishers.

ECR29 BUDAPEST (H) Budapest 8/10.8.2003 *coeff.5*   **S**

1	Toth/Toth	Peugeot 206	WRC	1h.44m.52.7s.
2	Benik/Somogyi	Ford Focus	WRC	1h.45m.52.7s.
3	Pech/Uhel	Ford Focus	WRC	1h.47m.52.3s.
4	'Asi'/Nandi	Mitsubishi Lancer Evo	A	1h.47m.53.6s.
5	Butor/Toth	Citroen Saxo	A	1h.52m.36.6s.
6	Szilagyi/Domonkos	Mitsubishi Lancer Evo	A	1h.52m.48.5s.
7	Herczig/Herczig	Citroen Saxo	A	1h.54m.20.6s.
8	Oroszlan/Oroszlan	Mitsubishi Lancer Evo	N	1h.55m.04.0s.

102 starters. 57 finishers.

ECR30 GEORGIA (GE) Tblisi 15/17.8.2003 *coeff.2*   **E**

1	Isik/Guleren	Fiat Punto	A	1h.57m.46.64s.
2	Avci/Yilmaz	Fiat Palio	A	1h.58m.33.31s.
3	Matveev/Mikhailov	Mitsubishi Lancer Evo	N	2h.03m.07.15s.
4	Zorin/Pogosyan	Subaru Impreza	N	2h.04m.39.00s.
5	Tavartkiladze/Kukhianidze	Honda Civic	A	2h.09m.28.33s.
6	Arjevanidze/Gambarashvili	Lada Samara	A	2h.12m.22.06s.
7	Ogbaidze/Iashvili	Citroen Saxo	N	2h.31m.00.41s.

19 starters. 7 finishers.

ECR31 KOSICE (SK) Kosice 15/17.8.2003 *coeff.2*   **E**

1	Cserhalmi/Krajnak	Ford Focus	WRC	1h.43m.00.9s.
2	Pech/Uhel	Ford Focus	WRC	1h.43m.10.8s.
3	Beres/Stary	Subaru Impreza	WRC	1h.44m.48.2s.
4	Jandik/Chrastecky	Mitsubishi Lancer Evo	N	1h.49m.34.6s.
5	Palko/Palko	Mitsubishi Lancer Evo	N	1h.50m.44.1s.
6	Beltowski/Wilk	Skoda Felicia	A	1h.59m.21.4s.
7	Spurek/Kovak	Mitsubishi Lancer Evo	N	2h.00m.50.4s.
8	Pelikanski/Dymurski	Peugeot 206	A	2h.01m.29.8s.

56 starters. 35 finishers.

ECR32 SOSSER SLIVEN (BG) Sliven 30/31.08.2003 *coeff.10*   **E**

1	Tzarski/Tevelekov	Ford Escort	WRC	2h.11m.39.2s.
2	Donchev/Manolov	Peugeot 306 Maxi	A	2h.12m.05.4s.
3	Marinov/Cholakov	Mitsubishi Lancer Evo	N	2h.13m.12.8s.
4	Gulerhan/Gucenmez	Mitsubishi Lancer Evo	N	2h.20m.00.6s.
5	Cilento/Oliva	Mitsubishi Lancer Evo	N	2h.20m.02.7s.
6	Ali Sipahi/Dincer	Mitsubishi Lancer Evo	N	2h.20m.03.2s.
7	Matveyev/Mikhailov	Mitsubishi Lancer Evo	N	2h.21m.21.4s.
8	Stoilov/Delev	Subaru Impreza	N	2h.23m.02.0s.

42 starters. 27 finishers.

ECR33 ALPI ORIENTALI (I) Udine 29/30.08.2003 *coeff.5*   **S**

1	De Cecco/Barigelli	Peugeot 206	WRC	2h.35m.54.2s.
2	Basso/Guglielmini	Fiat Punto	A	2h.37m.39.6s.
3	Rossetti/De Luis	Citroen Saxo	A	2h.38m.23.0s.
4	Bizzarri/Bosi	Renault Clio	A	2h.38m.42.9s.
5	Dallavilla/Canton	Fiat Punto	A	2h.39m.57.9s.
6	Longhi/Imerito	Subaru Impreza	N	2h.40m.16.2s.
7	Chiorboli/Campeis	Toyota Corolla	WRC	2h.40m.31.0s.
8	Fiorio/Brambilla	Subaru Impreza	N	2h.41m.09.6s.

81 starters. 45 finishers.

ECR34 BARUM (CZ) Zlin 29/31.08.2003 *coeff.20*

1	Pech/Uhel	Ford Focus	WRC	2h.34m.57.0s.
2	Campos/Magalhaes	Peugeot 206	WRC	2h.36m.08.4s.
3	Kopecky/Schovanek	Skoda Octavia	WRC	2h.36m.50.1s.
4	Cserhalmi/Palivec	Ford Focus	WRC	2h.39m.25.7s.
5	Trojan/Nesvadba	Skoda Octavia	WRC	2h.42m.28.5s.
6	Enge/Gross	Skoda Octavia	WRC	2h.43m.03.7s.
7	Jandik/Chrastecky	Mitsubishi Lancer Evo	N	2h.46m.16.8s.
8	Triner/Horniacek	Seat Cordoba	WRC	2h.46m.57.1s.

128 starters. 47 finishers.

ECR35 ULSTER (GB) Armagh 5/6.09.2003 *coeff.2*   **W**

1	Laukkanen/Riipinen	Subaru Impreza	WRC	2h.06m.11.2s.
2	McGarrity/O'Gorman	Subaru Impreza	WRC	2h.08m.01.8s.
3	Milner/Beech	Toyota Corolla	WRC	2h.08m.20.0s.
4	Latvala/Anttila	Ford Focus	WRC	2h.08m.42.8s.
5	McHale/Murphy	Subaru Impreza	WRC	2h.08m.50.5s.
6	Meeke/Senior	Opel Corsa	A	2h.11m.06.3s.
7	Hall/Egglestone	Mitsubishi Lancer Evo	A	2h.14m.39.4s.
8	Champion/Simmons	Ford Puma	A	2h.14m.59.4s.
9	White/Shinners	Mitsubishi Lancer Evo	N	2h.15m.02.8s.

86 starters. 52 finishers.

ECR36 BALKAN (SCG) Bajina Basta 5/7.09.2003 *coeff.2*   **E**

1	Martinovic/Markovic	Renault Clio	N	2h.09m.28.4s.
2	Brkic/Tomic	Mitsubishi Lancer Evo	N	2h.09m.33.4s.
3	Jereb/Kacin	Subaru Impreza	A	2h.12m.02.4s.
4	Zirojevic/Vujkov	Ford Escort	N	2h.15m.49.2s.
5	Jovanovic/Petrovic	Seat Ibiza	N	2h.18m.38.3s.
6	Podboj/Djakovic	Suzuki Swift	N	2h.20m.01.8s.
7	Komljenovic/Stefanovic	Mitsubishi Lancer Evo	N	2h.21m.53.3s.
8	Prlainovic/Spasic	Zastava Yugo	N	2h.22m.43.2s.

29 starters. 16 finishers.

ECR37

ECR39

ECR41

ECR38

ECR40

ECR42

ECR37 INA CROATIA (HR) Zagreb 12/14.09.2003 *coeff.10*				**E**
1	Pech /Uhel	Ford Focus	WRC	2h.35m.35.0s.
2	Jandik/Chrastecky	Mitsubishi Lancer Evo	N	2h.42m.40.3s.
3	Szilagyi/Domonkos	Mitsubishi Lancer Evo	A	2h.44m.14.9s.
4	Loncaric/Puzic	Mitsubishi Lancer Evo	A	2h.45m.57.0s.
5	Iliev/Yanakiev	Peugeot 206	A	2h.46m.13.2s.
6	Skalic/Skalic	Honda Civic	A	2h.51m.37.6s.
7	Perharic/Butorac	VW Golf KC	A	2h.51m.38.8s.
8	Grendene/Grendene	Opel Astra	N	2h.53m.33.9s.

51 starters. 34 finishers.

ECR39 COSTA SMERALDA (I) Porto Cervo 19/21.09.2003 *coeff.5*				**S**
1	Rovanpera/Pietilainen	Peugeot 206	WRC	2h.20m.47.4s.
2	Navarra/Fedeli	Subaru Impreza	WRC	2h.21m.40.4s.
3	Galli/Bioletti	Mitsubishi Lancer Evo	N	2h.23m.25.7s.
4	Grossi/Pavesi	Ford Focus	WRC	2h.25m.51.4s.
5	Cantamessa/Capolongo	Mitsubishi Lancer Evo	N	2h.27m.36.7s.
6	Rossetti/De Luis	Mitsubishi Lancer Evo	N	2h.30m.44.6s.
7	Fiorio/Brambilla	Subaru Impreza	N	2h.30m.53.0s.
8	De Dominicis/Bernacchini	Mitsubishi Lancer Evo	N	2h.32m.11.5s.

106 starters. 50 finishers.

ECR41 YU (SCG) Bajina Basta 19/21.09.2003 *coeff.5*				**E**
1	Jereb/Kacin	Seat Ibiza KC	A	1h.56m.55.2s.
2	Klemencic/Korpar	Mitsubishi Lancer Evo	N	2h.01m.42.1s.
3	Brkic/Tomic	Mitsubishi Lancer Evo	N	2h.01m.59.3s.
4	Marinov/Cholakov	Mitsubishi Lancer Evo	N	2h.02m.12.5s.
5	Cilento/Oliva	Mitsubishi Lancer Evo	N	2h.03m.17.9s.
6	Szollosi/Jankovics	Mitsubishi Lancer Evo	N	2h.03m.18.1s.
7	Peljhan/Somun	Subaru Impreza	N	2h.04m.54.1s.
8	Tabarelli/Pastoret	Ford Escort Cosworth	N	2h.07m.18.9s.

58 starters. 35 finishers.

ECR38 MESSINA (I) Messina 12/14.09.2003 *coeff.5*				**S**
1	Riolo/Marin	Toyota Corolla	WRC	1h.57m.01.7s.
2	Valli/Stefanelli	Subaru Impreza	WRC	1h.58m.27.1s.
3	L.Fontana/Settimo	Toyota Corolla	WRC	2h.00m.54.7s.
4	Lagana/Messina	Mitsubishi Lancer Evo	N	2h.03m.13.8s.
5	Sicilia/Cambria	Mitsubishi Lancer Evo	N	2h.03m.46.6s.
6	Bellini/Cangemi	Ford Escort Cosworth	N	2h.03m.48.8s.
7	Virag/Pozzi	Renault Clio	A	2h.03m.48.9s.
8	C.Fontana/Casazza	Toyota Corolla	WRC	2h.04m.32.8s.

59 starters. 28 finishers.

ECR40 MIKONA (SK) Rimavska Sobota 19/20.09.2003 *coeff.2*				**E**
1	Pech /Uhel	Ford Focus	WRC	1h.28m.10.8s.
2	Cserhalmi/Krajnak	Ford Focus	WRC	1h.28m.53.3s.
3	Beres/Stary	Toyota Corolla	WRC	1h.31m.27.5s.
4	Palko/Muller	Mitsubishi Lancer Evo	N	1h.36m.14.8s.
5	Trnovec/Karnik	Mitsubishi Lancer Evo	N	1h.38m.45.8s.
6	Surek/Kovac	Mitsubishi Lancer Evo	N	1h.41m.19.5s.
7	Konuch/Porubcan	Skoda Octavia	A	1h.41m.30.7s.
8	Beltowski/Wilk	Skoda Felicia	A	1h.43m.52.7s.

40 Starters. 29 finishers.

ECR42 GOLDEN TULIP (NL) Nijverdal 26/27.09.2003 *coeff.2*				**W**
1	Wevers/Poel	Toyota Corolla	WRC	1h.37m.42s.
2	Ampuja/Markkula	Toyota Corolla	WRC	1h.39m.48s.
3	Winkel/van Hoek	VW Golf KC	A	1h.42m.33s.
4	Poulsen/Fredriksen	Toyota Celica	A	1h.43m.37s.
5	Arthurs/Scholtalbers	Toyota Celica	A	1h.43m.45s.
6	Jonkers/Jonkers	Mitsubishi Lancer Evo	A	1h.44m.13s.
7	O'Donovan/Moynihan	Subaru Impreza	WRC	1h.45m.01s.
8	Vossen/Findhammer	Mitsubishi Lancer Evo	N	1h.45m.06s.

70 starters. 51 finishers.

In terms of competition, 2003 will long be remembered as the season when two drivers, competing in equal cars, fought out the battle for the title to the very end of the season and ending up with them equal on points. In addition to taking scores from the coefficient 20 events it was also possible to enter one extra event, the points from which could be added to the total. At the end of the season, therefore, Thiry entered the Condroz Rally (coefficient 10) in his home country Belgium. The championship hinged on this event, and Thiry took the title by having won five events to the four of Campos.

In 2004 the season will be based only on events which have previously been given coefficient 20 status. Whereas in 2002 there was an attempt to run a sub championship for Super1600 cars this was not a success, and in 2003 there was only trophy for the Drivers, title. For 2004 the other rounds of the former ECR will run only for regional geographic zones. This is the final year in which World Rally Cars can be used in these events, and it is expected that the ECR season, like with every regional championship, will be fought out using Group N or two-wheel drive cars.

2003 FIA European Champion
Bruno Thiry (B) 1400pts, 2 Miguel Campos (P) 1400, 3 Vaclav Pech (CZ) 42, etc.

2003 FIA Regional European Rally Cup Winners
NORTH Andreas Eriksson (S)
SOUTH Giandomenico Basso (I)
EAST Vaclav Pech (CZ)
WEST
SCANDINAVIAN WINTER CUP Janne Tuohino (FIN), Henning Solberg (N) and Eddie Horbing (N) - joint winners.

ECR43

ECR45

ECR47

ECR44

ECR46

ECR48

ECR43 ELPA (GR) Patra 26/28.09.2003 *coeff.20*

1	Thiry/Fortin	Peugeot 206	WRC	23m.51.2s.
2	Campos/Magalhaes	Peugeot 206	WRC	23m.57.4s.
3	Vasin/Shchukin	Peugeot 206	WRC	25m.16.0s.

Rally was stopped following the death of Dimitris Koliopanos
55 starters. 47 finishers (3 Classified).

ECR45 SATURNUS (SLO) Idrija 3/5.10.2003 *coeff. 2*   **S**

1	Spurek/Dratva	Mitsubishi Lancer Evo	N	2h.06m.38.4s.
2	Turk/Kumse	Ford Escort Cosworth	N	2h.06m.57.6s.
3	Loncaric/Puzic	Mitsubishi Lancer Evo	A	2h.07m.05.2s.
4	Klemencic/Korpar	Mitsubishi Lancer Evo	N	2h.07m.59.6s.
5	Mikulastik/Baran	Subaru Impreza	N	2h.08m.11.7s.
6	Szollosi/Jankovics	Mitsubishi Lancer Evo	N	2h.08m.17.3s.
7	Cilensek/Podbregar	Subaru Impreza	N	2h.09m.25.5s.
8	Jeram/Jeram	Zastava Yugo 55	A	2h.09m.59.2s.

89 starters. 55 finishers.

ECR47 VALAIS (CH) Martigny 23/25.10.2003 *coeff. 10*   **S**

1	Burri/Hoffmann	Subaru Impreza	WRC	3h.07m.58.7s.
2	Roux/Corthay	Ford Focus	WRC	3h.09m.59.1s.
3	Heintz/Scherrer	Subaru Impreza	N	3h.20m.47.2s.
4	Gonon/Dubuis	Honda Integra	N	3h.22m.16.8s.
5	Galli/Arcadi	Peugeot 206	A	3h.27m.51.4s.
6	Tornay/Bourgeois	Citroen Saxo	A	3h.29m.16.7s.
7	Bagnoud/Dietrich	Peugeot 206	A	3h.30m.18.5s.
8	Hotz/Robert	Citroen Saxo	N	3h.31m.58.5s.

83 starters. 44 finishers.

ECR44 ROTA DO VIDRO (P) Marinha Grande 3/5.10.2003 *coeff.5*   **W**

1	Araujo/ Ramalho	Citroen Saxo	A	2h.03m.07.6s.
2	Peres/Silva	Ford Escort Cosworth	A	2h.03m.48.9s.
3	Campos/Camacho	Peugeot 306 Maxi	A	2h.04m.47.4s.
4	Louro/Janela	Mitsubishi Lancer Evo	A	2h.05m.16.2s.
5	Chaves/Paiva	Renault Clio	A	2h.05m.28.7s.
6	Matos/Tavares	Peugeot 206	A	2h.10m.20.9s.
7	Bernardes/Reis	Opel Corsa	A	2h.10m.24.9s.
8	Pinto/Pereira	Citroen Saxo	A	2h.11m.50.7s.
10	Parente/Ferreira	Mitsubishi Lancer Evo	N	2h.12m.46.1s.

60 starters. 45 finishers.

ECR46 ANTIBES (F) Antibes 24/26.10.2003 *coeff. 20*   **W**

1	Thiry/Fortin	Peugeot 206	WRC	3h.13m.38.7s.
2	Campos/Magalhaes	Peugeot 206	WRC	3h.14m.03.8s.
3	Pech/Uhel	Ford Focus	WRC	3h.24m.10.6s.
4	Van Parijs/Peyskens	Mitsubishi Lancer Evo	A	3h.34m.05.5s.
5	Bartolini/Descamps	Mitsubishi Lancer Evo	N	3h.36m.38.6s.
6	Casier/Miclotte	Citroen Saxo	A	3h.39m.35.1s.
7	Fiandino/Badano	Peugeot 206	A	3h.40m.38.7s.
8	Verola/Bonnamy	Renault Clio	N	3h.44m.20.8s.

55 starters. 28 finishers.

ECR48 ADAC 3-STADTE (D) Straubing 24/25.10.2003 *coeff. 10*   **N**

1	Kahle/Gobel	Skoda Octavia	WRC	2h.12m.31.9s.
2	Wallenwein/Zeitlhofer	Mitsubishi Lancer Evo	A	2h.14m.09.1s.
3	Stohl/Minor	Mitsubishi Lancer Evo	A	2h.15m.59.1s.
4	Stolzel/Windisch	Skoda Octavia	WRC	2h.16m.25.2s.
5	Dobberkau/Bauer	Mitsubishi Lancer Evo	N	2h.16m.26.9s.
6	Solowow/Baran	Mitsubishi Lancer Evo	N	2h.16m.28.1s.
7	Gassner/Schrankl	Mitsubishi Lancer Evo	N	2h.16m.57.2s.
8	Carlstrom/Holmstrand	Mitsubishi Lancer Evo	N	2h.17m.11.5s.

68 starters. 41 finishers.

Janne Tuohino.

Bruno Thiry, 2003 European Champion.

ECR49 WALDVIERTEL (A) Horn 6/8.11.2003 *coeff. 5*   **W**

1	Baumschlager/Eichhorner	Mitsubishi Carisma	A	2h.16m.04.6s.
2	Hideg/Tajnafoi	Mitsubishi Lancer Evo	N	2h.19m.34.5s.
3	Gassner/Thannhauser	Mitsubishi Lancer Evo	N	2h.19m.41.4s.
4	Harrach/Kolbach	Mitsubishi Lancer Evo	A	2h.20m.12.1s.
5	Zellhofer/Novotny	Mitsubishi Lancer Evo	A	2h.21m.24.4s.
6	Lietz/Wicha	Mitsubishi Lancer Evo	N	2h.21m.32.2s.
7	Rosenberger/Schwarz	Lancia Delta Integrale	A	2h.22m.09.3s.
8	Kovar/Kohlbacher	Mitsubishi Lancer Evo	N	2h.23m.05.5s.

71 starters. 44 finishers.

ECR50 CONDROZ (B) Huy 15/16.11.2003 *coeff.10*   **W**

1	Loix/Smeets	Peugeot 206	WRC	2h.26m.03.8s.
2	Thiry/Fortin	Peugeot 206	WRC	2h.26m.12.7s.
3	Tsjoen/Chevaillier	Toyota Corolla	WRC	2h.26m.59.6s.
4	Snijers/Muth	Subaru Impreza	WRC	2h.31m.46.2s.
5	Van Parijs/Peyskens	Toyota Corolla	WRC	2h.34m.34.7s.
6	Munster/Leyh	Subaru Impreza	A	2h.37m.21.6s.
7	Bouche/Bourguignon	Mitsubishi Lancer Evo	N	2h.37m.42.6s
8	Bruyneel/Meert	Toyota Celica GT-4	A	2h.38m.12.8s.

174 starters. 110 finishers.

Fernando Rueda.

African

Rally Championship

African Champion in 2003 was the Spaniard Fernando Rueda, who lives in Cape Town and who has been in South Africa for 20 years. He had never rallied outside South Africa before and after a good position in the opening round he went to Zimbabwe, did well again and planned to continue in the series. He gained maximum championship points on the first four rallies, then missed Uganda where he became unbeatable on round five. This was the third year running a South African resident has won the title. "For me there were two main impressions. Firstly, how big is Africa! It took my crew 11 days travelling to come home from Rwanda." Secondly, I did not feel comfortable on road rallies, like in Rwanda. Our cars these days are so fast, so

Moses Lumala (left) with codriver Moses Matovu.

quiet, we need closed roads for these events. When this championship only has closed road stages, it will be fantastic!î The main change in the championship this year was that Namibia was replaced by Reunion.

Round 1 South Africa

The series started with this odd-ball event, in that the top three cars to finish were non homologated cars allowed under local championship rules and therefore ineligible to score points for the championship. Fernando Rueda headed the APC competitors despite a puncture. The overall winner was Serge Damseaux, consolation for retiring when leading on the final stage last year.

Round 2 Zimbabwe

This was an amazingly inspirational event run by enthusiasts determined not to let the country's difficulties affect their sport. Fuel, supplies, money were all stockpiled to make sure the event happened and was enjoyed by everyone who had the chance to be there. Rueda led from start to finish but had a battle with the Audi Quattro of Brendon Long before Long crashed.

Round 3 Zambia

This was Rueda's third successive vistory this year, after a close fight with Muna Singh

which was only resolved when Singh was slowed by suspension trouble. On his home event, eight times African champion, Satwant Singh fought back throughout the rally eventually to finish third. In the 1600cc Cup, consistent results brought Lauderdale into the lead in the category.

Round 4 Rwanda

As the championship progressively moved up country, they came to the first of the French speaking events and the first open road event in the series but Rueda was still unbeatable. Legs 1 and 2 were repeated, making the event easier for visiting drivers. Rueda led the rally all the way.

Round 5 Uganda

In his absence Rueda won the title! Lubega gained his lead over second placed driver Moses Lumala when the latter lost a lot of time changing a flat tyre, when his jack broke. Heartbreak for Burundi driver Rudi Cantanene who had repaired his car crashed at Rwanda only to retire 3km into the first section here!

Round 6 Safari Equator

A puncture for Rob Hellier in his old Evo III decided the result of the last mainland APC event of the season, and gave victory to Glen Edmunds in his Evo VI. A little earlier Alastair Cavenagh fell back with transmsission trouble. 18 year old Conrad Rautenbach from Zimbabwe clinched the 1600cc Cup. This event took on a major significance to Kenyan enthusiasts, to the extent of bringing the Safari name into the event's title. This event was also observed by the FIA, who were examining the feasibility of running greater distances of stages between service halts on world championship rallies.

Round 7 Reunion

This was something completely new in the ARC. The French Indian Ocean island off Madagascar was invited into the series as much to offer, through the other events in the championship, another range of rallies which the Reunion enthusiasts could tackle. This was the first ever asphalt event in the series, none of the regular APC drivers took part and indeed a two-wheel drive car won outright! Only homologated cars took the start.

Pascal Ardouin.

Round 1 TOTAL SOUTH AFRICA (ZA) 12/14.04.2003
Pretoria-Badplass. Closed roads - gravel - 297.00km.

4	Rueda/Botha	Mitsubishi Lancer Evo	N	3h.23m.31s.
6	Ryan/Carrahill	Subaru Impreza	N	3h.31m.09s.
7	Botha/Clark	Subaru Impreza	N	3h.34m.57s.
8	Du Plessis/Von Westernhagen	Subaru Impreza	N	3h.37m.10s.
9	Reyneke/Pheiffer	Subaru Impreza	N	3h.38m.54s.
10	Swart/Sime	Subaru Impreza	N	3h.40m.24s.
11	Dewit/Labuschagne	Toyota Corolla RSi	N	3h.42m.45s.
12	Watson/Miller	Toyota Corolla RSi	N	3h.44m.02s.

56 (27) starters. 28 (12) finishers. (eligible for ARC points)

LEADING RETIREMENTS

Himmell/Botes	Toyota Corolla Rsi	A	suspension
M.Singh/Sihoke	Subaru Impreza	A	clutch

Round 2 DUNLOP ZIMBABWE CHALLENGE (ZW) 23/25.05.2003
Harare. Closed roads - gravel - 274.79km.

1	Rueda/Botha	Mitsubishi Lancer Evo	N	3h.27m.37s.
3	M.Singh/Sihoka	Subaru Impreza	N	3h.44m.43s.
4	Himmel/Botes	Toyota Corolla RSi	A	3h.47m.55s.
6	Lauderdale/Dawe	Toyota Corolla RSi	N	3h.55m.54s.
12	Green/Exton	Toyota Corolla RSi	N	5h.39m.44s.

24 (10) starters. 12 (5) finishers.

LEADING RETIREMENT

Rautenbach/Marsh	Toyota Corolla RSi	N	water in engine

Fernando Rueda, 2003 African Champion.

Round 3 ZAMBIA (Z) 27/29.06.2003
Lusaka. Closed roads - gravel - 252.31km.

1	Rueda/Botha	Mitsubishi Lancer Evo	N	2h.41m.40.6s.
2	M.Singh/Sihoka	Subaru Impreza	N	2h.44m.33.0s.
3	S.Singh/Dearlove	Subaru Impreza	A	2h.49m.44.1s.
4	Robinson/Schireiber	Toyota Corolla RSi	A	2h.52m.25.0s.
5	Rautenbach/Marsh	Toyota Corolla RSi	A	2h.54m.45.0s.
6	Long/Rowley	Subaru Impreza	A	2h.55m.35.0s.
7	Lauderdale/Dawe	Toyota Corolla RSi	A	2h.56m.32.0s.
8	Nel/Nel	Toyota Celica	A	3h.03m.18.0s.

19 starters. 12 (8) finishers.

LEADING RETIREMENTS none

Round 4 RWANDA MOUNTAIN GORILLA (RWA) 1/3.08.2003
Kigale. Open road - gravel

1	Rueda/Botha	Mitsubishi Lancer Evo	N	4h.22m.15s.
2	Lumala/Matovu	Toyota Celica	A	4h.24m.56s.
3	Rautenbach/Marsh	Toyota Corolla RSi	N	4h.38m.44s.
6	Puggia/Cox	Peugeot 106	A	5h.00m.04s.
7	Mitraros/Paganin	Peugeot 106	A	5h.20m.00s.
9	Roberts/fiore	Toyota Celica	A	5h.44m.39s.
10	Mugwana/Khagram	Peugeot 205	A	5h.47m.39s.
12	Rutabingwa/Rugema	Peugeot 106	A	6h.34m.46s.

24 starters. 12 (8) finishers.

LEADING RETIREMENTS none

Round 5 TOTAL PEARL OF AFRICA UGANDA (EAU) 5/7.09.2003
Kampala. Open roads - gravel

1	Lubega/Musa	Mitsubishi Lancer Evo	A	2h.49m.32s.
2	Lumala/Buzabo	Toyota Celica	A	2h.56m.20s.
3	Rautenbach/Marsh	Toyota Corolla RSi	A	3h.07m.48s.
4	Ruparelia/Kasaija	MitsubishiLancer Evo	A	3h.08m.25s.
5	Kurji/Kadiri	Mitsubishi Lancer Evo	A	3h.14m.21s.
9	Lule/Mungyereza	Subaru Impreza	A	4h.09m.10s.
10	Blick/Kisooka	Mitsubishi Lancer Evo	A	4h.16m.33s.
11	Puggia/Daubie	Peugeot 106	A	4h.18m.21s.

21 starters. 11 (8) finishers. No group N finishers.

LEADING RETIREMENTS none

Round 6 KCB SAFARI EQUATOR RALLY KENYA (EAK) 9/11.10.2003
Mombasa. Open roads - gravel

1	Edmunds/Phillips-Carter	Mitsubishi Lancer Evo VI	A	3h.50m.24s.
2.	Hellier/Page-Morris	Mitsubishi Lancer Evo III	A	3h.56m.02s.
3	Anwar/Semhi	Mitsubishi Lancer Evo VI	N	3h.56m.47s.
4	Cavenagh/Cavenagh	Subaru Impreza	A	4h.17m.05s.
5	Rautenbach/Marsh	Toyota Corolla Rsi	A	4h.18m.18s.
6	Smith/Patel	Subaru Impreza	A	4h.20m.44s.
7	Manji/A,Khan	Subaru Impreza	A	4h.30m.58s.
8	van Tongeren/S.Khan	Subaru Impreza	A	4h.44m.24s.

29 (27) starters. 15 (15) finishers.

LEADING RETIREMENTS none

Round 7 REUNION (F) 7/8 .11.2003
St Denis. Closed roads, asphalt - 224.85km.

1	Ardouin/Paris	Peugeot 206 S1600	A	2h.52m.08.0s.
2	Maitre/Deschamps	Renault Clio RS	A	2h.52m.39.7s.
3	Grondin/Benard	Citroen Saxo VTS	A	2h.52m.53.8s.
4	Law Long/Reynes	Peugeot 206S1600	A	2h.55m.19.6s.
5	Bel/Tien Ken Seing	Subaru Impreza	A	2h.56m.21.6s.
6	Moullan/Patel	Mitsubishi Lancer	N	2h.58m.50.8s.
7	Unia/Stasica	Ford Puma	A	2h.59m.40.3s.
8	Ricquebourg/Pause	Mitsubishi Lancer	N	3h.01m.58.7s.

45 (45) starters. 27 (27) finishers.

LEADING RETIREMENT

Barbe/Renelleau	Toyota Corolla	WRC	differential

2003 FIA African Champion Fernando Rueda (E) 40pts, 2 Conrad Rautenbach (ZW) 20, Muna Singh (Z) & Moses Lumala (EAU) 10, Charlie Lubega (EAU), Glen Edmunds (EAK) and Pascal Ardouin (F) all 6, etc.
1600 Cup winner Conrad Rautenbach (ZW).

Suzuki maintained a presence in the 2003 APRC. This is the Ignis of the Australian brothers Atkinson.

Asia-Pacific

Rally Championship

Four drivers went into the final round of the championship able to win the title: Geof Argyle, Armin Kremer, Fumio Nutahara and Karamjit Singh. Last year's high hopes for the future of the APRC had been well founded, with a similar number of drivers registered for the series (14 in 2003), but there were still many problems. The biggest was the unexpected cancellation of two events. New Caledonia was cancelled for financial reasons, then China was cancelled due to the economic fallout after the SARS epidemic. The championship continued to be confusing because of the unique 'SuperRally' points system, whereby drivers were allowed to restart the next day, and score points for their performances after they restarted. This was a great idea and an encouragement for drivers who had to travel long distances only to retire early. It was, however, too complex for a championship in which the eligibility qualifications were unclear and with poor media promotion by the organisers and the FIA. It was never even clear who ran the secretariat! And then there were more problems en route. The political question regarding the world championship status

for Hokkaido caused concerns about the future constitution of the APRC, ending with Hokkaido being nominated for both championships in 2004. This was curious bearing in mind the two championships ran under different regulations. The late addition of India raised eyebrows. The timing was unfortunate in view of the long wait before the championship would be decided and too late for us to report! It was the first FIA championship event held in this sub-continent since 1990.

Round 1 Canberra

Crocker's win in Australia was very emotive, coming right after the death of his mentor Possum Bourne, a sad affair for Subaru Australia and the drivers who regularly competed in that country. While the Australian Group N championship drivers battled for the lead of the event, the race for the highest placed championship contender was a different battle altogether, with Kremer coming fifth, less than one second in front of Geof Argyle. The lead in the APRC race was closely fought between these two and also Fumio Nutahara. The rally started dry and dusty with cars running at three minute intervals, later the rains came and changed the nature of the stages

completely. The top three APRC crews finished within ten seconds of each other.

Round 2 Rotorua

Herbert's big event! This was Bruce's fifth win on this event, after which he proudly announced his retirement from the sport! The opening stages were run on the long, twisty Motu Road where Nutahara led initially, followed by Herbert then Argyle. On the second day Argyle's turbocharger broke and he fell well out of contention. From then on, Herbert was on his own. In the end there was a tie for best placed APRC driver between Nutahara and Singh, the extra points going to Nutahara for being quicker on the first stage of the event.

Round 3 Hokkaido

This event has been at the centre of the changes in the future 16-round world rally calendar! Winner was non championship driver Toshihiro Arai. Argyle and Kremer continued their rivalry on their own after Singh retired on the opening stage and Nutahara just after half distance. After the rains of 2002, this year's rally was run in mixed conditions. Two days after the end of the event, the FIA's World Rally Championship Commission voted to recommend Japan's entry in to the world series.

Round 4 Thailand

Held for the third time on the farm roads east of Bangkok, this was the fastest Rally of Thailand yet! There was a fierce battle in the first half of the event, with the lead changing hands eight times in the first nine stages. The competition for the overall lead was not the only hot thing at the rally, Karamjit Singh added "The weather was also even hotter than I am used to in Malaysia!" At the end of the event Singh had climbed up to third place in the championship, with no fewer than four drivers able to take the title at the final event in December. There was another very close battle for Group N, between Nutahara, Kremer and Taguchi, with the lead changing six times between them. After halfway Kremer pulled ahead and then became involved in a battle with second placed Argyle, the championship leader, which Kremer won on the first stage.

Note: Final round is the MRF INDIA (IND) 5/7.12.2003.

The three challengers to Karamjit's Crown:

Armin Kremer was the top points scorer in Canberra,

Geof Argyle at Hokkaido, and

Fumio Nutahara at Rotorua.

Round 1 SUBARU RALLY OF CANBERRA (AUS) 25/27.04.2003
Canberra. 22 Stages - gravel, 263.21km

1	Crocker/Foletta	Subaru Impreza	N	2h.50m.52.0s.
2	S.Pedder/Humm	Mitsubishi Lancer	N	2h.51m.26.2s.
3	Herridge/Macneall	Subaru Impreza	N	2h.52m.17.0s.
4	Ordynski/Stewart	Mitsubishi Lancer	N	2h.53m.56.5s.
5	Kremer/Berssen	Mitsubishi Lancer	N	2h.53m.56.7s.
6	Argyle/Smith	Mitsubishi Lancer	A	2h.53m.57.4s.
7	Nutahara/Hayashi	Mitsubishi Lancer	N	2h.54m.05.5s.
8	Neale/Neale	Mitsubishi Lancer	A	2h.55m.11.8s.

33 starters. 21 finishers.

LEADING RETIREMENTS & LAST STAGE COMPLETED

Evans/Evans	Subaru Impreza	N	transmission	0
Caldarola/Cecchini	Mitsubishi Lancer	N	engine	4
Hawkeswood/Fallon	Subaru Impreza	A	radiator	8
Kangas/Rabbett	Mitsubishi Lancer	N	rolled	10
R.Jones/Bult	Mitsubishi Lancer	N	engine	11
Schelle/McLoughlin	Suzuki Ignis	S1600	rear suspension	11
Schelle/McLoughlin	Suzuki Ignis	S1600	front suspension	17
Pedder/Feaver	Mitsubishi Lancer	N	accident	19

Round 2 ROTORUA (NZ) 11/13.07.2003
Rotorua. 15 Stages - gravel, 274.69km

1	Herbert/Ryan	Subaru Impreza	A	2h.58m.32.6s.
2	Nutahara/Hayashi	Mitsubishi Lancer	N	3h.00m.22.9s.
3	K.Singh/Oh	Proton Pert	A	3h.00m.22.9s.
4	Hawkeswood/Fallon	Mitsubishi Lancer	A	3h.00m.44.4s.
5	Mason/Smith	Mitsubishi Lancer	A	3h.02m.30.6s.
6	Kremer/Berssen	Mitsubishi Lancer	N	3h.02m.57.8s.
7	Smith/Smith	Mitsubishi Lancer	A	3h.03m.11.1s.
8	Caldarola/Cecchini	Mitsubishi Lancer	N	3h.05m.07.4s.

38 starters. 26 finishers.

LEADING RETIREMENTS & LAST STAGE COMPLETED

R.Jones/Bult	Mitsubishi Lancer Evo	N	steering	1
West/Cobham	Subaru Impreza	N	radiator	2
Bawden/McLachlan	Mitsubishi Lancer Evo	A	off road	3
Cangani/Prima	Mitsubishi Lancer Evo	N	mechanical	11

Round 3 HOKKAIDO (J) 12/14.09.2003
Hokkaido. 19 Stages - gravel, 272.33km

1	Arai/Sircombe	Subaru Impreza	N	2h.59m.55.1s.
2	Argyle/Smith	Mitsubishi Lancer Evo	A	3h.04m.02.3s.
3	Kremer/Berssen	Mitsubishi Lancer Evo	N	3h.05m.51.6s.
4	Kamada/Hiruta	Subaru Impreza	N	3h.06m.08.7s.
5	Carlsson/Andersson	Suzuki Ignis	S1600	3h.07m.30.0s.
6	Taguchi/Sakashita	Mitsubishi Lancer Evo	N	3h.10m.07.7s.
7	Watanabe/Ikeda	Mitsubishi Lancer Evo	N	3h.11m.20.0s.
8	Iwashita/Takeshita	Mitsubishi Lancer Evo	N	3h.11m.30.3s.

56 starters. 35 finishers.

LEADING RETIREMENTS & LAST STAGE COMPLETED

K.Singh/Oh	Proton Pert	N	gearbox	0
Caldarola/Cecchini	Mitsubishi Lancer Evo	N	accident	1
Doppelreiter/Floene	Mitsubishi Lancer Evo	N	gearbox	5
Herridge/Macneall	Subaru Impreza	N	engine	10
Taguchi/Stacey	Mitsubishi Lancer Evo	N	heavy landing	11
Nutahara/Hayashi	Mitsubishi Lancer Evo	N	heavy landing	11

Round 4 THAILAND (T) 1/2.11.2003
Rayong. 17 Stages (one cancelled), gravel - 261.47km

1	K.Singh/Oh	Proton Pert	A	2h.07m.47s.
2	Kremer/Berssen	Mitsubishi Lancer Evo	N	2h.08m.52s.
3	Argyle/Smith	Mitsubishi Lancer Evo	A	2h.08m.55s.
4	Taguchi/Stacey	Mitsubishi Lancer Evo	N	2h.09m.13s
5	Nutahara/Hayashi	Mitsubishi Lancer Evo	N	2h.09m.41s.
6	Tawatchai/Wongsakorn	Mitsubishi Lancer Evo	A	2h.13m.09s.
7	Atkinson/Atkinson	Suzuki Ignis	S1600	2h.14m.09s.
8	Narasak/Peerapong	Mitsubishi Lancer Evo	N	2h.15m.44s.

33 starters. 20 finishers.

LEADING RETIREMENTS & LAST STAGE COMPLETED

Caldarola/Cecchini	Mitsubishi Lancer Evo	N	gearbox	0
Green/Pedersen	Mitsubishi Lancer Evo	A	accident	6
Hawkeswood/Fallon	Mitsubishi Lancer Evo	N	engine	7
Doppelreiter/Floene	Mitsubishi Lancer Evo	N	engine	16

Strange environment 1. Nasser Al-Attiyah and Steve Lancaster clinched the title in Cyprus.

Middle East

Rally Championship

Thirty-two year old Nasser Al-Attiyah from Qatar returned after a four year absence from the sport, to win the 2003 Middle East championship at Troodos Rally, with one event to go. It is ten years since a Qatari last won the series. For Steve Lancaster, Al-Attiyah's codriver, this was his debut season in the Middle East series. Al-Attiyah is little known in motorsport but well respected in clay pigeon shooting, in which he has been Asian champion and well placed in the Olympics. He was professional in his approach, for example entering non championship events in Oman and Lebanon, to prepare himself for the Troodos Rally, which was slow and twisty, very different from other MERC events. The series featured a similar format to before, with one event (Troodos) being held in forest rally style and another (Lebanon) held on asphalt. The only change in the 2003 MERC calendar was that Bahrain was cancelled during the international conflict in the region. The season started with Abdullah Bakhashab as favourite but he had an unhappy season, while other drivers scored more through consistency than performance.

Round 1 Qatar

An exciting entry came from Abdullah Bakhashab, the 1995 Middle East champion, with a 206WRC, but he retired with damage after a heavy landing. The Qatari driver Al-Attiyah held the lead throughout the event. Abdullah Al-Qassimi finished second after delays with a blocked intercooler and differential trouble. In Group N, Misfer Al-Marri retired with a broken rear differential while the provisional Group N winner Khaled Qassimi was excluded for turbocharger offences and the category was won by the British driver Justin Dale.

Round 2 Lebanon

This sole all-asphalt MERC rally was a walkover for the Feghali brothers, known abroad for their JWRC challenges, this time driving World Rally Cars. Roger took the lead but had a puncture letting Abdo go ahead for a while. There was technical trouble: Philippe Kazan had provisionally won Group N in a Honda Civic but was excluded for brake offences, so Abdullah Al-Qassimi won the category. Bakhashab had a bad event, crashing off the road on the second stage. Al-Attiyah made his asphalt rally debut but retired off the road.

Round 3 Jordan

Postponed by two months from its original May fixture on account of the Middle East crisis, this event was run in the full heat of the Arabic summer coupled with the extra heat of stages held at sub-zero altitude close to the Dead Sea. A newly installed tracking system was used on this event to follow competitors in the open deserts. Transmission failure sealed the championship fate for Bakhashab which allowed Al-Attiyah to cruise to the finish. Coming into the championship frame was Andreas Tsouloftas in second place.

Round 4 Syria

This was a dramatic event! Held in the desert areas between Damascus and Palmyra, there was a superspecial for the first time used for live TV. The drama happened at the end of the event, on this section, when Al-Attiyah took a wrong route, and initially this promoted him to victory. In the end this was amended and he finished third, with Tsouloftas the

Strange environment 2. Cypriot driver Andreas Tsouloftas discovers the deserts in Jordan.

Group N challenger, Abdullah Al-Qassimi, seen in Lebanon.

winner. Earlier in the rally Al-Attiyah had a bad run, breaking his suspension and dropped to eighth. Then afterwards the Group N car of Abdullah Al-Qassimi was protested, unsuccessfully, but the delay prevented the car going to Cyprus for the Troodos Rally.

Round 5 Troodos

Based at Nicosia, the Troodos Rally saw the Middle East title claimed by Nasser Al-Attiyah. Before the start three drivers still had a chance of the title, including the Cypriot driver Tsouloftas following his win in Syria. He started the event behind Abdullah Al-Qassimi and Al-Attiyah on points. A lot of the drama happened before the start. Al-Attiyah's car was burned out in testing two days beforehand, needing another car to be flown from Britain and converted to gravel specification. Al-Qassimi could not start, preparation of his car delayed following a protest at the preceding round in Syria. Two other drivers failed to arrive at the start on time, Roger Feghali from Lebanon and Farouk Ghurab from Saudi Arabia, because of delays in shipping due to bad weather. Al-Attiyah led all the way, despite a delay when he went off the road.

Note: Final round Dubai(UAE) 3/5.12.2003. Nasser Al Attiyah (QA) cannot be beaten in the overall championship.

Nasser's spoils.

Round 1 TOYOTA QATAR INTERNATIONAL (Q) 26/28.02.2003
Doha. 19 Stages - gravel 248.68km

1	Al-Attiyah/Lancaster	Subaru Impreza	WRC	1h.42m.15.6s.
2	A.Al-Qassimi/Zakaria	Ford Focus	WRC	1h.48m.46.1s.
3	Dale/Bargery	Subaru Impreza	N	1h.53m.54.7s.
4	A.Al-Kuwari/A.Al-Kuwari	Mitsubishi Lancer Evo	N	1h.59m.25.9s.
5	Johnson/Line	Subaru Impreza	N	1h.59m.50.6s.
6	Al-Rabban/Al-Hajri	Mitsubishi Lancer Evo	N	2h.05m.00.9s.
7	Guloom/Guloom	Mitsubishi Lancer Evo	N	2h.11m.50.1s.
8	Boshier/Robinson	Mitsubishi Lancer Evo	N	2h.15m.52.3s.

20 starters. 11 finishers.

LEADING RETIREMENTS & LAST STAGE COMPLETED

Al-Marri/Hussein	Mitsubishi Lancer Evo	N	differential	3
Al-Sowaidi/Morrissey	Mitsubishi Lancer Evo	N	radiator	6
Bakhashab/Willis	Peugeot 206	WRC	engine	9
A.Al-Kuwari/N.Al-Kuwari	Mitsubishi Lancer Evo	N	fire	16
K.Al-Qassimi/Al-Warshaw	Mitsubishi Lancer Evo	N	excluded	19

Round 2 LEBANON (RL) 3/6.07.2003
Beirut-Jounieh. 21 Stages - asphalt 283.45km

1	R.Feghali/Chehab	Subaru Impreza	WRC	2h.46m.07.0s.
2	A.Feghali/Mattar	Toyota Corolla	WRC	2h.47m.12.7s.
3	Rahi/Ziade	Lancia Delta HF Integrale	A	3h.07m.12.4s.
4	'Marco'/Sawaya	VW Golf GTI KC	A	3h.09m.26.4s.
5	Saleh/Ghaziri	Toyota Celica GT4	A	3h.09m.50.0s.
6	A.Al-Qassimi/Khoury	Mitsubishi Lancer Evo	N	3h.13m.30.8s.
7	Elam/Khawam	Mitsubishi Lancer Evo	N	3h.13m.46.4s.
8	Germany/Chaaya	Lancia Delta HF Integrale	A	3h.14m.47.9s.

45 starters. 24 finishers.

LEADING RETIREMENTS & LAST STAGE COMPLETED

Bakhashab/Willis	Peugeot 206	WRC	accident	1
A.Al-Kuwari/Menhem	Mitsubishi Lancer Evo	N	accident	2
Al-Attiyah/Lancaster	Subaru Impreza	WRC	accident	5
Al-Marri/Hussein	Mitsubishi Lancer Evo	N	accident	10
Al-Sarraf/Al-Sarraf	Mitsubishi Lancer Evo	N	electrical	13

Round 3 JORDAN (HKJ) 24/26.07.2003
Amman. 20 Stages - gravel 256.66km

1	Al-Attiyah/Lancaster	Subaru Impreza	WRC	2h.51m.10.8s.
2	Tsouloftas/S.Laos	Mitsubishi Lancer Evo	A	3h.01m.38.0s.
3	A.Al-Qassimi/Al-Warshaw	Mitsubishi Lancer Evo	N	3h.07m.20.0
4	Al-Sowaidi/Morrissey	Mitsubishi Lancer Evo	N	3h.13m.59.8s.
5	Bustami/Al Hmoud	Mitsubishi Lancer Evo	A	3h.14m.08.7s.
6	Al-Marri/Hussein	Mitsubishi Lancer Evo	N	3h.17m.24.9s.
7	A.Al-Kuwari/Al-Hajri	Mitsubishi Lancer Evo	N	3h.25m.57.0s.
8	Al-Sarraf/Al-Sarraf	Mitsubishi Lancer Evo	N	3h.27m.16.5s.

38 starters. 18 finishers.

LEADING RETIREMENTS & LAST STAGE COMPLETED

K.Al-Qassimi/Al-Kandi	Mitsubishi Lancer Evo	N	oil cooler	3
Saleh/Matai	Toyota Celica GT4	A	driveshaft	4
Bakhashab/Willis	Peugeot 206	WRC	gearbox	8
A.Al-Kuwari/N.Al-Kuwari	Mitsubishi Lancer Evo	N	over time limit	9

Round 4 SYRIA (SYR) 10/12.09.2003
Damascus. 11 Stages - gravel, 216.29km

1	Tsouloftas/S.Laos	Mitsubishi Lancer Evo	A	1h.50m.03s.
2	K.Al-Qassimi/Al-Kandi	Mitsubishi Lancer Evo	N	1h.51m.27s.
3	Al-Attiyah/Lancaster	Subaru Impreza	WRC	1h.51m.31s.
4	A.Al-Qassimi/Zakaria	Mitsubishi Lancer Evo	N	1h.52m.27s.
5	A.Hamsho/A.Harryman	Subaru Impreza	WRC	1h.55m.59s.
6	Al-Marri/Hussein	Mitsubishi Lancer Evo	N	2h.00m.05s.
7	M.Hamsho/T.Harryman	Subaru Impreza	WRC	2h.02m.07s.
8	Al-Sarraf/Al-Sarraf	Mitsubishi Lancer Evo	N	2h.04m.42s.

34 starters. 17 finishers.

LEADING RETIREMENTS & LAST STAGE COMPLETED none

Round 5 TROODOS (CY) 31/10/2.11.2003
Nicosia, 13 stages, gravel. 229.10km

1	Al-Attiyah/Lancaster	Subaru Impreza	WRC	3h.40m.46.5s.
2	Tsouloftas/S.Laos	Mitsubishi Lancer Evo	A	3h.47m.18.2s.
3	Shiohatovich/Michael	Mitsubishi Lancer Evo	A	3h.58m.46.1s.
4	Armeftis/Constantinou	Mitsubishi Lancer Evo	N	4h.02m.31.1s.
5	Antoniades/Economides	Subaru Impreza 555	A	4h.03m.09.1s
6	Al-Kuwari/Hussain	Mitsubishi Lancer Evo	N	4h.03m.09.9s.
7	Koutsakos/P.Laos	Peugeot 306GTI	A	4h.11m.23.4s.
8	Parellis/Shialos	Opel Corsa	A	4h.22m.45.4s.

30 starters. 15 finishers.

LEADING RETIREMENTS & LAST STAGE COMPLETED none

International Championships

FIA CROSS COUNTRY

Round 1 BAJA ITALY (I) 14/16.03.2003   82s   48f
1	Masuoka/Picard	Mitsubishi	6h.29m.46s.
2	Peterhansel/Cottret	Mitsubishi	6h.32m.38s.
3	C.Sousa/Magne	Mitsubishi	6h.47m.43s.

Round 2 TUNISIA (TN) 5/13.04.2003   100s   56f
1	Schlesser/Lurquin	Schlesser	20h.13m.50s.
2	Biasion/Siviero	Mitsubishi	21h.24m.27s.
3	Misslin/Polato	Mitsubishi	21h.54m13s.

Round 3 BAJA PORTUGAL (P) 9/11.05.2003   75s   31f
1	C.Sousa/Magne	Mitsubishi	9h.53m.16s.
2	R.Sousa/Silva	Nissan	9h.58m.58s.
3	Barbosa/Ramalho	Mitsubishi	10h.23m.53s.

Round 4 MAROC (F) 5/9.06.2003   41s   31f
1	De Villiers/Thorner	Nissan	15h.38m.06s.
2	C.Sousa/Magne	Mitsubishi	16h.20m.54s.
3	Servia/Borsotto	Schlesser	16h.55m.04s.

Round 5 BAJA SPAIN (E) 18/19.07.2003   122s   75f
1	Alphand/Debron	BMW	9h.06m.59.053s.
2	Khalita/Tiefembach	BMW	9h.18m.14.535s.
3	Schlesser/Comolli	Schlesser	9h.22m.06.476s.

Round 6 ORIENT CAPPADOCE (F) 10/16.08.2003   15s   14f
1	C.Sousa/Magne	Mitsubishi	18h.42m.37s.
2	Komornicki/Marton	Mitsubishi	21h.12m.48s.
3	Gache/Garcin	Ford	21h.22m.24s.

Round 7 POUR LAS PAMPAS (RA) 1/5.09.2003   15s   11f
1	Schlesser/Lurquin	Schlesser	22h.14m.49s
2	C.Sousa/Magne	Mitsubishi	22h.19m.44s.
3	Strugo/Ferri	Mercedes	27h.04m.46s.

Round 8 UAE DESERT CHALLENGE(UAE)   45s   23f
20/24.10.2003
1	Peterhansel/Cottret	Mitsubishi	15h.19m.20s.
2	Schlesser/Lurquin	Schlesser	15h.35m.09s.
3	De Mevius/Guehennec	BMW	16h.29m.51s.

2003 FIA Cross Country Champion Carlos Sousa (P) 170pts,
2 Jean-Louis Schlesser (F) 147, 3 Jean-Pierre Strugo (F) 84,
4 Stephane Peterhansel (F) 67, 5 Lukasz Komornicki (PL) 66, etc.

Derek McGarrity, 2003 Toshiba Irish Tarmac Champion.

DEMPSTER

Carlos Sousa, 2003 FIA Cross Country Champion.

CODASUR/SOUTH AMERICA

Round 1 TRANS-ITAPUA (PY)   46s   26f
Encarnacin 12/13.04.2003
| Gorostiaga/Aguilera | Toyota Corolla WRC | 1h.39m.22.7s. |

Round 2 MISIONES (RA) Posadas 31.05/1.06.2003   16s   15f
| Gorostiaga/Aguilera | Toyota Corolla WRC | 1h.11m.57s. |

Round 3 CONCORDIA (BOL)   12s   f
Cochabamba 5/6.07.2003
| Malarczuk/Tomas | Mitsubishi Lancer Evo | 1h.40m.23s. |

Round 4 ERECHIM (BR) Erechim 30/31.08.2003   31s   21f
| Bertholdo/Zoffmann | Mitsubishi Lancer Evo | 1h.36m.11.5s. |

Round 5 PACIFICO (RCH)   55s   40f
Puerto Varas 18/19.10.2003
| Suriani/Rodriguez | Subaru Impreza | 1h.28m.42s. |

Note: Final round ATLANTICO (ROU) Punta del Este 20/30.11.2003.

TOSHIBA IRISH TARMAC

Round 1 CIRCUIT OF IRELAND (GB/IRL)   113s   67f
Enniskillen 19/21.04.2003
| McGarrity/Patterson | Subaru Impreza WRC | 2h.23m.06.4s. |

Round 2 KILLARNEY RALLY OF THE LAKES (IRL)   147s   41f
Killarney 3 /4.05.2003
| Donnelly/Kiely | Subaru Impreza WRC | 2h.29m.47.8s. |

Round 3 DONEGAL (IRL) Donegal 20/22.06.2003   151s   46f
| Nesbitt/O'Brien | Subaru Impreza WRC | 2h.32m.46.0s. |

Round 4 JIM CLARK (GB) Duns 4/6.07.2003   60s   36f
| Nesbitt/O'Brien | Subaru Impreza WRC | 2h.03m.42.1s |

Round 5 MANX INTERNATIONAL (GBM)   58s   31f
Douglas 31.07/2.08.2003
| Milner/Beech | Toyota Corolla WRC | 3h.01m.03.5s. |

Round 6 ULSTER (GB) Armagh 5/6.09.2003   79s   52f
| Laukkanen/Riipinen | Subaru Impreza WRC | 2h.06m.11.2s |

Round 7 CORK (IRL) Cork 4/5.10.2003   65s   40f
| Boland/Morrisey | Subaru Impreza WRC | 1h.55m.32.0s |

2003 Toshiba Irish Tarmac Champion Derek McGarrity 81pts,
Eamonn Boland 51, Austin McHale 51, Andrew Nesbitt 42pts, etc.
Group N winner Roy White (Mitsubishi Lancer Evolution)

MITROPA CUP

Round 1 ADAC-OBERLAND (D) 14/15.03.2003   51s   48f
| Zeltner/Zeltner | Mitsubishi Carisma | 1h.29m.38.1s. |

Round 2 PIRELLI LAVANTTAL (A) 4/5.04.2003   64s   39f
| Gassner/Thannhauser | Mitsubishi Carisma | 2h.11m.20.9s. |

Round 3 DUNLOP PYHRN EISENWURZEN   74s   52f
(A) 2/3.05.2003
| Zeltner/Zeltner | Mitsubishi Carisma | 1h.36m.13.5s. |

Round 4 CASTROL (A) 13/14.06.2003   72s   41f
| Gassner/Thannhauser | Mitsubishi Carisma | 2h.14m.17.2s. |

Round 5 BOHEMIA (CZ) 11/13.07.2003   129s   73f
| Turolo/Valmassoi | Mitsubishi Lancer | 2h.13m.49.3s. |

Round 6 ALPI ORIENTALI (I) 28/30.08.2003   81s   45f
| De Cecco/Bariggli | Peugeot 206 WRC | 2h.35m.54.2s. |

Round 7 BASSANO (I) 12/13.09.2003   102s   62f
| Zeltner/Zeltner | Mitsubishi Lancer | 1h.31m.57.6s. |

Ruben Zeltner, 2003 Mitropa Cup Winner.

Round 8 ADAC-3-STADTE (D) 23/25.10.2003 78s   41f
Gassner/Schrankl   Mitsubishi Lancer Evo   2h.16m.57.2s..

Round 9 DUE VALLI (I) Verona 14/15.11.2003   81s   42f
Tavano/de Colle   Renault Clio Williams   2h.01m.58.2s

2003 Mitropa Cup Winner Ruben Zeltner (D) 311pts,
2 Hermann Gassner (D) 279, 3 Stefano Tavano (I) 234,
4 Alberto Turolo (I) 233, 5 Andrea Cudicio (I) 218 etc.
F2 Winner Stefano Tavano (Renault Clio Williams)

NORTH AMERICAN RALLY CUP (NARC)

Round 1 SNO*DRIFT (USA) Atlantic, MI 24/25.01.2003 35s   23f
1   D.Higgins/Barritt   Mitsubishi Lancer Evo   2h.02m.15s2.
2   Laukkanen/Ripinen   Subaru Impreza WRX   2h.04m.16s3.
3   Milner/McMath   Subaru Impreza WRX   2h.08m.15s.

Round 2 PERCE-NEIGE MANIWAKI (CDN)   34s   22f
Maniwaki, QUE 7/9.02.2003
1   Erickson/Erickson   MitsubishiLancer Evo   2h.35m.59s.
2   L'Estage/Napert   Hyundai Elantra   2h.41m.49s.
3   Perusse/Raymond   Subaru Impreza WRX   2h.43m.55s.

Round 3 QUEBEC (CDN)   48s   32f
Quebec, QUE 26.02/2.03.2003
1   Richard/Johansson   Subaru Impreza WRX   2h.21m.39.5s.
2   Choiniere/Becker   Hyundai Tiburon   2h.24m.47.7s.
3   Comrie-Picard/Maxwell   Mitsubishi Lancer Evo   2h.24m.50.7s.

Round 4 RIM OF THE WORLD (USA)   32s   27f
Palmdale, CA 2/3.05.2003
1   D.Higgins/Barritt   Mitsubishi Lancer Evo   1h.27m.34s.
2   Lovell/Turvey   Subaru Impreza WRC   1h.30m.26s.
3   O'Sullivan/Edstrom   Mitsubishi Lancer Evo   1h.34m.01s.

Round 5 BIGHORN (CDN) Edson, ALTA 17/19.05.2003 28s   19f
1   McGeer/Davies   Subrau Impreza WRX   1h.37m.09s.
2   Comrie-Picard/Goldfarb   Mitsubishi Lancer Evo   1h.37m.48s.
3   Komorowski/Karzynski   Mitsubishi Eclipse   1h.44m.28s.

Round 6 ROCKY MOUNTAIN (CDN)   23s   19f
Calgary, ALTA 23/25.05.2003
1   McGeer/Davies   Subaru Impreza WRX   1h.38m.39s.
2   Richard/McCurdy   Subaru Impreza WRX   1h.39m.09s.
3   Erickson/Erickson   Mitsubishi Lancer Evo   1h.43m.33s.

Round 7 SUSQUEHANNOCK TRAIL (USA)   62s   37f
Wellsboro, PA 6/7.06.2003
1   D.Higgins/Barritt   Mitsubishi Lancer Evo   1h.54m.51s.
2   O'Neil/Gelsomino   Ford Focus   2h.01m.02s.
3   Choiniere/Becker   Hyundai Tiburon   2h.04m.59s.

Round 8 PACIFIC FOREST (CDN)   36s   16f
Merritt, BC 13/14.06.2003
1   McGeer/Becker   Subaru Impreza WRX   2h.00m.48s.
2   Komorowski/Karzynski   Mitsubishi Eclipse   2h.14m.20s.
3   Olsen/Shindle   Volkswagen Golf GTI   2h.17m.34s.

Round 9 BAIE DES CHALEURS (CDN)   39s   28f
New Richmond, QUE 4/6.07.2003
1   Richard/McCurdy   Subaru Impreza WRX   1h.50m.51s.
2   Comrie-Picard/Goldfarb   Mitsubishi Lancer Evo   1h.54m.58s.
3   Pilon/Pilon   Subaru Impreza   1h.57m.53s.

Round 10 OREGON TRAIL (USA)   32s   22f
Hillsboro, OR 12/13.07.2003
1   D.Higgins/Barritt   Mitsubishi Lancer Evo   1h.37m.27s.
2   O'Neil/Gelsomino   Ford Focus   1h.38m.16s.
3   O'Sullivan/Edstrom   Mitsubishi Lancer Evo   1h.39m.10s.

Round 11 MAINE FOREST (USA)   62s   37f
Rumford, ME 1/3.08.2003
1   D.Higgins/Barritt   Mitsubishi Lancer Evo   1h.40m.42s
2   O'Sullivan/Edstrom   Mitsubishi Lancer Evo   1h.42m.39s
2   Choiniere/Becker   Hyundai Tiburon   1h.42m.39s

Round 12 OJIBWE FOREST (USA)   33s   24f
Bemdji, MN 22/23.08.2003
1   D.Higgins/Barritt   Mitsubishi Lancer Evo   1h.58m.29s
2   Lagemann/Orr   Subaru Impreza WRX   1h.59m.21s
3   O'Sullivan/Edstrom   Mitsubishi Lancer Evo   2h.00m.17s

Round 13 DEFI STE-AGATHE (CDN)   55s   33f
Ste-Agathe, QUE 5/6.09.2003
1   Erickson/Erickson   Mitsubishi Lancer Evo   1h.29m.49s.
2   McGeer/Becker   Subrau Impreza WRX   1h.29m.58s.
3   Sprongl/Sprongl   MitsubishiLancer Evo   1h.30m.43s.

Round 14 WILD WEST (USA) Olympia, WA 6/7.09.2003 27s   22f
1   Hagstrom/Taskinen   Subaru Impreza WRX   2h.05m.47s.
2   Lagemann/Orr   Subaru Impreza WRX   2h.09m.13s.
3   O'Sullivan/Edstrom   Mitsubishi Lancer Evo   2h.11m.27s.

Round 15 LAKE SUPERIOR (USA)   34s   24f
Houghton, Mi 17/18.10.2003
1   D.Higgins/Barritt   Mitsubishi Lancer Evo   1h.50m.34s.
2   Lagemann/Orr   Subaru Impreza WRX   1h.51m.37s.
3   Hagstrom/Taskinen   Subaru Impreza WRX   1h.53m.05s.

Note: Final round TALL PINES (CDN) Bancroft, ONT 21/22.11.2003

RALLY SERIES OF NORTH AMERICA (RSNA)

Round 1 QUEBEC (CDN) Quebec City 26.02/2.03.2003 34s   22f
Richard/Johansson   Subaru Impreza   2h.21m.39.2s.

Round 2 CORONA (MEX) Leon 14/16.03.2003   45s.   16f
Ligato/Garcia   Mitsubishi Lancer Evo   4h.34m.19.9s.

Round 3 DE LOS 24 HORAS (MEX) Valle de Bravo 11/12.07.2003
no qualifying finishers

Round 4 WILD WEST (USA) Olympia, WA 6/7.09.2003   27s   22f
Gubelmann/Pace   Subaru Impreza   2h.24m.32s.

Note: Final round RAMADA EXPRESS (USA) Laughlin 11/14.12.2003.

WEST EURO CUP

Round 1 FINNSKOG (N)   76s   42f
Kongsvinger 21/22.02.2003 (ECR3)
Gallagher/Moynihan   Peugeot 206 XS   2h.55m.07.8s

Round 2 KILLARNEY RALLY OF THE LAKES (IRL)   70s   41f
Killarney 3/4.05.2003
Donnelly/Kiely   Subaru Impreza   2h.29m.47.8s.

Round 3 CHARLEMAGNE (F) Maubeuge 5/6.07.2003 92s   50f
Holton/Walsh   Toyota Celica GT-4   1h.39m.58.0s.

Round 4 MANX INTERNATIONAL (GBM)   58s   31f
Douglas 31.07/2.08.2003
Foss/Patterson   Nissan Almera   3h.35m.13.6s

Round 5 GOLDEN TULIP (NL)   70s   51f
Nijverdal 26/27.09.2003 (ECR42)
Arthurs/Scholtalbers   Toyota Celica GT-4   1h.43m.45.0s.

2003 West Euro Cup Winner Paddy White (IRL)(Subaru Impreza
WRC) 354 pts, 2 Henrik-Munk Hansen (DK) 259, 3 Derek McGarrity (IRL)
202, 4 Aaron McHale (IRL) 198, 5 Tom Holton (IRL) 190, etc.

Paddy White, 2003 West Euro Cup winner.

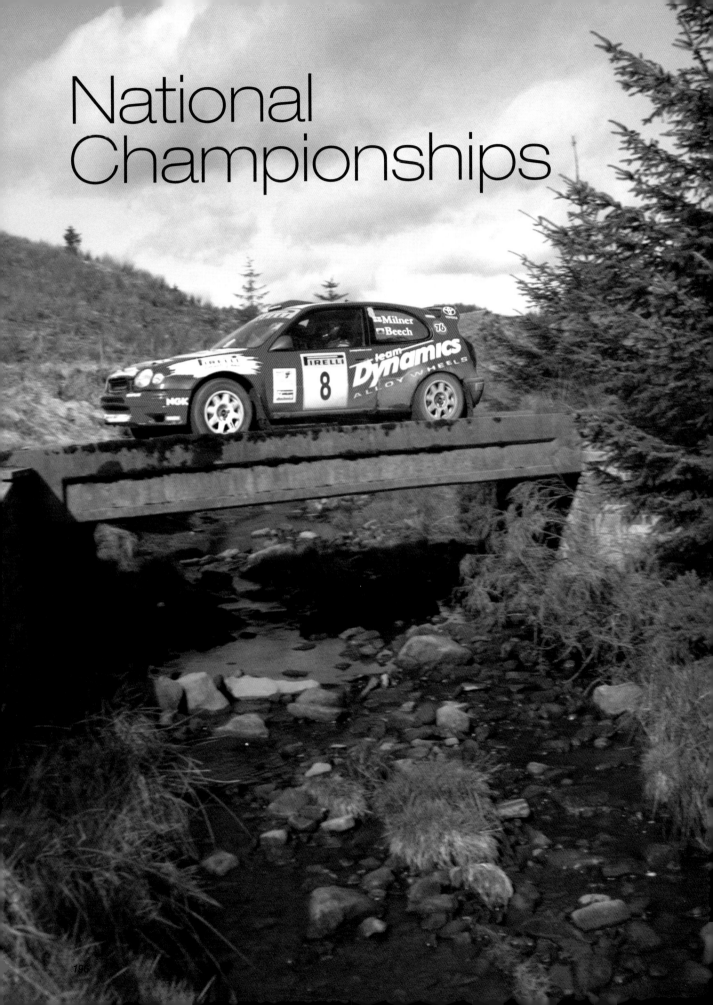

National Championships

Note The results given are the first crews scoring points in the relevant national championships, not necessarily the overall winner.

Key s = number of actual starters.
f = number of classified finishers.

A Austria

Round 1 IQ JANNER Pregarten 2/4.01.2003 (ECR1)   40s   27f
Wittmann/Feichtinger   Toyota Corolla WRC   2h.20m.03.3s.

Round 2 OMV-BURGENLAND   66s   34f
Oberwart 14/16.03.2003
Baumschlager/Eichhorner   Mitsubishi Carisma   1h.38m.57.8s.

Round 3 PIRELLI LAVANTTAL   64s   39f
Wolfsberg 4/5.04.2003
Kramer/Sappl   Mitsubishi Lancer Evo   2h.17m.00.3s.

Round 4 DUNLOP PYHRN EISENWURZEN   74s   52f
Kirchdorf 2/3.05.2003
Baumschlager/Eichhorner   Mitsubishi Carisma   1h.34m.32.7s.

Round 5 BOSCH SUPER PLUS   46s   36f
Pinggau 16/18.05.2003
Baumschlager/Eichhorner   Mitsubishi Carisma   1h.39m.41.4s.

Round 6 CASTROL Krappfeld 12/14.06.2003   72s   41f
Baumschlager/Eichhorner   Mitsubishi Carisma   2h.11m.38.8s.

Round 7 OMV Wein-Krumbach 4/6.09.2003   50s   29f
Baumschlager/Wicha   Mitsubishi Lancer Evo   1h.50m.59.4s.

Round 8 ARBO - STEIERMARK Admont 11/12.10.2003   62s   42f
Baumschlager/Eichhorner   Mitsubishi Lancer Evo   1h.33m.42.3s

Round 9 WALDVIERTEL Horn 6/8.11.2003 (ECR49)   95s   61f
Baumschlager/Eichhorner   Mitsubishi Lancer Evo   2h.16m.04.6s.

2003 Austrian Group A Champion Raimund Baumschlager 155pts, 2 Gottfried Kogler 83, 3 Ernst Haneder 67, 4 Stefan Reininger 53, 5 Hans Holzmueller 44, etc.
Group N-champion Beppo Harrach (Mitsubishi Lancer Evolution)
Diesel-champion Andreas Waldherr (VW Golf IV TDI KC)
Formula 2-champion Heinz Jakobitsch (Peugeot 306 GTI)

AUS Australia

Round 1 RESPECT YOURSELF FOREST   33s   28f
Bussleton, WA 29/30.03.2003
Crocker/Foletta   Subaru Impreza   1h.14m.17.8s.(heat 1)
Crocker/Foletta   Subaru Impreza   53m.23.1s.(heat 2)

Round 2 QUEENSLAND Caloundra 14/15.06.2003   38s   19f
Crocker/Foletta   Subaru Impreza   1h.26m.17.4s.(heat 1)
Crocker/Foletta   Subaru Impreza   1h.11m.56.3s.(heat 2)

Round 3 PREMIER STATE Sydney 4/6.07.2003   45s   30f
Crocker/Foletta   Subaru Impreza   51m.46.3s.(heat 1)
Ordynski/Stewart   Mitsubishi Lancer Evo   45m.43.3s.(heat 2)

Round 4 SOUTH AUSTRALIA   33s   20f
Barossa Valley 9/10.08.2003
Ordynski/Stewart   Mitsubishi Lancer Evo   1h.04m.11.6s.(heat 1)
Ordynski/Stewart   Mitsubishi Lancer Evo   54m.29.8s.(heat 2)

Round 5 RALLY OF MELBOURNE   44s   29f
Melbourne 3/5.10.2003
Evans/Evans   Subaru Impreza   1h.08m.02.8s.(heat 1)
Pedder/Humm   Mitsubishi Lancer Evo   1h.05m.04.3s.(heat 2)

Round 6 SAFARI TASMANIA Hobart 14/16.11.2003   24s   18f
Crocker/Foletta   Subaru Impreza   1h.16m.41.7s.(heat 1)
Kangas/Rabbett   Mitsubishi Lancer Evo   1h.05m.56.5s.(heat 2)

2003 Australian Champion Cody Crocker 199pts, 2 Ed Ordynski 168, 3 Juha Kangas (FIN) 148.5, 4 Simon Evans 142, 5 Dean Herridge 127, etc.
Privateer Cup winner Juha Kangas

B Belgium

Round 1 BOUCLES DE SPA   107s   74f
Spa 4/6.04.2003 (ECR8)
Tsjoen/Chevallier   Toyota Corolla WRC   1h.35m.49s.

Round 2 WALLONIE Jambes 3/4.05.2003   68s   37f
Tsjoen/Chevallier   Toyota Corolla WRC   2h.03m.30s.

Round 3 YPRES WESTHOEK   111s   52f
Ypres 27/29.06.2003 (ECR21)
Thiry/Turin   Peugeot 206WRC   2h.51m.21.3s.

Round 4 OMLOOP VAN VLAANDEREN   79s   58f
Roeselare 13/14.09.2003
Tsjoen/Chevallier   Toyota Corolla WRC   1h.46m.11.1s.

Round 5 HASPENGOUW Landen 26/28.09.2003   76s   53f
Snijers/Muth   Subaru Impreza WRC   1h.42m.37s

Round 6 CONDROZ Huy 15/16.11.2003 (ECR50)   174s   110f
Loix/Smeets   Peugeot 206 WRC   2h.26m.03.8s.

2003 Belgium Champion Pieter Tsjoen 44pts, 2 Patrick Snijers 23, 3 Bernard Munster 22, 4 Dominique Bruyneel 20, 5 Larry Cols 19, etc.
Super 1600 Winner Larry Cols
F2 Winner Larry Cols

BG Bulgaria

Round 1 INTERSPEED   38s   21f
Budva (SCG) 31.05/1.06.2003 (ECR16)
Donchev/Manolov   Peugeot 306 Maxi   2h.13m.03.2s.

Round 2 BULGARIA   53s   26f
Borovetz 13/15.06.2003 (ECR18)
Popov/Popov   Skoda Octavia WRC   2h.52m.23.8s.

Round 3 HEBROS Plovdiv 26/27.07.2003 (ECR27)   51s   32f
Popov/Popov   Skoda Octavia WRC   2h.28m.04.8s.

Round 4 SOSSER - SLIVEN   42s   31f
Sliven 30/31.08.2003 (ECR32)
Tsarski/Tevekelov   Ford Escort WRC   2h.11m.39.2s.

Round 5 STARI STOLITZI Shumen 6/7.09.2003   35s   24f
Tsarski/Tevekelov   Ford Escort WRC   1h.00m.17.5s.

Krum Donchev, 2003 Bulgarian Champion.

Round 6 YU Bajina Basta 13/14.09.2003 (SCG) (ECR41)   25s   18f
Marinov/Cholakov   Mitsubishi Lancer Evo   2h.02m.12.5s.

2003 Bulgarian Champion Krum Donchev 72.5pts, 2 Ilia Tsarski 58, 3 Ivan Marinov 51, 4 Jasen Popov 50, 5 Hristo Stoilov 43, etc.
Group N winner Ivan Marinov (Mitsubishi Lancer Evolution)
F2 Champion Krum Donchev (Peugeot 306 Maxi)

BR Brazil

Round 1 SANTA CATERINA Camboriu 29/30.03.2003   s   31f
Bertholdo/Zoffmann   Mitsubishi Lancer Evo   1h.29m.49.2s.

Round 2 MINAS GERAIS Ouro Branco 24/25.05.2003   s   50f
Sartori/Sartori   Mitsubishi Lancer Evo   48m52.6s.

Round 3 FARROUPILHA Porto Alegre 14/15.06.2003   s   23f
Fuchter/Gomes   Subaru Impreza   1h.02m.19.4s.

Round 4 RIO DE JANEIRO Porto Real 9/10.08.2003   s   f
Bertholdo/Zoffman   Mitsubishi Lancer Evo   1h.49m.14.1s.

Round 5 ERECHIM Erechim 30/31.08.2003   s   f
Fuchter/Furtado   Subaru Impreza   1h.34m.44.4s.

Round 6 GRACIOSA Curitiba 25/26.10.2003   42s   28f
Sartori/Sartori   Mitsubishi Lancer Evo   1h.44m.47.5s.

Round 7 SAO PAULO Indaiatuba 14/15.11.2003   29s   18f
"Marcola"/Tarcisio   VW Golf   1h.20m.09.5s.

2003 Brazilian N4 Champion Ulysses Bertholdo (Mitsubishi Lancer Evo)
Category A6 Winner Luis Tedesco (Fiat Palio)
Category N2 Luis Debes (VW Gol)

CDN Canada

Round 1 PERCE-NEIGE Maniwaki 7/9.02.2003   34s   22f
Erickson/Erickson   Mitsubishi Lancer Evo   2h.35m.59s.

Round 2 QUEBEC Quebec City 26.02/2.03.2003   48s   32f
Richard/Johansson   Subaru Impreza WRX   2h.21m.39.2s.

Round 3 BIG HORN Edson 17/19.05.2003   28s   19f
McGeer/Davies   Subaru Impreza WRX   1h.37m.09s.

Round 4 ROCKY MOUNTAIN Calgary 23/25.05.2003   23s   19f
McGeer/Davies   Subaru Impreza WRX   1h.38m.39s.

Round 5 PACIFIC FOREST Merritt 13/14.06.2003   36s   16f
McGeer/Becker   Subaru Impreza WRX   2h.00m.48s.

Round 6 BAIE DES CHALEURS   39s   28f
New Richmond 4/6.07.2003
Richard/McCurdy   Subaru Impreza WRX   1h.50m.51s.

Round 7 STE-AGATHE Ste-Agathe 5/6.09.2003   55s   33f
Erickson/Erickson   Mitsubishi Lancer Evo   1h.29m.49s.

Note: Final round TALL PINES Bancroft 21/22.11.2003. Tom McGeer cannot be beaten in the championship.

CH Switzerland

Round 1 LYON-CHARBONNIERES   30s   25f
(Lyon-Charbonnieres) (F) 13/14.04.2003
Jaquillard/Jaquillard   Toyota Corolla WRC   1h.43m.48.5s.

Round 2 CRITERIUM JURASSIEN   97s   71f
Saignelegier 2/4.05.2003
Althaus/Charpilloz   Ford Escort WRC   1h.35m.01s.

Round 3 TICINO Lugano 29/31.05.2003   124s   69f
Burri/Hofmann   Subaru Impreza WRC   1h.13m.22.5s.

Round 4 ALPES VAUDOISES   91s   68f
Lavey-Village 27/29.06.2003
Jaquillard/Jaquillard   Toyota Corolla WRC   1h.03m.42s.

Christian Jacquillard, 2003 Swiss Champion.

KAUFMANN

Round 5 COPPA d'Oro Alessandria (I) 18/20.07.2003   33s   16f
Jaquillard/Jaquillard   Toyota Corolla WRC   1h.26m.55.2s.

Round 6 RONDE JURASSIENNE   92s   69f
Coeuve 29/31.08.2003
Jaquillard/Jaquillard   Toyota Corolla WRC   59m.13.9s.

Round 7 VALAIS   83s   44f
Martigny 24./26.10.2003 (ECR47)
Burri/Hofmann   Subaru Impreza WRC   3h.07m.58.7s.

Swiss Champion Christian Jaquillard 169pts, Pietro Galfetti 112, Didier Germain 103, Patrick Heintz 92, Nicolas Althaus 89, etc.
Group N winner Devis Crimona (Renault Clio)

CN China

Round 1 SHANGHAI Shanghai 22/23.03.2003   54s   f
Cheng zihua/Deng Baolian   Subaru   1h.23m.39.8s.

Round 2 CHANGCHUN Changchun 16/17.07.2003   55s   f
Liu bin/Huang yu   Mitsubishi

Round 3 BEIJIN Beijin 16/17.08.2003   59s   f
Jian zhixiong/Ding jianping   Subaru

Round 4 LONGYOU Zhejiang 6/7.09.2003   54s   f
Cheng zihua/Deng biaohua   Subaru

2003 Chinese Champion Liu bin 83pts, 2 Cheng zihua 80, 3 Hua qinxian 76, 4 Wei hongjie 55, 5 Huang youkun 53, etc.

Liu bin, 2003 Chinese Champion.

CY Cyprus

Round 1 NICOSIA Nicosia 28.01.2003   16s   6f
Peratikos/Ekiskopou   Mitsubishi Lancer Evo   2h.09m.55.5s.

Round 2 LARNACA Larnaca 14.03.2003   30s   22f
Peratikos/Ekiskopou   Mitsubishi Lancer Evo   1h.49m.51.22s.

Round 3 ADONIS Paphos 30.03.2003   27s   10f
Peratikos/Ekiskopou   Mitsubishi Lancer Evo   2h.45m.21.1s.

Round 4 GERMASOGIA Limassol 7.09.2003   31s   12f
Peratikos/Episkopou   Mitsubishi Lancer Evo   1h.35m.56.7s.

Round 5 KYRENIA Nicosia 5.10.2003   30s   15f
Peratikos/Stavrinou   Mitsubishi Lancer Evo   1h.18m.18.2s.

Round 6 TROODOS Nicosia 31.10.2003   30s   15f
Tsouloftas/Laos   Mitsubishi Lancer Evo   3h.47m.18.2s.

2003 Cypriot Champion Andreas Peratikos 50pts, 2 Andreas Tsouloftas 27.5, 3 Pamos Timotheou 25, etc.

CZ Czech Republic

Round 1 SUMAVA MOGUL   90s   56f
Klatovy 14/15.03.2003 (ECR5)
Kresta/Hulka   Peugeot 206 WRC   1h.23m.49.9s.

Round 2 VALASSKA Vsetin 18/20.04.2003   91s   44f
Pech/Uhel   Ford Focus WRC   1h.45m. 45.1s.

Round 3 SEAT CESKY KRUMLOV   95s   55f
Cesky Krumlov 16/18.05.2003
Pech/Uhel   Ford Focus WRC   1h.37m.56.1s.

Round 4 BOHEMIA Mlada   129s   73f
Boleslav 11/13.07.2003 (ECR25)
Kresta/Tomanek   Peugeot 206 WRC   1h.54m.02.6s.

Round 5 BARUM Zlin 29/31.08.2003 (ECR34)   128s   47f
Pech/Uhel   Ford Focus WRC   2h.34m.57.0s

Round 6 PRIBRAM Pribram 26/28.09.2003   85s   56f
Kopecky/Schovanek   Skoda Octavia WRC   1h.55m.48.8s

Round 7 HORACKA Trebic 24/26.10.2003   96s   54f
Kopecky/Schovanek   Skoda Octavia WRC   1h.43m.33.5s.

2003 Czech Champion Vaclav Pech 129pts, 2 Karel Trneny 83, 3 Jan Kopecky 79, 4 Emil Triner 75, 5 Karel Trojan 68, etc.
Group N Champion Miroslav Jandik (Mitsubishi Lancer Evolution)

D Germany

Round 1 UBERLAND Schongau 14/16.03.2003   65s   47f
Zeltner/Zeltner   Mitsubishi Carisma   1h.29m.38.1s.

Round 2 PNEUMANT Wittenberg 2/4.05.2003   44s   30f
Kahle/Gobel   Skoda Octavia WRC   1h.45m.17.9s.

Round 3 SACHSENRING Zwickau 29/31.05.2003   38s   24f
Kahle/Gobel   Skoda Octavia WRC   1h.08m.25.2s.

Round 4 SAARLAND Merzig 20/21.06.2003 (ECR19)   52s   29f
Gassner/Schrankl   Mitsubishi Carisma   2h.05m.14.4s.

Round 5 EIFEL Daun 21/23.08.2003   56s   43f
Kahle/Gobel   Skoda Octavia WRC   1h.25m.40.3s

Round 6 CASTROL Possneck 19/21.09.2003   35s   26f
Kahle/Gobel   Skoda Octavia WRC   1h.03m.34.6s

Round 7 DREI-STADTE   68s   47f
Straubing 24/25.10.2003 (ECR48)
Kahle/Gobel   Skoda Octavia WRC   2h.12m.31.9s

German Champion Hermann Gassner 247pts, 2 Mathias Kahle 240, 3 Carsten Mohe 194, 4 Sandro Wallenwein 167, 5 Maik Stolzel 166, etc.
Super 1600 Champion Carsten Mohe (Renault Clio)

Jorgen Pilgaard, 2003 Danish Group A Champion.

DK Denmark

Round 1 HIMMERLAND Hobro 2/3.05.2003   71s   51f
Pilgaard/Pedersen   Peugeot 306 Maxi   57m.57s.

Round 2 RENAULT SAS Slagelse 28.06.2003   62s   36f
Madsen/Vestergaard   Renault Megane   1h.28m.26s.

Round 3 SNAPPHANERALLYT   28s   28f
Hassleholm (S) 15/16.08.2003
Jensen/Marx   Mitsubishi Carisma   53m.05s.

Round 4 FROST-MIKA SUPERBEST   54s   38f
Viborg/Hedeland 20.09.2003
Pilgaard/Pedersen   Peugeot 306 Maxi   42m.45s.

Round 5 AK RALLY Kalundborg 11.10.2003   58s   44f
Pilgaard/Pedersen   Peugeot 306 Maxi   48m.30s.

Round 6 BCA RALLY   62s   41f
Grindsted-Vejle 31.10/1.11.2003
Poulsen/Frederiksen   Toyota Celica GT-4   1h.46m.00s.

Danish Group A Champion Jorgen Pilgaard 95pts, 2 Brian Madsen 89, 3 Ib Cragh 60, 4 Steen Johansen 42, 5 Perden Andersen 40 etc.
Group N Champion Morten Karl (Mitsubishi Lancer Evolution)

E Spain

Round 1 MEDITERRANEO Villajoyosa 22/23.03.2003   83s   49f
Sola/Romani   Citroen Saxo S1600   2h.22m.10.0s.

Round 2 CANARIAS   37s   20f
Maspalomas 11/12.04.2003 (ECR9)
Fuster/Medina   Citroen Saxo KC   3h.08m.35.6s.

Round 3 CANTABRIA Santander 10/11.05.2003   90s   65f
Sordo/Castillo   Mitsubishi Lancer Evo   1h.33m.32.0s.

Round 4 RIAS BAJAS Vigo 31.05/1.06.2003   86s   51f
Fuster/Medina   Citroen Saxo KC   1h.32m.41.0s.

Round 5 ORENSE Orense 21/22.06.2003   83s   39f
Fuster/Medina   Citroen Saxo KC   1h.58m.05.0s.

Round 6 AVILES Aviles 5/6.07.2003   63s   45f
Fuster/Medina   Citroen Saxo KC   1h.53m.59.3s.

Round 7 NAVARRO Pamplona 4/5.10.2003   93s   55f
Ojeda/Fernandez   Peugeot 206 S1600   1h.36m.23.0s.

Round 8 COSTA DEL SOL Mijas 1/2.11.2003   89s   68f
Vinyes/Lorza   Peugeot 206 S1600   1h.34m.46.2s.

Note: Final round MADRID 22/23.11.2003. Miguel Fuster, Txus Jaio (Ford Focus WRC), Xavi Pons (Mitsubishi Lancer Evolution) cannot be beaten in the asphalt, gravel and Group N championships respectively

EAK Kenya

Round 1 NAIROBI Nairobi 1/2.03.2003   s   13f
Rose/Daykin   Mitsubishi Lancer Evo   1h.16m.40s.

Round 2 ELDORET Eldoret 12.04.2003   s   15f
Bailey/Kirk   Toyota Celica   1h.50m.34s.

Round 3 NAIROBI 2 Naibori 14/15.06.2003   20s   14f
Duncan/Haji   Toyota Landcruiser   1h.32m.09s.

Round 4 NAKURU Nakuru 19/20.07.2003   s   11f
Rose/Daykin   Mitsubishi Lancer Evo   1h.54m.25s.

Round 5 NYANZA Nyzanza 16/17.08.2003   s   10f
Edmunds/Carter   Mitsubishi Lancer Evo   1h.19m.24s.

Round 6 SAFARI EQUATOR Mombasa 9/11.2003   29s   15f
Edmunds/Carter   Mitsubishi Lancer Evo   3h.50m.24s.

Round 7 GURU NANAK 15/16.11.2003   25s   11f
Duncan/Haji   Toyota Landcruiser   1h.38m.15s.

Note: Final Round NANYUKI 6.12.2003.

Lubega (right) and Musa (left) winners of six rounds in the 2003 Ugandan Championship.

EAU Uganda

Round 1 CALTEX HAVOLINE ENERGY   18s   8f
Kampala-Lugazi 17/19.01.2003
Lubega/Musa   Mitsubishi Lancer Evo   1h.36m.11.8s.

Round 2 KOBIL Kampala-Mbarara 21/23.02.2003   18s   10f
Lubega/Musa   Mitsubishi Lancer Evo   2h.53m.27.8s.

Round 3 GARDEN CITY Kampala 28/30.03.2003   18s   9f
Lubega/Musa   Mitsubishi Lancer Evo   1h.50m.07.8§,

Round 4 UMÔSPOC CHALLENGE   14s   6f
Kampala 9/11.05.2003
Lubega/Musa   Mitsubishi Lancer Evo   1h.42m.51.8s.

Round 5 UMC CHALLENGE   18s   8f
Kampala 18/20.07.2003
Lumala/Matovu   Toyota Celica Turbo   1h.50m.02.1s.

Round 6 TOTAL PEARL OF AFRICA   21s   11f
Kampala 5/7.09.2003
Lubega/Musa   Mitsubishi Lancer Evo   2h.49m.32.1s.

Round 7 CASTROL MOGAS INDEPENDENCE   22s   12f
Kampala-Masaka 25/26.10.2003
Lubega/Musa   Mitsubishi Lancer Evo   1h.34m.33.1s

Note: Final standings not available on going to press.

EE Estonia

Round 1 ESTONIAN WINTER Tartu 17/18.01.2003   68s   49f
Raidam/Lepikson   Mitsubishi Lancer Evo   47m.06.2s.

Round 2 SARMA Gulbene (LV) 7/8.02.2003   76s   44f
Raidam/Lepikson   Mitsubishi Lancer Evo   51m.42.1s.

Round 3 TALLINN Tallinn 2/3.05.2003   75s   51f
Murakas/Kitsing   Ford Focus WRC   44m.18.9s.

Round 4 SOUTH ESTONIAN Voru 13/14.06.2003   53s   37f
Murakas/Kitsing   Ford Focus WRC   43m.48.9s.

Round 5 EOS Tartu-Otepa 4/5.07.2003   53s   32f
Martin/Park   Ford Focus WRC   1h.00m.34.6s.

Round 6 VIRUMAA Rakvere 22/23.08.2003   43s   33f
Murakas/Kitsing   Toyota Corolla WRC   52m.47.8s.

Round 7 PAIDE Jarvamaa 12/13.09.2003   41s   28f
Rauam/Poom   Subaru Impreza   52m.32.4s.

Round 8 SAAREMAA Kuressaare 17/18.10.2003   89s   54f
Rauam/Poom   Subaru Impreza   56m.07.8s.

2003 Estonian Champion Slava Popov 29 pts, 2 Priit Saluri 22, 3 Margus Murakas 19.

Group N Champion Ivar Raidam (Mitsubishi Lancer Evolution)

F France

Super 1600

Round 1 LYON-CHARBONNIERES   106s   75f
Lyon-Charbonnieres 11/13.04.2003
Jean-Joseph/Boyere   Renault Clio S1600   2h.03m.51.1s.

Round 2 AUXERROIS Auxerre 2/4.05.2003   46s   29f
Jean-Joseph/Boyere   Renault Clio 01000   1h.55m.48.0s.

Round 3 ALSACE VOSGES Mulhouse 23/25.05.2003   59s   43f
Tirabassi/Renucci   Renault Clio S1600   2h.25m.42.7s.
Round 4 ROUERGUE Rodez 27/29.06.2003   97s   50f
Robert/Bedon   Peugeot 206 S1600   2h.31m.27.8s.

Round 5 TERRE DE PARIS Chevanne 19.07.2003   12s   11f
Jean-Joseph/Boyere   Renault Clio S1600   1h.07m.48.4s.

Round 6 TERRE DES CARDABELLES   52s   27f
Millau 18/20.09.2003
Tirabassi/Renucci   Renault Clio S1600   2h.15m.36.3s.

Round 7 TOUQUET-PAS DE CALAIS   68s   51f
Le Touquet 10/12.10.2003
Tirabassi/Renucci   Renault Clio S1600   1h.59m.31.5s.

Note: Final round VAR Ste Maxime 21/23.11.2003.

Asphalt

Round 1 COEUR DE FRANCE Tours 4/6.04.2003   97s   53f
Rousselot/Mondesir   Subaru Impreza   1h.41m.57.6s.

Round 2 VINS-MACON Macon 9/11.05.2003   133s   80s
Bengue/Escudero   Peugeot 206 WRC   1h.37m.54.6s.

Round 3 MONTAGNE NOIRE Mazamet 25/27.07.2003   99s   61f
Bengue/Escudero   Peugeot 206 WRC   1h.11m.37.1s.

Round 4 MONT-BLANC Morzine 5/7.09.2003   101s   67f
Bengue/Escudero   Peugeot 206 WRC   2h.12m.04.1s.

Round 5 LA ROCHELLE La Rochelle 26/28.09.2003   109s   63f
Bengue/Escudero   Peugeot 206 WRC   1h.35m. 23.8s.

Round 6 CRITERIUM DES CEVENNES   218s   137f
Montpellier 14/16.11.2003
Rousselot/Mondesir   Subaru Impreza WRC   1h.47m.29.9s.

2003 French Asphalt Champion Alexandre Bengue, 2 Benoit Rousselot, 3 Jean Marie Cuoq, 4 Gilles Nantet, 5 Jean Pierre Landon, etc.

Gravel

Round 1 TERRE D'AUVERGNE   97s   55f
Issoire 18/20.04.2003
Richelmi/Barjou   Ford Focus WRC   1h.25m.09.4s.

Round 2 TERRE DE PROVENCE Digne 16/18.05.2003   140s   82f
Rousseaux/Legars   Subaru Impreza WRC   1h.22m.56.4s.

Round 3 TERRE DU DIOIS   98s   56f
Valence and Die 6/8.06.2003
Richelmi/Delorme   Ford Focus WRC   1h.39m.24.5s.

Round 4 TERRE DE LANGRES Langres 17/20.07.2003   107s   58f
Rousseaux/Legars   Subaru Impreza WRC   1h.23m.04.2s.

Round 5 TERRE Des Causses   105s   61f
Rouergat 29/31.08.2003
Richelmi/Delorme   Ford Focus WRC   1h.18m.32.5s

Round 6 TERRE DES CEVENNES Ales 3/5.10.2003   91s   46f
Richelmi/Barjou   Ford Focus WRC   1h.13m.22.1s.

Round 7 TERRE DU VAUCLUSE   126s   54f
Courthezon 7/9.11.2003
Albertini/Leon   Mitsubishi Lancer Evo   1h.42m.12.7s.

2003 French Gravel Champion Jean-Pierre Richelmi (Ford Focus WRC)

FIN Finland

Round 1 ARCTIC Rovaniemi 24/25.01.2003 (ECR2) 110s 55f
Tuohino/Tuohino   Ford Focus WRC   2h.16m.48.1s.

Round 2 OSUUSPANKKI Lapua 21/22.02.2003   85s 55f
Tuohino/Tuohino   Ford Focus WRC   49m.49.0s.

Round 3 VAAKUNA Mikkeli 14/15.03.2003   91s 56f
Lindholm/Heinonen   Peugeot 206 WRC   43m.36.8s.

Round 4 ABLOY ITARALLI Joensuu 6/7.06.2003   72s 41f
Lindholm/Tuominen   Peugeot 206 WRC   47m.38.5s.

Round 5 EXIDE Tampere 11/12.07.2003   79s 52f
Lindholm/Hantunen   Peugeot 206 WRC   37m.13.1s.

Round 6 UUSIKAUPUNKI Uusikaupunki 12/13.09.2003 64s 36f
Lindholm/Hantunen   Peugeot 206 WRC   46m.58.6s.

Round 7 VALVOLINE Riihimaki 3/4.10.2003   74s 43f
Lindholm/Tuominen   Peugeot 206 WRC   1h.06m.52.3s.

2003 Finnish Champion Sebastian Lindholm 100pts, 2 Janne Tuohino 87, 3 Jari Viita 61, 4 Jouni Ampuja 60, 5 Jarmo Mikkonen 46, etc.
Group A winner Sebastian Lindholm
Group N winner Hannu Hotanen (Mitsubishi Lancer Evolution)
Junior Champion Peti Kymalainen

GR Greece

Round 1 STEREAS ELLADOS   65s 36f
Agios Konstantinos 15/16.03.2003
Nasoulas/Maheras   Mitsubishi Lancer Evo   49m.48.8s.

Round 2 OLYMPIAKIO Pyrgos 5/6.04.2003   68s 32f
Nasoulas/Maheras   Mitsubishi Lancer Evo   2h.29m.27.3s.

Round 3 ACHAIOS Patra 3/4.05.2003   88s 79f
Efstathiou/Garyfalis   Renault Clio KC   47m.48.7s.

Round 4 D.E.TH (TIF-Thessalonikian Intl. Fair Rally) 87s 48f
Thessaloniki 14.09.2003
Tsolakidis/Lithopoulos Peugeot 306 Maxi   1h.57m.54.2s.

Round 5 ELPA Patra 26/28.09.2003 (ECR43)   87s 48f
Efstathiou/Garyfalis   Renault Clio KC   25m.35.1s.

Round 6 MAVRO DOPO Chalkis 11/12.10.2003   51s 23f
Tsolakidis/Lithopoulos Mitsubishi Lancer Evo   1h.18m.15.7s.

Round 7 OLYMPION Lamia 8/9.11.2003   51s 36f
Tsolakidis/Pavlidis   Subaru Impreza STi   1h.26m.18.26s.

2003 Greek Champion Sokratis Tsolakidis 97pts, 2 Panagiotis Hatzitsopanis 95, 3 Dimitris Nasoulas 81, 4 Kostas Bintzos 44, 5 Athanassios Eustathiou 43, etc.

H Hungary

Round 1 VALVOLINE Salgotarjan 28/30.03.2003   77s 55f
Benik/Somogyi   Ford Focus WRC   1h.00m.28.1s.

Round 2 VREDESTEIN Miskolc 25/27.04.2003   83s 49f
Toth/Toth   Peugeot 206 WRC   1h.14m.50.3s.

Round 3 FEHERVAR   76s 44f
Szukesfehurvar 23/25.05.2003 (ECR14)
Szabo/Kerek   Skoda Octavia WRC   1h.47m.19.2s.

Round 4 SAVARIA Szombathely 12/14.06.2003   56s 37f
Benik/Somogyi   Ford Focus WRC   1h.13m.21.4s.

Round 5 VESZPREM Veszprem 11/13.07.2003   72s 32f
Toth/Toth   Peugeot 206 WRC   1h.32m.36.2s.

Round 6 MICHELIN BUDAPEST   102s 57f
Budapest 8/10.08.2003 (ECR29)
Toth/Toth   Peugeot 206 WRC   1h.44m.52.7s.

Round 7 ALLIANZ HUNGARY Pucs 26/28.09.2003   92s 65f
Toth/Toth   Peugeot 206 WRC   1h.16m.27.7s.

Round 8 ZEMPLEN Tokaj 24/26.10.2003   69s 44f
Benik/Somogyi   Ford Focus WRC   53m.56.3s.

2003 Hungarian Champion Balazs Benik 135pts, 2 Janos Toth 105, 3 Gergely Szabo 75, etc.
Group N Champion Csaba Spitzmuller (Mitsubishi Lancer Evolution)
A6 winner Robert Bitor (Citroen Saxo KC)

HR Croatia

Round 1 OPATISJKA RIVIJERA   33s 21f
Mosqenicka Draga 7/8.03.2003
Loncaric/Puzic   Mitsubishi Lancer   57m.27.8s.

Round 2 INA MILLENIUM KVARNERSKI   42s 30f
Rijeka Opatija 21/22.03.2003
Pattison/Stefanovic   Ford Escort Cosworth   51m.34.5s.

Round 3 MARTINSKI Dugo Selo 27/28.06.2003   37s 25f
Loncaric/Puzic   Mitsubishi Lancer Evo   1h.16m.27.6s.

Round 4 INA CROATIA Zagreb 12/14.09.2003 (ECR37) 51s 31f
Loncaric/Puzic   Mitsubishi Lancer Evo   2h.45m.57.0s.

Round 5 ALLIANZ HUNGARY Mecsek (H) 26/28.09.2003 92s 65f
Franja/Bruner   Peugeot 306 S1600   1h.28m.45.5s.

Round 6 SATURNUS Idrija 3/5.10.2003 (ECR45)   89s 55f
Turk/Kumse   Ford Escort Cosworth   2h.06m.57.0s.

Round 7 POREC Porec 14/15.11.2003   63s 45f
Pulic/Santic   Peugeot 206 KC   59m.25.2s.

2003 Croatian Champion Nenad Loncaric, 2 Marko Lovak, 3 Mike Pattison, 4 Silvestr Mikulasti, 5 Gabor Takacs, etc.

I Italy

Round 1 TUTTA TERRA TOSCANA   84s 47f
Montalcino 28.02/2.03.2003
Galli/d'Amore   Mitsubishi Lancer Evo   2h.07m.42.28s.

Round 2 IL CIOCCO II   76s 45f
Castelnuovo di Garfagnana 21/22.03.2003 (ECR6)
Basso/Dotta   Fiat Punto S1600   2h.15m.53.2s.

Round 3 MILLE MIGLIA   88s 40f
Desenzano del Garda 4/5.04.2003 (ECR7)
Basso/Guglielmini   Fiat Punto S1600   3h.38m.20.8s.

Round 4 TARGA FLORIO Palermo 1/3.05.2003 (ECR11) 59s 43f
Andreucci/Andreussi   Fiat Punto S1600   2h.04m.05.4s.

Round 5 SAN MARINO   93s 53f
Serravalle (RSM) 30/31.05.2003 (ECR15)
Longhi/Imerito   Subaru Impreza WRX   3h.03m.46.9s.

Balazs Benik, 2003 Hungarian Champion.

Round 6 SALENTO Lecce 19/21.06.2003 (ECR20)   54s f
No Points awarded for Italian Championship following the death of Loris Roggia.

Round 7 SAN MARTINO DI CASTROZZA   53s 34f
San Martino di Castrozza 17/19.07.2003 (ECR26)
Andreucci/Andreussi   Fiat Punto S1600   2h.23m.05.5s.

Round 8 ALPI ORIENTALI   81s 45f
Udine 28/30.08.20U3 (ECR33)
Basso/Guglielmini   Fiat Punto S1600   2h.37m.39.6s.

Round 9 COSTA SMERALDA   108s 50f
Porto Cervo 19/20.09.2003 (ECR39)   Galli/Bioletti
Mitsubishi Lancer Evo   2h.23m.25.7s.

Round 10 ADRIATICO Ancona 17/18.10.2003   70s 49f
Andreucci/Andreussi   Fiat Punto S1600   1h.50m.49.7s.

2003 Italian Champion Paolo Andreucci 106pts, 2 Giandomenico Basso 94, 3 Renato Travaglia 79, 4 Piero Longhi 75, 5 Alessandro Fiorio 62, etc.
Super 1600 Winner Paolo Andreucci.
Group N Winner Piero Longhi (Subaru Impreza WRX STi)
Group N-2WD Winner Gabriele Tognozzi (MG ZR 160)
Group A Winner Fabio Bombardi (Nissan Sunny)
Diesel Winner Germano Ongaro (Seat Ibiza TDi)
Ladies Winner Luisa Zumelli (Renault Clio RS)

IND India

Round 1 COFFEE DAY Chikmagalur 23/25.05.2003 21s 15f
Kumar/Ramkumar   Honda City V-Tech   2h.38m.24.0s.

Round 2 MRF TAJ CHALLENGE Nashik 6/8.06.2003 14s 10f
Kumar/Sherif   Honda City V-Tech   1h.13m.40.0s.

Round 3 KERALA Cochin 29/31.08.2003   17s 13f
Kumar/Ramkumar   Honda City V-Tech   1h.23m.16.0s.

Round 4 POWER M1 CHALLENGE   16s 11f
Chandigarh 19/21.09.2003
Kumar/Ramkumar   Honda City V-Tech   1h.43m.46.0s.

Round 5 WIAA DE GOA Panjim 31.10/2.11.2003   8s 8f
Balu/Ramaswamy   Honda City V-Tech   1h.14m.25s.

Round 6 BANGALORE Bangalore 14/16.11.2003
Singh/Menon   Honda City V-Tech   1h.29m.13s.

Note: Final round MRF INDIA Mumbai 5/7.12.2003. V R Naren Kumar cannot be beaten for the overall championship

IRL Ireland

Round 1 MAYO Ballina 9.03.2003   132s 96f
Donnelly/Kiely   Subaru Impreza WRC   52m.35s.

Round 2 MONAGHAN Monaghan 27.04.2003   168s 84f
Barrable/O'Gorman   Subaru Impreza WRC   1h.16m.04s.

Round 3 CARLOW Carlow 11.05.2003   146s 96f
Barrable/O'Gorman   Subaru Impreza WRC   1h.06m.24s.

Round 4 CAVAN Cavan 25.05.2003   131s 88f
Donnelly/Toner   Subaru Impreza WRC   1h.23m.15s.

Round 5 LIMERICK Adare 1.06.2003   151s 103f
Donnelly/Toner   Subaru Impreza WRC   1h.11m.06s.

Round 6 RAVENS ROCK Kilkenny 29.06.2003   151s 103f
Donnelly/Toner   Subaru Impreza WRC   57m.47s.

Round 7 STONETHROWERS Clonmel 10.08.2003   152s 93f
Donnelly/Toner   Subaru Impreza WRC   1h.10m.12s.

Round 8 GALWAY Portumna 31.08.2003   131s 93f
Donnelly/Toner   Subaru Impreza WRC   1h.10m.16s.

Round 9 CLARE Ennis 21.09.2003   131s 96f
Harrison/Bell   Subaru Impreza   1h.01m.21s.

Round 10 DONEGAL HARVEST   151s   116f
Letterkenny 11.10.2003

Harrison/Bell	Subaru Impreza WRC	46m.46s.

2003 Irish National Champion Eugene Donnelly 156pts,
2 Michael Barrable 142, 3 Adrian McElvaney 120, 4 James Harrison 119,
5 Sean Gallagher 88, etc.
Group N Champion Mark Courtney (Mitsubishi Lancer Evolution)

J Japan

Round 1 SNOW IN HOKKAIDO   29s   23f
Hokkaido 31.01/02.02.2003

Kamata/Kitazawa	Mitsubishi Lancer Evo	23m.08.3s.

Round 2 MCA BARU Oita 12/13.04.2003   28s   23f

Katsuta/Kitada	Subaru Impreza	27m.02.6s.

Round 3 HIETSUKI Miyazaki 24/25.05.2003   35s   30f

Nutahara/Odagiri	Mitsubishi Lancer	27m.36.9s.

Round 4 KIRORO TRAVERSE KAMUINAINDRA   36s   25f
Akaigwa-Hokkaido 21/22.06.2003

Nutahara/Odagiri	Mitubishi Lancer	44m.58.8s.

Round 5 NORTH ATTACK Hokkaido 4/6.07.2003   52s   44f

Nutahara/Odegiri	Mitsubishi Lancer	54m.20.6s.

Round 6 NECOSTE SANGAKU   39s   35f
Saitama-Gunma 18/20.07.2003

Nishio-Gifu/Yamaguchi	Subaru Impreza	1h.09m.58.4s.

Round 7 MONTORE 2003 Gunma 26/28.09.2003   46s   32f

Katsuta/Kitada	Subaru Impreza	47m.12.7s

Round 8 HIGHLAND MASTERS   36s   27f
Nagano Gifu 24/26/10.2003

Nutahara/Odagiri	Mitsubishi Lancer Evo	1h.07m.06s.

2003 Japanese Champion Fumio Nutahara 540pts, 2 Norihiko Katsuta
401, 3 Masahisi Ishida 308, 4 Yujiro Nishio 273, 5 Masayuki Ishida 258, etc.

JAM Jamaica

Round 1 ST BESS St Elizabeth 6.07.2003   15s   11f

Panton/Morin	Toyota Celica	36m.38s.

Round 2 KIG St. Ann 17.08.2003   14s   10f

Panton/Morin	Toyota Celica	29m.08s.

Round 3 RAYNOR KING MEMORIAL Westmoreland 5.10.2003

Gore/Nelson	Mitsubishi Lancer Evo	29m.45s.

Note: Final round RALLY OF JAMAICA 6/7.12.2003.

LT Lithuania

Round 1 VISAGINAS Visaginas 17/18.01.2003   44s   32f

Girdauskas/Sosas	Mitsubishi Lancer Evo	56m.00.6s.

Round 2 VILNIUS Vilnius 10/11.05.2003   67s   36f

Lipeikis/Vaitkevicius	Mitsubishi Lancer Evo	50m.43.89s.

Round 3 ZEMAITIJA Siauliai 5/6.07.2003   65s   34f

Lipeikis/Vaitkevicius	Mitsubishi Lancer Evo	55m.01.88s.

Round 4 AUKSTAITIJA Ukmerge 1/2.08.2003   62s   37f

Lipeikis/Vaitkevicius	Mitsubishi Lancer Evo	51m.07.55s.

Round 5 APLINK LEITUVA   51s   33f
Kaunas-Vilnius 6/7.09.2003

Lipeikis/Vaitkevicius	Mitsubishi Lancer Evo	58m.57.54s.

Round 6 KAUNO RUDUO Kaunas 10/11.10.2003   64s   42f

Lipeikis/Honkanen	Mitsubishi Lancer Evo	48m.54.71s.

2003 Lithuanian and A,R 3500 Champion Rokas Lipeikis 116pts,
2 Arunas Strumskis 75, 3 Evaldas Cirba 63.
Class A , R 2000 Champion Evaldas Cirba
Class N2000 Champion Darius Vilimas
Class S 2000 Champion Zilvinas Jursys
Class A, R 1600 Champion Dovilas Ciutele
Class N 3500 Champion Arunas Strumskis

LV Latvia

Round 1 ESTONIAN WINTER (EE) Tartu 17.01.2003   65s   49f

Vasaraudzis/Simkus	Mitsubishi Lancer Evo	47m.47.1s.

Round 2 SARMA Gulbene 7.02.2003   76s   44f

Vasaraudzis/Spredzis	Mitsubishi LancerEvo	51m.55.1s.

Round 3 TALSI Talsi 17.05.2003   60s   35f

Lebedevs/Deklaus	Mitsubishi Lancer Evo	1h.02m.10.3s.

Round 4 CESIS Cesis 21.06.2003   50s   36f

Mezaks/Ronis	Ford Escort WRC	47m.18.9s.

Round 5 KURZEME   65s   39f
Liepaja 11/13.07.2003 (ECR24)

Vorobjovs/Ervalds	Mitsubishi Lancer Evo	1h.35m.12.1s.

Round 6 VIDZEME Sigulda 15.08.2003   40s   24f

Vasaraudzis/Spredzis	Mitsubishi Lancer Evo	59m.58.9s.

Round 7 LATVIA Riga 4.10.2003   55s   35f

Vasaraudzis/Spredzis	Mitsubishi Lancer Evo	1h.05m.34.4s.

Rokas Lipeikis, 2003 Lithuanian Champion.

ZALMANIS

Ivars Vasaraudzis, 2003 Latvian Champion.

2003 Latvian & Class A8 Champion Ivars Vasaraudzis 46pts,
2 Matiss Mezaks 28, 3 Aivis Egle 26.6, 4 Janis Vorobjovs 22.4, 3 Martins
Balodis 13, etc.
Class N4 winner Aivis Egle (Mitsubishi Lancer Evolution)
Class AN2000 winner Aivars Kivkucans (VW Golf KC)
Class R13 winner Raimonds Strokss (Audi 80)
Class R2000 winner Dans Lescs (Opel Kadett)
Class R1600 winner Maris Neiksans (Lada 2108)

MAL Malaysia

Round 1 PETANI Kedah 22/23.02.2003   18s   12f

Low/Zulhassan	Proton Wira 4WD	2h.03m.54s.

Round 2 LUMUT Perak 19/20.04.2003   27s   18f

Abdullah/Hassan	Proton Wira 4WD	1h.31m.12s.

Round 3 KANGAR Perlis 24/25.05.2003   27s   13f

Gunaseelan/Jayaselan	Proton Putra 4WD	2h.16m.38s.

Round 4 NEG SEMBILAN 21/22.06.2003   23s   13f

Gunaseelan/Jayaselan	Proton Putra 4WD	2h.16m.38s.

Round 5 MALAYSIA Melaka 8/10.08.2003   16s   8f

Hong/Chin	Perodua Kelisa 4WD	3h.26m.60s.

Round 6 SEPANG Salak 27/28.09.2003   33s   26f

Adbullah/Hassan	Proton Wira	1h.51m.04s.

2003 Malaysian National Champion Gunaseelan Rajoo 55pts,
2 Rozali Abdullah 48, 3 Kan Chee Hong 37, 4 Tengku Djan Ley 25,
5 Lim Leong Onn 22.
Class N4 Champion (FIA Homologated cars above 2000cc) Abdullah/Hasan
Class P12 Champion (above 2000cc) Rajoo/Rajoo
Class P11 Champion (1601cc to 2000cc) Aziz/Aziz
Class P10 Champion (1401cc to 1600cc) Hong
Class P9 Champion (Up to 1400cc) Onn/Kok

MEX Mexico

Round 1 CORONA Leon 13.03.2003   36s   15f

Ligato/Garcia	Mitsubishi Lancer Evo	4h.34m.19s.

Round 2 FERIA DE MAYO Morelia 5.05.2003   28s   24f

Izquierdo/Fuentes	Mitsubishi Lancer Evo	1h.07m.09s.

Round 3 SIERRA BRAVA Puebla 14.06.2003   32s   27f

Richter/Telleacha	Mitsubishi Lancer Evo	49m.41s.

Round 4 24 HORAS Valle de Bravo 12.07.2003   32s   25f

Richter/Telleacha	Mitsubishi Lancer Evo	2h.31m.19s.

Round 5 DE LA PLATA Taxco 23.08.2003   32s   28f

Richter/Telleacha	Mitsubishi Lancer Evo	1h.21m.59s.

Round 6 SIERRA DE LOBOS Leon 06.09.2003   20s   12f

Tejeda/Munnoz	Mitsubishi Lancer Evo	1h.03m.43s.

Round 7 MEDIANOCHE Cuernavaca 26.09.2003   39s   26f

Sanchez/D.Lopez	Audi A4	1h.07m.43s.

Round 8 RETO A LAS ALTURAS Toluca 18.10.2003   36s   24f

Richter/Telleacha	Mitsubishi Lancer Evo	38m.53s.

Note: Final round ACAPULCO Acapulco 28.11.2003.
Erwin Richter cannot be beaten in the championship.

MG Madagascar

Round 1 JOVENA Antananarivo 13.04.2003   17s   10f
Kely/Chinois   Toyota Celica GT-4   1h.04m.16s.

Round 2 BOINA Majunga 5/7.06.2003   13s   9 f
Kely/Chinois   Toyota Celica GT-4   1h.05m.16s.

Round 3 RIM Antananarivo 15/17.08.2003   16s   8f
Kely/Chinois   Toyota Celica GT-4   1h.27m.03s.

Note: Final round MOBIL Antananarivo 6/7.12.2003

N Norway

Round 1 MOUNTAIN RALLY
Valdres-Hallingdal 17/18.01.2003   72s   41f
H.Solberg/Menkerud   Mitsubishi Lancer Evo   1h.34m.53.7s.

Round 2 SNOFRESER Elverum 1.02.2003   112s   67f
K.Kolberg/K Pettersen   Hyundai Accent WRC   1h.09m.23.3s.

Round 3 FINNSKOG
Kongsvinger 21/22.02.2003 (ECR3)   68s   42f
H.Solberg/Menkerud   Mitsubishi Lancer Evo   2h.26m.25.0s.

Round 4 AURSKOG-HOLAND
Aurskog 21.06.2003   139s   105f
H.Solberg/Menkerud   Mitsubishi Lancer Evo   44m.43.7s.

Round 5 OSTFOLD Momarken 30.08.2003   133s   78f
Schie/Engen   Toyota Corolla WRC   57m.10.5s.

Round 6 NAF HAMAR & OMEGN   139s   100f
Jr.Hedemarken 20.09.2003
H.Solberg/Menkerud   Mitsubishi Lancer Evo   41m.23s.

2003 Norwegian Group A/WRC Champion Henning Solberg.
Group N04 Champion Eivind Steffensen
Group A 2wd Champion Erik Nordahl
Group N 2wd Champion Svein AndersMyrvang

NL The Netherlands

Round 1 DER STAVEREN ZUIDERZEE   25s   15f
Emmeloord 21/22.03.2003
Bijvelds/Bijvelds   Mitsubishi Lancer Evo   1h.36m.16s.

Round 2 KILLARNEY RALLY OF THE LAKES   70s   41f
Killarney 3 /4.05.2003 (IRL)
Henneky/v.Oorschst   Nissan Micra   3h.10m.09.2s.

Round 3 PARADIGIT ELE Veldhoven 23/25.05.2003   61s   36f
Van den Heuvel/Scholtaber   Mitsubishi Lancer Evo   1h.52m.09s.

Round 4 BHV EXPO Roosendaal 12/14.07.2003   30s   11f
De Winkel/Van Hoek   VW Golf KC   2h.22m.19s.

Round 5 EIFEL Daun 22/23.08.2003 (D)   56s   43f
De Winkel/Van Hoek   VW Golf KC   1h.28m.03.2s.

Round 6 GOLDEN TULIP   70s   51f
Nijverdal 26/27.09.2003 (ECR42)
De Winkel/Van Hoek   VW Golf KC   1h.42m.33s.

Round 7 CONDROZ Huy (B) 15/16.11.2003 (ECR50) 174s   110f
no points scoring drivers finished event

2003 Dutch Champion Jan De Winkel 367pts, 2 Gerhard Henneky 284, 3 Nelis Verkooijen 263, etc.
Group N Champion Nelis Verkooijen in Subaru WRX (N4)
F2 Champion Jan de Winkel.
National Champion Evert Bolderheij (Mitsubishi Lancer Evolution)

NZ New Zealand

Round 1 PROPECIA RALLY NZ   80s   46f
Auckland 9/13.04.2003 (WRC4)
Argyle/Smith   Mitsubishi Lancer Evo   4h.03m.46.6s.

Round 2 OTAGO Dunedin 10/11.05.2003   46s   29f
Bawden/McLachlan   Mitsubishi Lancer Evo   2h.09m.42s.

Round 3 ASCOT PARK SOUTHLAND   53s   35f
Invercarghl 31.05/1.06.2003
Bawden/McLachlan   Mitsubishi Lancer Evo   1h. 57m.35.0s.

Round 4 ROTORUA Rotorua 11/13.07.2003   38s   26f
Herbert/Ryan   Subaru Impreza   2h.58m.32.6s.

Round 5 HAWKES BAY Hastings 15/16.08.2003   82s   58f
Mason/Brensell   Mitsubishi Lancer Evo   1h.36m.46.0s.

2003 New Zealand Champion Bruce Herbert 166pts, 2 Geof Argyle 122, 3 Richard Mason 121, 4 Andrew Hawkeswood 83, 5 Todd Bawden 73.
Group N Champion Chris West (Subaru Impreza Sti)
Junior Champion Richard Mason (Mitsubishi Lancer Evolution)
Group N Chris West
Junior Champion Richard Marson
2wd Champion Deane Buist (Toyota Corolla)

P Portugal

Round 1 CASINO DA POVOA   43s   19f
Povoa De Varzin 7/8.02.2003
Araujo/Ramalho   Citroen Saxo KC   2h.42m.26.7s.

Round 2 PORTUGAL   60s   45f
Macedo de Cavaleiros 28/29.03.2003
Araujo/Ramalho   Citroen Saxo KC   2h.04m.12.7s.

Round 3 FC PORTO Fafe 24/25.05.2003   60s   30f
Peres/Silva   Ford Escort   1h.30m.31.2s.

Round 4 SATA ACORES   60s   30f
Ponta Delgada 3/5.07.2003 (ECR22)
Peres/Silva   Ford Escort   3h.36m.42.1s.

Round 5 VINHO DA MADEIRA   78s   35f
Funchal 31.07/2.08.2003 (ECR28)
Sa/Camacho   Peugeot 306 Maxi   3h.07m.57.0s.

Round 6 ROTA DO VIDRO   60s   45f
Marinha Grande 3/5.10.2003 (ECR44)
Araujo/Ramalho   Citroen Saxo KC   2h.03m.07.6s.

Round 7 CASINOS DO ALGARVE   60s   40f
Portimao 16/18.10.2003
Araujo/Ramalho   Citroen Saxo KC   1h.29m.56.9s.

Round 8 SPORT DAO LAFOES 14/15.11.2003   54s   43f
Araujo/Ramalho   Citroen Saxo KC   1h.35m.12.0s.

2003 Portuguese Champion Armindo Araujo 68pts, 2 Fernando Peres 32, 3 Vitor Lopes 23, etc.

Armindo Araujo, 2003 Portuguese Champion.

Bruce Herbert, 2003 New Zealand Champion.

Eduardo Dibos, 2003 Peruvian Group N winner.

PE Peru

Round 1 ASIA Lima 8.03.2003   24s   13f
Dasso/Hiraoka   Subaru Impreza WRX   59m.01s.

Round 2 HUARAL Lima 4.04.2003   26s   12f
Dasso/Rojas   Subaru Impreza WRX   1h.01m.24.s.

Round 3 PRESIDENT OF THE REPUBLIC   38s   23f
Lima 1.05.2003
Dibos/Bromberg   Toyota Celica GT-4   1h.12m.45.s.

Round 4 MANTARO VALLEY Huancayo 15.06.2003   29s   13f
Dibos/Bromberg   Toyota Celica GT-4   1h.41m.05.s.

Round 5 SACRED VALLEY Cusco 6.07.2003   29s   21f
Jochamowitz/Medina   Mitsubishi Lancer Evo   1h.10m.28.s.

Round 6 CANETE Lima 3.08.2003 Lima   21s   10f
Dibos/ Bromberg   Toyota Celica GT-4   1h.08m.04.s.

Round 7 AREQUIPA Arequipa 23.08.2003   22s   16f
Dibos/Bromberg   Toyota Celica GT-4   1h.17m.47.s.

Round 8 CHINCHA Ica 31.10.2003   25s   13f
Jochamowitz/Medina   Mitsubishi Lancer Evo   50m.35s.

2003 Peruvian National Tourism Champion
Raul Velit Jr (Toyota Corolla)
Group N Winner Eduardo Dibos
Super 1600 Winner Andy Ledgard (Toyota Corolla)

PL Poland

Round 1 ELMOT Swidnica 2/3.05.2003   65s   32f
Kuzaj/Lukas   Subaru Impreza WRC   1h.55m.16.4s.

Round 2 POLSKI   61s   36f
Klodzko-Polanica 30/31.05.2003 (ECR17)
Czopik/Wronski   Subaru Impreza WRC   2h.32m.03.7s.

Round 3 KORMORAN Olsztyn 27/29.06.2003   57s   25f
Kuzaj/Lukas   Subaru Impreza WRC   1h.34m.10.9s.

Round 4 RZESZOWSKI Rzeszow 7/10.08.2003   50s   39f
Czopik/Wronski   Mitsubishi Lancer Evo   1h.42m.45.7s.

Round 5 SLASKI Jastrzebie Zdroj 4/7.09.2003   61s   35f
Czopik/Wronski   Mitsubishi Lancer Evo   1h.37m.55.7s.

Round 6 WARSZAWSKI Warszawa 17/19.10.2003   45s   30f
Kuzaj / Lukas   Subaru Impreza WRC   1h.22m.48.7s.

2003 Polish Champion Tomasz Czopik 45(50)pts, 2 Sebastian Frycz 36 (39), 3 Leszek Kuzaj 34, 4 Michal Bebenek 29, 5 Maciej Lubiak 18(19), etc.
Group N Champion Sebastian Frycz (Mitsubishi Lancer Evolution)
1600 Trophy Champion Grzegorz Grzyb (Peugeot 206)

PY Paraguay

Round 1 MISIONES San Juan Bautista 8/9.03.2003   54s   20f
A.Galanti/Toyotoshi   Toyota Corolla WRC   2h.05m.23.1s.

Round 2 TRANS-ITAPUA Encarnacion 11/13.04.2003 82s   26f
Gorostiaga/Aguilera   Toyota Corolla WRC   1h.39m.21.7s.

Round 3 CORONEL OVIEDO   60s   23f
Coronel Oviedo 13/14.06.2003
A.Galanti/Toyotoshi   Toyota Corolla WRC   1h.05m.59.9s.

Round 4 CAAGUAZU Cawsguazu 13/14.06.2003   65s   30f
A.Galanti/Toyotoshi   Toyota Corolla WRC   1h.08m.42.1s.

Round 5 YBYCUI Ybycui 8/10.08.2003   73s   40f
A.Galanti/Toyotoshi   Toyota Corolla WRC   1h.27m.09.9s.

Round 6 PALERMO-SHELL TRANSCHACO   95s   6f
La Patria 25/27.09.2003
M.Galanti/Toyotoshi   Toyota Corolla WRC   8h.10m.38.s.

2003 Paraguayan Champion Alejandro Galanti 84pts,
2 Didier Arias 84, 3 Francisco Gorostiaga 54, etc.

R Romania

Round 1 BRASOV Brasov 4/6.04.2003   55s   32f
Ilna/Cimpeanu   Mitsubishi Lancer Evo   1h.21m.00.8s.

Round 2 SIROMEX Baia Mare 2/4.05.2003   52s   31f
Leu/Solomon   Hyundai Accent WRC   1h.17m.16.5s.

Round 3 HUNEDOARA Deva 23/25.05.2003   48s   31f
Leu/Solomon   Hyundai Accent WRC   52m.55.7s.

Round 4 BLITZ BANAT Timisoara 13/15.06.2003   39s   30f
Stan/Tiugan   Mitsubishi Lancer Evo   1h.43m.40.1s.

Round 5 ROMANIA Brasov 4/6.07.2003 (ECR23)   51s   27f
Girtofan/Pulpea   Seat Cordoba WRC   1h.44m.06.9s.

Round 6 LIQUI MOLY Sibiu 1/3.08.2003   45s   23f
Aur/Berghea   Mitsubishi Lancer Evo   1h.42m.17.0s.

Round 7 MAHLE & CARTEX ARGES   40s   22f
Pitesti 29/31.08.2003
Girtofan/Pulpea   Seat Cordoba WRC   1h.07m.51.9s.

Round 8 RAFO ONESTI Onesti 19/21.09.2003   33s   19f
Morar/Vararichi   Mitsubishi Lancer Evo   1h.32m.12.0s.

Round 9 MOL PREVENT HARGHITA   43s   25f
Odorheiul Secuiesc 10/12.10.2003
Marisca/Itu   Mitsubishi Lancer Evo   1h.15m.22.1s.

Round 10 MOBIL 1 Cluj 24/26.10.2003   40s   33f
Leu/Solomon   Hyundai Accent WRC   1h.02m.17.0s.

2003 Romanian Champion Mihai Leu 46pts, 2 Dan Morar 46,
3 Emanuel Ilina 44, 4 Dan Girtofan 39, Romulus Preda 35, etc.
Group N Champion Emanuel Ilina.

RA Argentina

Round 1 TRASLASIERRA   37s   30f
Mina Clavero 31.01/02.02.2003
Villagra/Villagra   Mitsubishi Lancer Evo   1h.11m.42.1s.

Round 2 ANDALGALA Andalgala 7/9.03.2003   48s   27f
Villagra/Villagra   Mitsubishi Lancer Evo   1h.22m.38.5s.

Round 3 CAPILLA DEL MONTE   46s   31f
Capilla del Monte 5/7.04.2003
Sanchez/Cretu   Subaru Impreza   1h.09m.36.6s.

Round 4 NEUQUEN Plaza Huincul 13/15.06.2003   42s   26f
J.P.Raies/Perez   Toyota Corolla   1h.16m.05.0s.

Round 5 CATAMARCA   53s   29f
San Fernando de Catamarca 18/20.07.2003
Villagra/Villagra   Mitsubishi Lancer Evo   1h11m.45.8s.

Mihai Leu, 2003 Romanian Champion.

DOBAI

Round 6	LA PAMPA Santa Rosa 15/17.08.2003	52s	26f
JP.Raies/Perez	Toyota Corolla	1h.08m.04.7s.	

Round 7	VUELTA DE LA MANZANA	53s	30f
General Roca 12/14.09.2003			
Perez Companc/Volta	Toyota Corolla	1h.11m.52.4s.	

Round 8	TUCUMAN Concepcion 3/5.10.2003	51s	33f
Perez Companc/Volta	Toyota Corolla WRC	1h.16m.38.0s.	

Note: Final round GRAN PREMIO Cutral-Co 20/23.11.2003. Juan Pablo Raies (Toyota Corolla WRC) Javier Badra (Renault Clio Williams) and Juan Manuel Solis (Fiat Palio 16V) cannot be beaten in the A8, A7 and A6 championships respectively.

RCH Chile

Round 1	VINA DEL MAR 28/30.03.2003	s	21f
Suriani/Rodriguez	Subaru Impreza	1h.23m.42.8s.	

Round 2	TALCA 23/25.05.2003	s	26f
Suriani/Rodriguez	Subaru Impreza	1h.15m.47.4s.	

Round 3	LA SERENA 20/22.06.2003	s	27f
Suriani/Rodriguez	Subaru Impreza	1h.31m.36.6s.	

Round 4	IQUIQUE 22/24.08.2003	s	18f
Suriani/Rodriguez	Subaru Impreza	1h.37m.11.5s.	

Round 5	SAN FELIPE 26/28.09.2003	s	22f
R.Ibarra/De Gavardo	Hyundai Coupe	1h.45m.29.4s	

Round 6	PUERTO MONTT 17/19.10.2003	s	36f
Suriani/Rodriguez	Subaru Impreza	1h.28m.42.3s.	

Round 7	SANTIAGO 14/16.11.2003	40s	29f
Innocenti/Galindo	Subaru Impreza WRX	1h.05m.43.2s.	

2003 Chilean Champion Walter Suriani (RA).

RI Indonesia

Round 1	GUDANG GARAM PRIMA XP	28s	f
Cikarang, West Java 29/30.03.2003			
Agung/Mboi	Mitsubishi Lancer Evo		

Round 2	GUDANG GARAM	31s	f
Sentul, West Java 24/25.05.2003			
Alim/Damarjati	Mitsubishi Lancer Evo		

Round 3	GUDANG GARAM KRATATAU	45s	f
Bandar Lampung, Sumatra 25/27.07.2003			
Agung/Mboi	Mitsubishi Lancer Evo		

Round 4	GUDANG GARAM	29s	*f
Makassar, South Sulawesi 26/28.09.2003			
Rifat Sungkar/Harilatu	Mitsubishi Lancer Evo		

2003 Indonesian National Champion Herry Agung.
Group N16 Champion M. Herry Prastomo (Timor S515i)
Group GR2 Champion Rizal Sungkar (Mitsubishi Lancer GTi)

RL Lebanon

Round 1	WINTER Jounieh 8/9.04.2003	16s	12f
A.Feghali/Matar	Mitsubishi Lancer Evo	35m.16s.	

Round 2	SPRING Faraya 3/4.05.2003	14s	9f
Bou Doumit/Njeim	Mitsubishi Lancer Evo	1h.05m.16s.	

Round 3	LEBANON Jounieh 3/6.07.2003	44s	21f
R.Feghali/Chehab	Subaru Impreza WRC	2h.46m.07s.	

Round 4	CEDARS Faraya 18/19.10.2003	15s	9f
Al-Attiyah/Chehab	Mitsubishi Lancer Evo	1h.12m.23s.	

Round 5 A L'ETRANGER

Rizal Sungkar, Indonesian Group GR2 Winner.

ROU Uruguay

Round 1	ROSARIO Rosario 17/18.05.2003	s	18f
Pita/Umpierrez	Mitsubishi Lancer Evo	45m.32.6s.	

Round 2	TACUAREMBO Tacuarembo 14/15.06.2003	s	13f
Mendez/Dotta	Mitsubishi Lancer Evo	1h.12m.06.7s.	

Round 3	DURAZNO Durazno 26/27.07.2003	29s	18f
Mendez/Dotta	Mitsubishi Lancer Evo	1h.10m.46.1s.	

Round 4	MINAS Minas 16/17.08.2003	26s	15f
Mendez/Dotta	Mitsubishi Lancer Evo	1h.12m.05.0s.	

Round 5	PAYSAND Paysand 4/5.10.2003	33s	23f
Fernandez/Diego	Hyundai Coupe KC	1h.01m.19.3s.	

Round 6	TREINTA Y TRES Treinta y Tres 1/2.11.2003	29s	f
Fresnedo/Benytez	Peugeot 206	1h.17m.54s.	

Note: Final round ATLANTICO Punta del Este 28/30.11.2003.

RUS Russia

Round 1	ZHIGULI Togliatt 17/19.01.2003	37s	23f
Zhigunov/Ter-Oganesiants	Mitsubishi Lancer Evo	1h.56m.10.8s.	

Round 2	SELIGER Peno 21/23.02.2003	51s	30f
Uspensky/Lotko	Subaru Impreza	1h.45m.53.2s.	

Round 3	SNOW LADOGA Lahdenpohja 7/9.03.2003	70s	45f
Zhigunov/Ter-Oganesiants	Mitsubishi Lancer Evo	1h.36m.39.8s.	

Round 4	KARELIA Lahdenpohja 6/8.06.2003	52s	21f
Zhigunov/Oganesiants	Mitsubishi Lancer Evo	1h.49m.23.4s.	

Round 5	KURZEME	48s	27f
Kurzeme 11/13.07.2003 (LV) (ECR24)			
Grjazin/Troshkin	Mitsubishi Lancer Evo	1h.35m.05.2s.	

Round 6	GUKOVO Gukovo 1/3.09.03	53s	27f
Uspensky/Lotko	Subaru Impreza WRX STI	2h.00m.34.8s.	

2003 Russian N4 Champion Andrey Zhigunov 75pts, 2 Sergey Uspensky 67, 3 Yuri Trutnev 39, 4 Denis Levyatov 36, 5 Alexander Jeludov 30.
Group N2 Champion Andrey Buneev (Citroen Saxo VTS)
Group R10 Champion Alexander Nikonenko (Lada 112 KC)

S Sweden

Round 1	VANNAS Vannas 14/15.02.2003	70s	43f
Johansson/Locander	Toyota Corolla WRC	1h.17m.41.2s.	

Round 2	SNOW RALLY SWEDEN	69s	63f
Leg 1 Ostersund 28.02.2003			
Horbing/Olsson	Ford Escort WRC	38m.10.7s.	

Round 3	SNOW RALLY SWEDEN	66s	43f
Leg 2 Ostersund 1.03.2003			
Eriksson/Svensson	Ford Focus WRC	1h.15m.29.9s.	

Round 4	SOUTH SWEDISH Leg 1 Vaxjo 23.05.2003	70s	52f
Radstrom/Skallman	Toyota Corolla WRC	45m.58.2s.	

Round 5	SOUTH SWEDISH Leg 2 Vaxjo 24.05.2003	63s	39f
Dale/Bargery	Hyundai Accent WRC	1h.05m.33.6s.	

Round 6	SNAPPHANERALLYT	56s	44f
Hassleholm 15/16.08.2003			
Radstrom/Skallman	Toyota Corolla WRC	47m.38.7s.	

Round 7	SILVERSTONE Koping 5/6.09.2003	58s	38f
Radstrom/Skallman	Toyota Corolla WRC	59m.45.3s.	

2003 Swedish Group A Over 2000cc Champion
Andreas Eriksson 58pts, 2 Mats Thorszelius 57, 3 Tobias Johansson 53, 4 Thomas Radstrom 52, 5 Mats Jonsson 41, etc.
Group N Over 2000cc Champion Stig Olov Walfridsson (Mitsubishi Lancer Evolution)
Group A Up to 2000cc Champion Per Gunnar Andersson (Renault Clio S1600)
Group N Up to 2000cc Champion Tobias Lindstrom (VW Polo)
Juniors Fredrik Eriksson (Peugeot 306)

Andreas Eriksson, 2003 Swedish Group A Over 2000cc Champion.

SCG Serbia & Montenegro

Round 1 INTERSPEED   21s   11f
Budva 30.05/1.06.2003 (ECR16)
Jereb/Kacin   Seat Ibiza KC   2h.10m.56.2s.

Round 2 HYUNDAI SREMSKI   32s   23f
Ruma 27/28.06.2003
Simic/Jelenic   Skoda Octavia WRC   46m.22.7s.

Round 3 ZEMUNSKI Zemun 1/2.08.2003   35s   27f
Jereb/Kacin   Seat Ibiza KC   46m.16.6s.

Round 4 G.A.G.A. FORD TARA OBREN TESIC   33s   26f
MEMORIAL Bajina Basta 22/23.08.2003
Simic/Jelenic   Skoda Octavia WRC   1h.03m.54.3s.

Round 5 BALKAN Bajina Basta 5/7.09.2003 (ECR36) 27s   15f
Martinovic/Markovic   Renault Clio Williams 2h.09m.28.4s.

Round 6 YU Bajina Basta 19/21.09.2003 (ECR41) 36s   20f
Jereb/Kacin   Seat Ibiza KC   1h.56m.55.2s.

2003 Serbian & Montenegran Champion Andrej Jereb 57pts,
2 Cedomir Brkic 47, 3 Mirko Martinovic 31, 4 Dragan Simic 28, 5 Vladan
Petrovic 17.
Group N Champion Cedomir Brkic (Mitsubishi Lancer Evolution)

SLO Slovenia

Round 1 VRANOV Vrarnov 5/6.04.2003   43s   35f
Pech/Uhel   Ford Focus WRC   49m.39.7s.

Round 2 MATADOR TATRY   54s   25f
Puchov 2/3.05.2003 (ECR10)
Pech/Uhel   Ford Focus WRC   1h.28m.58.0s.

Round 3 TRNAVA Trnava 13/15.06.2003   54s   39f
Pech/Uhel   Ford Focus WRC   29m.23.5s.

Round 4 VIHORLAT SNINA Snina 5/6.07.2003 37s   27f
Pech/Uhel   Ford Focus WRC   43m.26.5s.

Round 5 KOSICE Kosice 15/17.08.2003 (ECR31) 54s   35f
Cserhalmi/Krajnak   Ford Focus WRC   1h.43m.00.9s.

Round 6 HURBANOVO Hurbanovo 5/7.09.2003   35s   20f
Beres/Stary   Toyota Corolla WRC   49m.49.0s..

Round 7 MIKONA   40s   29f
Rimavska Sobota 19/20.09.2003 (ECR40)
Pech/Uhel   Ford Focus WRC   1h.28m.10.8s.

2003 Slovakian Champion Vaclav Pech 520pts,
2 Tibor Cserhalmi 420, 3 Josef Beres 404, etc.
Group N Champion Vladimir Palko (Mitsubishi Lancer Evolution)
F2 Champion Marcin Beltowski (Skoda Felicia KC)

T Thailand

Round 1 Kanchanaburi 8/9.03.2003   26s   13f
Tawatchai Pasomsam/
Wongsakorn Saied   Mitsubisi Lancer Evo 1h.11m.30s.

Round 2 Pak Chong 10/11.05.2003   27s   16f
Jirapat Promnog/
Panlop Meenil   Mitsubishi Lancer Evo 1h.04m.55s.

Round 3 Rayong 28/29.06.2003   29s   16f
Jirapat Promnog/
Panlop Meenil   Mitsubishi.Lancer Evo 1h.09m.10s.

Round 4 Rayong 23/24.08.2003   28s   20f
Tawatchai Pasomsub/
Wongsakorn Saied   Mitsubishi Lancer Evo 1h.04m.33s.

Round 5 Rayong 27/28.09.2003   28s   16f
Jirapat Promnog/
Panlop Meenil   Mitsubishi Lancer Evo 1h.04m.57s.

Round 6 THAILAND Rayong 31.10/2.11.2003   33s   19f
K.Singh/Oh   Proton PERT   1h.31m.18s.

2003 Thailand Champion Jirapat Promnog.
Group N Champion Chaichan Piriyaphrapsakul.

Volkan Isik, 2003 Turkish Champion.

TR Turkey

Round 1 EGE Izmir 26/27.04.2003   46s   34f
Yazici/Okan   Ford Focus WRC   1h.02m.13s.

Round 2 TOFAS Izmir 16/18.05.2003 (ECR12) 51s   32f
Yazici/Okan   Ford Focus WRC   3h.09m.49.5s.

Round 3 PIRELLI Istanbul 12/13.07.2003   63s   41f
Isik/Guleren   Fiat Punto S1600   52m.46s.

Round 4 YESIL BURSA Bursa 23/24.08.2003   59s   35f
Yazici/Okan   Ford Focus WRC   1h.11m.24.9s.

Round 5 HITIT Ankara 20/21.09.2003   s   39f
Sarihan/Celen   Ford Focus WRC   54m.55.0s.

Round 6 KOCAELI Izmit 11/12.10.2003   39s   26f
Isik/Guleren   Fiat Palio S1600   1h.16m.34.3s.

Note: Final round 7 KIBRIS 1/2.11.2003. Volkan Isik cannot be beaten in
the championship.

USA United States of Amercia

Round 1 SNO*DRIFT Atlantic, MI 24/25.01.2003 35s   23f
D.Higgins/Barritt   Mitsubishi Lancer Evo 2h.02m.15s.

Round 2 RIM OF THE WORLD   32s   27f
Parmdale, CA 2/3.05.2003
D Higgins/Barritt   Mitsubishi Lancer Evo 1h.27m.34s.

Round 3 SUSQUEHANNOCK   62s.   37f
Wellsboro, PA 7.06.2003
D Higgins/Barritt   Mitsubishi Lancer Evo 1h.54m.57s.

Round 4 PIKES PEAK   14s   13f
Colorado Springs, CO 26/27.06.2003
Lovell/Freeman   Subaru Impreza   11m.39.63s.

Round 5 OREGON TRAIL   32s   22f
Hillsboro, OR 12/13.07.2003
D Higgins/Barritt   Mitsubishi Lancer Evo 1h.37m.27s.

Round 6 MAINE FOREST Rumford, ME 1/2.08.2003 62s   37f
D.Higgins/Barritt   Mitsubishi Lancer Evo 1h.40m.42.0s.

Round 7 OJIBWE FORESTS   33s   24f
Bemidji, MN 22/23.08.2003
D.Higgins/Barritt   Mitsubishi Lancer Evo 1h.58m.29.0s.

Round 8 WILD WEST Olympia, WA 6/7.09.2003 27s   22f
Hagstrom/Taskinen   Subaru Impreza   2h.05m.47.0s.

Round 9 LAKE SUPERIOR   34s   24f
Houghton, MI 17/18.10.2003
D.Higgins/Barritt   Mitsubishi Lancer Evo 1h.50m.34.0s.

2003 SCCA Pro-Rally Champion David Higgins (GB) 155pts,
2 Lauchin O'Sullivan 96, 3 Ramana Lagemann 65, 4 Tim O'Neil 62,
5 Mark Utecht 51, etc.

ZA South Africa

Round 1 TOUR NATAL Durban 7/8.03.2003   48s   24f
Habig/Judd   VW Golf   2h.31m.57s.

Round 2 TOTAL SOUTH AFRICA   55s   28f
Pretoria-Badplass 10/12.04.2003
Damseaux/Paisley   Toyota Runx   3h.19m.41s.

Round 3 TOYOTA DEALERS CAPE   50s   32f
Cape Town 30/31.05.2003
Damseaux/Paisley   Toyota Runx   1h.38m.38s.

Round 4 SASOL Nelspruit 20/21.06.2003   69s   34f
Kuun/Hodgson   VW Golf   2h.18m.16s.

Round 5 VOLKSWAGEN Port   56s   37f
Elizabeth 18/19.07.2003
Damseaux/Paisley   Toyota Runx

Round 6 MOUNTAIN TRIAL   30s   27f
Aliwal North 15/16.08.2003
Lourens/Vermeulen   Toyota Corolla RXi   1h.47m.12s.

Round 7 SUBARU CAPE   53s   33f
Cape Swartlamp 19/20.09.2003
Damseaux/Paisley   Toyota Runx   1h.48m.21s.

Round 8 TOYOTA DEALERS   48s   24f
GREAT NORTH 10/11.10.2003
Kuun/Hodgson   VW Golf   2h.50m.21s.

2003 South African Champion Serge Damseaux 213pts, 2 Etienne
Lourens 194, 3 Enzo Kuun 149, 4 Schalk Burger 126, 5 Jan Habig 125, etc.
Group N Champion Schalk Burger (Subaru Impreza WRX)

Reunion

Round 1 SAINTE SUZANNE   76s   54f
Ste Suzanne 9.03.2003
Law Long/Reynes   Peugeot 206 S1600   25m.53.6s.

Round 2 ABC ENTRETIEN St Benoit 3/4.05.2003 102s   85f
Grondin/Benard   Citroen Saxo KC   31m.29s.

Round 3 ORANGE Ste Marie 4/5.05.2003   88s   60f
Ardouin/Paris   Peugeot 206 S1600   1h.38m.48.8s.

Round 4 1000 KM St Andre 8/9.06.2003   85s   56f
Ardouin/Paris   Peugeot 206 S1600   2h14m.27s.

Round 5 SFR St Benoit 18/19.07.2003   104s   68f
Ardouin/Paris   Peugeot 206 S1600   42m.20s.

Round 6 206 RC ELF ST LOUIS   100s   61f
St Louis 13/14.09.2003
Maitre/Descamps   Renault Clio S1600   1h.02m.31.2s.

Round 7 TOUR AUTO REUNION St Denis 7/9.11.2003 45s   27f
Ardouin/Paris   Peugeot 206 S1600   2h.52m.08.0s.

Note: Final round FIAT DINDAR St Denis 6/7.12.2003

2002 INTERNATIONAL CHAMPIONSHIPS

2002 North American Rally Cup

Round 18 TALL PINES (CDN)   50s   32f
Bancroft 22/23.11.2003
McGeer/Williams   Subaru WRX   1h.55m.29s.

North American Rally Cup Winner Tom McGeer
Group N Winner Patrick Richard (Subaru Impreza WRX)

2002 NATIONAL CHAMPIONSHIPS

CDN Canada

Round 10 TALL PINES Bancroft, ONT 22/23.11.2002   50s   32f
McGeer/Williams   Subaru WRX   1h.55m.29s.

2002 Subaru Canadian Rally Champion
Ratrick Richard (Subaru Impreza WRX)
Group N Winner Andrew Comrie-Picard (Mitsubishi Lancer)

F France

Round 7 VAR Sainte-Maxime 29.11.2002   97s   62f
Sarrazin/Renucci   Subaru Impreza WRC   2h.28m.50.0s.

MEX Mexico

Note: Acapulco 30.11.2002. (Cancelled).

Category D 1600 cc Alberto Pedroza/ Lizbeth Gonz·lez 2000
Renault Clio
Category B 2000cc Patrick Silve 2001 Renault Clio
2002 Mexican Champion Carlos Izquierdo (Mitsubishi Lancer Evo)
329 pts, 2 Rodrigo Ordonez 320, 3 Patrick Silve 205, 4 Fernando Couto
197, 5 Alejandro Pimentel 124 etc

P Portugal

Round 10 DAO LAFOES 22/23.11.2002
Campos/Magalhaes   Peugeot 206 WRC   1h.30m.50.5s

RA Argentina

Round 8 PETROLEO Y LOS DINOUSAURIOS   34s   20f
Plaza Huincul/Cutral-Co, 15/17.11.2002
G.Raies/Ya   Toyota Corolla WRC   1h.25m.18.0s.

2002 FIA CHAMPIONSHIPS

2002 Asia-Pacific

Round 6 Thailand (T) 29.11/1.12.2002
Rayong. Stages 16, gravel - 269.73km.

1	Caldarola/Agnese	Mitsubishi Lancer Evo	N	2h.38m.00s.
2	Lloyd/Gullick	Mitsubishi Lancer Evo	A	2h.41m.19s
3	Hantrakul/Sukosi	Mitsubishi Lancer Evo	A	2h.42m.23s
4	Jones/J.Judd	Mitsubishi Lancer Evo	N	2h.47m.22s.
5	Bunchaylua/Sombutwong	Honda Civic	A	2h.57m11s.
6	Warren/D.Judd	Mitsubishi Lancer Evo	N	3h.03m.28s.

22 starters. 10 finishers.

2002 FIA Asia-Pacific Champion 1 Karamjit Singh (MAL) 70pts,
2 Nico Caldarola (I) 48, =3 Reece Jones (NZ) & Warren Stuart (AUS) 25,
5 Possum Bourne (NZ) 24, etc.

2002 Middle East

Round 7 Dubai (UAE) 4/6.12.2002

1	Ben Sulayem/Spiller	Ford Focus WRC	A	1h.58m.33s.
2	A.Al Qassimi/Zakaria	Ford Focus WRC	A	2h.02m.32s.
3	K.Al Qassimi/Al-Warshaw	Mitsubishi Lancer Evo	N	2h.15m.48s.
4	Baker/Ahmadi	Toyota Celica GT-4	A	2h.22m.51s.
5	Fadhel/Naban	Mitsubishi Lancer Evo	N	2h.30m.05s.
6	Ghuloom/Ghuloom	Mitsubishi Lancer Evo	N	2h.33m.11s

33 starters. 13 finishers.

2003 Middle East Champion Mohammed Ben Sulayem (UAE)
56pts, 2 Abdullah Al Qassimi (UAE) 20, 3 Khaled Al Qassimi (UAE) 18,
4 Misfer Al Marri (QA) 13, 5 Abdulla Bakhashab (KSA) 12, etc.

It was announced on 17th November that RICHARD BURNS will be unable to contest the 2004 FIA World Rally. It was explained that he had suffered an Astrocytoma (brain tumour) and was undergoing treatment which hopefully will be successful.

RALLY CAR DEVELOPMENTS

Ford's Secret Air Accumulator System

This diagram shows how air is collected, having passed through the restrictor, turbocharger and intercooler, at moments when the engine does not need it. It is then stored in the reservoirs and returned to the engine when it is under acceleration, and could use more air than the restrictor allows. Initially the FIA confirmed that this system did not infringe the regulations, but later decided that the rules needed "clarification"!

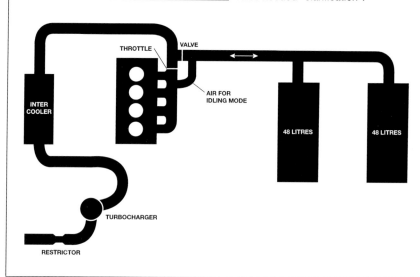

ERRATA - PIRELLI WORLD RALLYING 25

p123   Australia date = 31.10/3.11.2002
p126   both pictures credit GRIFFIN
p134   World Class Drivers,
           Philippe Bugalski, 2002 add after D,
           I Citroen Xsara WRC JC accident.
p135   Francois Duval, 2002, AUS, Ford Focus WRC
p139   Jani Paasonen, Fiat rally car Opel Ascona 2000 in 1995

p143   WRC Countdown, Ford X3FMC add GB for Stohl,
           add EJ02KMO Ginley: GB
           Peugeot, 47 add AUS for Gronholm.
           Skoda add 10 MBS97-68 Kresta: MC.
           Subaru, 02006 = PS02SSS
p162   JWRC, Sanremo and Great Britain,
           59/Kangas had codriver (b)

p163   Sanremo, 67/Carlsson, had codriver (b) with him
           and 68/Schelle codriver (b)
           71/Doppelreiter, codriver (b) nationality = N
           75/Niwa, codriver (d) nationality = J
p189   ECR, nationality of event ECR45 (A) and ECR46 is (B)
p197   both pictures credit KOMAROCK
p205   Poland, Sebastian Frycz

ACKNOWLEDGEMENTS

Published in England by
Martin Holmes Rallying
PO Box 117, Woking
Surrey, GU22 8YP

Written and compiled by Martin Holmes

The endless work of producing the book during the year was carried out by Ursula Partridge, assisted by Sally Holmes, Rosi & Keith Valters *(left, on their wedding day)*, Pauline Tindall and Colyn Partridge. With considerable help from many contributors. Thanks to all of you.

Did you recognise them all?
(left to right) Hakan Lindberg (S), Ove Andersson (S), Pat-Moss Carlsson (GB), Erik Carlsson (S), Alexandre Dardoufas (GR), Vassilis Despotopoulos (GR), Paddy Hopkirk (GB), Michele Mouton (F), Bjorn Waldegard (S).

Page layouts and maps by Heaton Ainsworth Limited
www.heatonainsworth.com
Reproduction by PH Media, St Austell.
Printed by St Ives (Roche) Limited, St Austell.
Bound by William Clowes, Beccles.

All photographs and illustrations used in this book are from the library of Martin Holmes Rallying taken either by Maurice Selden or the author, unless a special credit is given alongside.

Rear Cover photos *Selection of the Pirelli Champions from 2003 in International and National series: (foreground) Martin Rowe, 2003 FIA World Production Car Champion. (left to right) Txus Jaio (Spain, Ford), Hermann Gassner (Germany, Mitsubishi, VOIGT-NEUMEYER) Derek McGarrity (Irish Tarmac, Subaru, DEMPSTER), Kris Meeke (British Super 1600, Opel), Jonny Milner (British, Toyota), and Raimund Baumschlager (Austria, Mitsubishi, KOMAROCK).*

Once again we have also received considerable help from the many photographic contributors and colleagues in other countries, including journalists:

Argentina	Juan Cruz Mathus
Australia	Greg Yard
Austria	Werner Schneider
Belgium	Willy Weyens
Canada	Linda Epp
China	Ding Zhi Xiang
Croatia	Nenad Nikolic
Czech Republic	Pavel Vacha
Denmark	Ib Trebbien
Estonia	Rein Luik
Finland	Ralf Pettersson
France	Philippe Carles
Germany	Andrea Voigt-Neumeyer
Hungary	Andras Fekete
India	Zayn Khan
Indonesia	Helmy Sungkar
Ireland	Brian Patterson
Italy	Paolo Francalanchi
Japan	Tatsuo Tomita
Jordan	Ziad Louza
Kenya	Surinder Thatthi
Latvia	Liga Kalnacha
Lebanon	Antony Cauchy
Lithuania	Vidmantas Jankavicius
Malaysia	Azmarul
Mexico	Guy Lassauzet
Netherlands	Wim van Lagemaat
New Zealand	David Thomson
Norway	Jan Egil Jenssen
Paraguay	Gabriel Gonzalez
Peru	Daniel San Roman
Poland	Jacek Lewandowski
Portugal	Filipe Loureiro
Romania	Alexandru Dobai
Russia	Andrej Kleshchev
Serbia & Montenegro	Nenad Nikolic
Slovakia	Zdenek Weiser
Slovenia	Erik Loger
South Africa	Diether Kok
Spain	Esteban Delgado
Sweden	Thomas Lindberg
Switzerland	Annette Rothenmund
Thailand	Komar Johari
Turkey	Serhan Acar
Uganda	Geoffrey Kihuguru
USA	Sean Conlan
Uruguay	Mario Uberti
Zambia	Muna Singh
European	Zdenek Weiser
	David Limage
	Werner Schneider
Middle East	Neil Perkins
West Euro Cup	Jan Meester
South America	Juan Cruz Mathus

			FIA	ECR	GB
Jan	8-10	Janner	A	-	5W	-
	22-24	Arctic Lapland	FIN	H	-	-
	23-25	MONTE-CARLO	MC	WC/J	-	-
	28-30	U.A.E.	UAE	ME	-	-
	29-31	Arctic Lapland	FIN	-	10N	-
Feb	6-8	UDDEHOLM SWEDISH	S	WC/P	-	-
	12-15	Finnskog Norway	N	-	10N	-
	13-15	Swedish Snow	S	-	5N	-
	28	Sunseeker	GB	-	-	N
Mar	10-13	Bahrain	BRN	ME	-	-
	11-14	Italian Baja	I	CC/B	-	-
	12-13	Casino Povoa	P	-	2W	-
	12-14	CORONA MEXICO	MEX	WC/P	-	-
	12-14	Kenya Safari	EAK	A	-	-
	16-20	Baleares	E	H	-	-
	18-20	Ciocco + Valle del Serchio	I	-	5S	-
	25-27	Sumava Mogul	CZ	-	5E	-
Apr	1-3	Sanremo	I	H	-	-
	1-3	Mille Miglia	I	-	20	-
	3	Astra Stages	GB	-	-	N
	2-12	Tunisia	TN	CC	-	-
	3-4	Boucles de Spa	B	-	5W	-
	16-18	NEW ZEALAND	NZ	WC/P	-	-
	23-24	Pirelli	GB	-	-	O
	30-2 May	Matador Tatry	SK	-	5E	-
May	6-8	South Africa	ZA	A	-	-
	6-8	Targa Florio	I	-	5S	-
	6-9	Baja Vodafone 1000	P	CC/B	-	-
	7-8	Roush	GBM	-	-	N
	7-8	Horacka	CZ	H	-	-
	7-9	Canberra	AUS	AP	-	-
	7-9	Balkan	YU	-	2E	-
	13-15	South Swedish	S	-	10N	-
	14-16	CYPRUS	CY	WC	-	-
	15-16	Gwynedd Rally of Wales	GB	-	-	O
	17-20	Canarias	E	-	5W	-
	20-22	Jordan	HKJ	ME	-	-
	20-24	Saturnus	SLO	-	5S	-
	21-23	Fehervar	H	-	5S	-
	21-23	Interspeed	YU	-	10E	-
	28-30	New Caledonia	F	AP	-	-
	28-30	Trofeo Florio	I	H	-	-
	28-30	San Marino	RSM	-	10S	-
June	1-6	Orpi Maroc	F	CC	-	-
	3-5	Dunlop Zimbabwe Challenge	ZW	A	-	-
	3-5	Saarland	D	H	-	-
	3-5	Polski	PL	-	20	-
	4-5	RSAC Scottish	GB	-	-	-
	4-6	ACROPOLIS	GR	WC/J	-	-
	5	Mutiny	GB	-	-	N
	10-12	Ina Croatia	HR	-	10E	-
	16-18	Salento	I	-	10S	-
	18-20	Bulgaria	BG	-	20	-
	18-20	Saarland	D	-	5N	-
	25-27	TURKEY	TR	WC/J	-	-
	25-27	Hebros	BG	-	5E	-
July	1-3	Zambia	Z	A	-	-
	1-3	SATA Azores	P	-	10W	-
	2-3	Jim Clark Memorial	GB	-	-	O
	2-4	Lebanon	RL	ME	-	-
	2-4	Romania	RO	-	5E	-
	2-4	Jim Clark Memorial	GB	-	2N	-

			FIA	ECR	GB
	2-4	Ypres	B	H	-	-
	3-4	Ypres Westhoek	B	-	20	-
	5-8	Kormoran	PL	-	5N	-
	9-10	Rotorua	NZ	AP	-	-
	9-11	Bohemia	CZ	-	10E	-
	15	Swansea Bay	GB	-	-	N
	15-17	San Martino di Castrozza	I	-	5S	-
	15-18	Baja Espana	E	CC/B	-	-
	16-18	ARGENTINA	RA	WC/P	-	-
	23-25	Kosice	SK	-	2E	-
	28-31	Vinho da Madeira	P	-	20	-
	29-31	Manx	GBM	-	-	O
	30-1 Aug	Manx	GB	-	2N	-
Aug	6-8	NESTE FINLAND	FIN	WC/P	-	-
	6-8	Rwanda Mountain Gorilla	RWA	A	-	-
	6-8	Budapest	H	-	10S	-
	7-15	Orient	F	CC	-	-
	13-15	Lahti	FIN	H	-	-
	15-17	Georgia	GE	-	2E	-
	20-22	ADAC DEUTSCHLAND	D	WC/J	-	-
	26-29	Barum	CZ	-	20	-
	27-29	Alpi Orientali	I	H	5S	-
	27-29	Sosser Sliven	BG	-	10E	-
Sept	1-3	Syria	SYR	ME	-	-
	2-4	AnswerCall Direct Ulster	GB	-	2N	O
	2-5	Pearl of Africa Uganda	EAU	A	-	-
	3-5	JAPAN	J	WC/AP	-	-
	3-5	Pennino	I	CC/B	-	-
	10-12	Tofas	TR	-	20	-
	10-12	Oviedo	E	-	10W	-
	11-12	YU	YU	-	5E	-
	15-21	Por las Pampas	RA	CC	-	-
	17-18	Golden Tulip	NL	-	2W	-
	17-19	WALES RALLY GB	GB	WC/J	-	-
	24-26	Elba Storico	I	H	-	-
	24-26	ELPA	GR	-	20	-
	24-26	Rota do Vidro	P	-	5W	-
	29-2 Oct	Greek Ekali 4x4 Club	GR	B	-	-
Oct	1-3	D'ITALIA SARDINIA	I	WC/J	-	-
	2-3	Trackrod International Yorkshire	GB	-	-	O
	11-15	UAE Desert Challenge	UAE	CC	-	-
	13-15	Oman International	OM	ME	-	-
	15-17	TOUR DE CORSE	F	WC/P	-	-
	16-18	China Shaoguan	CN	AP	-	-
	21-23	Valais	CH	-	10S	-
	21-23	ADAC 3-Stadte	D	-	10N	-
	21-24	Anta da Serra 500 ˚ Portalegre	P	B	-	-
	21-24	Antibes	F	-	20	-
	23	Bulldog	GB	-	-	N
	22-24	500 Minuti	I	H	-	-
	29-31	CATALUNYA-COSTA BRAVA	E	WC/J	-	-
Nov	4-6	Waldviertel	A	-	2W	-
	5-7	Troodos	CY	ME	-	-
	5-7	Olympion	GR	-	2S	-
	5-7	Condroz	B	-	10W	-
	6	Tempest	GB	-	-	O
	6-7	Thailand	T	AP	-	-
	11-13	Tour de la Reunion	F	A	-	-
	12-14	TELSTRA AUSTRALIA	AUS	WC/P	-	-
	26-28	Var	F	H	-	-
Dec	1-3	Dubai	UAE	ME	-	-
	3-5	India	IND	AP	-	-

Key:

A = Africa	**H** = European Historic Sporting Trophy	**O** = British Rally Championship
AP = Asia-Pacific	**J** = Junior WRC	**P** = Production Car WRC
B = Baja	**ME** = Middle East	**WC** = World Rally Championship
CC = Cross Country	**N** = Kumho Tyres National	(Manufacturers and Drivers).
ECR = European (coefficient/zone: North, South, East, West)		

WORLD RALLY WINNING DRIVERS

Note: these records do not include outright winners of W2L-only events but do include WCD-only results and Sanremo 1986

WINS	DRIVER'S NAME	BIRTH	YEAR & EVENTS WON
1	Andrea Aghini (I)	29.12.1963 Livorno	1992 I
1	Pentti Airikkala (FIN)	4.09.1942 Helsinki	1989 GB
20	Markku Alen (FIN)	15.02.1951 Helsinki	1975 P
			1976 FIN
			1977 P
			1978 P, FIN, I
			1979 FIN
			1980 FIN
			1981 P
			1983 F, I
			1984 F
			1986 I, USA
			1987 P, GR, FIN
			1988 S, FIN, GB
1	Alain Ambrosino (F)	15.05.1951 Casablanca(MA)	1988 CI
1	Ove Andersssson (S)	3.01.1938 Uppsala	1975 EAK
3	Jean-Claude Andruet (F)	13.08.1942 Montreuil	1973 MC
			1974 F
			1977 I
20	Didier Auriol (F)	18.08.1958 Montpellier	1988 F
			1989 F
			1990 MC, F, I
			1991 I
			1992 MC, F, GR, RA, FIN, AUS
			1993 MC
			1994 F, RA, I
			1995 F
			1998 E
			1999 CN
			2001 E
1	Fulvio Bacchelli (I)	22.01.1951 Trieste	1977 NZ
1	Bernard Beguin (F)	24.09.1947 Grenoble	1987 F
17	Massimo 'Miki' Biasion (I)	7.01.1958 Bassano del Grappa	1986 RA
			1987 MC, RA, I
			1988 P, EAK, GR, USA, I
			1989 MC, P, EAK, GR, I
			1990 P, RA
			1993 GR
11	Stig Blomqvist (S)	29.07.1946 Orebro	1973 S
			1977 S
			1979 S
			1982 S, I
			1983 GB
			1984 S, GR, NZ, RA, CI
1	Walter Boyce (CDN)	29.10.1946 Ottawa	1973 USA
2	Philippe Bugalski (F)	12.06.1963 Cusset	1999 E, F
10	Richard Burns (GB)	17.01.1971 Reading	1998 EAK, GB
			1999 GR, AUS, GB
			2000 EAK, P, RA, GB
			2001 NZ
2	Ingvar Carlsson (S)	2.04.1947 Nykoping	1989 S, NZ
1	Roger Clark (GB)	5.08.1939 Narborough	1976 GB
1	Gianfranco Cunico (I)	11.10.1957 Vicenza	1993 I
7	Bernard Darniche (F)	28.03.1942 Cenon	1973 MA
			1975 F
			1977 F
			1978 F
			1979 MC, F
			1981 F
4	Francois Delecour (F)	30.08.1962 Cassel	1993 P, F, E
			1994 MC
1	Ian Duncan (EAK)	23.06.1961 Nairobi	1994 EAK
1	Per Eklund (S)	26.06.1946 Arvika	1976 S
2	Mikael Ericsson (S)	28.02.1960 Umea	1989 RA, FIN
6	Kenneth Eriksson (S)	13.05.1956 Appelbo	1987 CI
			1991 S
			1995 S, AUS
			1997 S, NZ
1	Guy Frequelin (F)	2.04.1945 Langres	1981 RA
15	Marcus Gronholm (FIN)	5.02.1968 Espoo	2000 S, NZ, FIN, AUS
			2001 FIN, AUS, GB
			2002 S, CY, FIN, NZ, AUS
			2003 S, NZ, RA
1	Josef 'Sepp' Haider (A)	26.08.1953 Dienten	1988 NZ
1	Kyosti Hamalainen (FIN)	16.09.1945 Helsinki	1977 FIN
2	Mats Jonsson (S)	28.11.1957 Karlstad	1992 S
			1993 S
1	Harry Kallstom (S)	30.06.1939 Sodertalje	1976 GR
23	Juha Kankkunen (FIN)	2.04.1959 Laukaa	1985 EAK, CI
			1986 S, GR, NZ
			1987 USA, GB
			1989 AUS
			1990 AUS
			1991 EAK, GR, FIN, AUS, GB
			1992 P
			1993 EAK, RA, FIN, AUS, GB
			1994 P
			1999 RA, FIN
1	Anders Kullang (S)	28.09.1943 Karlstad	1980 S
1	Piero Liatti (I)	7.05.1962 Biella	1997 MC
4	Sebastian Loeb (F)	26.02.1974 Haguenau	2002 D
			2003 MC, D, I
4	Timo Makinen(FIN)	18.03.1939 Helsinki	1973 FIN, GB
			1974 GB
			1975 GB
24	Tommi Makinen (FIN)	26.06.1964 Puuppola	1994 FIN
			1996 S, EAK, RA, FIN, AUS
			1997 P, E, RA, FIN
			1998 S, RA, FIN, I, AUS
			1999 MC, S, NZ, I
			2000 MC
			2001 MC, P, EAK
			2002 MC
2	Markko Martin (EE)	10.11.1975 Tartu	2003 GR, FIN

WINS	DRIVER'S NAME	BIRTH	YEAR & EVENTS WON
25	Colin McRae (GB)	5.08.1968 Lanark	1993 NZ
			1994 NZ, GB
			1995 NZ, GB
			1996 GR, I, E
			1997 EAK, F, I, AUS, GB
			1998 P, F, GR
			1999 EAK, P
			2000 E, GR
			2001 RA, CY, GR
			2002 GR, EAK
5	Shekhar Mehta (EAK)	20.06.1945 Kampala(EAU)	1973 EAK
			1979 EAK
			1980 EAK
			1981 EAK
			1982 EAK
18	Hannu Mikkola (FIN)	24.05.1942 Joensuu	1974 FIN
			1975 MA, FIN
			1978 GB
			1979 P, NZ, GB, CI
			1981 S, GB
			1982 FIN, GB
			1983 S, P, RA, FIN
			1984 P
			1987 EAK
1	Joaquim Moutinho (P)	14.12.1951 Porto	1986 P
4	Michele Mouton (F)	23.06.1951 Grasse	1981 I
			1982 P, GR, BR
7	Sandro Munari (I)	27.03.1940 Cavarzere	1974 I, CDN
			1975 MC
			1976 MC, P, F
			1977 MC
5	Jean-Pierre Nicolas (F)	22.01.1945 Marseille	1973 F
			1976 MA
			1978 MC, EAK, CI
1	Alain Oreille (F)	22.04.1953 Sarre-Union	1989 CI
7	Gilles Panizzi (F)	19.09.1965 Menton	2000 F, I
			2001 I
			2002 F, E, I
			2003 E
1	Rafaelle Pinto (I)	23.04.1945 Como	1974 P
1	Jesus Puras (E)	16.03.1963 Santander	2001 F
3	Jean Ragnotti (F)	29.08.1945 Carpentras	1981 MC
			1982 F
			1985 F
1	Jorge Recalde (RA)	9.08.1951 Mina Clavero	1988 RA
14	Walter Rohrl (D)	7.03.1947 Regensburg	1975 GR
			1978 GR, CDN
			1980 MC, P, RA, I
			1982 MC, CI
			1983 MC, GR, NZ
			1984 MC
			1985 I
1	Harri Rovanpera (FIN)	8.04.1966 Jyvaskyla	2001 S
2	Bruno Saby (F)	23.02.1949 Grenoble	1986 F
			1988 MC
25	Carlos Sainz (E)	12.04.1962 Madrid	1990 GR, NZ, FIN, GB
			1991 MC, P, F, NZ, RA
			1992 EAK, NZ, E, GB
			1994 GR
			1995 MC, P, E
			1996 RI
			1997 GR, RI
			1998 MC, NZ
			2000 CY
			2002 RA
			2003 TR
11	Timo Salonen (FIN)	8.10.1951 Helsinki	1977 CDN
			1980 NZ
			1981 CI
			1985 P, GR, NZ, RA, FIN
			1986 FIN, GB
			1987 S
1	Armin Schwarz (D)	16.07.1963 Oberreichenbach	1991 E
2	Kenjiro Shinozuka (J)	20.11.1948 Tokyo	1991 CI
			1992 CI
2	Joginder Singh (EAK)	9.02.1932 Kericho	1974 EAK
			1976 EAK
5	Petter Solberg (N)	18.11.1974 Spydeberg	2002 GB
			2003 CY, AUS, F, GB
1	Patrick Tauziac (F)	18.01.1955 Saigon(VN)	1990 CI
5	Jean-Luc Therier (F)	7.10.1945 Hodeng-au-Bosc	1973 P, GR, I
			1974 USA
			1980 F
3	Henri Toivonen (FIN)	25.08.1956 Jyvaskyla	1980 GB
			1985 GB
			1986 MC
1	'Tony' Fassina (I)	26.06.1945 Treviso	1979 I
10	Ari Vatanen (FIN)	27.04.1952 Joensuu	1980 GR
			1981 GR, BR, FIN
			1983 EAK
			1984 FIN, I, GB
			1985 MC, S
16	Bjorn Waldegard (S)	12.11.1943 Ro	1975 S, I
			1976 I
			1977 EAK, GR, GB
			1978 S
			1979 GR, CDN
			1980 CI
			1982 NZ
			1983 CI
			1984 EAK
			1986 EAK, CI
			1990 EAK
2	Achim Warmbold (D)	17.07.1941 Duisburg	1973 PL, A
1	Franz Wittmann (A)	7.04.1950 Ramsau	1987 NZ